Black Americans and the Civil Rights Movement in the West

RACE AND CULTURE IN THE AMERICAN WEST
QUINTARD TAYLOR, SERIES EDITOR

Black Americans and the
Civil Rights Movement in the West

Edited by
Bruce A. Glasrud
and **Cary D. Wintz**

Foreword by **Quintard Taylor**

UNIVERSITY OF OKLAHOMA PRESS : NORMAN

Publication of this book is made possible through the generosity of Edith Kinney Gaylord.

Library of Congress Cataloging-in-Publication Data

Names: Glasrud, Bruce A., editor. | Wintz, Cary D., 1943– editor.
Title: Black Americans and the Civil Rights Movement in the West / edited by Bruce A. Glasrud and Cary D. Wintz ; foreword by Quintard Taylor.
Description: Norman, OK : University of Oklahoma Press, 2019. | Series: Race and Culture in the American West ; Volume 16 | Includes bibliographical references and index.
Identifiers: LCCN 2018022537 | ISBN 978-0-8061-6196-9 (pbk. : alk. paper)
Subjects: LCSH: African Americans—Civil rights—West (U.S.)—History—20th century. | African Americans—West (U.S.)—History—20th century. | Civil rights movements—West (U.S.)—History—20th century. | West (U.S.)—Race relations—History—20th century.
Classification: LCC F596.3.N4 B53 2019 | DDC 323.1196/073078—dc23
LC record available at https://lccn.loc.gov/2018022537

Black Americans and the Civil Rights Movement in the West is Volume 16 in the Race and Culture in the American West series.

The paper in this book meets the guidelines for permanence and durability of the Committee on Production Guidelines for Book Longevity of the Council on Library Resources, Inc. ∞

Copyright © 2019 by Bruce A. Glasrud and Cary D. Wintz. Published by the University of Oklahoma Press, Norman, Publishing Division of the University. Manufactured in the U.S.A.

All rights reserved. No part of this publication may be reproduced, stored in a retrieval system, or transmitted, in any form or by any means, electronic, mechanical, photocopying, recording, or otherwise—except as permitted under Section 107 or 108 of the United States Copyright Act—without the prior written permission of the University of Oklahoma Press. To request permission to reproduce selections from this book, write to Permissions, University of Oklahoma Press, 2800 Venture Drive, Norman, OK 73069, or email rights.oupress@ou.edu.

Contents

List of Maps ■ vii

Foreword
  by Quintard Taylor ■ ix

Preface ■ xv

Part I: Prologue

1. Freedom Struggle: An Introduction
   by Bruce A. Glasrud and Cary D. Wintz ■ 3

2. Before *Brown* in the West
   by Jean Van Delinder ■ 7

Part II: The Far West

3. Civil Rights Movement in the Pacific Northwest
   by Kevin Allen Leonard ■ 23

4. The Struggle on Multiple Planes: California's Long Civil Rights Movement
   by Herbert G. Ruffin II ■ 38

5. Civil Rights Movement in Nevada
   by Elmer R. Rusco ■ 71

Part III: The Mountain States and the Desert Southwest

6. Breaking Racial Barriers: Civil Rights Movements in Montana and Wyoming
   by Kenneth G. Robison ■ 89

7. The Modern Civil Rights Movement in Colorado
   by George H. Junne Jr. ■ 107

8. Civil Rights in Utah: The Mormon Way
   by J. Herschel Barnhill ■ 122

9. Blacks and Whites Together: Interracial Leadership in the Phoenix, Arizona, Civil Rights Movement
   by Mary S. Melcher ■ 136

10. The Modern Civil Rights Movement in New Mexico
    by George M. Cooper ■ 153

Part IV: The Upper Midwest

11. Civil Rights in the Dakotas
    by Betti VanEpps-Taylor ■ 167

12. The Modern Civil Rights Movement in Iowa and Minnesota
    by Donald H. Strasser and Melodie Andrews ■ 181

13. Challenging the Color Line in Kansas and Nebraska: The Revolution at a Regional Nexus
    by James N. Leiker ■ 196

Part V: The South and the West Collide

14. Conceived in Segregation and Dedicated to the Proposition That All Men Were *Not* Created Equal: Oklahoma, the Last Southern State
    by Paul Finkelman ■ 213

15. The Civil Rights Movement in Texas
    by Alwyn Barr ■ 236

Part VI: Epilogue

16. Western Civil Rights since 1970
    by Albert S. Broussard ■ 255

Selected Bibliography ■ 271

Index ■ 279

Maps

United States West ■ xxii
Western Regions ■ xxii

Foreword

The civil rights movement continues to be iconic in United States history. The movement challenged long-standing inequities in American society including—at the core of these inequities—the denial of the right to vote to millions of black women and men across the South, my parents in Tennessee among them. Racial barriers came down through a massive civil disobedience campaign that eventually involved the efforts of tens of thousands of people, mostly black, and mostly in the South.

Few observers of the period, however, would have anticipated how that campaign, whose favorable outcome was by no means guaranteed, would soon be immortalized. By the late 1970s, powerful images would be used to tell a compelling story of the freedom struggle. These images include depictions of the March on Washington, Birmingham and Selma, Albany and Americus, and Mississippi's freedom summer in 1964, when three brave men were killed because they wanted to democratize the state. Those images are now embedded within hundreds of popular books, movies, documentaries, television miniseries, high school and university course materials, monuments, museums, presidential proclamations, and now even tours. Collectively they attest to the nearly irresistible power of memory over actual history.

Historians, however, have an obligation to research and interpret those events and to present them as accurately and comprehensively as we can. By the 1980s civil rights movement historians such as David Garrow and Taylor Branch portrayed the struggles of the 1960s as a single epic campaign dominated by an energized southern black community crucially backed by a liberal national political coalition headed by President Lyndon Baines Johnson. This campaign, inspired by heroic figures such as Martin Luther King and Fannie Lou Hamer, secured important new laws including the 1964 Civil Rights Act and the 1965 Voting Rights Act, ensuring equality and opportunity. Other historians such as Aldon D. Morris and John Dittmer challenged that view, arguing that the movement was bottom-up, meaning it could be best explained in terms of local initiatives from grassroots organizations across the South.[1]

Other approaches sought to broaden our understanding of the movement. Brenda Gayle Plummer and Mary Dudziak, for example, introduced the influence of international politics on U.S. civil rights, while legal historian Michael J. Klarman followed the role of the courts, especially the U.S. Supreme Court, in the struggle for equality. Peniel E. Joseph coupled the civil rights era with Black Power.[2]

In a 2005 essay in the *Journal of American History*, Jacquelyn Dowd Hall introduced the concept of the "long civil rights movement," extending the traditional chronology of the movement—the 1954 U.S. Supreme Court's *Brown v. Board of Education* decision to the 1965 Voting Rights Act—back to the New Deal and up to the rise of New Right conservatism in the 1970s. Other historians including Adam Fairclough, Nikhil Singh, and Tomiko Brown-Nagin have built on that notion in their work.[3]

Although earlier historians had noted individual civil rights struggles in the North such as Martin Luther King's 1966 campaign against Chicago housing segregation, Jeanne Theoharis and Komozi Woodard in 2003 shifted the focus of civil rights activity to the North (and the West). They argued that while the issues in the North were different—housing segregation, job discrimination, police brutality, and corrupt political machines that allowed African Americans to vote but limited their political influence—these struggles were no less important than those centered in the South. Numerous historians including Martha Biondi, Matthew J. Countryman, and Thomas J. Sugrue elaborated on these themes in their respective works.[4]

Despite the growing awareness that the civil rights movement was a national struggle and part of the effort to bring democracy and opportunity to millions throughout the nation, the West remained understudied. Only two historians, Robert Self and Matthew C. Whitaker, have examined in book-length detail the 1960s civil rights struggle in two major cities—Oakland and Phoenix—west of the one hundredth meridian.[5] In this volume, *Black Americans and the Civil Rights Movement in the West*, Bruce Glasrud and Cary Wintz finally attempt to fully integrate the West into this crucial national struggle.

This anthology brings together the work of sixteen historians who have provided either original articles or previously published pieces that highlight important aspects of the struggle for racial justice in the region. While the articles are understandably urban focused, they also address the impact of these struggles on entire states including those with small African American populations. Statewide campaigns in Montana, Wyoming, Utah, and the Dakotas, for example, employed strategies that differed significantly from those of civil rights advocates in major urban centers in California, Colorado, Washington, Oregon, or Texas. Those strategies were even more removed from those employed in the South, Midwest, or Northeast. Yet local people in the Dakotas, Oregon, or Nevada were just as committed to dismantling the racial barriers to their advancement as their counterparts in Mississippi or New York. Also, more than northerners and southerners, westerners reached out to create coalitions of whites, Latinos, Asians, and American Indians to pursue their civil rights goals, convincing them that a victory for African Americans would be a victory for all.

Each article illustrates the profound role of black women in these western civil rights campaigns. We are introduced to activists such as Rowena Moore, secretary of the Omaha, Nebraska, meat cutters' union, who fought for the rights of black women to work in the city's packinghouses; Lucinda Todd of Topeka, Kansas, the driving force behind the landmark *Brown v. Board of Education* case; Thelma Paige, the Dallas, Texas, plaintiff who, in 1942, used the courts to eventually equalize the salaries of black and white school teachers across Texas; and Beatrice Cannady, who almost single-handedly led the campaign for racial justice in Portland, Oregon. It is clear from these accounts that these women did not derive inspiration from the southern civil rights campaigns, as their efforts came long before the first Greensboro sit-ins on February 1, 1960.

In fact, each of these essays reminds us of the "long" civil rights campaign. Each contributor begins his or her account in the nineteenth or early twentieth centuries, indicating that African American westerners fully understood their grievances in their own region and sought to address them within their cities and states regardless of circumstances elsewhere in the nation. Their stories remind us that black westerners knew that racism in its varied manifestations—whether school segregation in Dallas or Los Angeles, job discrimination in Wichita or Seattle, or housing bias in Phoenix, Portland, or San Francisco—meant that the civil rights movement had to be fought in every corner of the United States including the American West.

In a 1973 interview five years after he had left Seattle, civil rights activist Rev. John H. Adams recalled the early days of the 1960s movement in a major American city far from the South. He declared that local civil rights advocates in Seattle were prepared to use the civil disobedience tactics already tested in cities like Montgomery, Greensboro, Atlanta, and Albany. Then he said, "By

1963, the Civil Rights movement finally had leaped the Cascade Mountains."[6] Bruce Glasrud and Cary Wintz illustrate how that was done in *Black Americans and the Civil Rights Movement in the West* and how the activities of well-known and virtually unknown people changed the region and ultimately the entire United States.

>Quintard Taylor
>The Scott and Dorothy Bullitt Professor of American History
>University of Washington, Seattle

Notes

1. See David Garrow, *Bearing the Cross: Martin Luther King, Jr. and the Southern Christian Leadership Conference* (New York: William Morrow, 1986); Taylor Branch, *Parting the Waters: America in the King Years, 1954–63* (New York: Simon & Schuster, 1989); Aldon D. Morris, *The Origins of the Civil Rights Movement: Black Communities Organizing for Change* (New York: Free Press, 1984); and John Dittmer, *Local People: The Struggle for Civil Rights in Mississippi* (Urbana: University of Illinois Press, 1994).
2. See Brenda Gayle Plummer, *Rising Wind: Black Americans and U.S. Foreign Affairs, 1935–1960* (Chapel Hill: University of North Carolina Press, 1997); and Mary L. Dudziak, *Cold War Civil Rights: Race and the Image of American Democracy* (Princeton, N.J.: Princeton University Press, 2000). See also Michael J. Klarman, *From Jim Crow to Civil Rights: The Supreme Court and the Struggle for Racial Equality* (New York: Oxford University Press, 2004); and Peniel E. Joseph, *Waiting 'Til the Midnight Hour: A Narrative History of Black Power in America* (New York: Henry Holt, 2006).
3. See Jacquelyn Dowd Hall, "The Long Civil Rights Movement and the Political Uses of the Past," *Journal of American History* 91, no. 4 (March 2005): 1233–66. See also Adam Fairclough, *Race and Democracy: The Civil Rights Struggle in Louisiana, 1912–1972* (Athens: University of Georgia Press, 1999); Nikhil Singh, *Black is a Country: Race and the Unfinished Struggle for Democracy* (Cambridge: Harvard University Press, 2004); and Tomiko Brown-Nagin, *Courage to Dissent: Atlanta and the Long History of the Civil Rights Movement* (New York: Oxford University Press, 2006).
4. Jeanne Theoharis and Komozi Woodard, eds., *Freedom North: Black Freedom Struggles Outside the South, 1940–1980* (New York: Palgrave Macmillan, 2003); Martha Biondi, *To Stand and Fight: The Struggle for Civil Rights in Postwar New York City* (Cambridge: Harvard University Press, 2003); Matthew J. Countryman, *Up South: Civil Rights and Black Power in Philadelphia* (Philadelphia: University of Pennsylvania Press, 2006); and Thomas J. Sugrue, *Sweet Land of Liberty: The Forgotten Struggle for Civil Rights in the North* (New York: Random House, 2008).
5. See Robert O. Self, *American Babylon: Race and the Struggle for Postwar Oakland* (Princeton, N.J.: Princeton University Press, 2003); and Matthew Whitaker, *Race Work: The Rise of Civil Rights in the Urban West* (Lincoln: University of Nebraska Press, 2005). Albert Broussard's *Black San Francisco: The Struggle for Racial Equality*

in the West, 1900–1954 (Lawrence: University Press of Kansas, 1993) is, as the title suggests, a precursor to later civil rights accounts as he frames the history of the black community in the first half of the twentieth century as a history of its collective campaign for racial justice.

6. Quoted in Quintard Taylor, *The Forging of a Black Community: Seattle's Central District from 1870 through the Civil Rights Era* (Seattle: University of Washington Press, 1994), 198.

Preface

The significance of the civil rights movement in the western United States led to the publication of this book, *Black Americans and the Civil Rights Movement in the West*. We contacted researchers familiar with both the civil rights movement and a particular state or region in the West. Hence most of the chapters in this book were written originally for this study, although we also included four previously published articles that covered their respective topics especially well. Each chapter focuses, as much as possible, on a western state or region, with particular emphasis on urban areas. Naturally, where and when it proved useful and appropriate, authors also considered rural areas. Each author was encouraged to focus his or her efforts on the years of the civil rights movement (or movements) in that state or region. We suggested to the authors that they likely would begin with the 1954 *Brown* decision, or focus on the "modern" movement of the mid-1940s to mid-1970s, but they were encouraged to start where they deemed appropriate for their area. Some authors discovered that an important relationship to the overall civil rights struggle had begun earlier or continued into the following decades. Each essay included five thousand to six thousand words, and the authors developed vital "further reading" lists while some utilized extensive endnotes. For the four previously published chapters, we retained the original documentation method.

The boundaries of the West are malleable. For this purpose, we define it as those states one removed westward from the Mississippi River, but including two northern "first tier states"—Iowa and Minnesota—due to their history, their midwestern location, and their similarity and relationship to the remaining "western" states. We also include Hawaii and Alaska as western, but for varied reasons did not utilize their studies for our book.

It is important to understand that the western civil rights struggle was not monolithic. Every locality in the West had a somewhat different story. As our authors located aspects of the story that related to or differed from the national or regional picture, they identified and described those. Two of the chapters are broader in scope. One, written by Oklahoma State University scholar Jean Van Delinder, traces the emergence of civil rights activity throughout the West in the years prior to the *Brown* decision of 1954. And the other, produced by Texas A&M University historian Albert S. Broussard, focuses on civil rights activities as they emerged in the years after the mid-1970s. Both are vital for understanding the western experience and the overall civil rights picture.

Previously, research on the topic of blacks and the civil rights movement in the West lagged and was a forceful reason for publication of this book. No single monograph examined this movement, and research publications discussing western civil rights efforts frequently lie tucked away in historical journals or as chapters in broader publications on the West. There are two solid exceptions to the paucity, and they begin with the 2003 publication edited by Jeanne Theoharis and Komozi Woodard, *Freedom North: Black Freedom Struggles Outside the South, 1940–1980*, in which the editors supplemented their emphasis on the North with two forays into the West. In their collection they included chapters from Robert O. Self, "'Negro Leadership and Negro Money': African American Political Organizing in Oakland before the Panthers," and Scot Brown, "The Politics of Culture: The US Organization and the Quest for Black 'Unity.'" Two years later Theoharis and Woodard published a broader-based study, *Groundwork: Local Black Freedom Movements in America*, which also included two essays on western localities: Reynaldo Anderson, "Practical Internationalists: The Story of the Des Moines, Iowa, Black Panther Party," and Robyn Ceanne Spencer, "Inside the Panther Revolution: The Black Freedom Movement and the Black Panther Party in Oakland, California." Their more specific northern-centered approach has been explored also by Thomas J. Sugrue in *Sweet Land of Liberty: The Forgotten Struggle for Civil Rights in the North*. A literary study that encompasses a much broader era, Blake Allmendinger's *Imagining the American West*, complements *Black Americans and the Civil Rights Movement in the West*. Also, Bruce A. Glasrud and Laurie Champion included a section on "Freedom and Civil Rights" in their literary anthology, *The African American West: A Century of Short Stories*. For a work that covers the broader pattern of black activities in the West turn to Herbert G. Ruffin II and Dwayne A. Mack's edited collection, *Freedom's Racial Frontier: African Americans in the Twentieth-Century West*.

Two studies edited by Ohio State University scholar Judson L. Jeffries limit their focus to one organization, the Black Panther Party, in the struggle for civil rights on the national level. In *Comrades: A Local History of the Black Panther Party* and *On the Ground: The Black Panther Party in Communities across America*, Jeffries and his authors included studies from the West. The valuable western-based contributions included Judson L. Jeffries and Malcolm Foley, "To Live and Die in L.A."; Charles E. Jones, "Arm Yourself or Harm Yourself: People's Party II and the Black Panther Party in Houston, Texas"; Jeffrey Zane and Judson L. Jeffries, "A Panther Sighting in the Pacific Northwest: The Seattle Chapter of the Black Panther Party"; Reynaldo Anderson, "The Kansas City Black Panther Party and the Repression of the Black Revolution"; and Bruce Fehn and Robert Jefferson, "The Des Moines, Iowa, African American Community and the Emergence and Impact of the Black Panther Party, 1948–1973." Jeffries's works significantly bettered our knowledge and understanding of the western civil rights struggles.

As a critical starting point to the overall western civil rights discussion, however, three prominent scholars of the black West have written pioneering overview chapters—Quintard Taylor, "The Civil Rights Movement in the West, 1950–70," in his *In Search of the Racial Frontier*; Albert S. Broussard, "Civil Rights," in his *Expectations of Equality*; and Douglas Flamming, "Fighting for Civil Rights," and especially "The Era of Black Nationalism," both of which can be found in his *African Americans in the West*. These authors brought years of historical experience and awareness in western African American studies to their depiction of the freedom struggles in the West. A bibliography can be located in Bruce A. Glasrud, "Civil Rights Revolution," in his bibliographical study of *African Americans in the West*.

A few scholars have published books on aspects of the western civil rights struggle. See for example Jean Van Delinder, *Struggles Before Brown: Early Civil Rights Protests and Their Significance Today*; Matthew C. Whitaker, *Race Work: The Rise of Civil Rights in the Urban West*; Robert O. Self, *American Babylon: Race and the Struggle for Postwar Oakland*; Albert S. Broussard, *Black San Francisco: The Struggle for Racial Equality in the West*; Quintard Taylor, *The Forging of a Black Community: Seattle's Central District from 1870 through the Civil Rights Era*; Scot Brown, *Fighting for US: Maulana Karenga, The US Organization, and Black Cultural Nationalism*; Gretchen Cassel Eick, *Dissent in Wichita: The Civil Rights Movement in the Midwest*; and Peniel E. Joseph, *Waiting 'Til the Midnight Hour: A Narrative History of Black Power in America*. See also Joseph's anthology, *The Black Power Movement: Rethinking the Civil Rights–Black Power Era*.

African American civil rights leaders and activists made an impact in the West, and have begun to be recognized nationally. On a Minnesota African American leader, see David Brauer, *Nellie Stone Johnson: The Life of an Activist*. From Arizona, Cloves C. Campbell Sr., the man who became that state's first black senator, left us his thoughts in *I Refused to Leave the 'Hood*. Seattle Panther leader Aaron Floyd Dixon published *My People Are Rising: Memoir of a Black Panther Party Captain* with a foreword from historian Judson L. Jeffries. Jeffries also captured the importance, ability, and contributions of an Oakland Black Panther leader in *Huey P. Newton: The Radical Theorist*. A broader study from Southern California that focuses on six black personalities is Emile Raymond, *Stars for Freedom: Hollywood, Black Celebrities, and the Civil Rights Movement*.

Publications of note that influenced the contributors to *Black Americans and the Civil Rights Movement in the West* as they wrote include the aforementioned study by Van Delinder, *Struggles Before Brown*. On the early movement in the West see also Jennifer A. Delton, *Making Minnesota Liberal: Civil Rights and the Transformation of the Democratic Party*, Mary L. Dudziak, "The Limits of Good Faith: Desegregation in Topeka, Kansas, 1950–1956," and Kristine McCusker, "The Forgotten Years of America's Civil Rights Movement: Wartime Protests at the University of Kansas." The golden state of California encompassed massive protests and events during the tumultuous years of civil rights activity; for information see Donna Jean Murch, *Living for the City: Migration, Education, and the Rise of the Black Panther Party in Oakland, California*. Also on California see Robert O. Self, *American Babylon: Race and the Struggle for Postwar Oakland*, and Josh Sides, "Building the Civil Rights Movement in Los Angeles."

Authors covered other western states and locales as well. For Utah turn to Thomas G. Alexander, "The Civil Rights Movement in Utah." Jamie Coughtry captured civil rights activities in Las Vegas, Nevada, in *Civil Rights Efforts in Las Vegas*. In *Storming Caesars Palace*, Annelise Orleck more specifically told *How Black Mothers Fought Their Own War on Poverty*. Quintard Taylor focused on "The Civil Rights Movement in the Urban West: Black Protest in Seattle." Black women played important roles; see Oklahoma activist Clara Luper's *Behold the Walls*; Merline Pitre's *In Struggle Against Jim Crow: Lulu White and the NAACP*; Elaine Brown's *A Taste of Power: A Black Woman's Story*; and Stefanie Decker's consideration of black women in Texas, "African American Women in the Civil Rights Era." Four northwest region African American women, leaders and activists in the Seattle-based CORE, Joan Singler, Jean Durning, Bettylou Valentine, and Maid Adams, published a much-needed work titled *Seattle in Black and White: The Congress of Racial Equality and the Fight for Equal Opportunity*.

Recently also, much attention has been given to the significance and emergence of the Black Power movement in the West. A few studies have been mentioned, but see also Lucas N. N. Burke and Judson L. Jeffries, *The Portland*

Black Panthers: Empowering Albina and Remaking a City. Black Panthers who emerged in Seattle also point out Jeffrey Zane and Judson L. Jeffries in "A Panther Sighting in the Pacific Northwest: The Seattle Chapter of the Black Panther Party." A broader history of the Black Panthers, focusing on the Oakland-based Panthers, is found in Joshua Bloom and Waldo E. Martin Jr., *Black Against Empire: The History and Politics of the Black Panther Party*. Peniel Joseph edited a thoughtful work, *The Black Power Movement: Rethinking the Civil Rights–Black Power Era*.

With all the previously published, solid studies, the question emerges, why this book? No one has yet written the definitive study of African American civil rights efforts throughout the West in this period. Other reasons for publishing *Black Americans and the Civil Rights Movement in the West* have been discussed above, but a more systematic answer should be made. First, we need to better understand and recognize our history, both its positive and negative elements. Writers and researchers have provided us with studies on aspects of the civil rights movement in the West. Much has been written, for example, about individual efforts within the western states and communities, but big gaps loomed, and we needed new approaches to the study of this movement as it emerged and contributed to African American civil rights experiences in the West.

Black Americans and the Civil Rights Movement in the West is comprised of a foreword written by University of Washington scholar Quintard Taylor; this preface; an introduction, "Freedom Struggle," fifteen articles; a bibliography; and an index. We emphasize the varied civil rights options and opportunities manifested by black westerners to facilitate their own particular situations. To further that goal, the basic articles are divided into four separate parts—"The Far West," "The Mountain States and the Desert Southwest," "The Upper Midwest," and "The South and the West Collide." Each chapter is introduced by the editors and related to the overall civil rights story and struggle in the United States West. The book, published by the University of Oklahoma Press, is part of Quintard Taylor's Race and Culture in the American West series.

Even though the focus of this book remains on the African American struggle for civil rights, other overlapping struggles for equal rights and social or political change are brought into the articles, especially in terms of their connection to the black struggle. Often concomitant with the black freedom struggle were efforts by various other groups such as Mexican Americans, Asian Americans, American Indians, and women's rights activists to seek more equitable treatment. These civil rights interrelationships have been looked at by numerous authors.

Mark Brilliant, in his book *The Color of America*, focuses on California multiracial movements as they interacted and encouraged the advancement of civil rights for numerous groups, including African Americans. Shana Bernstein, as her title indicates, discusses multiracial civil rights movements in *Bridges of Reform: Interracial Civil Rights Activism in Twentieth Century Los Angeles*. So too does Scott Kurashige, albeit focusing on Japanese Americans and African Americans, in *The Shifting Grounds of Race: Black and Japanese Americans in the Making of Multiethnic Los Angeles*. Brian Behnken points out the interrelationship of Mexican Americans and African Americans in *Fighting Their Own Battles: Mexican Americans, African Americans, and the Struggle for Civil Rights in Texas*, and in his informative edited collection *The Struggle in Black and Brown*, he includes examples from Texas and California. At this historical epoch, the remarkable women's rights movement was emerging also, and played a comparable role in the overall civil rights struggles as well as in the western African American civil rights movement.

Please note that we also include chapters on the period prior to 1954 as well as after 1970. Among additional features of particular interest in this study are an emphasis on major cities, a consideration of the influential role of women, and a discussion of the emergence of western-based Black Power and its ramifications. The prelude to *Brown* certainly is recognized, and the book covers the entire west, from the Pacific Ocean to first-tier states. However, due to space and research limits, neither Alaska nor Hawaii was a focus of an article for this book. For those interested in those states, Albert S. Broussard published an excellent article on Hawaii, "The Honolulu NAACP and Race Relations in Hawaii," and for Alaska, Everett Louis Overstreet, *Black on a Background of White: A Chronicle of Afro-Americans' Involvement in America's Last Frontier, Alaska*, is helpful. We should also mention that this study does not include a discussion of the civil rights efforts in Idaho, principally due to the fact that we could uncover no works that discussed that state's civil rights endeavors. For some historical information about the African American community in Idaho see two monographs by Mamie O. Oliver, *Idaho Ebony: The Afro-American Presence in Idaho State History* (1990), and *Blacks in Idaho's White Press* (2003).

Our book includes the important relationship of western civil rights to national and other regional efforts, such as those in the South, and an introductory overview of the western movement that emphasizes its special place in the U.S. civil rights movement. We also indicate misconceptions; for example, the first sit-ins took place in Oklahoma and Kansas, not North Carolina, and even earlier

(1947) in New Mexico. In general *Black Americans and the Civil Rights Movement in the West* covers the years from the 1940s to 1970s, but as noted, earlier chapters covering the years before *Brown* as well as after 1975 have been included.

Publishing a book takes considerable help and support; *Black Americans and the Civil Rights Movement in the West* was no exception. The book began with a discussion between the two editors at a meeting of the Western History Association. In the above process they spoke to Jay Dew, then editor at the University of Oklahoma Press. He encouraged our concept, and suggested publishing with the University of Oklahoma Press. This we decided was a good idea; unfortunately before the manuscript was completed, Dew moved to Texas. However, we were treated well when Kathleen Kelly took over our manuscript at the press. Manuscript editor Emily J. Schuster and copyeditor Kerin Tate readied the manuscript for a University of Oklahoma Press publication.

We also want to thank a number of other individuals. Without the hard work and ability of the individual authors, of course, the book would not have been feasible. We profusely thank the sixteen authors whose studies are featured in this book. Four of the articles were previously published; we thank the publishers of those works who enabled us to use those essays, which we minimally edited for volume consistency. Curtis Peoples, archivist with the Southwest Collection at Texas Tech University, prepared the two maps for us, which are a vital aid. Many thanks to University of Washington historian Quintard Taylor, the Scott and Dorothy Bullitt Professor of American History, who kindly agreed to write the foreword and allowed our book to be included in his first-rate University of Oklahoma Press series, Race and Culture in the American West. As usual, Pearlene V. Glasrud aided the process. Any errors or omissions, however, we realize are our own for which we remain responsible.

United States West

Western Regions

Maps by Curtis L. Peoples

Part I
Prologue

1

Freedom Struggle
An Introduction
Bruce A. Glasrud and Cary D. Wintz

From the 1940s to the 1970s, in an effort similar to that taking place in the rest of the nation as African Americans and their allies challenged oppression and discrimination, an African American civil rights movement emerged in the United States West. While such western efforts had occurred sporadically over the previous decades, segregation, unequal treatment, antiblack violence, and economic dislocation continued to thwart civil rights endeavors in the West. That was not all; overcrowded housing, residential discrimination, loss of employment opportunities, and segregated education further engaged western African American activists. Black aspirants joined civil rights organizations such as the National Association for the Advancement of Colored People (NAACP), the Congress of Racial Equality (CORE), and the National Urban League (NUL). Western activists often established their own local branches of these alliances or formed new associations. With their cadre of local officials and activists, numerous among them women and black professionals, they sought rights and opportunities comparable to that of their white counterparts. Western blacks benefitted from judicial decisions by the U.S. Supreme Court as well as by congressional actions that furthered their communities' civil rights aims.

In 1954, for example, due in large measure to the values, influence, and political skills of a former Californian and westerner, Earl Warren, President Dwight D. Eisenhower's newly appointed chief justice of the U.S. Supreme Court, the court declared in *Brown v. Board of Education of Topeka* that separate schools for white and black students were "inherently unequal." That momentous decision, encouraged by courageous and determined westerners from Kansas, overturned years of constitutionally allowed race-based school segregation in the United States. Even though the succeeding year the court declared that implementation only needed to proceed "with all deliberate speed," enabling school districts to delay desegregating their schools for years, such delays were not typical of all the twenty affected states. In Kansas for example, implementation soon followed.[1] In some respects school desegregation began what is now referred to as the modern civil rights movement, which continued through the 1970s. However, in the West, as in much of the rest of the nation, the movement for African American civil, political, and economic rights started earlier and continued later.

Overlooked in the numerous studies and works devoted to the civil rights movement is the fact that this movement for black rights took place in the western United States as assiduously as in the rest of the nation, and frequently civil rights protests and events in the West overshadowed those in the South and East. Perhaps Texas A&M University scholar Albert S. Broussard phrased the complex relationship of black westerners to the national picture most clearly when he wrote, "Like their counterparts in other parts of the nation, black westerners challenged hostile white attitudes and racial discrimination and exclusion by insisting that they, too, deserved to enjoy all of the rights and privileges of citizens under the United States Constitution."[2] In fact, much of what happened in the West predated the southern experience; the multiracial context of the West, as well as its varied social and political venues, shaped different trajectories in the conflicted western states.

The term "modern civil rights movement" is used to refer to the African American struggle for equal rights with the white majority in the mid-twentieth century. While the chronological boundaries of this movement are somewhat flexible, its period of greatest activity was from the mid-1940s to the mid-1970s, and it encompassed the legal and political battles, as well as the mass action struggle for voting rights, desegregation, educational opportunity, and other issues that obstructed black participation in the economic area. Certainly, in many western locales the movement can trace its roots to earlier in the twentieth century, and elements extend into the late twentieth century. But the greatest activity and advances occurred in the decades at the middle of the century.

As Hasan Kwame Jeffries phrased it, albeit for the larger national story, the civil rights movement was "a diffuse collection of local struggles."[3] The chronological parameters were not identical, but in each state the overall civil rights focus was similar. Recurring issues, such as segregation and desegregation, suffrage and political participation, racial violence, and equal opportunity, surfaced in each, alongside grassroots efforts and the emergence of black leadership. National and regional events, such as the desegregation of the armed forces, the *Brown* decision, civil disobedience and the sit-in movement, the civil rights acts, and the Voting Rights Act of 1965 became part of the story with their impact on communities in the West. Issues and events peculiar to each community and state in the region have been factors in the western civil rights movement. To some extent, protests and confrontations started in the West before the South or North. The civil rights effort in the West was not a trickle-down endeavor from the South or North. Rather, such activity frequently *began* in the West—for example, the sit-in movements. In the West, civil rights activities were more likely to involve interests other than black concerns, and they did not always follow a pattern. Black women emerged as leaders and activists in Seattle earlier than in the South; on the other hand, Seattle activists lagged. As one Seattleite noted, in 1963 "the Civil Rights movement finally had leaped the Cascade Mountains."[4] These similarities and differences are part of the story.

The western civil rights movement, though lesser known and studied, was important not only to the West but also nationally in a number of ways, not the least of which was the important role of women. But other factors such as the early sit-in and direct protest actions, and the effects of 1965 and 1966 events on the national scene, contributed to the rise of the civil rights movement in the West. In 1965 Los Angeles experienced the unexpected, albeit significant, Watts Riot, and in 1966 the Black Panther Party emerged in Oakland; later that year US started in Los Angeles. (It should be noted for the record that despite numerous erroneous statements about the nomenclature of "US," the letters do *not* stand for united slaves, as the Black Panthers labeled them, but for "us" as opposed to "them.") These events turned the western civil rights strategy to a focus on Black Power as a means to accomplish their goals; those ideas and strategies also began to permeate the remainder of the nation.

At this point, perhaps we should make one caveat, or at least offer it for consideration. That is the fact that "civil rights" may be a somewhat misleading and inaccurate term for encompassing this entire body of western efforts to improve the lot of African Americans with many varied goals, approaches, localities, and difficulties. As Robin D. G. Kelley put it so well, the term *civil rights* "falls short of capturing the wide scope and vision of the post–World War II black freedom movement, not just in the North but throughout the country."[5] As a result we use the phrase "civil rights" hesitantly but also purposefully, while acknowledging and reflecting on Kelley's observation. What one realizes is that the western civil rights efforts worked together with other protests—such as the Black Power movement—that fought for economic, social, educational, and even cultural privileges and necessities and encompassed the Struggle for

Black Liberation, a phrase that was sometimes used by activists and scholars in depicting the overall civil rights revolution in the United States West.

As important as these movements for African American rights and freedoms were in the West, the work is not yet fully accomplished. But a valiant effort effected change and affected many individuals and groups. Even as we wrote, pivotal civil rights actions transpired in the cities and rural regions of the West; they also continue to impact the entire nation.

Notes

1. Brown v. Board of Education of Topeka, 347 U.S. 483 (1954).
2. Albert S. Broussard, *Expectations of Equality: A History of Black Westerners* (Wheeling, Ill.: Harlan Davidson, 2012), xiii.
3. Hasan Kwame Jeffries, "Searching for a New Freedom," in *A Companion to African American History*, ed. Alton Hornsby Jr., (Malden, Mass.: Blackwell Publishing, 2008), 499–511; quotation on p. 503.
4. Quoted in Quintard Taylor, *The Forging of a Black Community: Seattle's Central District from 1870 through the Civil Rights Era* (Seattle: University of Washington Press, 1994), 198.
5. Robin D. G. Kelley, "Afterword," in *Freedom North: Black Freedom Struggles Outside the South, 1940–1980*, ed. Jeanne F. Theoharis and Komozi Woodard (New York: Palgrave Macmillan, 2003), 313–15; quotation on p. 314.

Further Reading

See selected bibliography, pp. 271–78.

2

Before *Brown* in the West

Jean Van Delinder

In this essay, Oklahoma State University sociologist Jean Van Delinder explores the diverse groups that settled in the West during the nineteenth and twentieth centuries. For blacks in the West, as for many of the other groups, segregation was a way of life. Many African Americans—who typically made up a small segment of the population—resided in segregated communities that looked after each other. Due to the U.S. Supreme Court ruling on *Brown v. Board of Education of Topeka* and other legal supports, blacks in the West pressured for equal rights through a variety of tactics, including an early use of sit-ins. Among Van Delinder's professional accomplishments is the exciting book *Struggles Before Brown: Early Civil Rights Protests and Their Significance Today*.

The modern national civil rights movement credits the 1954 Supreme Court case *Brown v. Board of Education of Topeka* as the beginning of organized protest against racial segregation. Dating the pursuit for civil rights to this period obscures western dissent that occurred prior to the 1950s. Referencing *Brown* also characterizes the civil rights movement as a conflict between the North and South, neglecting what was occurring in other regions, such as the West. The boundary in racial relations between the East and West is just as significant as that between the North and South. This chapter addresses the significance of pre-*Brown* protest in the West by examining regional variation in demonstrations and how protest was tempered by local customs or folkways.

The West is both an imaginary place and a geographical region, its boundaries ever changing as new states were created. The West captured people's imagination as a place where there was the potential to begin anew. When considering pre-*Brown* civil rights activism, the West is a sober reminder that racial discrimination was not just a southern problem, but a national one. As European settlers moved west, they brought white supremacist ideals along with their hopes and dreams. Nevertheless, the African American settlers found new ways to challenge racism and discrimination, eventually erasing the color line separating black from white.

Though the story of the modern civil rights movement focuses on challenges to legal and economic injustices suffered by African Americans, less obvious was their everyday lived reality, how their disenfranchisement included social practices based on prejudice and persistent beliefs about their social and moral inferiority. Black sociologist W. E. B. Du Bois categorized racial segregation or "Jim Crow" as the "color line"—an imaginary boundary separating black from white. As an all-inclusive system of exclusion, it justified African Americans' economic, political, and social inequality. Du Bois also recognized that the boundaries of the color line were recreated through everyday social interaction, something that could be challenged, and that the racial meanings associated with those boundaries were dependent on agreement by *both* whites and blacks. Disrupting these agreed-upon understandings of racial separation was a gradual process, involving numerous challenges and negotiations.

As a region, the West challenges conventional understandings of race due to the presence of four nonwhite groups of color: African Americans, Asian Americans, Latinos, and American Indians. These diverse racial and ethnic groups interacted differently with the dominant Anglo population, just as they were often thrown into competition with each other for jobs, housing, and social status. Even though Asians were usually signaled out, especially Chinese and Japanese laborers on the West Coast, African Americans still had to contend with significant racial discrimination and prejudice. Though they were granted citizenship status after the Civil War, it did not give them much of an advantage over other western ethnic and racial minorities. Closer examination of the West helps illustrate how racial segregation and the civil rights movement were much more complex and nuanced outside the South, and how social change itself is incremental and hard to see even while it takes place before our eyes.

Preexisting *Brown* protests included a range of events. There was a series of boycotts against southern Jim Crow streetcars starting in 1900 and ending in 1906. Between 1929 and 1941, northern African Americans organized "don't buy where you can't work" campaigns, boycotting white restaurants, grocery stores, clothing stores, and other stores that refused to hire blacks. Embryonic mass-based protest tactics included the mass march planned for Washington in 1941 (the March on Washington movement), lunch-counter sit-ins staged by CORE (Congress of Racial Equality, which emerged from the earlier FOR—Fellowship of Reconciliation) that same year in Chicago, and the first Freedom Ride in 1947. These earlier manifestations of protest point to the presence of black resistance and an insurgent ideology outside the South long before the 1950s.

Race and Democracy

The pre-*Brown* era cannot be understood without coming to terms with the inherent contradiction between racism and democracy. If democratic societies are based on the premise that its citizens freely elect its leaders, membership in those societies are based on the political franchise or the right to vote. The granting of voting rights to African American males with the passage of the Fifteenth Amendment in 1870 gave them the legal status of citizenship, though without any of its protections. Some even argued that once they were emancipated, blacks no longer possessed a special dependent status they had while slaves and therefore no longer needed the protection of the federal government. During this period, through the use of poll taxes, literacy tests, and other means of intimidation, southern states, controlled by the Democratic Party, were able to effectively disenfranchise African Americans. Given that their rights of citizenship were not supported, it is not surprising that many blacks began migrating in significant numbers after 1870. They moved north and west, where their voting rights were somewhat protected by the Republican Party during Reconstruction. However, as Republicans gained new voters in the West from white immigration, black votes were not as necessary. Attempts to regain voting rights would provide one basis for group action in the civil rights movement in the mid-twentieth century.

Racial Uplift in an Era of White Supremacy

Between 1880 and 1930, after the end of Reconstruction and before the beginning of the New Deal, the federal government sanctioned the emergence of a nationwide order of white supremacy. The racial dimensions of governmental policy sanctioned a tightening of racial segregation starting with the Civil Rights Cases of 1883, when the Supreme Court invalidated the 1875 Civil Rights Acts forbidding discrimination in public transportation. This decision was followed by the 1896 *Plessy v. Ferguson* decision, further reinforcing the second-class status of African American citizens not only in public transportation but in all facets of community life. Even during Reconstruction, between 1865 and 1877, the racial order both inside and outside the South meant a marginalized status for African Americans—politically, economically, socially—enforced by a culture of antiblack violence.

As a means to survive, blacks created their own separate institutions including churches, schools, and community and fraternal organizations. The cohesiveness of these segregated communities was both sustained and divided by an ideology of racial uplift, a highly individualistic response, in an era with little protection from local, state, and federal governments. As a self-help ideology, racial uplift emphasized the importance of image or representation. As a belief system it resonated with American individualism, isolating individual achievement from other contributing factors to their privileged status. It also divided the black community since black elites identified more with the goals and aspirations of whites than members of their own race. Black elites led by example, wherein their appearance mirrored what was valued in the white community—educated, well spoken, and economically prosperous. It also alleviated the guilt of elite blacks when a majority of African Americans were barely surviving.

In an era when blacks were being continuously characterized as unfit for citizenship, and speaking out brought unwanted violent attention from political authorities, black leaders counseled unadventurous approaches rather than direct confrontation to combat discrimination. By insisting that individual achievements benefited the entire race, racial uplift undermined collective responses to racism and demands for equal rights. Challenges to the racial uplift ideology as belonging to an older, more conservative generation gained momentum in the twentieth century with the rise of black militancy and the growth of a strong youth counterculture in the 1960s.

Race and the West:
Search for a Racial Promised Land

Though the prospect of free land and new beginnings drew settlers to the West, it nevertheless quickly became economically, politically, and socially dominated by white Europeans. Chronic shortages of labor in farming, mining, and manufacturing in the Far West (California, Oregon, Washington, Nevada, Montana, and Colorado) brought about the recruitment of Asians and Pacific Islanders as laborers along with the indigenous American Indian and Hispanic or Latino populations. African Americans who had journeyed west hoping to find their own promised land found instead stiff competition from other racial and ethnic minorities and a system of racial segregation that rivaled that of the South.

Race and the Frontier

Frederick Jackson Turner's famous frontier thesis, published in 1890, was constructed on mythological and individualistic notions of a white, male conquest of western territories, making nonwhites and most white women invisible. It romanticized the pastoral life at a time when it had all but disappeared as a viable way to earn a living in the rapidly industrializing American economy. It also marginalized the contributions of nonwhite groups in settling the West by prioritizing the rural rather than the urban experience. The frontier was defined by an ever-moving boundary between the settled East and the rough Wild West. In its fluctuating state, the frontier was also a disorderly region where there were negotiations and contests over land, as well as continuous redefinitions of gender roles and racial and ethnic divisions.

Black migration of any significance to the West began at the end of Reconstruction. Since the majority of African Americans settled in former slaveholding regions, Texas, and Indian Territory, tensions soon ensued over the power of the federal government to enforce suffrage and civil rights legislation. Texas was able to pass homestead legislation that, together with the common practice of not selling land to African Americans, effectively shut out ex-slaves. Black Californians found it difficult to claim a homestead, vote, serve on juries, testify in court, or marry a white person. Arizona (1912) and Oklahoma (1907) both adopted segregation statutes at statehood.

Even the rights of black soldiers serving in the military were circumscribed. In 1897 Montana passed a residency statute, which excluded any person living on an Indian or military reservation from becoming a resident. Iowa's 1844 constitution prohibited slavery but restricted "Negro" rights including suffrage, militia service, or ability to hold legislative office. Many states passed statutes prohibiting interracial marriages in the nineteenth century, and Nebraska amended its miscegenation laws in 1943 to include anyone of not only "Negro" but also Japanese or Chinese blood, reflecting the anti-Asian sentiment during World War II.

Nevada enacted four miscegenation laws and a school segregation statute over a period of almost one hundred years between 1865 and 1957. The education statute declared that blacks, Asians, and Indians were prohibited from attending public schools, and that a separate school would be established for them if "deemed advisable." The state's miscegenation law offered an extensive list of inappropriate marriage candidates by race and color for Caucasians, including blacks, Asians, and American Indians. Oregon enacted two different miscegenation laws, one passed in 1867 and another in 1930, prohibiting intermarriage between whites and blacks, Chinese, Kanakas, or any person having more than one-half Indian blood. Kanakas (literally "boy") is a derogatory term to refer to workers recruited from Hawaii and the South Pacific employed in agriculture and ranching.

In Minnesota, where the black population totaled only one-half of 1 percent of the state's population, antidiscrimination laws were passed between 1910 and 1940 making it lawful to refuse service to blacks in restaurants, hotels, and other public places along with restrictive covenants limiting their residential settlement to North Minneapolis. Minnesota also passed miscegenation laws even though it had a minuscule African American population.

Though there were black cowboys and homesteaders, far more African American men and women found jobs in the new urban economy, moving to cities like Minneapolis, Denver, San Francisco, Seattle, and Los Angeles, and smaller towns like Topeka, Kansas; Salt Lake City, Utah; Virginia City, Nevada; and Helena, Montana. Legitimate employment included domestic labor for women, and black men could find work as hotel waiters, railroad porters, messengers, cooks, and janitors. As their communities grew, they also established their own churches, fraternal organizations, and social clubs. Though racial segregation was not explicitly defined, as it was in the South, they were still subject to prejudice and discrimination. Their small numbers did not make them invisible to the dominant population. It also meant they were just as likely to be visible targets of unwanted attention, ranging from intimidation, harassment, and name calling, to physical violence.

Antiblack Violence in the West

Actually, African Americans were more likely to be lynched outside of the South, and the probability of an African American being lynched was more likely in western states than southern ones between 1900 and 1930. Wyoming ranks first, followed by New Mexico and Oregon. Even Nebraska, Missouri, and Iowa had significantly higher rates of lynching than the southern states of South Carolina, Virginia, and North Carolina. For example, in June 1920, three black circus workers were lynched in Duluth, Minnesota, a smaller city in northern Minnesota with a minuscule black population. Racial tensions were running high after U.S. Steel recruited black workers from southern plantations to fend off an impending strike for higher pay in the local steel mill. The end of World War I and the severe depression had hit this area hard during the winter of 1920, contributing to high unemployment and stagnant wages. The Duluth Works Steel Mill had been built in 1915 and was the region's major employer. The importation of the black workers meant the steelworkers' wages remained depressed at twenty five cents a day. That the three men were dragged from their jail cells and hung on a lamp pole at an intersection close to Gary, the black section of town, also sent a strong message its residents.

Though the specter of antiblack violence, prejudice, and segregation continued to circumscribe their movements in urban areas, blacks also found new avenues for gaining full citizenship by exercising their economic rights instead of fighting for their political ones. In Minneapolis, Minnesota, 80 percent of black men worked as porters, janitors, and night watchmen. As the Depression overwhelmed local charities, New Deal programs like the Civil Works Administration (CWA) assimilated black charities into a network of federal social societies. Employment through CWA organizations meant blacks were hired into jobs such as librarians and nurses that had previously been closed to them. These federal jobs also gave the black community protection and a way to fight racial discrimination in hiring.

The New Deal facilitated union organizing in Minnesota, and when the CIO integrated unions in the late 1930s, it provided an opportunity for black workers to unionize. One black leader in the Minneapolis labor movement, Cassius Allen, was able to become an independent businessman after working as a waiter at the Curtis Hotel in downtown Minneapolis. Others recognized that becoming involved in the labor movement was a way to fight discrimination. Nellie Stone Johnson, an elevator operator, saw working as a union activist as a way to unite Minneapolis's black community. Though some entrepreneurial individuals found union membership a way to become financially independent, union activism was also an avenue toward fighting for racial equality.

Early Legal Victories

Despite many setbacks to their economic and political rights, by the late 1930s there was a shift in favor of African American citizenship rights by challenges brought through the legal system. The Legal Defense and Education Fund (LDF) of the National Association of the Advancement of Colored People (NAACP), led by Charles Hamilton Houston and Thurgood Marshall, began to challenge barriers to political participation and unequal access to higher education in the 1930s. Their strategy was to dismantle segregation by exploiting its main weakness: the cost. Many states could barely afford to maintain separate institutions and most did not even attempt to make its separate institutions equal. The most obvious target was higher education, especially graduate and professional schools, which had low enrollments and were expensive to continue.

Successful challenges to segregated higher education included *Pearson v. Murray* (1935), a Maryland Court of Appeals decision, wherein Donald Murray became the first black applicant to matriculate into a southern law school—the University of Maryland Law School. Three years later, *Missouri ex rel. Gaines v. Canada* (1938) was heard before the U.S. Supreme Court, after the State of Missouri built a separate but unequal law school for Lloyd Gaines. This decision invalidated laws and practices among southern states forcing African American students to attend separate, inadequate graduate schools or out-of-state schools.

Ten years after the Gaines case, Lois Sipuel was barred from attending law school at the University of Oklahoma. With the help of the LDF, she successfully sued the Oklahoma State Regents in the Supreme Court Case *Sipuel v. Oklahoma State Regents*, 1948. Two years later in *McLaurin v. Oklahoma State Regents* (1950), the plaintiff, George McLaurin, also challenged University of Oklahoma. He wanted to pursue a doctor of education degree, but since the university did not provide separate facilities he was isolated from the professor and other students, forced to sit outside the classroom and at a separate table in the cafeteria. He petitioned the U.S. District Court for the Western District of Oklahoma to be allowed to sit in the same classroom as the other students. McLaurin appealed to the U.S. Supreme Court and won his case. The same day in *Sweatt v. Painter* (1950), the Supreme Court ruled in another law school case from Texas that law schools cannot be "separate and equal." Texas had hastily established a separate law school so they could deny Heman Marion Sweatt admission to the previously all-white University of Texas School of Law. The court ruled that the separate law could not provide a legal education "equal" to that available to white students.

Other important Supreme Court decisions include *Alston v. School Board of City of Norfolk* (1940), which resulted in pay equalization for African American teachers. In *Smith v. Allwright* (1944), Thurgood Marshall argued that the Texas Democratic primary system allowed whites to structurally dominate the politics of the one-party South and that the system violated the Fourteenth and Fifteenth Amendments. In so ruling, *Smith* overruled a unanimous nine-year-old decision in *Grovey v. Townsend* that upheld the Texas Democratic Party's race-based restrictions on voting in primaries because it was a private, not a public organization. The overthrow of the Democratic white primaries in Texas was the result of several years of planning by the local NAACP and black leadership. African

Americans learned practical skills in how to challenge white supremacy and took hope from the several Supreme Court victories as they began to migrate to the West in significant numbers in the late 1930s and 1940s.

The Second Great Migration and World War II

World War II brought a redefinition of status not only for women, but also for African Americans. In 1944 social scientist Gunnar Myrdal noted that "there is bound to be a redefinition of the Negro's status in America as a result of this war."[1] Wartime labor shortages pulled African American men and women to the West, while the widespread use of the mechanized cotton picker pushed them out of the rural South. Unlike earlier western migrations, theirs was an urban destination. Leaving behind subsistence sharecropping and farming, large numbers of African Americans headed to cities in the North, Midwest, and especially the West.

During the first half of the twentieth century, black migration was primarily to the North. This First Great Migration was facilitated by accessible transportation via the railroad lines, drawing rural blacks to menial manufacturing jobs in cities like St. Louis, Chicago, and Detroit. After 1941 their destination changed in favor of the West, based on the promise of living wages protected by the federal government through Executive Order 8802—implementing the Fair Employment Practices Commission (FEPC). By requiring that companies with government contracts not discriminate on the basis of race or religion meant that African Americans could now compete for jobs that had been only available to white males. This Second Great Migration began during World War II and eventually brought five million African Americans to the West, many of whom found work in Los Angeles's massive defense industries.

This second wave of migration also differed from the earlier one in that it drew more black people from southern cities than rural areas. They also brought with them a diversity of experiences with racism and a variety of skills in challenging discrimination. Migrants from New Orleans brought with them a legacy of affiliation with organized labor and even communism. As in Minneapolis, New Orleans's blacks found an opportunity to combat discrimination through union activism. The 1892 New Orleans general strike demonstrated that black and white dockworkers could unite through shared interests. Though the unions remained segregated, there was a form of interracial solidarity based on the recognition that by cooperating they improved working conditions for both groups. As unskilled laborers, dockworkers were easily replaced. By working with black unions, white labor unions could protect all of their jobs and circumvent the potential for strikebreakers to be brought in.

Houston migrants had experienced a low rate of racial violence, some occupational opportunities, and a high rate of civil rights activism. The Houston NAACP fought for integrated buses and were outspoken about police brutality in the 1930s and 1940s. In the early 1940s, black teachers walked off their jobs until the Houston School Board equalized their salaries. When a black dentist and NAACP member named Dr. Lonnie Smith was not able to vote in the Democratic primary, his case was eventually argued by Thurgood Marshall before the U.S. Supreme Court, resulting in the landmark decision *Smith v. Allwright* in 1944.

The West was also a place where experiments with economic boycotts conducted by college and high school students were met without much resistance by whites in the late 1940s and 1950s. Sit-ins and boycotts were staged in post–World War II Omaha, challenging discriminatory practices. In 1948, the DePorres Club, a group of African American high school students and white college students at Creighton University in Omaha, participated in a successful sit-in at a restaurant in downtown Omaha. They refused to leave until the owner agreed to serve African Americans. They also targeted local businesses, including Eppley Airfield, for not hiring black workers.

At the same time, college students at the University of New Mexico staged sit-ins in Albuquerque in 1947. The sit-ins were organized after a university law student named George Long was turned away at a nearby restaurant. University students quickly organized sit-ins to boycott the restaurant, forcing the management to change its policy. Three months later university students integrated a downtown Walgreens. Then George Long worked with Herbert Wright, the first black student body president, to write an antidiscrimination ordinance based on one in Portland, Oregon. The Albuquerque Civil Rights Ordinance was enacted by the city commission in February 1952. It prohibited discrimination in places of public accommodations and allowed businesses to be fined for violations. This ordinance was a community-based effort, the result of a cooperative alliance between student and off-campus organizations, such as the NAACP, the Ministerial Alliance, the GI Forum, labor unions, and the Catholic Archdiocese. Three years after the ordinance was passed, the state legislature enacted a similar statute. The ordinance is believed to be one of the earlier municipal ordinances passed in the United States since the beginning of World War II.

Around eight thousand blacks lived in Albuquerque in 1950, and most were employed as unskilled laborers. After the 1952 Civil Rights Ordinance was passed, the NAACP had branches in Roswell, Hobbs, Clovis, Carlsbad, and Las Cruces with a college chapter at the University of New Mexico. Alamogordo integrated its teaching staff in 1953 followed by the desegregation of the Hobbs school system in 1954.

Similar boycotts against public accommodations took place a decade later in Oklahoma and Kansas. Once again drawing on organizational and personal networks, in 1958 the NAACP Youth Council staged sit-ins in July at the Dockum Rexall Drug store in Wichita, Kansas. Led by Ron Walters, president of the local NAACP Youth Council, the Wichita sit-ins lasted three weeks. Across the state line in Oklahoma, Clara Luper, an NAACP Youth Council leader and local high school teacher, staged sit-ins at Katz Drug Store in Oklahoma City. Sit-ins quickly spread to Tulsa and Enid as well. Like the sit-ins in Albuquerque, local businesses quickly desegregated.

Though blacks in New Mexico, Kansas, and Oklahoma all experienced different levels of discrimination in education, housing, and employment, targeting public accommodations brought reluctant but sympathetic reactions from whites. Though they were not full members of society, being denied service in a public restaurant challenged notions of fairness and equality by people in the West.

From Migrants to Militants: The Rise of a Postracial Society

After 1947, wartime jobs disappeared and other employment opportunities fled to suburbs as inner cities deteriorated. Living in the city now meant high unemployment, substandard housing, and failing schools; the black population once again was faced with disenfranchisement. The existing civil rights organizations that had dismantled racial segregation were ineffective in combating these new forms of economic and political discrimination. By the mid-1960s, a more militant, Black Nationalist ideology began to resonate with young urban blacks replacing the "nonviolence" ethics of their parents' and grandparents' generations. Though these older generations had won formal citizenship rights, they still lacked significant political and economic power. Dissatisfied with the status quo and restless for change, during the latter years of the civil rights movement many began to question the future of American democracy in general.

The migration of black families out of the South during World War II transformed other social practices related to civil rights activism. The post–World

War II "baby boom" created an unprecedented number of urban young people who had access to higher education, were marginalized by existing civil rights organizations, and found racial uplift ideology irrelevant. A new generation of young blacks growing up in these cities faced a different world than their parents; they sought to develop new forms of tactics to address them. In Oakland, California, where the ideology of the Black Panther Party was starting to become verbalized, its membership "consisted of recent migrants whose families traveled north and west to escape the southern racial regime, only to be confronted with new forms of segregation and repression."[2]

Black Power represented a shift away from biracial coalitions and racial uplift ideology. It also indicated disillusionment with democracy to create consensus about the importance of racial equality. During the pre-*Brown* era, civil rights activists sought justice by working through democratic institutions and processes. In the 1950s and early 1960s, blacks and whites had worked together through such groups such as the National Association for the Advancement of Colored People (NAACP), the Congress for Equality (CORE) and the Southern Christian Leadership Conference (SCLC) to eliminate racial discrimination in order to build a desegregated society. Even with landmark civil rights legislation in the 1960s, blacks still faced lower wages than whites, contended with higher crime rates in their neighborhoods, and attended dilapidated inner-city schools.

Young blacks in particular saw the civil rights movement as unable to generate significant changes to the racial status quo. They wanted to enjoy the same economic and political rights whites had. Perhaps more important, they wanted to take control of the civil rights movement, which they thought was ineffective and only assuaged whites' guilt: significant change could only come from within the black community. Though black separatism and militancy had a long tradition in the black community, it was marginalized. However, with the Black Power movement it gained traction, especially among young, educated, and urban black people.

Though the term "Black Power" was not new, it was popularized by Stokely Carmichael as the Student Nonviolent Coordinating Committee (SNCC) evolved from an inclusive community activist organization into a black-only social change organization. Never a formally organized social movement and lacking central leadership, by the late 1960s Black Power ideology had made a definite mark on American culture and society.

Briefly, Black Power took issue with how white ideals of social progress had been imposed on them. They needed to take control of their own destiny by forming all-black political parties in order to build their own power base. Urging blacks to build their own institutions to combat racism raised both black and white fears about resegregation, undoing the victories of the civil rights movement. Many saw Black Power as a nationalist movement, a paramilitary organization bent on violence. Some even saw it as a threat to American democracy.

Though the Black Power movement did not sustain its early momentum, nor did it end discrimination or racism, it did signal a coming of age for black youths who demanded self-determination from the black community.

Conclusions

Civil rights activism had numerous manifestations throughout the United States prior to 1954, the year of the *Brown* decision. Racial segregation is commonly associated with the South and northern cities, but it was widespread throughout the West, a region often overlooked in the pre-*Brown* era. During the first part of the twentieth century, racial inequality was more likely to be addressed through negotiations facilitated by community organizations rather than marches and other public demonstrations commonly associated with the civil rights movement. The first national organization targeting racial equality, the NAACP, was organized in 1909–10, and soon there were local chapters throughout the United States, even in the sparsely populated West. The emergence of black protest literature emerged with the Harlem Renaissance of the 1920s, which also had a far-reaching influence on black communities throughout the United States.

The West is also a place that allowed black people to search for a racial promised land. But the presence of significant numbers of racial and ethnic groups—American Indians, Asians, and Hispanics or Latinos—intensified efforts by white elites to sustain their racial hegemony. To maintain their political and economic power, they even racialized other white immigrant groups that might threaten their privileged status. The influx of over a million newly displaced people in the 1930s gave rise to the pejorative term of "Okie," which referred to any poor white who happened to migrate to California, whether or not they originally came from Oklahoma.

The initial lure of living wages and stable employment brought African Americans to the West. Even though they still had to contend with racism and discrimination, they invented new strategies to contend with them. They also inspired other ethnic groups to seek empowerment, such as *El Movimiento*, an extension of the Mexican American civil rights movement, which began in the 1940s. As the New Deal gave new federal protections prohibiting racial and gender discrimination in employment, African Americans were able to secure jobs in the booming defense industry. By the end of World War II as they once again found themselves expendable, they also witnessed significant progress in winning legal challenges to segregation. It would be up to the next generation, those who had grown up in South Central Los Angeles, Denver's Five Points, or Seattle's Central District, to find new ways to overcome racism and poverty.

Notes

1. Josh Sides, *L.A. City Limits: African American Los Angeles from the Great Depression to the Present* (Berkeley: University of California Press, 2003).
2. Donna Jean Murch, *Living for the City: Migration, Education, and the Rise of the Black Panther Party in Oakland, California* (Chapel Hill: University of North Carolina Press, 2010).

Further Reading

Delton, Jennifer A. *Making Minnesota Liberal: Civil Rights and the Transformation of the Democratic Party.* Minneapolis: University of Minnesota Press, 2002.

Du Bois, W. E. B. *The Souls of Black Folk.* New York: Bantam, 1989.

Glasrud, Bruce A., ed. *Anti-Black Violence in Twentieth Century Texas.* College Station: Texas A&M University Press, 2015.

Hine, Darlene Clark. *Black Victory: The Rise and Fall Of The White Primary In Texas.* Columbia: University of Missouri Press, 2003.

Katznelson, Ira. *Fear Itself: The New Deal and the Origins of Our Time.* New York: W. W. Norton, 2013.

King, Desmond, and Stephen Tuck. "De-centering the South: America's Nationwide White Supremacist Order after Reconstruction." *Past and Present* 194 (2007): 214–53.

Meier, August, and Elliott Rudwick. *CORE: A Study in the Civil Rights Movement, 1942–1968.* New York: Oxford University Press, 1973.

Murch, Donna Jean. *Living for the City: Migration, Education, and the Rise of the Black Panther Party in Oakland, California.* Chapel Hill: University of North Carolina Press, 2010.

Rosenberg, Daniel. *New Orleans Dockworkers: Race, Labor, and Unionism, 1892–1923.* Albany, N.Y.: State University of New York Press, 1988.

Sides, Josh. *L.A. City Limits: African American Los Angeles from the Great Depression to the Present.* Berkeley: University of California Press, 2003.

Taylor, Quintard. *In Search of the Racial Frontier: African Americans in the American West 1528–1990.* New York: W. W. Norton, 1998.

Taylor, Quintard, and Shirley Ann Wilson Moore, eds. *African American Women Confront the West: 1600–2000.* Norman: University of Oklahoma Press, 2003.

Van Delinder, Jean. *Struggles Before Brown: Early Civil Rights Protests and their Significance Today.* Boulder: Paradigm, 2008.

Woodward, C. Vann. *The Strange Career of Jim Crow.* New York: Oxford, 1974.

Part II

The Far West

Geographically the four states of the far west are defined by their location west of the Rocky Mountains. California and Nevada were part of the 1848 Mexican cession, while Oregon and Washington became U.S. territory through the Oregon Compromise. Both were free territories and attracted relatively few African Americans prior to World War II. In 1940 the African American populations in these states ranged from less than 1 percent of the population in Washington, Oregon, and Nevada to less than 2 percent in California. By 1970 this had increased to 7 percent in California and almost 6 percent in Nevada, but remained between 1 percent and 2 percent in Washington and Oregon. In all four states African Americans were primarily located in urban centers, especially Los Angeles and the Bay Area in California, which attracted many black migrants from the South who sought an escape from southern racism and better economic opportunity through jobs in defense and other industries. While the West did not have the level of de jure segregation that characterized the South, racism and segregation persisted.

3

Civil Rights Movement in the Pacific Northwest

Kevin Allen Leonard

Until World War II, African Americans in the Pacific Northwest were few in number, and they faced long-standing white antagonism. However, jobs became available as the war progressed, and in the cities of Seattle, Spokane, and Portland, the black population increased. They still faced discrimination, and beginning in the 1960s, with help from CORE and the NAACP, began working to eradicate segregation and discrimination. Later Black Power became an option and was used by some in the black community. Kevin Leonard, formerly professor of history at Western Washington University, currently is chair of the history department at Tennessee State University; among his publications is the award-winning book, *The Battle for Los Angeles: Racial Ideology and World War II.*

Two years after his October 1942 release from the U.S. Army, John L. Vaughns, a native of Fairfield, Texas, moved to Spokane, Washington. Like many other African Americans, Vaughns took the jobs that were available to him while attempting to gain access to better paying positions. In the late 1940s, he worked in a shoe shine parlor in downtown Spokane. By 1952, he had begun working as a helper in the Union Iron Works. In the fall of 1955, he began work at the Kaiser Aluminum Company's plant at Mead, north of Spokane. Shortly before the end of his thirty-day probationary period at Kaiser, Vaughns was let go. A statement by his supervisor led Vaughns to believe that he had been fired because he was an African American. Employment discrimination on the basis of race was illegal in the state of Washington, and Vaughns filed a complaint with the

Washington State Board Against Discrimination in Employment (WSBADE). The WSBADE considered Vaughns's complaint on December 28, 1955, and soon ruled in his favor. The supervisor was reprimanded, and Vaughns was rehired and assigned to work under a different supervisor. Vaughns ended up working at Kaiser until he retired at the age of fifty-nine in 1975.

Although Vaughns regained his job at Kaiser and overcame the discrimination he faced, the statements of WSBADE executive director Glen Mansfield highlight some of the difficulties that African Americans faced in the Pacific Northwest in the 1950s and 1960s. In his announcement of the decision in the Vaughns case, Mansfield stated that "Kaiser Aluminum's over-all employment practices have always been in complete compliance with the law." He insisted that "this case was definitely not a reflection on company practices or policies, which are excellent, but was rather the possible default of one supervisor."[1] Mansfield's words reflect the fact that the officials of the state agency charged with enforcing the law against employment discrimination were extremely cautious in their actions. Evidence suggests that neither Mansfield nor the majority of appointees to the WSBADE in the 1950s were deeply committed to the eradication of employment discrimination.

African Americans faced racial discrimination in the Pacific Northwest from the earliest days of U.S. colonization of the region. Individual African Americans and white supporters of racial equality had worked to end discrimination even as early as the 1850s. Civil rights organizations formed in the Northwest in the early twentieth century, and they achieved some successes in the years prior to World War II. Even though many historians have argued that World War II set the stage for the emergence of a mass movement in the 1950s and 1960s, there was relatively little in the way of mass mobilization in the Northwest in the 1950s. This was in part due to the fact that both Oregon and Washington had relatively small black populations and both states had enacted fair employment legislation in 1949. Ironically, this legislation seems to have both encouraged and prevented further civil rights activism. Little evidence suggests that the *Brown* decision of 1954, the Montgomery Bus Boycott of 1955–56, or even the sit-ins of 1960 in the South had a great impact on civil rights activism in the Northwest. Instead, African Americans worked through state and municipal legislative bodies to try to end discrimination in housing, employment, and access to public accommodations without connecting their struggle to the southern civil rights movement. Black residents of Portland also fought to protect their neighborhoods and homes from redevelopment projects.

The Freedom Rides, however, did finally resonate in the Northwest, helping to lead to the establishment of a vibrant CORE chapter in Seattle that succeeded in gaining access to employment in grocery and department stores for black residents of that city. Marches also occurred in other cities, most notably Spokane. By the middle years of the 1960s, however, the coalitions that had been built by CORE, the NAACP, and the Urban League in Seattle frayed, and Black Power organizations emerged and became highly visible in the struggle for the elimination of discrimination and community empowerment. Some of the community service projects established by Black Power organizations continued to operate throughout the 1970s, and African Americans consolidated political power in several Northwest cities in the 1970s.

Many of the white Americans who participated in the colonization of the Pacific Northwest in the 1830s and 1840s brought with them deep hostility toward African Americans. The white men who established the provisional government in Oregon in 1843 prohibited slavery in the territory under their jurisdiction. The next year the government's legislative committee passed a law excluding African Americans from the territory. A similar law was passed by the territorial legislature after Congress formally established Oregon Territory. An exclusion clause was included in the state constitution of 1859. The constitution also denied African Americans the right to vote. Despite white efforts to exclude African Americans from Oregon, a small number of black people moved to the Northwest. After Washington Territory was established in 1853, most African Americans settled north of the Columbia River. By 1860, 154 African Americans lived in the region. Even though the ratification of the Thirteenth, Fourteenth, and Fifteenth Amendments to the U.S. Constitution after the Civil War prevented enforcement of exclusion measures in Oregon, pervasive discrimination persisted.

In part because of Oregon's reputation for hostility to African Americans, the black population of the Northwest remained quite small well into the twentieth century. However, some African Americans did migrate to the region's larger cities, particularly Seattle and Portland, after the Civil War. The 1900 census, for example, counted 775 African Americans in Portland and 406 in Seattle. Some of these black residents believed that their small numbers protected them from the kind of discrimination they had faced either in the South or in northeastern or midwestern cities. Nonetheless, the presence of racial prejudice was apparent to most black residents of the Northwest. Despite the small number of African Americans in these cities, by the 1890s the communities were large enough to support newspapers that exposed racial discrimination and fought for the rights of African Americans. Horace Cayton founded the *Seattle Republican*, which published continuously between 1894 and 1917. Edward Cannady and nine other men established the *Advocate* in Portland in 1903. Cannady's partners steadily abandoned the enterprise, but in 1912 Cannady married Beatrice Morrow, and the couple continued to publish the newspaper for more than twenty years. The Cannadys were involved in the establishment of an NAACP branch in Portland. In 1915, when the Portland premiere of D. W. Griffith's film *The Birth of a Nation* was announced, Beatrice Morrow Cannady, acting in her capacity as secretary of the local NAACP branch, announced the branch's opposition to the film. Cannady argued that the film should be suppressed because its negative depictions of African Americans would endanger the harmonious relations between Portland's black and white residents. Cannady also led the protest when the film returned to Portland in 1918, 1922, and 1931. The *Advocate* also raised questions and concerns about suspicious killings that may have been lynchings. For example, in 1924 the newspaper called for federal action to investigate the killing and mutilation of Timothy Pettis in Marshfield. An NAACP branch in Spokane was founded in 1919. However, branch members devoted most of their energy to supporting the national NAACP's campaigns against segregation and lynching.

The migration of thousands of African Americans to Portland, Seattle, Tacoma, and Spokane during World War II made it impossible for black residents of these cities to ignore the pervasive racial discrimination they faced. The black population of Seattle more than doubled during the war, and more than twenty thousand African Americans moved to Portland during the war. Some African Americans successfully fought racial discrimination at Boeing in the early years of World War II, although black workers at Boeing and at other employers were assigned to the worst jobs and were often paid less than their white counterparts. The Seattle branches of the NAACP and the National Urban League grew dramatically during the war. Seattle Mayor William F. Devin appointed a Civic Unity Committee in 1944. In November of that year, the Spokane Committee on Race Relations (SCRR) was founded. Both committees were intended to improve race relations so that race riots could be avoided.

In 1945 the Spokane NAACP branch and the SCRR cooperated to investigate charges of discrimination against African American soldiers stationed at an army air base in Walla Walla. In the aftermath of World War II, the local branch of the NAACP also protested the mistreatment of African Americans stationed at Geiger Army Airfield. The black community in Spokane, however, was deeply divided.

The NAACP, for example, opposed funding for the Booker T. Washington Community Center because it was a segregated facility.

Activists associated with the NAACP and with the race relations committee proposed state fair employment legislation soon after World War II, when opposition in Congress led to the demise of the President's Committee on Fair Employment Practice. Such legislation passed in both Washington and Oregon in 1949. However, neither law provided for a strong enforcement mechanism. For many years, gubernatorial appointees to the WSBADE were only weakly committed to fair employment. Legislative appropriations to WSBADE were inadequate. WSBADE ruled in favor of the employer in twenty-three of the first twenty-four cases it decided. Mansfield boasted in 1956 that "not once has it become necessary to call a public hearing or to issue a 'cease and desist' order under the provisions of the statute."[2]

Dissatisfaction with WSBADE prompted activism among leftists in Seattle. In 1950, left-leaning residents, most of them white, organized the Citizens Committee for Fair Employment. This committee waged boycotts of Safeway stores and Frederick and Nelson, a downtown department store. A few years later, the Seattle branch of the National Negro Labor Council picketed Sears, leading the department store to hire its first black employees. NAACP and Urban League leaders criticized the leftists' protest actions. The persecution of leftists in the early 1950s made it possible for moderate organizations such as the NAACP and the Urban League to dominate civil rights activities in Seattle for most of the 1950s. Through its negotiations with individual employers, the Urban League placed African Americans in local banks, breweries, and some retail stores.

The NAACP was also the most prominent civil rights organization in Washington's second-largest city, Spokane. Pressure on the school board succeeded in the summer of 1951, when the board agreed to hire Eugene H. Breckenridge as an English and math teacher at Havermale High School. At the same time the NAACP was working through legal challenges to end employment discrimination by the school district, the organization's Spokane branch was also working cooperatively with the Brotherhood of Sleeping Car Porters to protest against housing discrimination by Spokane realtors.

The Urban League in Portland also worked to gain employment opportunities for African Americans. E. Shelton "Shelly" Hill, the industrial secretary, and other Urban League leaders convinced 180 Portland employers to hire black workers in the 1950s. In that decade, the Portland Fire Department hired its first black firefighter, and the Oregon Bureau of Labor hired its first African American deputy commissioner. Reed College hired its first black faculty member. The *Oregonian* employed its first African American sports writer, and Sears and Montgomery Ward both hired black employees for duties other than custodial work. By 1953, however, the Portland Urban League had begun to concentrate its energy on housing. The Urban League determined that only 3 percent of Portland's rental housing was open to African Americans, and most of these available rental units were dilapidated. When African American families moved into previously all-white neighborhoods, the Urban League praised their courage. Such families often faced verbal abuse and threats of violence. The Urban League used these incidents to educate white Portland about the extent of segregation in the city. In 1953 and again in 1955 Portland's leading daily newspaper, the *Oregonian*, published articles that publicized African Americans' struggle to gain access to housing.

Prior to World War II, many of Portland's black residents had found homes in the Albina district in the city's northeastern section. Albina's black population increased dramatically after 1948, when the flooding Columbia River destroyed Vanport, which had been built to provide housing for shipyard workers during the war. After the war, large portions of Albina were targeted for redevelopment by city officials. Some African Americans initially expressed cautious support for redevelopment. For example, when the building of Memorial Coliseum in the southern portion of Albina was first proposed, Portland NAACP president Phil Reynolds expressed his support, even though his house was slated for demolition. In the spring of 1957, the year after voters approved the project, Reynolds told the *Oregonian* that the construction of the coliseum would "help break up the Negro ghetto . . . providing the Negroes are not just shifted into a similar area."[3] It soon became clear to civil rights leaders that city officials were doing little to assist the hundreds of African Americans who were displaced by the construction project. The city paid property owners when it took their land for redevelopment projects, but it had no legal obligation to provide assistance to displaced tenants. In 1957, however, the NAACP and other groups demanded that city officials assist the renters who were forced to find new homes. Mayor Terry Schrunk ordered the Portland Commission on Inter-Group Relations to coordinate the relocation of the residents displaced by the coliseum project, but he refused to commit city funds to the assistance of these displaced residents. The city also approved plans to expand Emanuel Hospital in Albina. As a result of these redevelopment projects, many black-owned businesses were forced to move or close, and more than 1,100 houses were demolished. Hundreds of black families were forced to move.

Washington's legislature extended its ban on racial discrimination to the sale and rental of housing in 1957. The action of Washington's legislature and the struggles faced by African Americans who were displaced by redevelopment projects led civil rights leaders in Portland to press the Oregon legislature to pass fair housing legislation. The Oregon legislature complied, and Oregon and Washington were the only two far western states that had banned housing discrimination by 1957. African American community leaders and other civil rights activists, however, were dissatisfied with the weakness of the 1957 fair housing act, which did not cover many dwelling units and which provided no serious penalty for realtors who violated the law. Lobbying by civil rights activists led the Oregon legislature to pass a stronger fair housing act in 1959. This act made it illegal for real estate agents and landlords to discriminate in selling or renting any residential property.

African American experiences with redevelopment in the 1950s led some leaders to become more assertive in defending and preserving the neighborhoods in which most African Americans were forced to live. In 1960, for example, Portland NAACP President Mayfield Webb joined with black ministers and activists to denounce the Central Albina Plan, which would have demolished every structure in a thirty-five-block portion of the district. Webb and the other community leaders proposed an alternative—the Albina Neighborhood Improvement Program (ANIP), and they convinced city officials to invest in housing and neighborhood improvement instead of demolition. Under the aegis of ANIP, residents of the area rehabilitated more than three hundred homes and developed a park.

The *Brown* decision and the Montgomery Bus Boycott did not have a great effect on civil rights activism in the Pacific Northwest. School segregation was illegal in both Washington and Idaho prior to 1954, although de facto school segregation occurred in Seattle. However, the sit-ins and freedom rides of the early 1960s inspired both African Americans and some white allies to take action. A group of Seattle residents had tried to form a chapter of the Congress of Racial Equality (CORE) in 1957, but they were not able to attract enough supporters. By 1961, however, as Seattleites saw newspaper reports and television footage of violence against Freedom Riders in the South, a second group of Seattle activists coalesced into a CORE chapter. At first, CORE members collected money to send Seattle residents south to participate in the Freedom Rides. Soon, however,

CORE members decided to mount a direct challenge to discriminatory practices in Seattle. While the NAACP and Urban League continued to work through judicial and legislative channels for the elimination of racial discrimination, the black and white members of CORE committed themselves to nonviolent direct action. Although the public face of CORE was often an African American man, black and white women did much of the behind-the-scenes work that allowed for successful demonstrations.

The members of this new CORE chapter chose Safeway as the target of their first protest. Safeway operated three supermarkets in the Central District, where most of the city's African Americans lived due to housing discrimination. Approximately 80 percent of the customers at the three Central District stores were African Americans, but only six of Safeway's 1,700 King County employees were black, and the company had never promoted a black employee to a managerial position. CORE and NAACP members distributed leaflets in the Central Area in August 1961. These leaflets urged African Americans, "Don't Shop Where You Can't Work!" CORE established a training program for potential supermarket employees and made certain that African Americans had applied to work for Safeway. Following the guidelines for action established by CORE's national leaders, representatives from Seattle CORE, the NAACP, and the Baptist Ministers Alliance attempted to negotiate with Safeway representatives. When the negotiations did not lead to the hiring of black workers, CORE and NAACP members began picketing outside Safeway stores in the Central District in late October 1961. This direct-action effort led to Safeway's hiring of dozens of African Americans over the next year. Over the next several years, CORE initiated similar campaigns designed to convince dairies, drugstores, and department stores to hire African Americans.

In late 1962, CORE members began their campaign to end employment discrimination by the Bon Marché, a large Seattle department store patronized by many working-class residents. Rev. Mance Jackson, the pastor of Bethel Christian Methodist Episcopal Church on Twenty-Third Avenue, was the public face of the Bon Marché campaign. However, the campaign was largely organized by Jean Durning, a white CORE member who had given birth to her second child just weeks before she was asked to coordinate the campaign. Durning remembered, "Even though I had a brand-new baby, I was the only logical candidate. I was still recovering. I was too busy. But the task needed to be done. I agreed."[14] As part of this campaign, CORE asked all "fair-minded people" to cancel their Bon Marché charge cards, and activists planned to picket the store on June 15, 1963. In the week preceding the planned protest, managers at the Bon Marché hired more than thirty African Americans. Rather than cancel the protest, its organizers redirected its focus away from a single employer. Instead of picketing the Bon Marché, more than 1,200 people participated in a march that concluded in a downtown rally.

In its early protests, Seattle CORE worked cooperatively with other civil rights organizations, particularly the NAACP. This pattern of cooperation led in 1963 to the formation of the Central Area Civil Rights Committee (CACRC). The CACRC included CORE, the NAACP, and the Urban League and coordinated much of the activism that occurred in Seattle in the mid-1960s.

In 1964 CORE and its CACRC allies embarked on their Drive for Equal Employment in Downtown Seattle, or DEEDS. Civil rights activists distributed leaflets, staged a rally, and initiated a boycott of downtown stores that began on October 19, 1964, and lasted until January 1965. DEEDS did not meet its ambitious goal of placing more than 1,200 African American employees in downtown stores and offices, but it did encourage a growing number of African Americans to agree that militant action was needed to end racial discrimination in Seattle.

CORE worked not only to end employment discrimination but also to eliminate housing discrimination in Seattle. The Washington legislature had passed legislation outlawing racial discrimination in housing in 1957, but the state supreme court declared this legislation unconstitutional in September 1961. Civil rights activists responded to the supreme court's decision by establishing the Fair Housing Listing Service (FHLS) in 1962. More than twenty different groups, including civil rights organizations and churches, participated in the FHLS. Individual activists distributed thousands of leaflets informing Central District residents of the FHLS. By 1963 more than 140 homes were included on the list of properties available to any qualified buyer.

The gradual and voluntary approach of the listing service, however, did not satisfy many activists, who recognized that racial discrimination prevented African Americans from buying the overwhelming majority of houses for sale in the city. Most of these activists were affiliated with CORE, and disagreements over strategies and tactics for ending housing discrimination strained CORE's relationships with the NAACP and the Urban League. CORE sought to publicize discrimination by real estate agents and to apply pressure to agents and homeowners who refused to sell to African Americans. During 1963 CORE conducted tests to show that real estate agents were engaging in racial discrimination. In these tests, a black couple would visit an agent's office. Then a white couple of a similar age and economic background would visit the agent's office. These tests allowed CORE members to determine that discrimination was widespread. Agents frequently refused to show African American couples the homes in which they were interested; they often informed the couples that the house had already been sold. Agents also quoted the black couples a higher price or down payment than the white couples. CORE used similar methods to test discrimination in the rental of houses and apartments.

On July 1, 1963, four hundred people, led by Rev. Mance Jackson and Rev. Samuel McKinney, marched from McKinney's church, Mount Zion Baptist Church, to city hall to protest housing discrimination. Thirty-five protesters broke away from the march and occupied the mayor's office for nearly twenty-four hours. This protest helped to persuade the city council to establish a Human Rights Commission, which was directed to draft an open housing ordinance. Activists kept applying pressure to city officials. On July 20, 1963, nearly three hundred demonstrators staged a sit-in in the city council's chamber.

At the same time, in July 1963, CORE launched "Operation Windowshop." In this action, CORE encouraged African American home buyers to look outside the Central District for homes or to attend open houses in new developments. On July 28, 1963, the first day of Operation Windowshop, the Seattle Real Estate Board placed an advertisement in both daily newspapers questioning the legitimacy of the demonstration. Most real estate offices closed and cancelled advertising in the *Times* and the *Post-Intelligencer*.

On August 28, 1963, the same day as the historic March on Washington, one thousand Seattle residents marched from First AME (African Methodist Episcopal) Church to the federal courthouse in downtown Seattle. Speakers, including Reverends Jackson and McKinney, criticized the city council for its failure to pass a fair housing ordinance. Two days after a rally on the playground at Garfield High School on October 20, 1963, the council finally enacted an ordinance that made discrimination in the sale or rental of housing a misdemeanor punishable by a fine. A petition drive succeeded in the placing of a referendum on the ordinance before the voters in March 1964. Only 53,453 Seattle residents voted in favor of the fair housing referendum, while 112,448 voted against it. Even though two-thirds of the voters rejected the open housing ordinance, historian Quintard Taylor has noted, the debate over the housing ordinance convinced a growing number of white Seattleites to reconsider their opposition to open housing. Taylor observed that there was a significant increase in housing listed with the FHLS after the referendum.

Two weeks after the referendum, on March 22, 1964, CORE began sit-ins at the offices of Picture Floor Plans Inc., a Seattle real estate agency. Some of these demonstrations resulted in physical confrontations. CORE voted to suspend its sit-ins at its May 12, 1964, meeting, and the Seattle Real Estate Board obtained a restraining order to prevent further demonstrations. Many CORE members were uncomfortable with the Picture Floor Plans sit-ins, and the demonstrations deepened the rift between CORE and more gradualist civil rights organizations such as the NAACP and the Urban League.

The sit-ins, the Freedom Rides, and other demonstrations in the South inspired African Americans in Spokane, even though a CORE chapter was not established in Washington's second-largest city. Some individuals challenged discriminatory practices in the early 1960s. For example, Mrs. Willie Williams filed a complaint with the WSBADE in 1961 against real estate agent A. H. Smick and his employer, the Walter L. Gainor Company. The WSBADE ruled in favor of Williams, but it could only request that the real estate agency comply with the state law, which was ruled unconstitutional a few months later. Eventually Williams was able to purchase a home in a "nonsegregated" neighborhood. Mass protest occurred in Spokane in the fall of 1963, when Jangaba Augustine Johnson, a Fulbright scholar from Liberia studying at Gonzaga University, was denied service at Wheeler's Barbershop in downtown Spokane. With the assistance of Carl Maxey of the local NAACP branch, Johnson filed a complaint with the WSBADE, which investigated and concluded that John M. Wheeler, the owner of the barbershop, had discriminated against Johnson. Students from Gonzaga also picketed outside the barbershop. Wheeler decided to close his barbershop rather than to serve black customers.

Throughout the 1960s, civil rights activists in both Portland and Seattle worked to address not only discrimination in employment and housing but also the de facto school segregation that resulted from housing discrimination. In 1957, 80 percent of the students at Eliot Elementary in Portland's Albina district were African Americans. Eight years later, more than 90 percent of the students at Eliot, Boise, and Humboldt elementary schools in Albina were black. The Portland NAACP offered a number of recommendations for ending segregation, including the construction of new schools located between racially segregated neighborhoods, the closing of two nearly all-black schools, the redrawing of attendance district lines, and the use of busing. In response, the Portland Public Schools conducted its own eighteen-month study. Although the report that resulted from this study acknowledged the existence of racial disparities in the schools, it expressed support for the continuation of the neighborhood school model and opposition to busing. Despite the Portland NAACP's condemnation of the report, the school board implemented some of its policy recommendations, including the Model Schools Program (MSP). The MSP funneled additional funding to the nine model schools, all but one of which had student bodies with large black majorities. The program reduced class sizes and teacher turnover rates. However, the MSP, which continued until 1972, did not stop the ongoing process of segregation.

In Seattle, the NAACP filed suit against the school board in 1962. The lawsuit was settled out of court in 1963, when Seattle became the first large city in the United States to implement a districtwide desegregation plan. At the center of this plan was the Voluntary Racial Transfer (VRT) program, which was designed to send 1,400 of the 7,000 black students in Seattle to schools outside of the Central District. In its first year, however, only 238 black students participated in the VRT program, and only seven white students transferred into schools in the Central District. The Central Area Civil Rights Committee endorsed actions similar to those proposed by the Portland NAACP. For example, CACRC called for the closing of the aging Horace Mann School, whose student body was 97 percent black in 1964. CACRC leaders believed that the closure of the school would require the school board to send the displaced students into largely white schools. The proposal, however, revealed division within the black community, as hundreds of parents called for the construction of a new school to replace Horace Mann. Despite the division apparent in 1964, the community united against school segregation one final time in 1966. The CACRC planned a boycott of the schools to express the community's dissatisfaction with school segregation. On March 31 and April 1, 1966, nearly 4,000 elementary and secondary school students attended Freedom Schools instead of the segregated Seattle public schools. More than half of all the black students in the public schools participated.

Divisions within the civil rights movement in the Northwest were apparent in the first half of the 1960s. For example, tensions between the NAACP and CORE surfaced when CORE members picketed Picture Floor Plans. These divisions became even more apparent when the Black Power movement emerged. By 1966, Seattle CORE was deeply divided. Many black members of the organization resented the presence of white people in the organization and came to believe that white people should only be working with other white people to end racism.

African Americans in the Northwest took a number of different courses of action in the second half of the 1960s. In Portland, some young black people, frustrated by their lack of access to jobs and by mistreatment at the hands of the police, took to the streets in 1967 and 1969. In a 1968 report, the City Club of Portland concluded that the rioting in Portland in 1967 was similar to the rioting that had occurred in cities across the country during that summer. Federal programs designed to reduce poverty and to improve the lives of poor people alienated some African Americans and led them to embrace Black Power ideology and programs. For example, the Portland Development Commission did not include African Americans in its 1967 application for $15 million in Department of Housing and Urban Development (HUD) funding through the Model Cities program. This snub led some community leaders to express their opposition to the program.

Black Power ideology appealed to younger African Americans who had come of age in the years of boycotts, protest marches, and sit-ins. Some were disillusioned by the slow pace of change in the mid-1960s and were therefore receptive to the ideas that had been expressed by Malcolm X and that were being expressed by Black Power leaders such as Stokely Carmichael and H. Rap Brown. Carmichael spoke at the University of Washington and at Garfield High School in the spring of 1967. Carmichael's speech had a profound impact on some of the members of the audience. Aaron Dixon, who heard the speech, recalled, "I walked out of the auditorium transformed. I was not the same person who had entered. From that day forward, I looked at the world and everyone around me with anger and rage."[5]

Dixon, who graduated from Garfield in the spring of 1967, entered the University of Washington in the fall of that year. In early 1968, Dixon and several other UW students founded the Black Student Union (BSU) at UW. BSU officers E. J. Brisker, Larry Gossett, and Dixon then began working to establish black student unions at Seattle high schools and community colleges. On March 6, 1968, BSU leaders demonstrated that they were able to marshal community support for some of their positions. When Rev. John Adams, the pastor of First AME Church, presented the CACRC's proposal to close Central District schools to force school integration, he was met with opposition organized by BSU members, who had gathered signatures from 1,100 people who opposed the plan.

Shortly after the assassination of Martin Luther King Jr. in April 1968, twenty BSU members from Seattle attended the second annual West Coast BSU convention at San Francisco State. These BSU members were deeply impressed by a speech by Bobby Seale, the chairman of the Black Panther Party for Self-Defense. The following week Panther leaders Seale, George Murray, and Kenny Denman from San Diego came to Seattle. The Seattle chapter of the Black Panther Party (BPP), established in April 1968 and led by Aaron Dixon, was the first chapter outside California.

While Dixon concentrated most of his energy on managing the affairs of the BPP chapter in Seattle, other members of the BSU at UW took action. On May 20, 1968, the BSU began picketing outside the administration building. The protesting students demanded the admission of more black students and greater support for current black students. BSU members entered the building that afternoon and refused to leave, trapping UW President Charles Odegaard in his office. Odegaard agreed to most of the demonstrators' demands—the doubling of black enrollment, the recruitment of African American faculty and staff, and the establishment of a black studies major.

Like many other BPP chapters, the Seattle chapter grew rapidly in the months following its establishment. Nearly three hundred people joined the chapter in 1968. However, Dixon and other party leaders found that many people were attracted to the Panther uniform but were reluctant to accept the party's discipline. By 1970, the chapter's membership had dwindled to twenty-five, about half of whom were women.

By 1969, Black Panther Party chapters in both Seattle and Portland were devoting much of their energy to the provision of community services. BPP chapters in both cities began serving breakfasts to children from poor families in 1969. The program in Portland served between 75 and 125 children each day during the work week. Demand was so great in Seattle that by 1970 the Panthers were serving breakfast at five different locations. The Seattle free breakfast program continued to operate until 1977. The Seattle chapter also delivered free groceries to needy families. The BPP chapters in both cities opened free health clinics, and the Portland chapter also operated a dental clinic. The Seattle Panthers established a liberation school in 1970 and began a pesticide program to deal with cockroach infestations in public housing.

In the early 1970s, as the Black Panther Party focused on providing services to the black community, tensions with the police eased, and some African Americans focused on electoral politics. Black Power did not take root in Spokane, where the NAACP remained the most important civil rights organization. However, in the early 1970s, attorney Carl Maxey and other members of Spokane's African American community formed Concerned Black Citizens (CBC). CBC criticized city officials for excluding African Americans and poor people from the planning for Expo '74. As a result of quiet organizing in the community and coalition-building efforts, James Chase won election to the Spokane City Council in 1975, becoming the first black city council member since the 1890s. In November 1981, Chase won election as mayor of Spokane. Chase's achievement was remarkable in part because less than 2 percent of Spokane's population was black.

Notes

1. "Ousted Negro Worker Will Be Rehired," *Seattle Times*, January 10, 1956, 13. Additional information about Vaughns was obtained from his obituary, which was published in the Spokane *Spokesman Review* on April 19, 2000, and from sources obtained through Ancestry.com.
2. Quoted in Howard Alan Droker, "The Seattle Civic Unity Committee and the Civil Rights Movement 1944–1964," PhD diss., University of Washington, 1974, 126.
3. *Oregonian*, April 7, 1957, quoted in Stuart McElderry, "Building a West Coast Ghetto: African-American Housing in Portland, 1910–1960," *Pacific Northwest Quarterly* 92, no. 3 (Summer 2001): 144.
4. Joan Singler, Jean Durning, Bettylou Valentine, and Maid Adams, *Seattle in Black and White: The Congress of Racial Equality and the Fight for Equal Opportunity* (Seattle: University of Washington Press, 2011), 67.
5. Aaron Dixon, *My People Are Rising: Memoir of a Black Panther Party Captain* (Chicago: Haymarket Books, 2012), 58.

Further Reading

Dixon, Aaron. *My People Are Rising: Memoir of a Black Panther Party Captain*. Chicago: Haymarket Books, 2012.
Gibson, Karen J. "Bleeding Albina: A History of Community Disinvestment, 1940–2000." *Transforming Anthropology* 15, no. 1 (2007): 3–25.
Johnson, Ethan, and Felicia Williams. "Desegregation and Multiculturalism in the Portland Public Schools." *Oregon Historical Quarterly* 111, no. 1 (Spring 2010): 6–37.
Mack, Dwayne A. *Black Spokane: The Civil Rights Struggle in the Inland Northwest*. Norman: University of Oklahoma Press, 2014.
Mangun, Kimberley. "'As Citizens of Portland We Must Protest': Beatrice Morrow Cannady and the African American Response to D. W. Griffith's 'Masterpiece.'" *Oregon Historical Quarterly* 107, no. 3 (Fall 2006): 382–409.
McElderry, Stuart. "Building a West Coast Ghetto: African-American Housing in Portland, 1910–1960." *Pacific Northwest Quarterly* 92, no. 3 (Summer 2001): 137–48.
Taylor, Quintard. *The Forging of a Black Community: Seattle's Central District from 1870 through the Civil Rights Era*. Seattle: University of Washington Press, 1994.
Zane, Jeffrey, and Judson L. Jeffries. "A Panther Sighting in the Pacific Northwest: The Seattle Chapter of the Black Panther Party." In *On the Ground: The Black Panther Party in Communities across America*, edited by Judson L. Jeffries. Jackson: University Press of Mississippi, 2010.

4

The Struggle on Multiple Planes
California's Long Civil Rights Movement
Herbert G. Ruffin II

In this thoroughly researched and critical chapter, Syracuse University historian Herbert G. Ruffin II explores the long civil rights movement for African Americans in California. Ruffin argues persuasively that blacks in California were particularly affected by World War II, as he phrased it, the war that "forever changed black California." California was a large state, with numerous important urban areas, including Los Angeles, San Francisco, San Diego, and Oakland, that frequently changed the parameters of the civil rights movement in not only California, but the nation as a whole, particularly the North. The effort in California, as in other parts of the West, was dependent on influential, dedicated, and charismatic leaders. Ruffin, the author, also has published an important book-length study set in California, *Uninvited Neighbors: African Americans in Silicon Valley, 1769–1990* and a co-edited work, *Freedom's Racial Frontiers: African Americans in the Twentieth-Century West*.

World War II (1941–45) forever changed black California. The Golden State's African American population exploded in the 1940s, growing from 124,306 black residents in 1940 to 462,172 in 1950. By 1970, this population grew to 1,400,143, making black Californians a sociopolitical force.[1] In the 1940s, most of this population was drawn to California by factory and shipyard employment in wartime defense industries. Others were drawn by the quest for a promised land in urban spaces rumored to be racial paradises uncommon in their native communities directly impacted by Jim Crow (legally authorized racial discrimination), such as Arkansas, Louisiana, Mississippi, Oklahoma, and Texas.[2]

During World War II, most African Americans discovered that California was not absent a color line. In fact, blacks discovered that it was a place where most socioeconomic and political structural relations were dictated by what is now called James Crow, Esquire (racial discrimination not by law but by deliberate custom) in housing, employment, education, and police misconduct.[3] This white supremacist treatment sparked the formation of stronger black communities and spurred a freedom rights movement designed to make metropolitan areas like Los Angeles and San Francisco live up to African American expectations.[4] Their base expectations were fair opportunity and equality before the law. This is the history that black California scholars have been mining since the late 1980s. Prior to 2003, urban histories that centered black Californians in their narratives tended to examine the state's early-twentieth century narrative up to the passage of California's Fair Housing Act of 1963 (a.k.a. Rumford Act). The exceptions were Lawrence De Graaf, Gerald Horne, and Raphael Sonenshein, as well as Lonnie G. Bunch, Lawrence P. Crouchett, and Martha Kendall Winnacker, who researched black suburbanization in Orange County, the black revolt in Watts, politics and race in postwar Los Angeles, and surveys on black Los Angelenos and the East Bay African American community. Utilizing what historian Joe William Trotter referred to as overlapping "theoretical frameworks of race relations, ghetto formation, and proletarianization," or race and class approach, historians such as Albert Broussard, Delores Nason McBroome, Shirley Ann Wilson Moore, Gretchen Lemke-Santangelo, and Quintard Taylor developed the modern foundation for black California history as a black migration study that preserves the agency of African descendants and places them at the center of their stories.[5]

Since 2003, a new generation of scholarship has emerged to expand the telling of black California in content and in chronology from 1945 to 2000. Coming out of this tradition are historians such as Robert Bauman, Kevin Allen Leonard, Donna Murch, Herbert Ruffin, Robert Self, and Josh Sides, whose research has enhanced our understanding of black community formation, black political expression, and black transformation in the East Bay Area, South Bay Area, and in Los Angeles, to name a few focuses and locales.[6] Accompanying this coverage is an ever-increasing body of work on the contemporary black Californian experience that is written from the viewpoint of scholars in other disciplines such as Clyde Woods (black studies, cultural anthropology, and cultural studies), Laura Pulido (ethnic studies and geography), Clora Bryant (musicology and oral history), and George Lipsitz (black studies and sociology), to name a few.[7] Written from the traditions mentioned, this chapter argues that California's civil rights movement has to be extended back at least to the start of the Great Migration (1915) and from there brought forward to 1978 when the movement began to move forward in a counterclockwise motion. That is, as an example, while a few black activists prospered and moved from the city, those blacks left behind in urban centers and without successful black leaders remained in poverty and faced discrimination.[8]

The Initial Pursuit of the Dream

Black Californians have addressed racial discrimination as a social justice collective since the gold rush (1848–63). This was the period that the California Colored Convention launched an aggressive abolitionist and freedom rights campaign for the repeal of California's fugitive slave law, antiblack testimony law, antiblack homesteading law, unfair education law, and unfair public accommodations law. Key to launching this battle were African American institutions such as the family, black church, "separate schools," barbershops, and newspapers like *Mirror of the Times*, *Pacific Appeal*, and *The Elevator*. By 1863, these institutions played crucial roles in the defeat of the state's fugitive slave law, antiblack testimony law, and antiblack homesteading law. Unfortunately, these early victories led to premature optimism about black freedom.

Similar to the legal battle led from 1935 to 1968 by the National Association for the Advancement of Colored People (NAACP) to end Jim Crow, California Colored Convention leaders such as African Methodist Episcopal (AME) reverend Peter Williams Cassey understood that defeating racial exclusion in the state's public school system would cause the system to crumble. From 1852 to 1890, desegregation victories in 1866 and 1874 led to the *Wysinger v. Crookshank* (1890) California Supreme Court decision that allowed African American and American Indian youth to attend public schools. Three years later, the state barred publicly accommodated segregation.[9] For black Californians, this ended legal racial discrimination in the Golden State on the eve of Jim Crow. This also created a different black experience prior to 1941 in California, as its communities were too minute to justify the cost for the formation of separate but "equal" facilities during the period that the landmark case *Plessy v. Ferguson* (1896) federally imposed "separate but equal." Thus, as Jim Crow gained strength in the South, his equally oppressive "brother" James Crow was forming in western states and in territories west of Austin, Texas.

Although they lacked the strength of numbers, black Californians continued their fight against racial discrimination in the state's early years of James Crow. From 1890 to 1940, most continued to organize their lives as a collective to survive increasingly ambivalent race relations. They did so in clustered communities that underwent the ghettoization process during the 1940s such as Watts (Los Angeles), Western Addition (San Francisco), and West Oakland. More important, political tactics that traditionally outlined the modern civil rights movement emerged in California, urging nonviolence, civil disobedience, direct action, legal battles, suffrage, and the quest for black empowerment fully eighty-four years before the *Brown v. Board of Education* (1954) verdict. Citing early events in juxtaposition with those of the 1940s presents a necessary context for comprehending the civil rights movement as it occurred in urban California and for understanding the use of civil rights tactics pioneered much earlier in nineteenth-century California.

The Birth of a New Era

During the early twentieth century, the urgency felt during the California Colored Convention struggle reemerged during the First Great Migration (1915–40). The component that triggered this mood was the state's African American population explosion from 21,645 in 1910 to 124,306 in 1940.[10] The foundation for California's civil rights movement had been laid in 1913, with the statewide tour of W. E. B. Du Bois, who was NAACP board member and editor of *The Crisis Magazine*.[11] His tour had the purpose of promoting the fledgling civil rights organization. A year later, NAACP chapters were formed in Los Angeles and Northern California communities. By 1915, the chapters had developed into a statewide civil rights juggernaut during the protest of the motion picture *The Birth of a Nation* (1915), which carefully projected black stereotypes "as menacing savages" and "glorified the Ku Klux Klan." California's race relations were already detestable: Chinese Americans were restricted to Chinatowns, Japanese were restricted from immigrating into the United States, Japanese Americans were contained within Japantowns, the California Alien Land Law of 1913 excluded most Asian descendants from landownership, most Mexican Americans and immigrants were restricted to barrios and temporary farm labor, and American Indians were housed on reservations.[12] Now *The Birth of a Nation* was stirring up hostility toward African Americans. In its inaugural year, the film was viewed by twenty-five million Americans already "deeply enmeshed in a culture of lynchings, Jim Crow segregation, and wide spread anti-black sentiment."[13]

The NAACP was fully aware that a public controversy would only boost ticket sales. They attempted to censor the film before it went national. The protest began in Los Angeles on February 8, 1915, several days before the New York City premiere. It failed to pressure policymakers and business executives into censoring the film and preventing its nationwide release.

The Bay Area movement began at San Francisco after the film went national. The initial protest in San Francisco was led by newly formed civil rights groups such as the Negro Equity League, the Negro Welfare League, and the Equal Rights League. Although each group saw the film as a force potentially harmful to local race relations, they were gridlocked by disagreements over strategies and tactics. Initially the black press advised its readers to ignore the film, but after several months, made an about face and pressed the local NAACP to join in the struggle. From this emergence of new groups, the NAACP proved to be the most flexible and durable in the Bay Area, and thus functioned as the umbrella organization in leading the charge.[14] In California, the San Francisco effort received praise from the national NAACP "for exhibiting more concern than Southern Californians over the movie's potential impact on race relations."[15] Following countless hours and endless energy involved in demonstrating and petitioning public officials, this struggle resulted in California

TABLE 4.1. African American Urban Populations in Selected California Cities, 1910–19400

City	1910	1920	1930	1940
Oakland	3,055	5,489	7,503	8,462
Los Angeles	7,599	15,579	38,894	63,774
Richmond	29	—	—	270
San Francisco	1,642	2,414	3,803	4,846
Santa Clara County	262	335	536	730

Sources: U.S. Bureau of the Census, *Negro Population, 1790–1915* (Washington, D.C.: GPO, 1918), 95–105; U.S. Bureau of the Census, *Fourteenth Census of the United States*, vol. 2, Population, 1920 (Washington, D.C.: GPO, 1922), 47; and U.S. Bureau of the Census, *Sixteenth Census of the United States, 1940, Population*, vol. 2, *Characteristics of the Population* (Washington, D.C.: GPO, 1943), part 1, 629, 636, 657, 787; part 5, 1041; part 6, 1026, 1044, 1053; part 7, 400; also see Taylor, *In Search of a Racial Frontier*, 193, 223.

banning the film, and, nationally, the release of a compromise version, which agreed to have "some of the movie's harshest moments deleted, including a scene proposing that blacks be sent back to Africa as a remedy for the nation's ills."[16]

The Birth of a Nation was rereleased in California theaters in 1923–25, and again in 1930. Every time the film came back it sparked immediate protest and growth in NAACP membership. Protesters included seasoned activists like journalists Charlotta Spears Bass and Delilah Beasley. New activists to the cause, such as Byron Rumford, a policymaker, and Tarea (Ty) Hall Pittman, a civil rights activist, scored long-lasting impacts against James Crow during the Great Depression (1930s) and post–World War II periods (1945–68), respectfully.[17] White liberals did not join the protest until its waning hours in 1930.

Beyond the *Birth of a Nation* controversy, California NAACP chapters served their local communities, offering a broad range of political tactics and social services. During the interwar period, the local NAACPs battled against racial injustice in education, employment, housing, minstrelsy, police brutality, public accommodations, and suffrage. Also, similar to the Colored Convention movement and the *Birth of a Nation* controversy, California chapters immeasurably impacted the national civil rights movement, staging demonstrations, financially supporting the passage of the Dyer Anti-Lynching Bill, and publicly protesting the East St. Louis race riot (1917). During the 1930s, nonviolent protest and direct-action activism continued in California with local NAACPs supporting the struggle of the Brotherhood of Sleeping Car Porters (BSCP) for increased wages and better labor conditions for African American porters, raising money for the Scottsboro Defense Committee (1935), and supporting civic appeals for low-income public housing.[18]

The Modernization of California's Civil Rights Movement

The modernization of California's civil rights movement occurred from 1922 to 1941 when the movement was challenged by black nationalism and black proletarianization (or the rise of the African American urban working class). The former occurred in 1921–23 after Marcus Garvey toured California promoting his Universal Negro Improvement Association (UNIA). During Garvey's tours, he astounded African descendants at places like Oakland's Liberty Hall with Pan-African rhetoric promoting black political and economic self-determination, black pride, black unity, and black redemption and regeneration as reverse migrants coming back to an independent Africa.[19]

The later expression caused the most controversy, because on the surface it appeared to support *The Birth of a Nation*'s white supremacist positions that blacks were inferior to whites, and that they were the reason why the United States had a race relations problem in the first place, that could be solved by *involuntarily* sending them back to Africa. California civil rights leaders also railed against the UNIA's push for separatism and African descendants accommodating Jim Crow in residential segregation, which to Garvey was the foundation of black nation building in the United States. For working-class Californians, the UNIA represented an alternative and legitimate path to freedom that was ignored by the middle-class, integrationist movement that was aspiring to civil rights.

Many activists such as Delilah Beasley and Frances Albrier were affiliated with both organizations. They selectively chose freedom tactics that suited their individual needs. The animosities between the NAACP and UNIA were arguably suppressed on the West Coast by distance and the pursuit of freedom by any nonviolent means. Beasley and Albrier were both empowered by the UNIA's emphasis on race redemption and regeneration. This involvement led to Beasley renewing her intent to become a journalist. She subsequently became a reporter for the *Oakland Daily Tribune*.[20] For Albrier, the movement provided her with several public activist platforms in the form of the Black Cross Nurses and the Women's Auxiliary, for which she was vice president in 1923. To Albrier, integration would never occur if the only base of power that African Americans had was a political base that served the dominant culture by exploiting and marginalizing people of color and women.[21]

What made the UNIA attractive to black Californians was its lack of emphasis on racial pluralism. For Garveyites, the term "black" became an uplifting term representing beauty and power; Pan-Africanism and Pan-Asianism were addressed by guest lecturers who advocated for Global South solidarity and the rise of sociopolitical independent movements to upend European colonialism; and capitalism was not seen as an impediment to black self-determination, which was an emerging belief in the mainstream freedom rights struggle. Central to this growing belief was capitalism's negative impact on the development of African America, and questionable finances associated with the UNIA and its Black Star Line, which first caught the ire of Division 156 members in Los Angeles in 1921.[22] The retarded development of black California communities stretches back to the 1870s when blacks were institutionally steered into clustered communities, many of which became ghettoes after the 1940s. In these spaces, most black Californians were chronically unemployed and underemployed in jobs that their ancestors occupied several generations earlier as domestics, laborers, and service workers, with only a small middle-class population successfully obtaining jobs as entrepreneurs, farmers, and skilled tradesmen.[23] As rapidly as African American businesses had formed in the 1920s, under the inspiration of Garvey's black economic model, most black businesses just as rapidly folded during the Great Depression (1929–ca. 1941). Black California communities filled this economic void by boycotting and leveraging their growing importance to demand access to industrial employment.

This proletarianization process began several years after the UNIA came to challenge California's civil rights movement in the mid-1920s, starting with service industry workers such as the Brotherhood of Sleeping Car Porters (BSCP). Central to the BSCP were twelve thousand Pullman porters pejoratively named "George," after the company's founder. In California, they were restricted to this industrial sector, because the Pullman Company was one of the few railroad companies that hired African Americans.[24] For many California blacks, working for Pullman placed the porter in African American middle-class standing, because porters were well paid, well traveled, and the personification of urban sophistication.[25] For Alameda County NAACP cofounder and BSCP vice president C. L. Dellums, African American middle-class standing did not matter as long as injustices in the workplace continued to place black workers at the whims of owners, managers, and workers of European descent. Porters from San Diego to Sacramento were on the frontlines of institutional discrimination in industrial employment, constantly confronted by discriminatory work practices such as "running in charge, doubling out . . . P.M. time," and depending on tips for the majority of their pay.[26] Running in charge meant that a porter could be assigned the duties of the conductor, along with his own work, and receive only a tenth of the conductors pay, and 20 percent of what he would normally earn.[27]

The BSCP was organized by A. Philip Randolph in a push for porters to have the right to collectively bargain for better wages and improved work conditions. In 1925, BSCP chapters formed throughout California. By the late 1920s, black porters became a force in California politics and economy, especially after the BSCP took a strike vote against the powerful and exclusionist American Federation of Labor (AFL) in April 1928, to force the National Board of Mediation to declare a state emergency. For African Americans, this was the first time that "big bluff" politics were successfully applied in the California freedom rights movement. Leading this charge were Randolph and BSCP officers like Dellums. Following the guidelines of the Railway Labor Act, the BSCP avoided a national emergency, as President Calvin Coolidge was given no reason to exercise his authority to appoint an emergency board to suppress the strike vote. In the interest of preserving uninterrupted economic growth of AFL affiliates, its president, William Green, granted the BSCP thirteen charters.[28]

During the 1920s, the proletarianization of black Californians led to the fight for fair housing. Prior to World War II (1941), most black Californians, with the exception of servants, were restricted to living in clustered communities such as Southwest Santa Ana and Northside San Jose—the exception to this was Watts in southeast Los Angeles, which was already forming into a ghetto.[29] In California, a fragmented fair housing struggle began in the cities with the largest black populations: Los Angeles and Oakland. In Los Angeles the struggle had already begun in 1916 with a black police officer, Homer L. Garrott, winning the right to live in Angeles Park against opposition from the subdivision's developer, Title Guarantee Company.[30] In the 1920s, the struggle expanded into a movement in Watts. Since its inception in 1903, Watts had been a diverse working poor community made up of African Americans, Mexican Americans, and European immigrants. By 1920, Watts's Central Avenue had become the beacon for 38 percent of the African American migrant population resettling in California from the South.[31] What attracted them was the pursuit of the California dream, best articulated by black Los Angeleno propagandist Jefferson L. Edmonds. According to Edmonds, if blacks came to California they would be free "from extralegal violence . . . that shaped and limited African American life in the South."[32] However in practice, even though black homeownership rates were comparably higher in California than in the Northeast and Midwest, most black Californians had to pursue their dreams in restricted communities that were getting blacker, poorer, and more dilapidated as time went on.[33] In the Bay Area, the fair housing movement in 1920s Oakland resulted in the Alameda County NAACP ending Oakland City Council's attempt to pass restrictive housing ordinances in the California Supreme Court in 1927.[34] A year later, the same court undermined this ruling in a Los Angeles case that upheld restrictive real estate and banking practices in California. It also ruled "that even when blacks lived in neighborhoods before the restrictions were established, they must vacate properties under covenants."[35] For Californians of color, restrictive racial housing covenants were not legally defeated until 1948, when Los Angeles NAACP's Loren Miller joined forces with Thurgood Marshall to win the landmark verdict in *Shelley v. Kraemer*.[36]

In 1929, the Great Depression temporarily halted black Californians' momentum for economic empowerment and fair housing. During the 1930s, working people, activist mothers, and activist youths worked as a collective to usher in a new brand of freedom politics built on the foundation of self-help and civil rights tactics that incorporated the politics of black empowerment, fair employment, fair housing, labor unionization, and suffrage. From 1929 to 1934, black Californians survived the Depression by heavily relying on their community institutions. Black women were especially eminent in the field of community activism, private caregiving, and the day-to-day operations of black community institutions. Shared experience rather than formal authority gave activist women community recognition and credibility in a patriarchal climate.[37] Many of these women were "activist mothers" widely recognized as movers and shakers in grassroots community activism that extended from the black women's club movement of the 1890s into the present.[38]

Organizations like Oakland's Linden Street branch of the Young Women's Christian Association (YWCA) were critical to California blacks surviving the first half of the Great Depression. During the late 1920s and 1930s, this segregated YWCA "operated as a community center, offering members religious training, recreational activities, adult education classes, counseling services, and vocational training." According to historian Gretchen Lemke-Santangelo, during the 1930s the "Y" also functioned as a temporary shelter, and "a job placement and [welfare] agency."[39] Other organizations that performed important functions for the health of black California communities were the National Council of Negro Women (NCNW), National Urban League, Booker T. Washington Community Center, Fannie Wall Children's Home, Garden City Women's Club, Home for the Aged and Infirm Colored People, and black churches. With the exception of the black church, many multipurpose and overburdened African American agencies did not survive the 1930s. Almost all were trying to compensate for the dire socioeconomic condition that faced black California. In 1929, blacks were 1.4 percent of the total state population and represented 4.3 percent of the California Relief Administration caseload. This increased to 17.3 percent in October 1933. During this same period, California blacks sought more public assistance than whites at a four-to-one ratio, and twice as much as other nonwhites. During the Depression, African Americans survived in California as extreme hustlers: working multiple odd jobs, taking in boarders, saving their earnings, and forming stronger, more self-determined collective communities.[40]

During the Great Depression, the formation of stronger black California communities and a radicalized civil rights struggle led to more effective collective approaches in voting. Prior to this period, the electoral process in every black

California community—except for South Central Los Angeles, which voted African American Frederick M. Roberts into the California state assembly in 1918—was largely symbolic. In the 1930s, after sixty-plus years of benign neglect from the Republican Party and the lure of New Deal economic benefits, California African Americans shifted their allegiance to the Democratic Party.[41] This realignment was rooted in the black Left's push for third-party politics, most loudly heard during the 1920s from freedom rights icons W. E. B. Du Bois, A. Philip Randolph, and California's C. L. Dellums. As a collective, black Californians gradually joined in with millions of other blacks to unseat the Republican Party in 1932, which strengthened the liberal wing of the national Democratic Party, a process that historian Douglas Flamming referred to as "one of the most significant political realignments in American history."[42]

In black California, this process was most starkly dramatized in Los Angeles, where a college-educated political upstart by the name of Augustus F. "Gus" Hawkins defeated Frederick Roberts for state assembly. The Depression negatively impacted most people, compressing the socioeconomic differences between African, Asian, European, Mexican, and American Indians. This led to a radicalizing political-economic environment where labor unionism, socialism, and communism flourished to an unprecedented degree. In this environment, Hawkins represented a new wave of liberal politicians that appealed to an eclectic coalition of working people, unionists, utopians, EPIC (End Poverty in California), black college graduates, and civil rights–minded followers of Father Divine's Peace Mission.[43]

Hawkins's victory over Roberts paralleled the rise of progressive liberalism, centered on President Franklin Delano Roosevelt's New Deal administration. Its programs temporarily gave most American citizens economic relief, while rescuing capitalism through government-regulated reforms to U.S. industries and banking.[44] For black Californians, the New Deal was their first Reconstruction period. Unlike the Reconstruction of the U.S. South, it was the first time that the majority of black Californians were granted the opportunity to receive federal relief funds and were allowed to work in federal jobs. In the early industrial cities of Los Angeles and San Francisco, many blacks found the Works Progress Administration and the National Youth Administration to be most responsive to their needs.[45]

The National Youth Administration was sponsored by Roosevelt's Works Progress Administration (1935–39) and Work Projects Administration (1939–43). The National Youth Administration had an all–African American advisory board headed by educator and civil rights leader Mary McLeod Bethune. The head of California's Division of Negro Affairs was Vivian Osborne Marsh. Marsh's platform for activism and recruiting was the California Federation of Colored Women's Clubs. Bethune, along with Marsh, used the National Youth Administration to reallocate funds from solvent New Deal programs to underresourced black programs. According to historian Quintard Taylor, "Between 1935 and 1941, the National Youth Administration created more than two thousand jobs in California for black youths, and sponsored the education of over four hundred black college and graduate students who completed their education. Moreover, over one thousand women and men received training in sheet metal, machine, and radio and aircraft production and repair that served them well in the state's World War II defense plants."[46]

During the New Deal era, black Californians attempted to curb their increasing dependency on state government for socioeconomic assistance by agitating for work in manufacturing industries where workers had the right to collective bargaining. According to historian Bruce Nelson, "On the West Coast, before the renaissance of unionism in 1933 and the founding of [International Longshoremen's and Warehousemen's Union] in 1937, there was little accommodation between blacks and whites."[47] This was especially true in the shipping industry. Prior to the 1930s, only a small segment of black Californians fully underwent the proletarianization process: the Pullman porters. The first half of the Great Depression temporarily halted the gradual expansion of labor radicalism in California African American communities. This was reignited during Roosevelt's first one hundred days in office in 1933. What sparked their interest in labor unionism was the passage of the controversial National Industrial Recovery Act of 1933, which protected workers' rights to organize and engage in collective bargaining under Section 7(a).[48]

In 1934, black Californians' participation in the Big Strike of 1934 set the foundation for the strengthening of their working-class communities. The Big Strike began on May 9, 1934, after months of negative tensions between the AFL's International Longshoreman Association (ILA) and the Industrial Association of San Francisco. This immediately led to an unauthorized general strike on the West Coast. Ten thousand to fifteen thousand ILA members went on strike to address better wages, lesser work hours, control over their conditions, and the right to organize in noncompany unions.[49] The strike was led by rank-and-file ILA member, Harry Bridges, a democratic socialist from Australia who believed in racial equality. This was not the same sentiment held by most white workers who saw black workers as social inferiors and as economic competition. On the West Coast, AFL unions such as the ILA systematically privileged the white workers with the "brother-in-law system." This system gave whites access to skilled and semiskilled jobs through bribes or the "shape-up," and "kept white labor 'in tow' by offering jobs to African Americans if the white workers complained about the shape-up."[50] At the start of the Big Strike, this resulted in only twenty-three African American ILA members working on the waterfronts of Portland, Tacoma, San Francisco, and San Pedro in Los Angeles.[51] Understanding that black workers were essential to Big Strike's success, Bridges met with Dellums and the black community on several occasions. This resulted in the tentative agreement that black workers would not break the lines if they had the fair opportunity to join the ILA and take part in waterfront employment. Because of that agreement, and because of growing support for labor radicalism fueled by worsening socioeconomic dislocations, the strike was cautiously embraced in the African American community.[52]

The Big Strike was most effective in the Bay Area. There it lasted through July 1934 as a general uprising of 125,000 workers walked off their jobs and effectively shut down San Francisco for three to four days. The strike ended with workers negotiating for the right to organize and collectively bargain on the waterfront. This included the ILA winning union recognition and control of the hiring hall on West Coast docks, which conditionally improved race relations: African American workers were given the opportunity to become ILA members, and thus work on the docks in auxiliary units. In these units, blacks could not vote for better jobs, wages, or work conditions, nor could they oppose company-controlled hiring halls whose primary function was the closed-shop agreement. Bay Area blacks were granted two representatives on the Alameda County Central Labor Council—Dellums and Ishmael Flory of the Dining Car Cooks and Waiters Union.[53]

The emergence of desegregated unions that evolved after the Big Strike gradually proletarianized black Californians. This included Los Angeles, which—along with Portland, Oregon—exhibited the worst forms of racism at its docks, and had the worst incidents of corporate resistance to the labor movement.[54] With that stated, black Californians became effective bloc voters and were consciously building proactive communities that fit within the emergent welfare state. In 1937, their increased interest in the labor movement was a driving force in the establishment of the International Longshoremen's and Warehousemen's Union (ILWU) of the Congress of Industrial Organizations (CIO). The ILWU, founded by Bridges, was the model labor union in dealing with race, because it "banned racial discrimination [in its constitution] twenty years before the U.S. Supreme Court found the courage to do so."[55] In final sum, the impact of the Big Strike on black California communities varied. For African American workers affiliated with the BSCP and dock work, the impact was huge, but it had less impact in areas where unionism was weak, such as areas dominated by agricultural pursuits like Pomona and San Jose, and in cities striving to become union-free such as Los Angeles.[56] Regardless of how black Californians were impacted, by 1941 their structure for political expression fundamentally changed, fluidly intersecting the politics of black empowerment, direct action, fair housing, labor unionism, legal equality, nonviolence, civil disobedience, and suffrage.

The California Dream and the Dream Deferred, 1941–1968 and Beyond

California civil rights legacy found its greatest expression during World War II and the postwar period from 1942 to 1968. In the twentieth century, the full maturation of the black freedom struggle to eradicate James Crow was abetted by the unprecedented growth of its African American population. This period is referred to as the Second Great Migration. It was launched on June 25, 1941, the date that the March on Washington movement pressured President Roosevelt into issuing Executive Order 8802. This policy outlawed segregation in defense industries with federal government contracts. It was enforced by the Fair Employment Practices Commission (FEPC) and War Manpower Commission, which set a modern precedent for the federal government to combat legal segregation.[57]

The success of the MOWM set a new precedent that opened industrial jobs to a critical mass of African Americans. In California, this included the explosion of its black population from 124,306 residents to 337,866. Most of this population resettled in the Golden State for industrial employment, which in turn made black Californians into a sociopolitical force dedicated to the Double-Victory movement (1941–45) against racism at home and fascism abroad. This was especially true in cities where black men and black women had a notable presence in the wartime industries of aircraft production and in shipbuilding. Air production took place throughout San Diego, and in Los Angeles at Consolidated-Vultee (Los Angeles), Douglas (Long Beach), Lockheed-Vega (Santa Monica), and North American Aviation (Inglewood). The bulk of black workers found employment in shipbuilding at California Ship, Consolidated Steel, and Western Pipe and Steel in Los Angeles, and in the Bay Area at

Marinship (near Sausalito), Moore Drydock and Bethlehem-Alameda (Oakland), and Kaiser (Richmond), which had four shipyards.[58] In these places, clustered communities became overcrowded black communities segregated at Fillmore and Western Addition in San Francisco, Logan Heights in San Diego, North Richmond, South Central Los Angeles, and West Oakland, to name a few (see table 4.2). For black Californians, restrictive housing was the first space that signaled to them that California had a color line that was getting worse the more the state's population grew.

California's color line was also found in employment. Most blacks continued to work as domestics and manual laborers, and in service-related industries, while during the war, a rapidly growing population worked in wartime industries. For black Californians, getting the opportunity to work in industrial employment was a major step in getting out of economic depression and compressing the "wage differentials between African American and white workers."[59] Even though unprecedented thousands of blacks worked as industrial workers, in 1943 more than thirty thousand worked in auxiliary units that were segregated within International Brotherhood of Boilermakers of the exclusionist AFL. Similar to the ILA, in 1937 the Boilermakers used internal segregation in their unions by restricting blacks to auxiliary unions designed to have them pay full union dues to work on the shop floor in temporary low- to semiskilled jobs with only moderate pay and without full union benefits and protections. This practice expanded during the war, with the Boilermakers controlling 65 percent of the dockworkers on the West Coast except for Seattle-Tacoma. In 1943, blacks fought back, especially after more than 950 African American workers were fired by California and Portland shipbuilders for protesting labor segregation within Boilermaker-affiliated unions. One of the people fired was San Francisco NAACP president Joseph James. He joined with other black workers to mount a collective assault against the Boilermakers. They first requested FEPC involvement. During West Coast hearings in November, the FEPC ordered all shipbuilders to break up their auxiliary systems and reminded them that they risked losing their lucrative contracts if caught discriminating. Every shipbuilder complied except for the Boilermakers. Emboldened by the FEPC ruling, black workers filed class action lawsuits with James's suit against Marinship carrying over into California Supreme Court. In 1944, the court ordered the Boilermakers to dismantle the auxiliary unions and integrate black workers within their membership.[60] A year later, the war ended.

TABLE 4.2. African American Population Growth in California by Metropolitan Area, 1940–1970

City	1940 (%)	1950	1960	1970 (%)	% Increase
Older Industrial Metropolitan Areas (Established before 1940)					
Los Angeles	63,774 (4.2)	171,209	334,916	503,606 (17.9)	790
Oakland	8,462 (2.8)	47,562	83,618	124,710 (34.5)	1,474
San Francisco	4,846 (0.8)	43,502	74,383	96,078 (13.4)	1,983
Older Civic/University Cities (Established before 1940)					
Berkeley	3,395 (4.0)	13,289	21,850	27,421 (23.5)	808
Sacramento	1,468 (1.4)	4,538	12,103	27,244 (10.7)	1856
World War II–era Industrial Metropolitan Areas (Established during the 1940s)					
Long Beach	610 (0.4)	4,267	9,531	18,991 (5.3)	3113
Richmond	270	13,374	14,388	28,633	1,060
San Diego	4,143 (2.0)	14,904	34,435	52,961 (7.6)	1278
Late-Blooming, Agricultural to Industrial Metropolitan Areas (Established after 1950)					
Bakersfield	1,025 (3.5)	1,492	8,218	9,243 (13.3)	902
Fresno	2,002 (3.3)	5,300	10,485	15,875 (9.6)	793
Late-Blooming, Postsuburban-Postindustrial Metropolitan Areas (Established after 1950)					
Anaheim	11 (0.1)	74	48	2,711 (1.2)	24,645
Ontario	38 (0.3)	215	492	1,133 (1.8)	2982
Pomona	104 (0.4)	217	880	10,648 (12.2)	10,238
Riverside	881 (2.5)	805	3,938	7,222 (5.2)	820
San Bernardino	660 (1.5)	1,931	8,061	14,586 (14.0)	2210
San Jose	291 (0.4)	591	1,955	11,161 (2.5)	3835
Santa Ana	158 (0.5)	433	1,759	6,731 (4.3)	4260

Sources: Taylor, *In Search of the Racial Frontier*, 267, 285–86; Ruffin, *Uninvited Neighbors*, 77; Gibson and Jung, "Historical Census Statistics . . . by Race . . . for Large Cities and Other Urban Places in the United States: California," working paper no. 76 (February 2005), https://www.census.gov/population/www/documentation/twps0076/twps0076.html.

Immediately after World War II, black workers like Joseph James were the first people fired when downsizing occurred in defense industries, despite many having high skill levels and advanced educations. In California the years following the war were not a great transformation period for the average black worker. The black middle-class growth that was notable during the war abruptly halted in the postwar period because of central city deindustrialization, military base closures, and chronic un- and underemployment. The main victims of this process were African American migrants in their midtwenties, whose pursuit of "gold" in the form of socioeconomic advancement, instantly became "frustrated optimism."[61] In places such as postwar Compton in Los Angeles, African Americans rapidly became victims of white flight, capital flight, and redlining. For many black youth, such as future Black Panther Party leaders Huey P. Newton and Alprentice "Bunchy" Carter, this divestment of inner-city California led to an undefined post-proletarian culture before the emergence of Black Power in 1966. This was best illustrated in the rise of street gangs that took the place of labor unions for dislocated workers seeking a balanced sense of masculinity, self, and financial security.[62]

Many African Americans fought the Golden State's hardening color line with the intent to make California live up to their expectations. How hard they fought—and what they fought for—depended on the size of the black population, and where and when the struggle was waged. In postwar San Francisco, a segment of the struggle was led by Rev. Howard Thurman (1944–53), who introduced to the movement a spiritual, anti-imperialistic form of interracial and nonviolent civil disobedience tactics that he learned from Indian leader Mohandas Gandhi while on a delegation in India in 1936. In 1949, his pioneering book, *Jesus and the Disinherited*, "presented the basic goal of Jesus' life as helping the disinherited of the world change from within so they would be empowered to survive in the face of oppression." This profoundly influenced how civil rights leaders James Farmer and Dr. Martin Luther King Jr. approached the civil rights movement.[63]

Whereas, in postwar Orange County, African Americans fought discrimination in coalitions with Mexican Americans, whose much larger population made it worth the cost for the white power structure to legally segregate them with separate facilities. This coalition's greatest feat occurred in 1947, when the California Supreme Court case *Mendez v. Westminster* set the precedent for the landmark U.S. Supreme Court case *Brown v. Board of Education* (1954). The case defeated "separate but equal" in California public education, and "put the Constitution on the side of racial equality and galvanized the nascent civil rights movement into a full revolution."⁶⁴ *Mendez* was led by the NAACP's Thurgood Marshall and Sylvia Mendez's attorney David Marcus, who used social scientific evidence to support the "argument that segregation resulted in feelings of inferiority among Mexican-American children that could undermine their ability to be productive Americans."⁶⁵ Implicit in this argument was that blacks also attended the Westminster school district, but in smaller numbers that would make it harder to make the argument that they were legally segregated, because the segregation that they were victimized by was by custom. Unlike Phoenix (1953), Topeka (1954–55), Pasadena (1963), and Berkeley (1964), racially imbalanced public school districts would not be effectively addressed in California until after 1965, which was after the passage of the Civil Rights Act of 1964, and the same year that the NAACP and the American Civil Liberties Union effectively linked residential housing patterns to separate and unequal education. It was also the same year that municipal busing plans were established, and that civil rights lawyers Loren Miller of Los Angeles and Maurice Hardeman of Santa Clara County became municipal judges.⁶⁶

In postwar Los Angeles, a broad-based civil rights battle ensued for fair education, fair employment, fair housing, fair political representation, and fair police treatment. In direct-action and labor movement campaigns, this struggle was led by groups that often clashed over tactics, such as the Los Angeles NAACP and the Communist Party USA–sponsored Civil Rights Congress (CRC) (1946–52). The CRC in particular reconnected the civil rights movement to the international realm, linking American racism "to United States Cold War foreign policy in the decolonizing world."⁶⁷ This occurred before it and radical activists statewide were purged from mainstream civil rights organizations such as the NAACP, and before the CRC was suppressed during the "climate of fear and repression linked to the Red Scare" (1947–ca. 1957).⁶⁸

In electoral politics, the bloc voting tactic that elected Los Angeles's Frederick Roberts and Gus Hawkins to office continued with Hawkins maintaining his state assembly position during the Second Great Migration period. In the process, Hawkins blazed a trail for modern black public officials, namely, William Byron Rumford (California assemblyman, Berkeley and West Oakland, 1949–67); Benjamin Franklin "Ben" Gross (Milpitas mayor, 1966–72); Ron Dellums (U.S. congressman, 1970–98, and Oakland mayor, 2006–present); Tom Bradley (Los Angeles mayor, 1973–93); Maxine Waters (California assemblywoman, Los Angeles, 1976–90, and U.S. congresswoman, 1990–present); and Willie Brown (California assembly speaker, 1980–95, and San Francisco mayor, 1996–2004).⁶⁹

Black Los Angelenos also formed coalitions with Latinos to overcome racial gerrymandering. In 1949, this resulted in Mexican American Edward Roybal being elected onto the Los Angeles City Council—a first for a Mexican American since 1881.[70]

Finally, in minute black communities, African Americans fought for acknowledgment and inclusion. In 1947, their civil rights battle was led by the Santa Clara County NAACP. They pressured San Jose city into observing Negro History Week, fought unfair housing with NAACP-endorsed realtors like Mary Anne Smith, and created an interracial forum to improve local race relations. In 1951, the NAACP's momentum came to an abrupt halt after their unsuccessful battle with minstrelsy, which split the chapter in San Jose and Palo Alto, and stalled direct-action politics in the county everywhere except the San Jose suburb of Milpitas.[71]

Similar to hundreds of postwar western communities, Milpitas underwent the process of urbanization, suburbanization, and industrialization overnight. Throughout California, this development was anchored by industries in entertainment (Anaheim), high technology (Palo Alto), and manufacturing (Milpitas). In Milpitas, this agricultural town benefited from the postwar decline of the automotive industry in inner-city America. In the Bay Area, Ford Motor Company's assembly operations were targeted in 1950 to be downsized and relocated from Richmond in five years. Before they could displace their senior black workforce, Ben Gross and several UAW Local 560 members negotiated for 196 to 350 African American workers to maintain their jobs. They effectively argued for solidarity in the workplace and secured a guarantee from Ford that its members would retain their seniority rights in the new location as an incentive to move to the new plant.[72] The latter half of this agreement resulted in the "creation of an interracial cooperative housing complex near the newly built plant in Milpitas called the Sunnyhills Cooperative—probably the first planned interracial community in the U.S."[73]

In postwar America, Local 560 was an unusual union, in that it was strong in spite of the systematic attack on labor rights following the passage of the Taft-Hartley Act (1947) and red baiting purges.[74] In the 1950s and '60s, many Local 560 members penetrated Milpitas's power structure as civil servants, profoundly impacting that city, which from 1954–68 was arguably the most democratic and diverse suburb in California. In this period, Milpitas had a 15 percent African American population, a black judge nominated to Santa Clara County municipal court in Maurice Hardeman (1964), and the first African American mayor of a predominantly white U.S. city in Ben Gross (1966).[75] This occurred in suburban metropolitan San Jose where the overall black population lingered below 1 percent from 1850 to 1960; this also happened in the suburban metropolitan areas of Anaheim–Santa Ana, Los Angeles–Long Beach, San Diego, Sacramento, San Bernardino–Riverside, and San Francisco–Oakland, which together in 1970 contained "nearly 70% of the state's population."[76]

Prior to the 1990s, being affiliated with the suburbs stereotypically meant being a homeowner. Components of this status included living in relatively new housing tracts in tightly controlled municipalities, with a comfortable income, high occupational status, and the disposable income to enjoy entertainment geared toward conspicuous consumption. According to historian Lawrence De Graaf, postwar suburbs also were centers of economic growth, which generated on a national average "more than three-fourths of all new manufacturing and retail jobs between 1950 and 1970."[77] In the United States, this was the golden age of suburbanization—an experience that people of color were not invited to participate in. For most of this period, the Federal Housing Authority (FHA) promoted white suburbanization by systematically denying home loans to people they considered to be high economic risks because they were not of the right complexion. During this period of the welfare state being privatized, Californians of color were redlined, which profoundly restructured race relations in a damaging manner through divesting and restricting people of color to central cities, and investing and allowing whites-only access into newly developed suburbs.[78]

Following the passage of the 1949 National Housing Act, which renewed the federal government's commitment to urban divestment through slum clearance and urban renewal, a statewide fair housing campaign was launched. In this period, assemblymen Gus Hawkins and William Byron Rumford effectively pushed policy makers to extend the life of California's FEPC into the postwar period and to extend its coverage to include fair housing. Their efforts were emboldened in 1951 by a multiracial civil rights coalition chaired by Dellums called the California Committee for Fair Employment Practices (CCFEP) and a new wave of young, civil-rights-oriented Democrats, led by Governor Edmund G. "Pat" Brown (1958–66). From 1959 to 1963, this coalition spearheaded the passage of a fair employment practices bill, a fair higher education bill (a.k.a. California Master Plan), and three fair housing bills in the Hawkins Act, Unruh Act, and California Fair Housing Act (a.k.a. Rumford Act), which covered public-assisted housing, fair business transactions in housing, and single-family housing.[79] The passage of these bills made California central to the success of the national fair housing, fair education, and civil rights movements.

Paralleling the many fair housing campaigns being waged throughout postwar California were rapidly expanding and fragmenting civil rights efforts with the common cause of abolishing the state's hardening color line. This evolved from a few small strikes sparked by the Greensboro, North Carolina, sit-ins of February 1960 in support of southern blacks, which later spread to spirited efforts to address local racism and social injustices. From 1960 to 1965, this campaign was led by local African American residents in clustered and concentrated communities, and students and faculty at California colleges and universities, among them University of California, Berkeley; University of California, Los Angeles; and Stanford University. In 1961, California residents and high school and college students worked with Freedom Riders, Congress of Racial Equality (CORE), and Student Nonviolent Coordinating Committee (SNCC) activists in Mississippi to register African American voters. Direct-action campaigns led to San Jose State College being pressured into enrolling black students who had been unjustly expelled for demonstrating at southern schools, as was the case with St. John Dixon from Alabama State College.[80] In San Diego, under the direction of black social worker Percy Steele (1953–63), the Urban League effectively was committed to addressing racism in interracial coalitions with white Americans and Mexican Americans. This led to several innovative programs to get black people jobs outside of the industrial sector that was controlled by powerful trade unions. In 1964, this program migrated with Steele to the Bay Area during his tenure as President and CEO of the Bay Area's Urban League (1964–90).[81] As this was occurring, organizations fighting for fair employment such as San Francisco CORE, and individuals fighting within collectives, such as Berkeley High School student Tracy Sims, received greater headlines for targeting unfair employment practices at chain stores, department stores, and grocery stores such as Woolworth's, Kress, and Safeway. From 1963 to 1965, this activity resulted in many fair employment agreements associated with Oakland CORE, local NAACPs, and Slate (a radical student organization at University of California, Berkeley), making the Bay Area the focal point of the civil rights campaign in the West.[82] According to Judge Hardeman, the culmination of affirmative action and fair employment agreements has resulted in arguably the greatest racial change in California from 1960–80, change that has seen major growth in economic opportunities in industrial, service, and skilled trade work for African Americans.[83]

As momentous as the California civil rights movement was, it dramatically lost momentum in 1964. This was the year that the Civil Rights Act of 1964 was enacted, the Vietnam War began, and California voted to repeal the state's recently passed Fair Housing Act with Proposition 14 by an initiative 2–1 vote, which went as high as 3–1 in many white suburban communities.[84] This result was an about-face of the spirit Dr. King attempted to instill on February 16, 1964, at the Negro Consolidated Realty Board of Los Angeles installation banquet, in which he warned that fair housing's repeal would be "one of most shameful developments in our nation's history." He also condemned people who said that "civil rights cannot be legislated, [while] asserting that segregation can be." After this legislation was passed, in 1965 it became Article I, Section 26 of the California Constitution, which forbade fair housing from being legislated and discussed.[85] In 1965, this law *in practice* trumped the Civil Rights Act of 1964, exacerbating the already harsher and more violent racial climate emerging throughout the Golden State. In this climate, California's civil rights activists responded to the state's freedom rights crisis in several ways.

In places with smaller African American communities such as San Jose and in predominantly white colleges and universities (PWCUs), while many young activists contemplated confronting racism with insurgency, seldom did they go this route *in these spaces* because civil rights lawsuits and nonviolent direct-action demonstrations and protests continued to be viable options in combating racial discrimination.[86] In PWCUs, prior to the creation of Educational Opportunity Programs in 1968, few students at public California PWCUs were African American, and of those who were, most were athletes. From 1960 to 1967, many participated in black student groups such as the Afro-American Association, considered "California's first indigenous Black nationalist organization"; the Revolutionary Action Movement; and the Soul Students Advisory Council for cultural support, political expression, and economic empowerment within and outside the walls of higher learning.[87] During California's Black Power era (1962–77), this political expression fueled the formation of black student unions and black studies departments based on the San Francisco State model, black student-athletic activism for fair campus housing, fraternity and sorority reform, and curriculum reform based on the "revolt of the Black athlete" or San Jose State model. It also prompted the diversification of communities with small African American populations through movements partly modeled on the black freedom movement such as the American Indian movement, antiwar movement, Chicano movement, environmental justice movement, feminist movement, and hippie movement.[88] Whereas, in communities with large African American populations sharply impacted by the Second Great Migration and postwar inequities, the civil rights struggle went into decline and morphed into the more urgent and urban Black Power movement.

In Watts, this resulted in a six-day revolt against police brutality, rising poverty, unfair education, and unfair housing. The revolt started on the evening of August 11, 1965, following the arrest of Marquette Frye and his mother and brother by California Highway Patrol officers (CHP). A standout student, Frye was stopped for alleged reckless driving while drunk. Tensions brewed after his mother, Rena Frye, had come onto the scene with other Watts residents following. CHP officers panicked as the crowd grew larger, which resulted in the mother being mistreated by CHP officers and arrested along with her sons. What ensued afterward was arguably the most unforeseen urban rebellion in U.S. history that resulted in 34 deaths, "almost all of whom were African American; 1,000 more were injured, and 4,000 were arrested." Moreover, the property damage was estimated to be $200 million in an area larger than Manhattan and San Francisco.[89] What made this such a pivotal moment was its duration, intensity, and the revelation to the U.S. public that the California dream was no more than a mirage for most African Americans. This was the reality that fueled former Afro-American Association member Maulana Karenga's black nationalism. Karenga is best known for establishing the US Organization ("us African people"), and the Kawaida thought and practice that forms the intellectual and spiritual foundation for the Pan-African holiday Kwanzaa.[90] Black cultural nationalism was the US Organization's resolution to Los Angeles's urban crisis, a phenomenon that swept across America from 1964 to 1969, including San Francisco's Hunter's Point in 1966.

In Oakland, urban rebellions never materialized because the Black Panther Party organized an already determined African American community, which was becoming enhanced by federal War on Poverty programs. They convinced enough flatland residents that spontaneous violence "placed the people at a decided disadvantage and left them vulnerable to the military might of the state."[91] On October 15, 1966, Huey P. Newton and Bobby Seale cofounded the Panthers on the premise of being a black revolutionary organization for political and economic change. Their answer to the urban crisis was multipronged: their ten-point platform stated their principles, emphasizing what black people "needed" and "wanted." Social programs such as the children's breakfast program and the Intercommunal Youth Institute composed their base for community empowerment, and the ideas in revolutionary psychiatrist Frantz Fanon's thesis *The Wretched of the Earth* (1963) formed the basis for their community control. This included addressing how to combat police and state oppression, and organizing the black working poor, or the post-proletariat that the Panthers conceptualized as the lumpen proletariat.[92] According to Seale,

> if you didn't organize the lumpen proletariat, if the organization didn't relate to the lumpen proletariat and give a base for organizing the brother who's pimping . . . hustling, the unemployed, the downtrodden, the brother who's robbing banks, who's not politically conscious. . . . if you didn't relate to these cats, the power structure would organize these cats against you.[93]

Newton and Seale's black nationalism was shaped by personal experience and participation in California's thriving black student movement (1962–65). By spring of 1966, Newton and Seale had left the black student movement—as Karenga had done earlier—"over their chronic unwillingness, or inability, to translate ideas into action."[94] Their last straw with the movement happened after Soul Students Advisory Council rejected their request for the group to aggressively address the miseducation of African American students at Merritt College (Oakland), and position itself in California's vanguard in addressing police brutality using armed self-defense and community control tactics patterned on Malcolm X's Organization of African American Unity.[95] This project was overwhelmingly rejected by Bay Area black nationalists at Merritt College, San Francisco State, and University of California at Berkeley. While Newton and Seale supported the Soul Students Advisory Council's quest for black faculty at Merritt and for black studies, what they were requesting went far beyond mere reforms in education, employment, and housing.[96] Later in 1966, Newton and Seale's cohort put themselves on the path toward addressing most of their concerns through the official establishment of the Black Panther Party for Self-Defense.

Black Panther Party membership exploded into California chapters after Seale delivered Executive Mandate Number One (or the Panther's ten-point platform) to a national audience at California's state capitol building at Sacramento on May 2, 1967.[97] Within this document, the point that came to define most of the Panther legacy is Point 7, which demanded "an immediate end to police brutality and murder of Black people."[98] Structurally, the Panthers reinforced Point 7 with police patrols, law books, shortwave radios, and publicly displayed guns, which were legal in California until 1968. After 1968, even though the organization expanded nationwide, it struggled to survive and thrive into the early 1970s. Their attraction to revolutionary nationalists of African, Asian, European, Latino, and Native descent occurred immediately following Newton's conviction (October 28, 1967) in the death of Oakland police officer William Frey, in which the Panther movement "took up the rallying cry 'Free Huey.'"[99] To law enforcement officials and the Federal Bureau of Investigation, the Panthers became a national security threat, which resulted in what appeared to members to be endless Counter Intelligence Program (COINTELPRO) attempts to discredit and destroy them.[100]

Within the organization, the Panther's revolutionary edge was dulled by 1970. The organization was deeply impacted by agents provocateurs, battle fatigue within membership, crippling internal conflicts, male chauvinism, and arrests, murders, and resignation of key leaders.[101] Arguably the Panther's darkest moment in this period occurred at the University of California, Los Angeles in 1969, during a shootout that resulted in the death of Southern California chapter Panther leaders Bunchy Carter and John Huggins by a black nationalist rival, over a heated dispute as to who would be the first director of the campus's new Afro-American Studies Center.[102]

Following the release of Newton in June 1970, Panther leadership abruptly shifted its politics from revolutionary nationalism to intercommunalism, or aligning with like-minded organizations conceptualized as "communities of the world" that took the place of nations.[103] During this postrevolutionary phase, the Panthers consolidated their operations in Oakland and became more focused on social programs and coalitions. Under the Central Committee leadership of Elaine Brown (1974–77) the reform arc extended to women, such as art historian Phyllis Jackson, who became a Panther leader, and key members penetrated the East Bay's public policy apparatus as civil servants and endorsed political candidates such as C. L. Dellums's nephew Ron Dellums for U.S. Congress. Similar to the California civil rights movement, which ended after the passage of the Fair Housing Act of 1968, the black freedom movement hatched during the 1910s officially ended at the end of Brown's term as Panther chairwoman and the landmark *Regents of the University of California v. Bakke* (1978) verdict that "declared affirmative action constitutional but invalidated the use of racial quotas."[104] It was at this juncture that California's struggle for racial equality began to move forward counterclockwise, much as it did when California's civil rights movement began in 1915.

Notes

1. Campbell Gibson and Kay Jung, "Historical Census Statistics on Population Totals by Race, 1790 to 1990, and by Hispanic Origin, 1970 to 1990, for the United States, Regions, Divisions, and States: California—Race and Hispanic Origin: 1850 to

1990," working paper no. 56 (Washington, D.C.: U.S. Census Bureau, September 2002), 37, https://www.census.gov/content/dam/Census/library/working-papers/2002/demo/POP-twps0056.pdf.
2. Albert S. Broussard, *Black San Francisco: The Struggle for Racial Equality in the West, 1900–1954* (Lawrence: University Press of Kansas, 1993), 138; Herbert G. Ruffin, *Uninvited Neighbors: African Americans in Silicon Valley, 1769–1990* (Norman: University of Oklahoma Press, 2014), 73–80; and Quintard Taylor, *In Search of the Racial Frontier: African Americans in the American West, 1528–1990* (New York: W. W. Norton, 1998), 256.
3. "James Crow" is discussed in Herbert G. Ruffin, "Which Came First, Jim or James Crow?: De Jure Racial Discrimination Revisited," in *The Encyclopedia of Diversity and Social Justice* (Lanham, Md.: Rowman & Littlefield Publishers, 2015).
4. The concept of freedom rights is discussed in Hasan Kwame Jeffries, *Bloody Lowndes: Civil Rights and Black Power in Alabama's Black Belt* (New York: New York University Press, 2009), 4.
5. Quote is from Joe William Trotter, *The Great Migration in Historical Perspective: New Dimensions of Race, Class, and Gender* (Bloomington: Indiana University Press, 1991), 17. Also see Robert L. Allen, *The Port Chicago Mutiny* (New York: Amistad Press, 1993); Frederick E. Anderson, *The Development of Leadership and Organization Building in the Black Community of Los Angeles from 1900 through World War II* (Saratoga, Calif.: Century Twenty One Publishing, 1980); Broussard, *Black San Francisco*; Lonnie G. Bunch III, *Black Los Angelenos: The Afro-American in Los Angeles, 1850–1950* (Los Angeles: California Afro-American Museum, 1988); Lawrence P. Crouchett, *William Byron Rumford, the Life and Public Services of a California Legislator: A Biography* (El Cerrito, Calif.: Downey Place Publishing House, 1990); Lawrence P. Crouchett, Lonnie G. Bunch, and Martha Kendall Winnacker, *Visions toward Tomorrow: The History of the East Bay Afro-American Community, 1852–1977* (Oakland: Northern California Center for Afro-American History and Life, 1989); Douglas Henry Daniels, *Pioneer Urbanites: A Social and Cultural History of Black San Francisco* (Berkeley: University of California Press, 1991); Lawrence B. De Graaf, "The City of Black Angels: Emergence of the Los Angeles Ghetto, 1890–1930," *Pacific Historical Review* 39, no. 3 (August 1970): 323–52; Lawrence B. De Graaf, *Negro Migration to Los Angeles, 1930 to 1950* (San Francisco: R and E Research Associates, 1974); Lawrence De Graaf, Kevin Mulroy, and Quintard Taylor, *Seeking El Dorado: African Americans in California* (Seattle: University of Washington Press, 2001); Douglas Flamming, *Bound for Freedom: Black Los Angeles in Jim Crow America* (Berkeley: University of California Press, 2005); Garden City Women's Club, *History of Black Americans in Santa Clara Valley* (Sunnyvale, Calif.: Lockheed Missiles & Space, 1978); David Hausler, *Blacks in Oakland, 1852–1987* (Oakland: privately published, Oakland Public Library, 1987); Joyce Henderson, *C. L. Dellums: International President of the Brotherhood of the Sleeping Car Porters and Civil Rights Leader* (Berkeley: Regents of the University of California, 1973); Gerald Horne, *Fire This Time: The Watts Uprising and the 1960s*

(Cambridge, Mass.: Da Capo Press, 1997); Marilynn S. Johnson, *The Second Gold Rush: Oakland and the East Bay in World War II* (Berkeley: University of California Press, 1993); Rudolph M. Lapp, *Afro-Americans in California* (San Francisco: Boyd & Fraser, 1979); Delores Nason McBroome, *Parallel Communities: African Americans in California's East Bay 1850–1963* (New York: Garland Publishing, 1993); Bruce Nelson, "The 'Lords of the Docks' Reconsidered: Race Relations among West Coast Longshoremen, 1933–61," in *Waterfront Workers: New Perspectives on Race and Class*, ed. Calvin Winslow (Chicago: University of Illinois, 1998), 155–92; Gretchen Lemke-Santangelo, *Abiding Courage: African American Migrant Women and the East Bay Community* (Chapel Hill: University of North Carolina Press, 1996); Raphael Sonenshein, *Politics in Black and White: Race and Power in Los Angeles* (Princeton, N.J.: Princeton University Press, 1993); Emory J. Tolbert, *The UNIA and Black Los Angeles: Ideology and Community in the American Garvey Movement* (Los Angeles: UCLA Center for Afro-American Studies, 1980); Emory J. Tolbert and Lawrence B. De Graaf, "'The Unseen Minority': Blacks in Orange County," *Journal of Orange County Studies*, Fall 1989–Spring 1990, 54–61; Gordon B. Wheeler, *Black California: The History of African-Americans in the Golden State* (New York: Hippocrene Books, 1993); and Shirley Ann Wilson Moore, *To Place Our Deeds: The African American Community in Richmond, California, 1910–1963* (Berkeley: University of California Press, 2000).

6. Robert Bauman, *Race and the War on Poverty: From Watts to East L.A.* (Norman: University of Oklahoma Press, 2008); Kevin Allen Leonard, *The Battle for Los Angeles: Racial Ideology and World War II* (Albuquerque: University of New Mexico Press, 2006); Donna Jean Murch, *Living for the City: Migration, Education, and the Rise of the Black Panther Party in Oakland, California* (Chapel Hill: University of North Carolina Press, 2010); Ruffin, *Uninvited Neighbors*; Robert O. Self, *American Babylon: Race and the Struggle for Postwar Oakland* (Princeton, N.J.: Princeton University Press, 2003); Josh Sides, *L.A. City Limits: African American Los Angeles from the Great Depression to the Present* (Berkeley: University of California, 2006). See also Mark Brilliant, *The Color of America Has Changed*; Scott Kurashige, *The Shifting Grounds of Race*; and Shana Bernstein, *Bridges of Reform* to situate California more broadly in a multiracial context. For citations, see bibliography.

7. Ingrid Banks, Gaye Johnson, George Lipsitz, Ula Taylor, Daniel Widener, and Clyde Woods, eds., *Black California Dreamin': The Crises of California's African-American Communities* (Santa Barbara: UC Santa Barbara Center for Black Studies Research, December 2012), 19–56; Laura Pulido, *Black, Brown, Yellow, and Left: Radical Activism in Los Angeles* (Berkeley: University of California, 2006); Clora Bryant, *Central Avenue Sounds: Jazz in Los Angeles* (Berkeley: University of California, 1999).

8. The "forward counterclockwise motion" concept is explained in Matthew C. Whitaker, *Race Work: The Rise of Civil Rights in the Urban West* (Lincoln: University of Nebraska Press, 2007).

9. See Ruffin, *Uninvited Neighbors*, 35–47.

10. Gibson and Jung, "Historical Census Statistics ... by Race ... for the United States, Regions, Divisions, and States: California," working paper no. 56 (September 2002), 37.
11. Broussard, *Black San Francisco*, 76; Lonnie G. Bunch III, "'The Greatest State for the Negro': Jefferson L. Edmonds, Black Propagandist of the California Dream," in De Graaf, Mulroy, and Taylor, *Seeking El Dorado*, 136; Flamming, *Bound for Freedom*, 142–52; and Taylor, *In Search of the Racial Frontier*, 222.
12. Crouchett, *Visions toward Tomorrow*, 32; and Ruffin, *Uninvited Neighbors*, 49.
13. Quoted from Kwame Anthony Appiah and Henry Louis Gates Jr., eds., "Birth of a Nation," in *Africana: The Encyclopedia of the African and African American Experience* (New York: Basic Civitas Books, 1999), 237. Also see Matthew Frye Jacobson, *Whiteness of a Different Color: European Immigrants and the Alchemy of Race* (Cambridge: Harvard University Press, 1998), 118; and Taylor, *In Search of the Racial Frontier*, 238.
14. Broussard, *Black San Francisco*, 77–81.
15. Taylor, *In Search of the Racial Frontier*, 239.
16. Appiah, "Birth of a Nation," 237.
17. Broussard, *Black San Francisco*, 81; Crouchett, *Visions toward Tomorrow*, 26–29; Hausler, *Blacks in Oakland, 1852–1987*, 87; and McBroome, *Parallel Communities*, 59.
18. Broussard, *Black San Francisco*, 82–83, 166; James Goodman, *Stories of Scottsboro* (New York: Pantheon Books, 1994), 210; and McBroome, *Parallel Communities*, 67, 80–81.
19. Broussard, *Black San Francisco*, 85–86; Winston James, *Holding Aloft the Banner of Ethiopia: Caribbean Radicalism in Early Twentieth Century America* (Brooklyn: Verso Books, 1998), 122–94; John T. McCartney, *Black Power Ideologies: An Essay in African-American Political Thought* (Philadelphia: Temple University Press, 1992), 80–88; Ruffin, *Uninvited Neighbors*, 67; Tolbert, *The UNIA and Black Los Angeles*; and Cary D. Wintz, *African American Political Thought: 1890–1930* (New York: M. E. Sharp, 1996), 199–218.
20. McBroome, *Parallel Communities*, 56–57; Hausler, *Blacks in Oakland, 1852–1987*, 94; and Wheeler, *Black California*, 203.
21. McBroome, *Parallel Communities*, 56–57. Also see Crouchett, *Visions toward Tomorrow*, 33; and Shirley Ann Wilson Moore, "Your Life Is Really Not Just Your Own: African American Women in Twentieth-Century California," in De Graaf, Mulroy, and Taylor, *Seeking El Dorado*, 215–25.
22. Flamming, *Bound for Freedom*, 235–39.
23. See "African Americans in Los Angeles"; "African Americans in Oakland"; "African Americans in Sacramento"; "African Americans in San Diego"; "African Americans in San Francisco"; and "African Americans in Santa Clara County" in *U.S. Census* (Online) from 1900–1940, Ancestry.com; and Ruffin, *Uninvited Neighbors*, 55.
24. Eric Arnesen, "Charting an Independent Course," in *Labor Histories: Class, Politics, and the Working Class Experience*, ed. Eric Arnesen, Julie Greene, and Bruce Laurie (Urbana: University of Illinois Press, 1998), 284–308; Joyce Henderson, *C. L. Dellums*, 8–28; Andrew E. Kersten, *A. Philip Randolph: A Life in the Vanguard* (New York:

Rowman & Littlefield, 2007); Herbert G. Ruffin, "A. Philip Randolph," in *Icons of Black America*, ed. Matthew C. Whitaker (Westport, Conn.: Greenwood Press, 2011), 727–40; and Jack Santino, *Miles of Smiles, Years of Struggle: Stories of Black Pullman Porters* (Chicago: University of Illinois Press, 1989), 7–30.
25. Santino, *Miles of Smiles*, 14.
26. Ibid., 23.
27. Henderson, *C. L. Dellums*, 14.
28. Henderson, *C. L. Dellums*, 26–27, 47–48; and McBroome, *Parallel Communities*, 67–68.
29. See Albert Broussard, "Black San Francisco as a Model for Examining the Urban West" (filmed presentation), in Program in African American Culture Archives, National Museum of American History, *A Quest for Freedom: The Black Experience in the American West* (Washington, D.C.: Smithsonian Institution, 2001); Flamming, *Bound for Freedom*, 350–53; Ruffin, *Uninvited Neighbors*, 57–59; Sides, *L.A. City Limits*, 11–35; and Tolbert, "The Unseen Minority," 58.
30. Flamming, *Bound for Freedom*, 153–56.
31. Campbell Gibson and Kay Jung, "Historical Census Statistics on Population Totals by Race, 1790 to 1990, and by Hispanic Origin, 1970 to 1990, for Large Cities and Other Urban Places in the United States: California—Race and Hispanic Origin for Selected Cities and Other Places: Earliest Census to 1990," working paper no. 76 (Washington, D.C.: U.S. Census Bureau, February 2005), https://www.census.gov/population/www/documentation/twps0076/twps0076.html; and Gibson and Jung, "Historical Census Statistics . . . by Race. . . for the United States, Regions, Divisions, and States: California," working paper no. 56 (September 2002), 37.
32. Bunch, "The Greatest State for the Negro," 136. Also see Flamming, *Bound for Freedom*, 55–58, 93–125.
33. Taylor, *In Search of the Racial Frontier*, 232–35.
34. McBroome, *Parallel Communities*, 39.
35. Taylor, *In Search of the Racial Frontier*, 235.
36. Amina Hassan, "Loren Miller (1903–1967)," Blackpast.org, http://www.blackpast.org/aaw/miller-loren-1903-1967; Shelley v. Kraemer, 334 U.S. 1 (1948).
37. Lemke-Santangelo, *Abiding Courage*, 153.
38. Lemke-Santangelo, *Abiding Courage*, 174; Ruffin, *Uninvited Neighbors*, 45–47, 66–68.
39. Quoted in Hausler, *Blacks in Oakland, 1852–1987*, 54. Also see Crouchett, *Visions toward Tomorrow*, 23.
40. Hausler, *Blacks in Oakland, 1852–1987*, 70, 117; Crouchett, *Visions toward Tomorrow*, 35.
41. Douglas Flamming, "Becoming Democrats: Liberal Politics and the African American Community in Los Angeles, 1930–1965," in De Graaf, Mulroy, and Taylor, *Seeking El Dorado*, 279–90; Ruffin, *Uninvited Neighbors*, 69–70.
42. Flamming, "Becoming Democrats," 279.
43. Ibid., 294.

44. David M. Kennedy, *Freedom from Fear: The American People in Depression and War, 1929–1945* (New York: Oxford University Press, 1999), 363–80.
45. See Broussard, *Black San Francisco*, 120–27; Flamming, "Becoming Democrats," 290–91; Eric Foner, *A Short History of Reconstruction, 1863–1877* (New York: Harper & Row, 1990), 82–123, 199–216, 238–60; and Taylor, *In Search of the Racial Frontier*, 103–33, 228–31.
46. Taylor, *In Search of the Racial Frontier*, 230–31.
47. Nelson, "Lords of the Docks," 157.
48. Art Preis, *Labor's Giant Step: Twenty Years of the CIO* (New York: Pathfinder Press, 1972), 12.
49. Ibid., 31.
50. Quoted in McBroome, *Parallel Communities*, 73.
51. Nelson, "Lords of the Docks," 157.
52. McBroome, *Parallel Communities*, 74.
53. McBroome, *Parallel Communities*, 73–76; and Preis, *Labor's Giant Step*, 31–32.
54. See Gerald Horne, "Black Fire: 'Riot' and 'Revolt' in Los Angeles, 1965 and 1992," in De Graaf, Mulroy, and Taylor, *Seeking El Dorado*, 385; and Nelson, "Lords of the Docks," 163–84.
55. Jonathan Dembo, "The West Coast Teamsters' and Longshoremen's Unions in the Twentieth Century," *Journal of the West* 25, no. 2 (1986): 27–35; and Nelson, "Lords of the Docks," 159–62.
56. Horne, "Black Fire," 385; Nelson, "Lords of the Docks," 163; and Ruffin, *Uninvited Neighbors*, 48–70.
57. Broussard, *Black San Francisco*, 145–46; Kennedy, *Freedom from Fear*, 765–76; Ruffin, "A. Philip Randolph," 733–34; Ruffin, *Uninvited Neighbors*, 82–83; Sides, *L.A. City Limits*, 3–4; and Taylor, *In Search of the Racial Frontier*, 255–56.
58. Taylor, *In Search of the Racial Frontier*, 254–55.
59. Gretchen Lemke-Santangelo, "Deindustrialization, Urban Poverty, and African American Community Mobilization in Oakland, 1945 through the 1990s," in De Graaf, Mulroy, and Taylor, *Seeking El Dorado*, 347.
60. See Broussard, *Black San Francisco*, 158–65; McBroome, *Parallel Communities*, 106–12; Ruffin, *Uninvited Neighbors*, 80–83; and Taylor, *In Search of the Racial Frontier*, 257–60.
61. Marilynn S. Johnson, *The Second Gold Rush: Oakland and the East Bay in World War II* (Berkeley: University of California Press, 1993), 30–59, 235–40; and Lemke-Santangelo, "Deindustrialization, Urban Poverty, and African American Community Mobilization in Oakland, 1945 through the 1990s," 345–54.
62. Horne, "Black Fire," 385–87; Sides, *L.A. City Limits*, 169–98.
63. PBS, *This Far by Faith: African American Spiritual Journeys* (2003), http://www.pbs.org/thisfarbyfaith/people/howard_thurman.html; Johnetta Richards, "Thurman, Howard (1900–1981)," Blackpast.org, http://www.blackpast.org/aaw/thurman-howard-1900-1981; Sudarshan Kapur, *Raising Up a Prophet: The African American Encounter with Gandhi* (Boston: Beacon Press, 1992), 83–96.

64. Quote was originally applied to the *Brown* verdict in PBS, "Brown v. Board of Education (1954)," The Supreme Court, http://www.pbs.org/wnet/supremecourt/rights/landmark_brown.html.
65. United States Courts, "Mendez v. Westminster Background," United States Courts, http://www.uscourts.gov/educational-resources/get-involved/federal-court-activities/mendez-westminster-re-enactment/mendez-westminster-background.aspx.
66. Hassan, "Loren Miller (1903–1967)"; PBS, "Brown v. Board of Education (1954)"; Ruffin, *Uninvited Neighbors*, 82–83; and Taylor, *In Search of the Racial Frontier*, 215; Stanford Law School–Robert Crown Law Library, "Jackson v. Pasadena City School District," Supreme Court of California Resources, http://scocal.stanford.edu/opinion/jackson-v-pasadena-city-school-dist-27149; Whitaker, *Race Work*, 113–22. Also see Jonathan Kozol, *Savage Inequalities: Children in America's Schools* (New York: Harper Perennial, 1992); Kozol, *The Shame of the Nation: The Restoration of Apartheid Schooling in America* (New York, Broadway, 2006); and *San Jose Mercury News*, "Why Court Ruled Against San Jose," May 18, 1984.
67. Quoted in Daren Salter, "Civil Rights Congress (1946–1956)," Blackpast.org, http://www.blackpast.org/aah/civil-rights-congress-1946-1956. Also see Sides, *L.A. City Limits*, 139–46.
68. A&E Television Networks, "Red Scare," HistoryChannel.com, http://www.history.com/topics/cold-war/red-scare.
69. Crouchett, *William Byron Rumford*; Alton Hornsby Jr., and Angela Hornsby-Gutting, "Brown, Willie Lewis, Jr. (1934–)," Blackpast.org, http://www.blackpast.org/aah/brown-willie-lewis-jr-1934; Office of Maxine Waters, "U.S. Congresswoman Maxine Waters," http://waters.house.gov/; Ruffin, *Uninvited Neighbors*, 134–36; Samantha Nicholas Kealoha, "Dellums, Ronald Vernie (1935–)," Blackpast.org, http://www.blackpast.org/aah/dellums-ronald-vernie-1935; Sonenshein, *Politics in Black and White*.
70. Kevin Allen Leonard, "In the Interest of All Races: African American and Interracial Cooperation in Los Angeles during and after World War II," in De Graaf, Mulroy, and Taylor, *Seeking El Dorado*, 329.
71. Ruffin, *Uninvited Neighbors*, 87–91, 98–101, 122–37.
72. Ibid., 122–37.
73. Quoted from Herbert G. Ruffin, "The Search for Significance in Interstitial Space: San Jose and Its Great Black Migration, 1941–1968," in *Black California Dreamin': The Crises of California's African-American Communities* (Santa Barbara: UC Santa Barbara Center for Black Studies Research, December 2012), 38.
74. See Kevin Boyle, *The UAW and the Heyday of American Liberalism, 1945–1968* (Ithaca: Cornell University Press, 1995), 61–131.
75. Ruffin, *Uninvited Neighbors*, 122–37.
76. Lawrence B. De Graaf, "African American Suburbanization in California, 1960 through 1990," in De Graaf, Mulroy, and Taylor, *Seeking El Dorado*, 407.
77. De Graaf, "African American Suburbanization," 407.

78. Broussard, *Black San Francisco*, 239–45; De Graaf, Mulroy, and Taylor, *Seeking El Dorado*, 343–449; Murch, *Living for the City*, 15–70; Ruffin, *Uninvited Neighbors*, 92–122; Self, *American Babylon*; and Sides, *L.A. City Limits*, 95–130.
79. Ruffin, *Uninvited Neighbors*, 107–15; and Martin Schiesl, ed., *Responsible Liberalism: Edmond G. "Pat" Brown and Reform Government in California, 1958–1967* (Los Angeles: Edmond G. "Pat" Brown Institute of Public Affairs, 2003), 101–24.
80. Ruffin, *Uninvited Neighbors*, 144–48.
81. Albert S. Broussard, "Percy H. Steele, Jr., and the Urban League: Race Relations and the Struggle for Civil Rights in Post–World War II San Diego," *California History* 83, no. 4 (2006): 7–23, http://ch.ucpress.edu/content/83/4/7.
82. Taylor, *In Search of the Racial Frontier*, 289.
83. Terry H. Anderson, *The Pursuit of Fairness: A History of Affirmative Action* (New York: Oxford University Press, 49–160); and Ruffin, *Uninvited Neighbors*, 119–20, 215.
84. De Graaf, "African American Suburbanization," 415.
85. Quotes are in Ruffin, *Uninvited Neighbors*, 93.
86. Ibid.
87. David Hilliard, ed., *The Huey P. Newton Reader* (New York: Seven Stories Press, 2002), 45–46; Peniel E. Joseph, "Black Studies, Black Student Activism, and the Black Power Movement," in *The Black Power Movement: Rethinking the Civil Rights–Black Power Era* (New York: Routledge, 2006), 259–62; Murch, *Living for the City*, 71–127; Bobby Seale, *Seize the Time: The Story of the Black Panther Party and Huey P. Newton* (New York: Random House, 1970), 12–25, 30, 46.
88. Martha Biondi, *The Black Revolution on Campus* (Berkeley: University of California Press), 43–78; Douglas Hartmann, *Race, Culture, and the Revolt of the Black Athlete: The 1968 Olympic Protests and Their Aftermath* (Chicago: University of Chicago Press, 2004); Joseph, "Black Studies," 264–77; Jeffrey O. G. Ogbar, "Rainbow Radicalism: The Rise of the Radical Ethnic Nationalism," in *The Black Power Movement: Rethinking the Civil Rights–Black Power Era*, ed. Peniel E. Joseph (New York: Routledge, 2006), 193–228; Pulido, *Black, Brown, Yellow, and Left*; Ibram H. Rogers, *The Black Campus Movement: Black Students and the Racial Reconstitution of Higher Education, 1965–1972* (New York: Palgrave Macmillan, 2012), 89–126; Fabio Rojas, *From Black Power to Black Studies: How a Radical Social Movement Became an Academic Discipline* (Baltimore: Johns Hopkins University Press, 2010), 45–92; Ruffin, *Uninvited Neighbors*, 163–200; Herbert G. Ruffin, "'Doing the Right Thing for the Sake of Doing the Right Thing': The Revolt of the Black Athlete and the Modern Student-Athletic Movement, 1956–2014," *The Western Journal of Black Studies* (Fall 2014).
89. Quoted in Horne, "Black Fire," 377, also see 377–81; and Taylor, *In Search of the Racial Frontier*, 299–303.
90. Molefi Kete Asante, *Maulana Karenga: An Intellectual Portrait* (Malden, Mass.: Polity Press, 2009); Scot Brown, *Fighting for Us* (New York: NYU Press, 2003), 33–36, 74–106, 159–62; Maulana Karenga, *Kawaida and Questions of Life and Struggle*

(Los Angeles: University of Sankore Press, 2008); and Keith A. Mayes, *Kwanzaa: Black Power and The Making of the African-American Holiday Tradition* (New York: Routledge, 2009), 47–134.
91. Quoted in Charles E. Jones, ed., *The Black Panther Party Reconsidered* (Baltimore: Black Classic Press, 1998), 40. Also see Murch, *Living for the City*, 121–51; Self, *American Babylon*, 217–55; William L. Van Deburg, *Modern Black Nationalism: From Marcus Garvey to Louis Farrakhan* (New York: New York University Press, 1997), 127; and Rhonda Williams, *The Politics of Public Housing: Black Women's Struggles Against Urban Inequality* (New York: Oxford University Press, 2004), 155–228.
92. Murch, *Living for the City*, 127–31;
93. Quoted in Seale, *Seize the Time*, 30.
94. Murch, *Living for the City*, 126.
95. Hilliard, *The Huey P. Newton Reader*, 45.
96. Murch, *Living for the City*, 125–27; and Seale, *Seize the Time*, 19–34.
97. Seale, *Seize the Time*, 147–49; Huey P. Newton, *War Against the Panthers: A Study of Repression in America* (New York: Harlem River Press, 1996), 32–33; Jones, *The Black Panther Party Reconsidered*, 308–9; and Hilliard, *The Huey P. Newton Reader*, 67–72.
98. Quoted in Hilliard, *The Huey P. Newton Reader*, 58.
99. Associated Press, "Huey Newton Killed; Was a Co-Founder Of Black Panthers," *New York Times*, August 23, 1989.
100. Newton, *War against the Panthers*, 31–32; and Seale, *Seize the Time*, 367.
101. Paraphrased from Jones, *The Black Panther Party Reconsidered*, 1. Also see Murch, *Living for the City*, 169–228; and Newton, *War against the Panthers*, 9, 22–23, 54, 86.
102. Murch, *Living for the City*, 176–78; and Taylor, *In Search of the Racial Frontier*, 307.
103. Hilliard, *The Huey P. Newton Reader*, 160–75.
104. Quoted from *Encyclopaedia Britannica*, "Bakke decision," http://www.britannica.com/EBchecked/topic/495961/Bakke-decision; and Blackpast.org, "University of California Regents v. Bakke, 1978," http://www.blackpast.org/primary/university-california-regents-v-bakke-1978.

Further Reading

See selected bibliography, pp. 271–78.

5

Civil Rights Movement in Nevada
Elmer R. Rusco

Civil rights actions in Nevada, unfortunately known in the black community and elsewhere as "the Mississippi of the West," were needed, and as Elmer R. Rusco points out, with the help of some white leaders and a struggle for effective state legislation, successful civil rights activity occurred. A significant portion of the Nevada African American community resided in the two major cities, Reno and Las Vegas. In Las Vegas, employment and fair salaries in the casinos received successful attention. Elmer Rusco was a professor of political science at the University of Nevada, Reno. He is the author of *"Good Time Coming?": Black Nevadans in the Nineteenth Century* and coeditor of *Ethnicity and Race in Nevada* with Sue Fawn Chung. This chapter was part of a special edition of the *Nevada Public Affairs Review*.

Nevada law regarding race has gone through three stages. Nevada began its life as a territory and state with laws explicitly discriminating on a racial basis. There were no laws banning private discrimination, and apparently none were considered. Most of the state's active involvement in discrimination was eliminated during the nineteenth century, but only one law outlawing discrimination by a public agency—a statute requiring the university not to discriminate in admissions—was enacted in that century. Not until the 1950s were the remnants of the previous century's racist laws completely eliminated, however. In the third stage, during the twentieth century, laws against discrimination by private

---

Originally published in *Nevada Public Affairs Review* 2 (1987), 75–81. Reprinted with permission of the Nevada Center for Surveys, Evaluation, and Statistics.

individuals in public accommodations, employment, and housing were enacted. The effort to secure these antidiscrimination laws is referred to as the civil rights movement. No full account of this movement in Nevada yet exists, but this summary is offered to fill a gap in this vital development.

Private Discrimination in Nevada

One of the important facts about private discrimination on a racial basis in Nevada in this century is the absence of significant documentation of such discrimination. William Horgan, chairman of the Nevada Advisory Committee to the United States Civil Rights Commission, noted in 1960:

> We have come to realize that Nevada, because of its small population, is different from many other states in that very little research into the problems with which we are concerned has been done here.[1]

There can be no doubt that much private discrimination existed by the 1950s, however. In fact, it was not uncommon to find Nevada described by both blacks and whites as the "Mississippi of the West" during the 1950s and 1960s. While discrimination or segregation by law had not existed since the nineteenth century, the name was applied to the state at least partly because of the openness of private discrimination. For example, Mrs. Alice Smith, cofounder with her husband of the Reno-Sparks branch of the National Association for the Advancement of Colored People, remembered in 1971 that:

> as you walked by in the windows of restaurants you would see a little sign that stated "No Negroes Allowed," "No Colored Trade Solicited" and the most attractive and impressive and aggravating one also, to me was a sign that was on east Fourth Street [in Reno] on a restaurant and it read like this: "No Indians, dogs or Negroes allowed."[2]

It is clear that major casinos and other tourist-oriented businesses in both the Las Vegas and Reno-Sparks areas refused to serve black customers until the 1960s. For example, it was well documented that prominent black entertainers, including Sammy Davis Jr., could not stay in the Las Vegas hotels where they were the star attractions in the 1940s and 1950s. This situation led to the establishment of the Moulin Rouge, a nondiscriminatory casino located on the southern edge of the Westside, the center of black population in Clark County. In Reno, only a small black-owned club and the New China Club, owned by Chinese-American Bew Hong (Bill) Fong, admitted black customers until the 1960s. El Capitan Casino in Hawthorne conspicuously excluded black customers until the passage of the federal Civil Rights Act in 1964. Nevada also earned the title of "Mississippi of the West" by its slowness to act against private discrimination; significant legislation in this area was not enacted until after the major civil rights statutes had been passed by Congress.

Civil Rights Organizations

Nevada developed few civil rights organizations before or during the 1960s, and some of these appeared only after major civil rights legislation had been passed. Significant civil rights efforts were made only by organizations centered in the black community, led by three branches of the NAACP. There is no evidence of such activities by organizations representing other racial or ethnic minorities in the 1950s and 1960s. A few short-lived interracial groups were organized to lobby for civil rights (such as Reno's Society to Underwrite Racial Equality—SURE) but chapters of the Congress of Racial Equality, the Urban League, and similar groups were never organized in Nevada. The National Conference of Christians and Jews organized in Southern Nevada in 1958 but was not present in the northern part of the state until 1962. The American Civil Liberties Union did not appear until 1966.

NAACP branches were organized only in the three counties with significant black populations. The 1950 census of population, for example, reported that 91.6 percent of the state's black population lived in Clark, Washoe, and Mineral Counties. The concentration of the black population in these three counties has continued to this date.

Early Civil Rights Efforts

What was apparently the first civil rights proposal in the state legislature was introduced in 1939. Assembly Bill 88, which would have required equal rights for Nevadans, was introduced by the Clark County delegation, by request. On the thirtieth day of the session, the Social Welfare Committee gave it a do-not-pass recommendation and the assembly as a whole, reportedly by a unanimous vote, moved that it be "indefinitely postponed." This bill probably originated with the NAACP branch in Las Vegas, because in the fall of 1939 this branch, joined by two other groups, asked the Las Vegas City Commission to bar discrimination in city-owned facilities.

The next civil rights bill was not introduced until the 1947 Session, when assemblyman E. R. "Boots" Miller of White Pine County sponsored a bill to bar discrimination by race in public accommodations. Miller, elected as an independent and describing himself as a LaFollette Progressive, introduced the measure on his own initiative. He was unsuccessful in getting it out of committee, however, losing a vote to withdraw the bill and assign it to another committee by a vote of 12 to 23 on March 12, 1947. The bill was eventually reported out of committee but assigned to another one, which killed it.

Similar measures to ban discrimination in public accommodations or to repeal the antimiscegenation statute failed in every legislative session from 1949 through 1957, with the exception of 1951, when no civil rights measures were introduced. All were introduced in the assembly, although none passed that body.

From 1949 on, civil rights bills probably were sponsored by the NAACP. In 1949, a hearing on a public accommodations bill attracted fifty persons and revealed support from the NAACP, church groups, the Progressive Party, and the Reno-Sparks Young Women's Christian Association. Also, a petition favoring the bill was sent to the legislature from the University of Nevada (whose sole campus was then in Reno), with 274 signatures, mostly from students; this may have represented as much as 15 percent of the student body that year.

During the 1950s, there were some efforts to promote civil rights by boycotts or local governmental action. In 1954 the West Coast Regional Welfare Conference cancelled a scheduled meeting in Las Vegas because black members could not secure nondiscriminatory housing there, and a regional conference of the Girl Scouts scheduled for Las Vegas was also cancelled during the 1950s in protest against discrimination. Efforts to get city councils to ban discrimination failed in both Sparks and Las Vegas during the 1950s. In both cases, the mayors said that they thought local governments should not tell businesses what to do.

Civil rights efforts intensified in 1958. The Nevada Advisory Committee to the national Civil Rights Commission created in 1957 was appointed; attorney and former Reno Chamber of Commerce president William Horgan was its chairman. During the 1958 campaign for governor, both candidates addressed the issue. Incumbent Governor Charles Russell met with NAACP leaders and pledged to appoint a study committee with representatives from minority groups if he was reelected. His Democratic challenger, Grant Sawyer, talked of support for the goal of nondiscrimination.

The Sawyer Administration: Civil Rights Becomes an Issue

Grant Sawyer, who was elected governor in 1958 and reelected in 1962, consistently backed civil rights legislation. Sometimes he was not willing to go as far as civil rights advocates wanted him to, but he was courageous in advocating and working for civil rights legislation throughout his eight years as governor. During his first legislative session, the miscegenation statute, which had been declared unconstitutional the year before in the Bridges case, was repealed. This session also repealed the law forbidding the employment of "Mongolians" on public works and enacted a measure forbidding discrimination in employment by state, county, or municipal agencies or by persons contracting with such agencies. These bills were noncontroversial and attracted little public attention. Governor Sawyer proposed to establish an appointed state human relations commission to study discrimination, but the bill, although it passed the assembly in a weakened form, died in a Senate committee.

The 1960 session likewise refused to adopt Sawyer's bill to create a study commission. The assembly again approved it but once again it died in a Senate committee. However, this session did approve a law to forbid discrimination in apprenticeship programs operating under the state Apprenticeship Council, with little public notice. Two significant extralegislative efforts to advance nondiscrimination occurred in 1960. In Las Vegas, the threat of a sit-in and demonstrations on the Las Vegas Strip by the NAACP against discrimination was taken seriously. After personal intervention by Governor Sawyer and behind-the-scenes efforts by newspaper publisher Hank Greenspun and others, an agreement by business leaders of Las Vegas to end discrimination in public accommodations in major businesses was reached, and the demonstration was called off. It was reported in the *Las Vegas Sun* on March 26, 1960, that "the local NAACP yesterday announced it was cancelling a mass demonstration by 300 Negroes set for tonight at 6, because 'We have received assurances from the majority of downtown and Strip businesses that the policy of racial discrimination in Las Vegas has ended.'"[3]

In northern Nevada, a determined effort led by the Reno-Sparks branch of the NAACP attempted to use the 1960 Winter Olympics, which were to be held at Squaw Valley, near Lake Tahoe, to end discrimination in public accommodations. Many labor and civil rights groups in California joined the effort, and California attorney general Stanley Mosk and Nevada attorney general Roger Foley requested action to end such discrimination. At a meeting called by Governor Sawyer, agreement was reached that discrimination in public accommodations would be suspended during the Olympics. Unfortunately this advance proved to be only temporary; previous patterns of racial discrimination returned after the Olympics.

In the 1961 legislative session, the Sawyer administration made an ultimately successful effort to secure creation of a state study group, the Equal Rights

Commission (ERC). In 1961 the NAACP made its strongest effort yet to ban discrimination in public accommodations, employment, and housing. This comprehensive measure was supported by the state Council of Churches and the Clark and Washoe County ministerial associations, the Anti-Defamation League, the state League of Women Voters, the state American Federation of Labor–Congress of Industrial Organizations, the Reno Young Women's Christian Association, the state Advisory Committee mentioned earlier, and various individuals, including the Rev. H. Clyde Mathews Jr., a Baptist minister to the Reno-Sparks Indian Colony who began to play a prominent role in the civil rights movement at this point. NAACP leaders who were active included attorney Charles Kellar of Las Vegas, who drafted the NAACP bill, Las Vegas dentist Dr. James B. McMillan, and Reno-Sparks branch President Eddie B. Scott.

As it became clear to civil rights leaders during the 1961 session that the pattern of Senate hostility to civil rights legislation with enforcement provisions was likely to hold, they decided to resort to public demonstrations. On March 27, the legislature was picketed. A few days later there was a sit-in at Reno's Overland Hotel that attracted much attention, plus picketing of other Reno businesses—Harrah's and Harold's casinos, the Nevada Bank of Commerce, and the New China Club (whose owner was accused of secretly opposing civil rights legislation). Although many legislators attacked the demonstrations and sit-ins, the Senate responded to them by unanimously passing the measure creating the Equal Rights Commission.

Efforts to Secure Meaningful Legislation: 1963–1965

The year 1962 was one of unrelieved frustration for the civil rights movement. The creation of the ERC should have led to a succession of public hearings to establish the existence of discrimination and to build support for legislation imposing penalties on violators, but this did not happen in a timely fashion. The first chairman of the ERC, William Horgan, resigned because the agency had so little authority. His successor, Robert Bailey of Las Vegas, was not appointed until months later. Another of the original members of the agency, Bishop Robert J. Dwyer of Reno, was sidelined by illness for several months in 1962, and the governor's office did not find anyone to fill a fifth position on the ERC until the fall of 1962. Meanwhile, subpoenas to appear and testify before the ERC sometimes were successfully resisted. For example, in May 1962 a district court in Las Vegas annulled subpoenas that had been issued by the ERC on the ground that the full commission had not authorized them.

As a result of all these problems, the ERC held only four full-scale hearings to document discrimination during the year and a half between the end of the 1961 session and the beginning of the 1963 session. All four were held after the general election of 1962 and after the Advisory Committee to the Civil Rights Commission had held three hearings. The last was held in January 1963, with the legislature's opening only a few weeks off. The ERC report to the 1963 legislature, therefore, was weak on evidence and was not accompanied by widespread public awareness of discrimination. It made no specific proposals for legislation and was largely ignored.

Attempts to move on other fronts were also frustrated. In January 1962, the Coordinating Council of the NAACP asked Governor Sawyer to use the State Gaming Commission to enforce nondiscrimination in public accommodations. The reasoning behind this request was that the state could make nondiscrimination a condition for the issuance of a gaming license. Since the state issued such licenses as a matter of privilege, not right, and imposed strict rules on licensees in other areas, it could validly require nondiscrimination. In spite of an opinion by the state attorney general that the law authorized some activity against discrimination by the Gaming Commission, Governor Sawyer and the commission refused to act. The governor argued that the legal authority to act in this area was dubious and that in any case the commission did not have the personnel or funds to take on a major new task.

The Reno-Sparks branch of the NAACP attempted to get the City of Reno to require nondiscrimination in public accommodations by businesses licensed by the city. The Reno city attorney advised the council that it was doubtful that the city had authority in this area, and the council declined to act. Moreover, the mayor and council also declined to initiate meetings with local businesses to discuss such issues. The late report of the ERC prevented the working out of a legislative proposal that could be supported by a broad coalition of groups. Governor Sawyer, in his address to the legislature, made no specific requests because the report had not yet been made. He recommended only that the legislators should give "most serious consideration" to the proposed amendments. The governor evidently planned to introduce his own bill, modeled on the federal civil rights proposal currently before the Congress, but did not do so.

On January 26, 1963, the civil rights movement's proposals for the session were presented to key legislators and Governor Sawyer, as amendments to the 1961 law that had created the ERC. They eventually became Assembly Bill 338, which was introduced March 1. Assemblywoman Flora Dungan of Las Vegas held a hearing of her Social Welfare Committee on March 14, at which the measure was endorsed by Robert Bailey for the ERC; Eddie Scott of Reno and Marion Bennett and J. David Hoggard of Las Vegas for the NAACP; Charles Springer, state chairman of the Democratic Party, representatives of the Nevada Council of Churches and the Clark County ministerial association; the presidents of the student body and the Panhellenic Council at the University of Nevada, Reno; UNR professors Erling Skorpen and James Hulse; Bertha Johnson of Las Vegas; and the Reverend Mathews, chairman of the Advisory Committee to the United States Civil Rights Commission.

When AB 338 came up for a floor vote on March 27, it was voted down, 13 to 23. At this point, civil rights supporters resorted to picketing the legislature, and various legislators claimed that these tactics doomed any civil rights legislation for that session. However, the assembly later passed a much weaker civil rights bill, AB 536, which merely declared that discrimination on racial grounds in employment, housing, and public accommodation constituted a violation of a "civil right." The meaning of this was unclear. An amendment adopted by the assembly stated specifically that the bill in no way enlarged the jurisdiction of the courts of the state, so the bill probably would not have allowed suits for damages. Characteristically, AB 536 passed the assembly April 22 by a vote of 27 to 4 but died in a Senate committee.

Probably no civil rights bill could have passed the Senate in 1963. State Senator James Slattery of Storey County, chair of the committee to which civil rights bills were assigned, went out of his way to state his opposition to such legislation. With Senator William Dial, a Republican from Ormsby County, he introduced a bill to abolish the ERC and another bill to replace the commission with a legislative study commission. On his own he introduced a bill to outlaw discrimination against Irish-American citizens, presumably in an attempt to ridicule civil rights backers. In declaring his intention on the floor of the Senate to bottle up the bill to create a legislative commission, Slattery said, "I feel that the colored people in this state have never been so well off." Further, he claimed that the houses of "colored people" in Las Vegas were "better than mine" and that "colored people drove better cars than he did."[14]

The last attempt in 1963 to salvage a weak civil rights bill failed when the Senate Finance Committee refused to report out AB 536 at the very end of the session. When the civil rights lobbyists tried to get senators to introduce a new measure the week before expected adjournment, the Senate divided along partisan lines. In party caucuses the Democrats favored introduction while

Republicans opposed it. After the 1963 session, Governor Sawyer took action of his own. On May 23, he sent a memorandum to the heads of all state boards and regulatory agencies, reminding them of the public policy of the state against discrimination, embodied in the 1961 law creating the Equal Rights Commission. The memorandum stated:

> It is imperative that this policy be implemented to the fullest extent possible by all state boards and regulatory agencies and by the persons with whom the state does business. I would respectfully suggest that you advise each applicant, present licensee, and persons with whom you do business of this policy in writing.[5]

Sawyer also asked each agency head to report to him what actions they had taken to implement and enforce the nondiscrimination policy.

In August, Sawyer asked the state attorney general for an opinion on the extent of his authority to enforce nondiscrimination policies by licensees of the state. On August 12, Attorney General Harvey Dickerson issued an opinion stating that the governor had "no power . . . to instruct regulatory commissions and licensing boards to revoke licenses, or take similar action when discrimination is found in an area over which such commissions and boards exercise jurisdiction." This opinion went on to say that the "Legislature has failed to enact legislation to adequately guarantee civil rights in Nevada. It is upon this body and not the Governor that the onus must fall."[6]

Civil rights advocates, meanwhile, adopted more militant tactics. The Las Vegas branch of the NAACP announced in July 1963 that it would hold a demonstration on the Las Vegas Strip just before a nationally televised prize fight between Floyd Patterson and Sonny Liston. A period of intense negotiation, which involved the governor's office and the ERC, followed this announcement. When seven of the major Strip hotels offered to meet with NAACP leaders if no demonstration occurred, the leaders called off the demonstration at the last minute. Talks between the hotels and civil rights leaders followed, including discussions on July 31, August 7, August 13, and August 14, which involved the ERC.

In 1964, civil rights advocates again met frustration. When the ERC subpoenaed Lindsay Smith, owner of El Capitan Casino in Hawthorne, to appear at a commission hearing, he replied with a suit charging that the commission was unconstitutional, that it had defamed him and invaded his privacy, and that he was entitled to damages of more than $250,000. The suit produced a temporary restraining order that relieved Smith of testifying before the commission, but ultimately the state supreme court upheld the authority of the commission to exist and to compel the attendance of witnesses and the production of documents in order to investigate the extent and nature of discrimination in the state. Thus, the authority of the ERC even to investigate discrimination in the state was not upheld until three years after its creation.

The 1965 Session: Victory at Last

The 1965 session finally enacted a law banning discrimination in employment and public accommodations. The civil rights movement had to wait three more sessions, however, to secure a law barring discrimination in housing. Suggestions are made at the end of this article about why partial victory was achieved in 1965 when 1963 brought only defeat, but the importance of one factor is obvious. In 1964, Congress passed the national Civil Rights Act, dealing with employment and public accommodations. Governor Sawyer, who had been urging such a law in vain for several sessions, in his address to the 1965 session pointed out clearly the significance of the new law. He told the legislators:

> The federal legislation, as a matter of fact, is the law of the land. Its most controversial title, public accommodations, has been held constitutional by the United States Supreme Court. The argument, therefore, is no longer as to the merits of the civil rights legislation . . . It is no longer then a question of *what* is going to be done, but simply a question of *who is* going to do it.[7]

Given this situation, the governor suggested that advocates of state control of public policy should now embrace civil rights legislation. "Many of us are concerned about the right of states to resolve their own problems," he said. "Here is an opportunity to preserve such rights . . . I am confident you will enact not only the morally inescapable legislation but, in this case, the expedient legislation."[8]

As in 1963, there was some confusion over the nature of the proposals. The first civil rights bill, Assembly Bill 159, introduced by several members of the Clark County delegation, embodied the approach favored by Chairman Robert Bailey of the ERC. This bill made discrimination in public accommodations on the basis of race or sex a misdemeanor and also authorized the aggrieved person to seek damages of up to $250. Local governments were authorized to enact similar ordinances, provided that the penalties for violation did not exceed those of state law. In the area of employment, the bill would have made several kinds of discrimination by employers, unions, or employment agencies "unlawful practices," but no penalties were provided for engaging in such practices. Various provisions of the bill defining unlawful employment practices were weaker than those of the federal statute. In the case of both public accommodations and employment discrimination, the bill would have authorized the ERC to issue cease and desist orders and ask district courts to enjoin discriminatory acts. According to newspaper accounts, Bailey favored a role for the ERC as conciliator in discrimination cases.

The civil rights leaders believed that AB 159 was much too weak to be taken seriously. Clyde Mathews, in a February 4 letter to Governor Sawyer and Lieutenant Governor Paul Laxalt, warned that "the minority people in this State today are saying that A.B. 159 is purely political and a stall."[9] As a result, although curiously an almost identical bill was introduced on February 19 by assemblymen Close and Bunker of Clark County, the approach originally favored by Bailey was not taken seriously; neither bill emerged from committee.

The vehicle for civil rights legislation eventually became AB 404, introduced on February 23 by Close and Bunker. This bill was modeled essentially on the federal legislation, which was the approach favored by Governor Sawyer. It passed the assembly by a vote of 24 to 2 on March 18, with one member voting "absent." On March 30, the bill passed the Senate by a vote of 12 to 4, with one senator voting "absent." The Senate had made minor changes in the assembly bill, and the differences had to be resolved by a conference committee. The final version of AB 404 was signed by Governor Sawyer on April 5. At a signing ceremony attended by about fifty proponents of civil rights, the *Las Vegas Sun* reported that Governor Sawyer declared that the bill was "one of the greatest landmarks in all legislation in the history of Nevada."[10]

Behind the bare summary outlined above lay the fact that the two most important party leaders in the state had backed the legislation. Governor Sawyer had of course been in favor of civil rights legislation for some time. In the 1963 session Lieutenant Governor Laxalt, while not opposing civil rights, had not endorsed the key bill when it came before the Senate. In the 1965 session, he had endorsed the bill before it came up for a floor vote. At a rally on the Capitol steps on March 22, Laxalt said that "The time for Nevada to put into law an adequate civil rights law is now: A.B. 404 as it passed the Assembly and with the necessary financing is such a law." Reverend Mathews said later that he wrote this statement, and he claimed much of the credit for persuading the lieutenant governor to endorse civil rights as a result of a series of conversations over the previous two years.[11] Mathews, a Republican, was given a state position after Laxalt became governor in 1967; in 1968 he ran unsuccessfully for his party's nomination for Nevada's congressional seat. It is not certain what factors went into Laxalt's decision, but clearly his stand influenced several Republican senators. The most vociferous opponent of civil rights in the previous session, Senator Slattery, while he voted against the bill in 1965, began his floor speech on the issue by "thanking Eddie Scott, Reverend Clyde Mathews, and James Anderson," the chief civil rights lobbyists, "for the fine way they conducted themselves in trying, as proponents of this bill, to pass it." He said that he continued to think the bill was unnecessary and that he would vote against it, but he said: "I know the votes are garnered."[12]

Another civil rights measure, which merely conformed Nevada law to the requirements of the United States Constitution, was approved in 1965. Assembly Bill 424 was introduced on February 25 by Republican assemblymen Edward Fike of Clark County and Coe Swobe of Washoe County. It voided provisions in agreements relating to real property that contained restrictions on a racial basis ("restrictive covenants"). The U.S. Supreme Court had declared such agreements to be unenforceable (though not illegal) in 1947, and this bill merely restated existing law. It was amended in the assembly on March 29 to give owners of property with restrictive covenants the right to file affidavits with county recorders declaring such restrictions void. In amended form, AB 424 passed the assembly by a vote of 24 to 6 on March 31 and the Senate without a recorded vote on April 2. It was approved by the governor April 9.

The Fair Housing Act

The legislature did not include housing in the civil rights legislation of the state until 1971, although Congress had taken this step in 1968 and the Supreme Court had also, in that year, recognized the continuing validity of a Reconstruction statute applying to housing. Joseph Crowley, describing the passage of the 1971 act, concluded that by that time, the proposal had become "relatively uncontroversial" and "aroused almost no public opposition."[13]

Several elements contributed to the late passage of this bill. As he had done with earlier civil rights proposals, Laxalt at first would not support the fair housing bill. In his 1967 address to the legislature he declared that the bill was not needed and that voluntary approaches to such discrimination as existed were to be preferred. However, he endorsed increased funding for the ERC.

Pressured later in 1967 to include fair housing as a subject to be considered in a special session, Laxalt announced the appointment of a fact-finding committee and said that he would back fair housing legislation in 1969 if the committee said that a problem of discrimination existed. The committee made such a finding and the governor backed fair housing in the 1969 session, but the bill died in the Senate. His successor, Donal "Mike" O'Callaghan, endorsed fair housing and it finally passed the legislature in 1971.

Nevada's first black legislator, Republican assemblyman Woodrow Wilson of Las Vegas, was elected in 1966 and became the chief legislative proponent of the fair housing bill. Contrary to expectations, his presence did not initially make a significant difference.

Conclusions and Analysis

The purpose of this brief account has been simply to recount the most important facts about the struggle to secure legislation outlawing discrimination on a racial basis in Nevada. However, some interpretation and analysis is in order. It is abundantly clear over more than two decades that the assembly was much more favorable to civil rights than the Senate. What may not be so clear is that this difference apparently was related to their apportionment bases and to interrelated partisan differences.

Until reapportioned under federal court order in the late 1960s, the Nevada legislature was among the most malapportioned legislative bodies in the country, from the standpoint of the one-person, one-vote standard, which the U.S. Supreme Court applied to all state legislatures in the landmark decision of *Reynolds v. Sims* in 1964. "Before reapportionment, 8 percent of the voters were theoretically able to elect a senate majority and 29.1 percent, an assembly majority; voters in the small counties had disproportionate power in both houses."[14] The malapportionment was greatest in the Senate; from 1917 in practice and from 1950 according to the state constitution, each county had had one senator, while the more populous counties had had multiple assemblymen (although each county was guaranteed an assemblyman, regardless of population).

The black population of the state was highly concentrated in the two metropolitan counties (together composing more than half the total state population) and in only one of the rural counties. As noted above, 91.6 percent of the black population of the state lived in Clark, Washoe, and Mineral Counties in 1950. By 1960 the black population had become even more concentrated, because the chief growth had been in the Westside of Las Vegas and adjacent areas in North

Las Vegas; 96.8 percent of the black population lived in these three counties. The residents of most of the rural counties had very little contact with black Nevadans; in 1960 only Elko had as many as one hundred black residents.

Rural-county members of the assembly were clearly less likely than their counterparts from Clark and Washoe Counties to vote for civil rights legislation. During the numerous assembly floor votes on civil rights bills from 1947 through 1963, two-thirds of the votes cast by rural-county members of the assembly favored civil rights, while over nine-tenths of all the votes cast by Clark County members and nearly 80 percent of those cast by members from Washoe County favored civil rights. The high proportion of pro–civil rights votes is accounted for by the fact that a number of issues being voted on were noncontroversial, as noted above. While the mechanisms at work are unclear, it is highly probable that rural-county voters were less favorable to civil rights legislation than voters in the metropolitan counties. Since these rural-county voters were even more overrepresented in the Senate than in the assembly, it is not surprising that the upper house was less hospitable to civil rights in this period than the lower house. A comparable measurement of Senate votes is not available, because of the small number of floor votes and the propensity of senators to be absent or cast no vote if a bill clearly has majority support.

Malapportionment also interacted with partisanship. From the 1937 through the 1963 sessions of the legislature, Democrats controlled the assembly every session while the Republican Senate majorities were lopsided (usually more than two to one), and the Democrats had a majority in the 1965 session only because an independent senator chose to vote with them on organizational questions. Partisan differences between members of the assembly in votes on civil rights bills from 1947 through 1963 were evident. Nearly 80 percent of all votes cast by Democrats were for civil rights, while less than two-thirds of the votes cast by Republicans favored civil rights. Combined with the effect of malapportionment, this fact helps to explain why civil rights measures almost never made it to the floor in the upper house while the assembly favored such legislation in several sessions.

A crucial element in the belated approval of legislation outlawing discrimination in employment and public accommodations, as noted above, was a change in the attitudes of key Republicans. Reverend Mathews, a leading civil rights advocate, believed that the forced reapportionment of the legislature during the late 1960s may have had significant impact. He suggested that Senator Slattery may have moderated his stance because he expected to run for reelection in a district predominantly based in Washoe County in 1966.[15] In fact, Slattery was reelected to the Senate in that year from just such a district.

To summarize, one of the reasons why Nevada was once called the "Mississippi of the West" was its obvious reluctance to enact legislation banning private discrimination by race. Eventually, however, laws were passed banning discrimination in public accommodations, employment, and housing, and a state agency is charged with enforcing civil rights laws. It seems highly likely that the high concentration of the black population in the two metropolitan counties, the malapportionment of the legislature, and the interaction of partisanship with malapportionment help to explain why Nevada came so late to the civil rights fold. No attempt will be made here to evaluate how effective such legislation has been, although it is obvious that overt discrimination in public accommodations is part of the past.

Notes

1. William P. Horgan to W. N. Campbell, March 8, 1961, Papers of Governor Grant Sawyer, State Archives, Carson City.
2. Bureau of Governmental Research, *Voices of Black Nevada* (Reno: University of Nevada, Reno, 1971), 88.
3. Alan Jarlson, *Las Vegas Sun*, March 26, 1960, p. 1
4. *Carson Nevada Appeal*, January 25, 1963; Nevada Legislature, *Journal of the Senate* (Carson City: State Printing Office, 1963), 451.
5. *Las Vegas Review Journal*, April 2, 1963; Attorney General, *Official Opinions of the Attorney General* (Carson City: State Printing Office, 1963), 33.
6. Attorney General, *Official Opinions* (1963), 33.
7. Nevada Legislature, *Journal of the Assembly* (Carson City: State Printing Office, 1965).
8. Joseph N. Crowley, "Race and Residence: The Politics of Open Housing in Nevada," in *Sagebrush and Neon: Studies in Nevada Politics*, ed. Eleanore Bushnell (Reno: Bureau of Governmental Research, 1976), 59.
9. H. Clyde Mathews Jr., *Oral Autobiography of a Modern-Day Baptist Minister* (Reno: Oral History Project, University of Nevada, Reno, 1965).
10. *Las Vegas Sun*, April 6, 1965.
11. Mathews, *Oral Autobiography*, 187–89.
12. Ibid.
13. Crowley, "Race and Residence," 59.
14. Bushnell, Eleanore, ed., *Impact of Reapportionment on the Thirteen Western States* (Salt Lake City: University of Utah Press, 1970), 187
15. Mathews, *Oral Autobiography*, 197.

Further Reading

Attorney General. *Official Opinions of the Attorney General*. Carson City: State Printing Office, 1962.

———. *Official Opinions of the Attorney General*. Carson City: State Printing Office, 1963.

Bureau of Governmental Research. *Voices of Black Nevada*. Reno: University of Nevada, Reno, 1971.

Bushnell, Eleanore, ed. *Impact of Reapportionment on the Thirteen Western States*. Salt Lake City: University of Utah Press, 1970.

Committee on Human Rights for the Western States. National Bar Association. Papers of Governor Grant Sawyer, State Archives, Carson City, 1957.

Coray, Michael S. "African-Americans in Nevada." *Nevada Historical Society Quarterly* 35 (1972), 239–57.

Crowley, Joseph N. "Race and Residence: The Politics of Open Housing in Nevada." In *Sagebrush and Neon: Studies in Nevada Politics*, edited by Eleanore Bushnell. Reno: Bureau of Governmental Research, University of Nevada, Reno, 1976.

Fitzgerald, Roosevelt. "The Evolution of a Black Community in Las Vegas, 1905-1940." *Nevada Public Affairs Review* 2 (1987), 23–28.

Horgan, William P. Letter to W. N. Campbell, March 8. Papers of Governor Grant Sawyer, State Archives, Carson City, 1961.

Mathews, H. Clyde, Jr. *Oral Autobiography of a Modern-Day Baptist Minister*. Reno: Oral History Project, University of Nevada, Reno, 1965.

Nevada Legislature. *Journal of the Assembly*. Carson City: State Printing Office, 1939.

———. *Journal of the Assembly*. Carson City: State Printing Office, 1947.

———. *Journal of the Assembly*. Carson City: State Printing Office, 1949.

———. *Journal of the Assembly*. Carson City: State Printing Office, 1965.

———. *Journal of the Senate*. Carson City: State Printing Office, 1963.

———. *Journal of the Senate*. Carson City: State Printing Office, 1965.

Orleck, Annelise. *Storming Caesars Palace: How Black Mothers Fought Their Own War on Poverty*. Boston: Beacon Press, 2005.

Overstreet, Everett Louis. *Black Steps in the Desert Sand: A Chronicle of African-American Involvement in the Growth of Las Vegas, Nevada*. Las Vegas: Native Son Bookstore, 1999.

Rusco, Elmer R. *"Good Time Coming?" Black Nevadans in the Nineteenth Century*. Westport, Conn.: Greenwood, 1975.

Rusco, Elmer R., and Sue Fawn Chung, eds. *Ethnicity and Race in Nevada*. Reno: Public Affairs Review, 1987.

Supreme Court. *Opinions of the Supreme Court of Nevada*. Carson City: State Printing Office, 1963.

Part III

The Mountain States and the Desert Southwest

"The Mountain States and the Desert Southwest" is the largest section in terms of the number of essays and the geographical area covered. It is also one of the most diverse regions, combining the former Mexican territories of Arizona, New Mexico, Colorado, and Utah with the northern Great Plains of Wyoming and Montana. None of the states in this region entered the United States prior to the Civil War. African American migration into this region accelerated in the twentieth century, in part due to the presence of military bases in the region. In all the states in this section, African American population was relatively small, ranging from 2.3 percent to 3.5 percent in Arizona and Colorado to less than 1 percent in Utah, Montana, and Wyoming. In addition, African Americans were outnumbered by Mexican Americans and American Indians in each state. While the African American civil rights movement in these states was impacted by these demographics, it did not prevent an active and effective struggle for equal rights.

6

Breaking Racial Barriers
Civil Rights Movements in Montana and Wyoming

Kenneth G. Robison

In the mountain states of Montana and Wyoming racial prejudice and discrimination existed despite their small African American communities. In 1960 Wyoming was the least populous and least diverse state in the nation. However, at least in Montana, discrimination began crumbling during World War II, due in part to the influx of black soldiers. In the cities of Casper, Great Falls, Helena, and Missoula, white and black individuals, such as Alma Jacobs and Mike Mansfield, aided the movement to eradicate racial intolerance. Overall the mountain states made "significant progress" in their endeavors to improve civil rights, as Kenneth G. Robison pointed out in his insightful article. Robison, a retired captain in the U.S. Navy and an independent historian residing in Great Falls, has published articles about Montana African Americans in *Montana Magazine* and Blackpast.org. Robison also is author or coauthor of nine books, including *Yankees and Rebels on the Upper Missouri*.

Montana: Breaking Racial Barriers

One day in the mid-1950s, Arlyne Reichert invited her friend Alma Jacobs to lunch at Schell's Townhouse in downtown Great Falls, Montana. Jacobs responded with resignation, "I'd love to join you, but I don't think they'll let me in." And the Schell restaurant did not! Not even the director of the Great Falls Library would be admitted to a downtown restaurant in Jim Crow–era

Great Falls. After all, Jacobs was African American. This was a typical scene and problem throughout Montana in the 1950s.

How had Jim Crow found such an insidious home so far north under the Big Sky? Discrimination in Montana, from its frontier beginnings, extended beyond African Americans to include the far more numerous American Indians. The roots of black discrimination took hold during the Civil War–founding of Montana Territory in 1864 when the remote region became the exile of choice for thousands of Border State and southern secessionists. While many returned to their homes after the war, the persistence of prejudice remained, even causing the Montana territorial legislature to pass school segregation in 1872. Although repealed in 1895, nostalgia for the South lingered into the twentieth century with the Daughters of the Confederacy erecting a prominent fountain in Helena, the state capital, in 1916 honoring Confederate veterans.

Montana passed a miscegenation law in 1909 prohibiting marriage between whites and "Negroes, Chinese," later adding Japanese. People participating in such a marriage, including officials and those assisting, could be punished with a $500 fine and six months in jail. Provisions were added in 1921 that nullified interracial marriages legally performed in other jurisdictions. Montana's antimiscegenation laws remained in effect until 1953.

After a one-year study, the Montana Advisory Committee on Civil Rights declared in 1959 that there was no evidence of civil rights problems in Montana except in isolated instances. The committee, chaired by Dean Robert E. Sullivan of Montana State University Law School, added, "Charges of discrimination, particularly against Indians, are largely due to local concerns and economic pressures that have little or nothing to do with discrimination because of race, color or creed."

Three years later the same committee heard testimony that "The environment for Negroes in this town [Great Falls] is unbearable," with serious problems in discrimination in restaurants, taverns, and housing. The committee agreed that there was discrimination against blacks in Great Falls.

Civil rights problems for African Americans in Montana in the 1950s centered on access to jobs, union membership, and public facilities, and in some cities housing. Montana did have a long tradition of relative racial harmony in public schools and voting booths. Earlier in the nineteenth century Montana had small numbers of black homesteaders, ranchers, and cowboys, but by midcentury few lived in rural areas or small towns.

Montana's population in 1960 was 650,738 with 1,467 African Americans and 21,181 American Indians. While the black population in 1960 was the largest it had been for four decades, the earlier major black population centers of Butte, Helena, and Missoula had dropped dramatically. In 1960 Cascade County (Great Falls with Malmstrom Air Force Base) had 517 black residents, Yellowstone (Billings) 235, Valley (with Glasgow Air Force Base) 156, Deer Lodge (with 67 blacks in Montana State Prison) 102, Silver Bow (Butte) 82, Lewis and Clark (Helena) 71, and Missoula County 54 black residents. Military assignment of black air force personnel and their families became a major factor in postwar Montana.

Passage of the Civil Rights Act of 1964 set the stage for enforcement of constitutional rights guaranteed after the Civil War but never fully enforced. Montanans played a surprising key role in the passage by the U.S. Senate of the Civil Rights Act, Public Law 88–352 (78 Stat. 241), which outlawed discrimination in employment practices, public places, and accommodations, and accelerated desegregation of public schools. The Senate, under Majority Leader Mike Mansfield (D-Mont.) and with an important role played by Montana's junior senator Lee Metcalf (D-Mont.), began action on a civil rights bill (H.R. 7152) that the House of Representatives had passed.

The Senate took up the House bill on February 26, 1964, and Mansfield placed it directly on the Senate calendar, rather than assigning it to a committee chaired by a civil rights opponent. Senator Richard B. Russell (D-Ga.), the bill's opposition leader, raised objection. Critically, the Senate's presiding officer, Senator Lee Metcalf of Montana, overruled Russell's objection, and this brought the bill to the Senate floor for debate, keeping the bill alive. Senator Metcalf had been selected by Mansfield the previous year to serve as acting president pro tempore to replace an aging Senator Carl Hayden. Mansfield foresaw that the only way to defeat filibusters by southern senators was to outmaneuver them through parliamentary procedures.

Metcalf had Mansfield's trust and a keen knowledge of Senate procedure, and he carried an air of authority that few could ignore. He presided over all important Senate votes and floor debate on the Civil Rights Act in the spring of 1964.

Both Mansfield and Metcalf despised racism and its inequalities and believed that discrimination limiting Montana's 21,181 American Indians and 1,467 African Americans was wrong. They viewed the Civil Rights Act as the starting point to remedy racial problems even though many of their constituents held mixed views on pending civil rights legislation.

On June 10, 1964, after seventy-five days of filibustering by opponents, Mansfield forced a vote for cloture, limiting each senator to just one more hour. Despite efforts by opponents to reject the cloture vote, Metcalf overruled them and cloture passed the Senate by 71 to 29, the first time the Senate had ever invoked cloture on a civil rights bill.

The civil rights bill was brought to a final vote on June 19, 1964, before a packed public gallery, passing 73 to 27. Mansfield's leadership and Metcalf's skill successfully controlled the longest debate in Senate history. On July 2, 1964, President Lyndon B. Johnson signed into law the Civil Rights Act of 1964. Without Montana's two U.S. senators, the Civil Rights Act likely would not have been passed that year.

Eight years later, on June 6, 1972, Montanans ratified a new constitution. In the words of Arlyne Reichert, Great Falls delegate to the Constitutional Convention, "the time was right . . . the era was conducive to change." She also emphasized that no person holding political office could serve as delegate to the convention. Boldly inserted among the provisions of the new Montana Constitution was Article II, a Declaration of Rights that presented a strong statement of equality. Section 4 of that declaration defined individual dignity: "The dignity of the human being is inviolable. No person shall be denied the equal protection of the laws. Neither the state nor any person, firm, corporation, or institution shall discriminate against any person in the exercise of his civil or political rights on account of race, color, sex, culture, social origin or condition, or political or religious ideas."

In 1973, just two decades after the Reichert-Jacobs lunch incident in Great Falls, Jacobs was serving as Montana state librarian and was admitted at restaurants throughout Montana. Change had been slow in coming, but it had been accelerated by national and state legislation. Armed with powerful new legislation in the Civil Rights Act of 1964 and the Montana Constitution of 1972, the stage was set for progress at the local level in Montana's towns and cities. It was in cities like Great Falls, Helena, and Missoula that long-lingering problems existed and the struggle for change took place.

Great Falls

It was a typical sunny day in Great Falls, Montana's largest city, in 1955, and on the surface all seemed well. The local economy was booming, fueled by the three largest employers, the Anaconda Copper and Zinc Refinery, Great Northern Railway Repair Facility, and Great Falls Air Force Base. The morning shift at the Anaconda Refinery clocked in with no black faces among the 2,500 highly paid employees, all members of the Mine, Mill, and Smelter Workers Union. African Americans could not join that union or other local unions, thus they were shut out of good jobs.

Black airmen from the air base, visiting downtown on their day off, as well as local black residents like Alma Jacobs, could not enjoy lunch at the town's restaurants or get haircuts at local barbershops. They could be seated only in theater balconies and at times were totally excluded. In the evening black airmen were not welcome in the city's restaurants, bars, and nightclubs. Only on the seedy lower Southside could those airmen find refuge in the bars, cafes, and brothels and at one black-owned nightclub, the Ozark Club. How had Jim Crow become institutionalized in Great Falls, Montana?

As Great Falls formed in the late 1880s, military veterans from Civil War service and black Indian Wars regiments formed the core leadership of the black community. During the first decade, while Great Falls was under strong Republican Party influence, respected black veterans had made notable strides, serving on juries, winning public election as town site constable, and serving on the small police force.

Later in the 1890s, as the Democratic Party gained control with the help of rapidly growing labor unions, unofficial though pervasive segregation and discrimination became institutionalized, placing many constraints on African Americans. Black residents were confined to live on the lower Southside of Great Falls, a dense and ethnically diverse working-class neighborhood. The exclusive Northside allowed only white residents.

Without union membership, blacks were excluded from the highest paying jobs. By 1900, even the barbers' union excluded black barbers. Black residents worked as porters and dining car waiters for the Great Northern and Milwaukee Railroads, as janitors and stewards in downtown service industries, and as domestics in white homes. Blacks lived on the Southside in black hotels, railroad porters' quarters, and modest family homes, and they worshiped at black churches.

The original social hub of the African American community was the Union Bethel African Methodist Episcopal (AME) Church, organized by the first black residents of Great Falls. From 1891, when the AME Church opened, through good times and bad, the church served as the cultural, social, political, and religious heart of the black community. In the 1920s a black Baptist church opened. The women of Union Bethel were the church's "soul" through their loyalty, hard work, and dedication. By the early 1920s, black churchwomen formed the Dunbar Art and Study Club. The Dunbar Club joined with those of other towns in the Montana Federation of Colored Women's Clubs (NFCWC).

The outbreak of World War II brought thousands of workers to Great Falls. Soldiers arrived to operate two new U.S. Army bases, Gore Field Air Base, where the Seventh Ferrying Group was stationed at the militarized civilian airport, and the newly constructed Great Falls Army Air Base, home of the Second Bomber Group. These major commands also required large numbers of civilian workers. The population of Great Falls exploded from 30,000 in 1940 to about 45,500 in 1944.

The war was a catalyst for growth and change in the black community. By early 1943, several hundred black soldiers arrived at the bases. They wanted fun in their off-duty hours, but they were not welcome at Great Falls restaurants, nightclubs, or even the new United Service Organization (USO) Club. Black servicemen came to the black churches, and hastily organized a small black USO Club. However, black soldiers found fun, music, and dancing at the Ozark Club, which was transforming into an interracial nightclub after a decade as a colored-only club. Leo LaMar, born to a black mother and Chinese father in Chicago, owned and operated the Ozark Club. Although change was never easy and never quickly attained, Leo LaMar and his Ozark Club, where "Everyone's welcome," played an important part in transforming the Great Falls community.

Wartime Great Falls was not the same place it had been in the prewar years. Black civic organizations such as the NAACP, led by Leo LaMar, and particularly the Dunbar Club, led by church women such as Emma Riley Smith and her daughter, Alma Smith Jacobs, fought for civil rights in Great Falls and in Montana. The efforts of the Dunbar Club were magnified by support from other clubs in the NFCWC. For example, in 1945, Dunbar Club members wrote letters to President Harry Truman and Montana congressmen supporting civil rights legislation, joined the mayor and the NAACP in opposing discrimination against young black figure skaters by a southern-born instructor at the Great Falls Skating Club, and successfully protested a local theater's refusal to sell tickets to blacks. In 1950, after the integration of U.S. armed forces, the members of the Dunbar Club served on an interracial committee to open access to local establishments for black airmen stationed at by then renamed Malmstrom Air Force Base.

Alma Smith Jacobs personally broke racial barriers when she was named catalog librarian at the Great Falls Public Library in 1946 and then was appointed director of the library in 1954. By 1960, the black community in Great Falls had grown significantly for the first time in four decades, with 311 residents in the city and another 206 blacks stationed at Malmstrom AFB. Housing began to open throughout the city, and unions finally began to open membership. Churches of all denominations increasingly welcomed black members, and no longer were blacks denied access to restaurants and nightclubs.

Pressure for change clashed directly with persistent Jim Crow institutions in Great Falls. Slow but steady progress was made as black leaders and heroes began to emerge, highlighted by the key role played by Alma Jacobs and the arrival of black athletes like John Roseboro and Eddie Reed to play for the popular Great Falls Baseball Club in the Pioneer League for rookies destined for the major leagues. Popular Eddie Reed, a talented veteran of Negro League baseball, remained in Great Falls after his baseball days, marrying a member of the local black community. For thirty years, when Eddie Reed attended baseball games, he drew cheers from the crowd each evening as he was introduced.

Baseball brought another young man to Montana, and in the mid-1960s Charlie Pride settled in Great Falls just as his career as a country western star began to take off. To this day, when Pride performs in Great Falls he engages in affectionate banter with friends in the audience.

Remarkable Alma Jacobs assumed an increasingly powerful leadership role in the community, quietly but firmly working to break down racial barriers by gaining respect and influence as she led the community to construct a state-of-the-art library and as she served on the Great Falls Interracial Council. In addition, Jacobs became a leader in northwest regional and national library associations and in 1973 was named Montana State Librarian. She was named Great Falls Woman of the Year in 1957 while her mother, Emma Smith, was named Great Falls Mother of the Year a decade later. Today, the plaza entrance to the library is named The Alma Jacobs Memorial Plaza "for an exceptional librarian and community leader."

The integrated air force expanded missions at Malmstrom AFB. As the base's black population grew, it accelerated the pressure for lasting change in the town. While the U.S. Air Force did not keep race-based records, the black population averaged from 5 to 10 percent of base strength in the decades following World War II, with black residents ranging from 200 during the early years and from 500 to 1,200 in later years. By the late 1950s there were some 1,000 blacks in the base population of 10,000. In addition, in later decades an increasing number of mixed-race families were assigned to the base.

For the first time, retiring black personnel joined the large air force retirement community in Great Falls. With their training and experience, black retirees brought diversity and vigor to the town as they began second careers. Typical of these retirees in the 1970s were Philip Caldwell, who founded the nondenominational Mount Olive Church of Christ and led the local NAACP, Frank and Mary Ghee, who assumed leading positions in the Union Bethel AME Church and black Masonic and integrated veterans organizations, and Robert Harris, who also led the local NAACP and became active in the city's advisory commissions and charitable groups.

The growing black base population brought increasing numbers of inner-city blacks to Great Falls. At times racial tensions flared although never beyond relatively minor incidents on the base. Black Power never became a factor at the base or in the town. In the late 1960s as racial tensions rose, fueled by Vietnam War sentiment in all military services, occasional racial incidents erupted at Malmstrom AFB. In October 1969, tensions rose among the five hundred black airmen when young Captain Terry B. Marsh, a collegiate all-American and member of the Great Falls mayor's committee on community relations was denied a "plum" assignment. Claims of bias triggered an investigation that found no evidence of discrimination, yet the matter spotlighted sensitivity on all matters involving race on the base.

Jet Magazine reported, "Incidents of discrimination in housing, employment and sometimes racial brawling have also been reported [at Malmstrom], but a number of the problems seem to be derived as much from the changing attitudes of the black servicemen as from the actual events."

Two years later racial tensions between black and white airmen erupted at Malmstrom AFB, resulting in three minor injuries during an incident at the Airman's Club. This culminated in a series of interracial scuffles. Seventy-five blacks gathered in front of the dining hall the next evening throwing rocks and breaking barracks windows. In the face of armed base riot squads and firemen, the blacks retreated from confrontation to express grievances that they were being discriminated against both on base and in town. Most complaints were registered by newly arrived, lower-ranking airmen. The base and missile wing commanders and members of the Human Relations Committee met with the crowd, and after a long discussion the crowd dispersed peacefully. Two more meetings followed at the base theater with both black and white airmen attending, while a newly formed Office of Contemporary Affairs worked on specific grievances.

Great Falls would never be the same with increasing black presence and pressures for change. Although never easy, change would come, and among the many signs of progress a young air force wife, Geraldine W. Travis, became the first African American elected to the Montana legislature in 1974. She was elected to the House of Representatives from District Forty-Three, representing the Malmstrom community of 5,500 residents.

From her arrival in Great Falls in 1967 with her husband and children, Travis worked to promote civil rights for African Americans, women, and children. In 1968 she was one of the rechartering members of the Great Falls branch of the NAACP and was a founder of the Montana Chapter of the National Council of Negro Women and the Montana Women's Political Caucus, serving as president. In 1972 she became involved in the Shirley Chisholm presidential campaign, voting for Chisholm as one of twenty Montana delegates at the Democratic National Convention. Travis served as a member of the Montana Advisory Committee to the U.S. Civil Rights Commission, and remained active in Montana state and local affairs until moving to Arizona in 1989.

As the years passed, greater racial harmony and opportunities came for blacks both in the air force and in Great Falls. Symbolic of civil rights progress was the assignment of Colonel Anthony J. Cotton to command the 341st Missile Wing at Malmstrom AFB in 2009. On Black Heritage Evening in 2010, Colonel Cotton spoke eloquently to a packed hall at the Great Falls Public Library about his life experiences as the great-grandson of slaves and the grandson of sharecroppers.

Helena

In 1948 the *Pittsburgh Courier* surveyed state capitals around the country to show "the extent to which democracy is being practiced in the United States." Norman C. Howard, a leader of the black community in Helena, Montana, and George S. Schuyler, a black socialist, wrote about the paradoxical racial situation in Montana's capital city and the lives of the seventy-five African Americans in the population of about sixteen thousand in Helena. By 1948 Helena's black population had dwindled from a high of five hundred two decades earlier. The *Pittsburgh Courier* observed, "On one hand they (colored people) enjoy a large measure of freedom and live the good American life. On the other hand they are subjected to the restrictions all too familiar elsewhere in our 'Land of the Free.'"

Unlike Great Falls, black residents of Helena could live in all but the most affluent residential areas, and most owned their homes. While in earlier times most of Helena's blacks attended St. James AME Church, by the 1940s many were welcomed at white churches. One black nurse worked at the hospital, treating patients of all races, and black patients received equal treatment.

There was no color line in the public schools of Helena, which had come a long way from 1910 when a portrait of General Robert E. Lee in his Confederate uniform was prominently displayed at Helena High School. Black students studied and played alongside their white classmates. An exclusive high school club, the "3-7-77," welcomed a black sophomore, an honor few white sophomores earned. The three black students in high school attended school parties and dances.

Star athlete Raymond C. Howard, son of Norman Howard, experienced discrimination at Helena High School. Despite being class president and one of the greatest athletes in school history, Ray couldn't date white girls and was never invited to private parties. If he stopped in the hallway to talk to a white girl, an administrator might say, "You know that's not too good an idea Ray. You'd better be careful."

As a black boy growing up in Helena, Howard learned that there were subtle but clear cultural ways to behave. In his words, "All black kids were taught by family don't get in way of white people when walking downtown. Get off the sidewalk. Be as invisible as possible." The old days of "yes boss" were passing, and Howard believed Helena had a good reputation with blacks, partly because blacks and whites both knew their roles.

On the other hand, Jim Crow lurked throughout the town. But one small hotel would accept black guests, and the only public restaurants open to blacks were the Northern Pacific Station, the bus depot, and one Chinese restaurant. With relatively few blacks, change in Montana came more quickly than in big cities. Change in Helena began to come in the 1950s as more restaurants opened to blacks, with varied reaction from white customers—some looked and left, others stayed and accepted change. By word of mouth, the black community closely tracked each change as it came to Helena including which restaurants would serve and which would not.

No labor union in Helena would accept black members. Local unions suggested that blacks seek memberships in Chicago locals. The exclusive Montana Club employed twelve black bartenders, as well as barmaids and checkroom girls—none belonging to a union. When the union brought pressure on these employees to join a Chicago local, the blacks refused, and club management successfully warned the union to leave their employees alone. The Montana Club jobs were the best in town and paradoxically, the club never hired a white bartender.

At a time when organized labor aggressively worked to unionize every worker, the black workers of Helena and throughout Montana were excluded. A black mechanic working in a garage in Helena applied for membership in a local union, and when this was refused, the garage owner successfully ignored the union. Helena blacks demanded either admittance to local unions or the right to work without joining a union. So rather than be "embarrassed" by the presence of a black member, unions simply did not bother the worker, even though he was working in a unionized job.

Blacks voted and some held such city jobs as laborers, truck drivers, parking attendants, and janitors. In addition to the important Montana Club jobs, blacks worked as postal custodians, registered nurses, flying instructors, janitors, domestics, caterers, and at Fort Harrison Veterans Hospital. Mainly, young blacks left for jobs on the West Coast.

Missoula

Arrival of the 25th Infantry Regiment at nearby Fort Missoula in the late 1880s greatly increased black presence in Missoula. Although relations between the town and the black regiment were generally good, servicemen faced discrimination in restaurants and nightspots. While Missoula's public schools were integrated with a small black student population, for three decades since its founding in 1893 the University of Montana (UM) had no black graduates.

This changed when James W. Dorsey, the son of a 25th Infantry soldier, became the first black to graduate from the university. Born at Fort Missoula in 1897, Dorsey played football and track and worked as a janitor, sign painter, and decorator to put himself through UM. Graduating with a bachelor of arts degree in psychology in 1922, five years later he received a law degree from the law school. James Dorsey soon moved on to practice law in Milwaukee's much larger black community. Yet, he was not forgotten by UM, and four decades later he was honored as a Distinguished Alumnus.

African American Naseby "Doc" Rhinehart came to Missoula in 1931 from Milwaukee to play football, basketball, and track and field. After graduating in 1935 from the university, Rhinehart was hired to serve as head athletic trainer. Rhinehart stayed on at UM for forty-seven years, retiring in 1982, after developing one of the first athletic training programs in the nation. The university's athletic training room is named in Rhinehart's honor.

By 1950 the military was gone, and the local black community had dwindled to a small number. The 3,500 students at the university traditionally included only a small number of blacks.

In 1953 all-star athletes Ray Howard of Helena and Rudolph "Zip" Rhodes of Kalispell accepted basketball scholarships at the university, where they joined white Montanans on the "Fabulous Frosh" team. Ray and Zip were the only two blacks on campus their first two years. Two other blacks had started school in 1953, but didn't last long; as Ray Howard recalled, "they were too lonely and left." At that time the football program began recruiting black athletes, mostly from California, so the numbers slowly increased later in the 1950s.

In Missoula some restaurants and hotels wouldn't let Howard, Rhodes, and trainer Rhinehart eat and stay. More trouble came on the road as the basketball team traveled to Mountain States Skyline Conference towns like Denver, where the united team would walk out if their teammates were refused service. At the time there were few black athletes in the Skyline Conference extending along the Rocky Mountains from Montana to New Mexico. At UM, Howard couldn't sit at the same table to have coffee with girls—if he did so fraternity boys would get upset and ostracize the girls.

Ray Howard graduated from the university in 1958, and despite strenuous efforts no Montana school would hire him. He was so angry that he moved to Red Deer, a small Canada town, where he was hired to teach high school, coach, and serve as part-time counselor.

After an eleven-year pastorate of a Chicago Methodist church, in 1968 Ulysses S. Doss took a vacation to visit a friend, UM's campus minister, in Missoula, and he never left. The trip forever changed Doss's life, and it led directly to greater diversity at the university. Doss brought impeccable credentials leading faith-based and neighborhood grassroots organizations in Chicago, to his new job establishing the university's new Black Studies/African American Studies program, Montana's first.

In 1968 just eight black students attended UM. These students, with white friends and American Indian students, rallied on the campus for a black studies program. Doss was hired, and for twenty-five years he taught classes, recruited minority students, counseled students of all races, and supervised acquisition of a black studies library. He worked diligently to recruit black students by promising them three things: an education, an opportunity, and a challenge, and he assured them, "You will not be alone." His first year, he recruited thirty-seven black students, and that number peaked at more than one hundred. Dr. Doss tirelessly lectured throughout Montana, often facing Montanans' "show-me" skepticism as he explained the black mentality.

In 2009, UM honored Professor Doss for his distinguished career on the forty-first anniversary of the Black Studies program. Approximately seventy alumni from fourteen states attended this reunion. Some alumni recalled sitting on the floor of Doss's "Gandhi and King" class, which was so popular that at times twenty students were without seats.

The Jim Crow discrimination for African Americans in Montana began crumbling during World War II. It accelerated with the integration of the armed forces and the strenuous efforts of groups like the Montana Federation of Colored Women's Clubs and individuals like Alma Jacobs and Ulysses Doss, as well as sports stars like Raymond Howard and Eddie Reed. Powerful new legislation, most notably the Civil Rights Act of 1964 and the Montana Constitution of 1972, reflected the changing attitudes of Montanans and the nation as racial politics rose to preeminence in social consciousness.

Access to restaurants, bars, and nightclubs started slowly, but gathered steam. Removal of housing restrictions followed. Dissolution of the Colored Women's Clubs in 1971 after black women finally were welcomed into the General Federation of Women's Clubs reflected success at integration after their good fight for equal rights. Decline in black church attendance reflected the freedom of blacks to attend the church of their choice. Acceptance of blacks into union membership increased access to good paying jobs. Increased access to advanced universities opened career paths. Talented young blacks could compete for good jobs, or they could leave Montana for the West Coast just as many young whites did to find the good jobs lacking in Montana.

Jim Crow had been challenged. Change and equal rights were coming to Montana. Attitudes were changing under the Big Sky.

Wyoming: Equality for Some

Wyoming's early path to equal rights differed from that of Montana, yet prejudice and discrimination were rampant also in the Equality State. Wyoming had earned the nickname when its first territorial legislature in 1869 passed an "Act to Grant to the Women of Wyoming the Right of Suffrage, and to Hold Office." Woman suffrage, white and black, was adopted by an all-Democratic legislature and signed by Republican Governor John A. Campbell as an inducement to spur migration into the new territory. Most Wyoming women cast their ballots on September 2, 1870.

Wyoming remained among the early western leaders in gender equality with the 1894 election of the first woman in the state, Estelle Reel Meyer, as Superintendent of Public Instruction, and the 1924 election of the first woman governor in the United States, Nellie Tayloe Ross, who was elected to complete the term of her deceased husband. Additionally, William Jefferson Hardin, a black man from Cheyenne, was elected to the Wyoming territorial legislature in 1879. Yet, Wyoming joined Montana and other Rocky Mountain states as the Inequality State for racial and ethnic minorities. In 1887 Wyoming established a local school district option for school segregation, and in 1908 imposed a miscegenation statute prohibiting intermarriage of whites with blacks or Asians.

In 1960 Wyoming was the least populous and the least racially diverse state in the nation. Wyoming had one Indian reservation, the Wind River Indian Reservation, and a smaller American Indian population than Montana, 4,020 versus 21,181. Wyoming's black population in 1960 was 2,183, while Montana had 1,467.

World War II–era ethnic and racial tensions flared in farming and railroad communities, with the former focused on importation of Mexican wartime farm laborers. Prejudice toward blacks closely coincided with state government failure to outlaw discrimination in public hotels and restaurants. Racial incidents flared up in other ways including a "beautiful baby" contest in Casper, with factions encouraging black women to enter their children in the contest, and more dominant factions asking for withdrawal. As this local contest became a national story, and as notions of "beauty" were challenged, racism created embarrassment for Casper, Wyoming.

While the black population was growing slowly in the postwar era in both states, primarily because of U.S. Air Force installations, both states shared similar racial prejudice and discrimination problems. Symptomatic of the environment in Wyoming in the 1950s was an incident in a small café at Cheyenne's Plains Hotel when an African American serviceman and his wife were refused service. Witnessing and outraged by this event were Dr. Francis Barrett and Teno Roncalio, the former a son of Republican U.S. Senator Frank A. Barrett, the latter a rising figure in the state Democratic Party. Both men determined to work toward change.

Racial discrimination flared at a rural school near Pinedale when Norman Barlow, a prominent rancher and Republican state senator promoted hiring African American Juanita Simmons as teacher. Despite impressive teaching credentials, Simmons was not hired.

The Plains Hotel and similar incidents stimulated discussion in both political parties of racial justice in the "less than equality" state. These racial incidents helped mobilize support for measures to promote racial justice. This sentiment extended across party lines and the climate seemed right for civil rights initiatives. Barlow, Barrett, Roncalio, and others converged on Cheyenne, spurred on by

Republican Governor Milward Simpson. In his "State of the State" speech to the 1955 legislature, Simpson reviewed the articles in Wyoming's constitution and asked for passage of civil rights measures to reinforce the call for fair and equal treatment of its citizens, regardless of race and ethnicity.

In response to Governor Simpson's call for greater racial equality, Barlow and other bipartisan legislators introduced civil rights bills designed to deal with school segregation, miscegenation, and public accommodations.

The national civil rights debate and the powerful decision in *Brown v. Board of Education* (1954), which struck down racial segregation in public education, influenced Wyoming. The legislature quickly repealed the school segregation option. Sponsors introduced bills aimed at repealing miscegenation laws, although these did not pass until 1965. Bipartisan House Bill 86 was introduced to prohibit "distinction, discrimination or restriction because of race, religion, color or national origin, and providing for civil action." This public accommodations bill was killed in the House.

Governor Simpson pressed the 1957 legislature for civil rights action including public accommodations. At this time Wyoming was one of the few states outside the South that failed to guarantee all citizens equal access to public accommodations. Bipartisan senators introduced a Senate bill in January 1957. After that failed, the House began work on a civil rights bill protecting minorities, Catholics, and Jews. The House passed the bill, and Senator Barlow introduced another civil rights bill in the Senate with the language: "no person of good deportment shall be denied the right to life and liberty because of race, color, creed or national origin or for any reason whatsoever." Governor Simpson signed the Barlow bill forming the Wyoming Civil Rights Act of 1957.

The Civil Rights Act had passed, but enforcing it proved problematic with enforcement in the hands of county and prosecuting attorneys. The fines and consequences of discrimination were simply too slight. The powerful federal Civil Rights Act in 1964 became law, although Milward Simpson, by then a U.S. Senator, voted against it. The bipartisan civil rights movement was crumbling, and Wyoming was becoming divided.

The most serious racial incident in postwar Wyoming further divided Wyomingites. In October 1969, the highly successful University of Wyoming (UW) football program was flying high under coach Lloyd Eaton, a native of South Dakota. The UW team was scheduled to play Brigham Young University, operated by the Church of Jesus Christ of Latter-day Saints (LDS, the Mormons) in Laramie. Willie Black, chancellor of UW's Black Students Alliance, learned of the LDS racial policy barring black men from the priesthood and organized a demonstration for the football game. Fourteen African American players on the Wyoming team decided to protest by wearing black armbands during the game. Eaton met with the players and sternly warned them not to wear the armbands. When they persisted in their plan, Coach Eaton fired the players for violating his prohibition against demonstrating, greatly affecting the players' careers and jeopardizing his own career. The university went through turbulent times in the face of adverse national publicity.

In the postwar civil rights movement, Teno Roncalio, Norman Barlow, Milward Simpson, and other Wyoming leaders were able to cobble together enough of a consensus on racial policy to enact the modest Civil Rights Act of 1957, sort of a marker that the Equality State was trying to come to grips with their civil rights problems.

With a population of 563,626 in 2010, modern Wyoming remains the least populous and second least densely populated of the fifty states, while Montana had 989,415 residents. The minority population of both Wyoming and Montana has grown significantly, with 31,932 American Indians, including mixed race, in the former and 76,783 in the latter. The black population in both states has increased also with 6,648 in Wyoming, including mixed race, and 6,505 in Montana. Laramie County, Wyoming, with Frances E. Warren AFB, was home to 2,897 blacks and mixed race. Cascade County, Montana, with Malmstrom AFB, had 1,661 black and mixed-race residents.

Both states have made significant progress overcoming discrimination since the 1950s, with public policy and personal attitudes changing to achieve racial equality and harmony. Yet, small but persistent groups such as the Ku Klux Klan, though diluted in numbers and hostility, still aim for separatism with racial superiority themes.

Perhaps the most fitting reflection of the state of the racial situation in both Montana and Wyoming is a meeting of the KKK and the NAACP in Casper, Wyoming, in September 2013—perhaps the first ever meeting in the nation of these two historically opposed organizations. After months of negotiations, John Abarr from Great Falls, Montana, organizer for the United Klans of America, stepped into a room at the Parkway Plaza Hotel to meet Jimmy Simmons, president of the NAACP branch in Casper. Abarr presented his Klan as a nonviolent Christian group focused on political issues, yet he argued for a separatist existence between whites and blacks and feigned ignorance of decades of Klan terror. He agreed that recent beatings of black men in Gillette, Wyoming, were terrible and constituted hate crimes. Ending the meeting by joining the NAACP, Abarr shut his briefcase, shook hands with Simmons, and walked briskly away.

Further Reading

Ashworth, William. "Racism Stirs Black Airmen at Air Force Base: Racial Tension Increases on Montana Air Force Base." *Jet Magazine*, October 23, 1969, 14–17.

Behan, Barbara, and Ken Robison. *National Register of Historic Places Nomination Form: Union Bethel African Methodist Episcopal Church, Great Falls, Montana*. May 15, 2003.

BlackPast.org Remembered & Reclaimed. "Geraldine Washington Travis" by Ken Robison; "Alma Smith Jacobs" by Carla W. Garner. http://www.blackpast.org.

Davenport, Loralee. *A Journey toward Sovereignty and Security: The African American Community of Butte, Montana from 1885–1955*. N.p., June 2001.

———. "The Pearl Club: Black Women and Community Building in the Mining City." In *Motherlode: Legacies of Women's Lives and Labors in Butte, Montana*, edited by Janet L. Finn and Ellen Crain, 142–53. Butte, Mont.: Clark City Press, 2005.

Fugleberg, Jeremy. "Ku Klux Klan and NAACP Leaders Meet in Wyoming." *Missoulian*, September 2, 2013.

Hallberg, Carl V. "Ethnicity in Wyoming." *Annals of Wyoming* 63, no. 4 (Fall 1991): 136–39. https://archive.org/details/annalsofwyom63141991wyom.

Ibach, Kim, and William Howard Moore. "The Emerging Civil Rights Movement: The 1957 Wyoming Public Accommodations Statute as a Case Study." *Annals of Wyoming* 73, no. 1 (Winter 2001): 2–13. https://archive.org/details/annalsofwyom7314200Iwyom.

Lang, William L. "The Nearly Forgotten Blacks on Last Chance Gulch, 1900–1912." *Pacific Northwest Quarterly* 70 (April 1979): 50–57.

Larson, T.A. *History of Wyoming*. 2nd. ed. Lincoln: University of Nebraska Press, 1990.

———. *Wyoming: A Bicentennial History*. New York: W. W. Norton, 1977.

Montana Historical Society. "Montana Federation of Colored Women's Clubs." Major Collection 281.

"Montana is 48th State to Pass King Holiday." *Jet Magazine*, March 4, 1991, 15.

"Montana's First Black Legislator Scores Big During First Quarter." *Jet Magazine*, July 10, 1975, 22.

Ogden, Karen. "Uncovering Black History in Montana." *Great Falls Tribune*, February 5, 2007.

Riley, Peggy. "Women of the Great Falls African Methodist Episcopal Church, 1870–1910." In *African American Women Confront the West, 1600–2000*, edited by Quintard Taylor and Shirley Ann Wilson Moore, 122–39. Norman: University of Oklahoma Press, 2003.

Robison, Kenneth G. "Breaking Racial Barriers: 'Everyone's Welcome' at the Ozark Club, Great Falls, Montana's African American Nightclub." *Montana the Magazine of Western History* 62, no. 2 (Summer 2012): 44–58.

Schuyler, George, Jr., and Norman C. Howard. "Democracy, U.S.A. . . . How It Works in Your State Capital. Old Jim Crow Still Lurks on Some of Fair Helena's Corners." *Pittsburgh Courier*, November 11, 1948.

Smurr, J. W. "Jim Crow Out West." In *Historical Essays on Montana and The Northwest*, edited by J. W. Smurr and K. Ross Toole, 149–203. Helena, Mont.: Western Press, 1957.

Thompson, Lucille Smith, and Alma Smith Jacobs. *The Negro in Montana 1800–1945: A Selective Bibliography*. Helena: Montana State Library, 1970.

Thompson, Lucille W. "Early Montana Negro Pioneers: Sung and Unsung." *Montana Business Quarterly*, Summer 1972.

7

The Modern Civil Rights Movement in Colorado

George H. Junne Jr.

In Colorado, as University of Northern Colorado historian George H. Junne Jr. shows, the black population increased during the 1940s, with an increase in wages and housing along with that fact. A coexisting Chicano movement took place as well, sometimes leading to acrimony. But civil rights progress occurred; with support from and black membership in the NAACP, National Urban League, and Black Panthers, improvements in housing, employment, and school integration took place in the 1960s and 1970s. Yet some black Coloradans today believe that Colorado civil rights have retreated during the past thirty years. In addition to this article, George Junne Jr. published *Afroamerican History: A Chronicle of People of African Descent in the United States*, as well as *Blacks in the American West and Beyond—America, Canada, and Mexico: A Selectively Annotated Bibliography*.

"Let freedom ring from the snowcapped Rockies of Colorado!"
Rev. Dr. Martin Luther King Jr., August 28, 1963

In 2014, Denver's I-News, an arm of Rocky Mountain PBS, released a 128-page report titled *Losing Ground*. The eighteen-month investigation acknowledged that during the 1980s and 1990s, minority gains of the 1960s and 1970s had eroded. The report used six decades of U.S. Census Bureau information plus interviews of persons going back to the 1960s, the years of observable struggle. Still, "after the civil rights movements of the 1960s, Colorado was one of the more equitable places in the nation for minorities."[1] This article provides relevant history and details some of the levels of attainment that today's Coloradans are trying to recoup.

When one searches for books and articles on civil rights, there seems to be a dearth of material on Colorado. When materials do surface, the focus is primarily on Denver at the expense of other communities. However, Denver is the state capital and is home to the largest community of the state's black residents. In reality, "Denver, like other cities in the west, was not a city where civil rights failed or stalled. Instead, Denver citizens experienced their own version of the movement with its own distinctive victories and defeats, collisions and conquest."[2]

African Americans were not alone in seeking civil and human rights and would sometimes work with others. As the United States began moving into the 1960s, the civil rights movement was expanding on a national level. In Colorado, as well as in other communities, civil rights became associated primarily with African Americans. In the Rocky Mountain State, active Latinos remember the time differently. In a documentary film titled *La Raza de Colorado: El Movimiento*, professor David Sandoval recalled that both the Chicano movement and the African American movements worked together for social change linking civil rights and cultural preservation. Flo Hernandez-Ramos, a prominent businesswoman, remembered that both movements worked for the betterment of their own groups but collectively worked for the advancement of all peoples of color.

To complicate matters, there were some Latinos that did not push for busing or integration, seeing no benefits for themselves. One of the dynamic leaders, Rudolfo "Corky" Gonzales, and his followers believed that integration was a product of a black inferiority complex and, like some others, felt that school integration was "a form of cultural assault, forced assimilation which breaks up the development of a growing community power based on self-awareness and independence."[3] The topic of civil rights in Colorado, therefore, was not a simplistic one.

Before World War II, blacks in Colorado, mostly in Denver and because of larger numbers, began to fight for their civil and human rights. They were slowly gaining access to public arenas such as restaurants, theaters, and hotels. However, World War II caused the expansion of citizen rights as the war industries provided work for skilled and unskilled laborers. Following the war, more job opportunities opened up in Colorado in construction and the expansion of older and newer military facilities. More African Americans were moving into the state, particularly to Denver and Colorado Springs.

Many African Americans who chose to settle in the Centennial State were ex-service people who had military pensions and benefits and who could afford both homes and education, doubling the black population between 1950 and 1960. By the latter decade, black income rose to 75 percent of white income. Those advances were not always welcomed. However, it was not until the 1960s and 1970s that African Americans experienced significant changes in housing, employment, and school integration.

African American women also had difficulty in finding employment in Colorado, but conditions began to change following World War II. Before the 1940s, for instance, none of Colorado's state universities with nursing programs admitted them. By 1950, there were twenty-eight black nurses. Also in 1950, there appeared to be only two black librarians in Denver. The teaching profession also showed gains in the Denver Public Schools system. There were forty-eight women teachers in 1950 and by 1960, there were 126 employed in Denver's primary and secondary schools.

Around the state, many whites refused to even consider race-mixing in schools. One of the extreme comments came from a superintendent in Weld County, north of Denver. He said that he did not believe that the Weld County residents would "want their children to sit along side of dirty, filthy, diseased, infested Mexicans."[34] However, change was occurring, much of it associated with housing.

By the 1960s, many African Americans were moving out of Denver's Five Points, where they were forced to live, into the previous white enclave of Park Hill. There was violence, and in spite of the fact that some whites formed the Park Hill Action Committee to stop the influx, by 1970 Park Hill was one of the most integrated communities in the country.

One of the most important and famous civil rights cases that received national attention, decided in the 1970s, was *Keyes v. School District No. 1, Denver, Colorado*. The parents of black and Latino students who were attending Park Hill schools sued the school board for creating a segregated system. It was the first Supreme Court desegregation case that focused on a school system not in the American South. African American and Park Hill resident Wilfred Keyes, along with seven others, sued Denver schools, claiming that their system violated the constitutional rights of their children. Park Hill had turned down desegregation plans that included busing. After considering the evidence, federal district judge William Doyle, agreeing with some of Keyes's assertions, ordered the busing of three thousand students, about 3 percent of the total, for fall 1969.

Since 1960, residents claimed that the Denver school system was practicing racial discrimination, which was unconstitutional. As the Keyes case slowly went through the court system, the district court decided that just because one part of the school system practiced racism, it did not mean that the whole system was involved. In 1972, however, the U.S. Supreme Court ruled, "when part of a school system is found to be segregated, a 'prima facie case of unlawful segregative design' becomes apparent."[5]

The case was first tried during 1969–70 until the Supreme Court issued its final judgment in June 1973. Because Park Hill schools were segregated through its school board, the court ruled that it constituted de jure segregation. Further, the plaintiffs in the case did not have to prove that de jure segregation existed across the schools under the board of education, but with proof it existed in one area of the Denver school system, other areas could be influenced.

In a 7–1 decision, the Supreme Court held that "discriminatory actions of school boards could lead to segregation, even in states lacking a statutory or constitutional mandate for dual schooling." The school system attempted to argue that social forces, not laws, had caused racial imbalance with the system. However, the court listed a variety of "racial inspired" policies, including minority faculty and staff assignments and gerrymandering school zones, that led to segregation. The court's findings would lead to forced busing.

During 1968, the Denver School Board adopted an integration plan by 5 to 2 that included busing. There was violence, including the bombing of about a third of the school buses. Antibusing politicians were elected to the school board in 1969 and in the meantime, there was "white flight" to the suburbs. Residents then passed an antibusing referendum by a 69 percent margin.

In an article, famous author Calvin Trillin wrote about this topic. According to him, the assassination of Dr. Martin Luther King Jr. was part of the impetus that led the Denver School Board to tackle school integration. He noted that black children were most affected by de facto segregation. The integrationist coalition formed in Denver after King's death moved for integration while at the same time, some criticized the plan for not going far enough. For the upcoming school board elections, all candidates said they were for integration, but some claimed they just did not want integration "dictated by law." Voluntary integration would be fine. Plus, the conservatives stated that they did not want to destroy the neighborhood schools, which the Denver School Board "used to manipulate boundaries to avoid having to send white children to predominantly black schools."[6]

There was an attempt to show that the Park Hill schools constituted an independent school system within the Denver school system. However, the defendants were not able to show that was the situation, and the court decided that "common sense dictates the conclusion that racially inspired school board actions have an impact beyond the particular schools that are the subjects of these actions." Also, the court ruled that segregated schools outside the Park Hill area were not segregated because of housing patterns and demographics, but because of deliberate policies. The situation in Park Hill was clearly saturating the whole district.

While the 1960s was a time for fighting school segregation, Denver's African American community was still making strides. In 1965, Rachel B. Noel was the first African American to be elected to the Denver Public School Board and the first African American woman to be elected to public office in Colorado. She presented the board with the "Noel Resolution" in April 1968, requesting that the superintendent develop an integration plan for Denver's schools. The board passed the resolution in 1970, with threats being made against Noel and her family. The Supreme Court would echo her position in the *Keyes v. Denver* case. From 1976 through 1984, Noel served on the University of Colorado Board of Regents, chairing that body for one year.

One of the people that Rachel Noel assisted in being elected to the Denver Public School Board of Education was Omar D. Blair, a civil rights advocate. He grew up in Denver when blacks had to use the fire escapes to enter and exit movie theaters in Denver and could only swim once a week in the swimming pool. He was able to attend UCLA for two years and was a member of the 332nd fighter group, the Tuskegee Airmen, rising to captain. Afterward he was a grievance officer at the Rocky Mountain Arsenal and later returned to the air force in 1970 as an equal opportunity investigator.

Blair was elected to the Denver Public School Board of Education in 1973 and served twelve years. It was a combative period at times because of the 1969 court-ordered busing of Denver's schoolchildren for racial balance. There were some Denverites, including some board members, who insisted that Denver's children would suffer from being bused to nonneighborhood schools. To refute that, Blair created the Knight Fundamental Academy, "a back-to-basics elementary magnet school" in a retiree neighborhood. Because he was board president, Blair had administrators recruit the best teachers. According to him, children of all socioeconomic levels from all over Denver went there and not a single parent complained that their children were being bused.

While some on the board were arguing about busing, Blair and his probusing colleagues quietly worked to get computers in Denver schools, opened a career education center, and got one school named for Dr. Martin Luther King Jr. Blair's name is on the Blair-Caldwell Library, a branch of the Denver Public Library system.

Forced busing in Denver did not achieve all its desired results, unfortunately. Judge Richard Matsch ruled in September 1995 that Denver could abandon school busing, even though Denver's public schools were more segregated than ever. In 1968, there were 63,398 white students attending public schools in the city, but in 1994, there were only 18,000, as white families enrolled their children in private schools or moved to the suburbs. Middle-class black and Latino families began to enroll children in Catholic schools, comprising a quarter of the 11,000 students there. After all the hopes for achieving equal education for all K-12 students, the *New York Times* reported, "While the city enjoys an economic and cultural renaissance, the public school system has become a dumping ground for poor and disadvantaged children. Ten percent of the students are in special education, one-fourth lack proficiency in English, and two-thirds qualify for subsidized lunches."[7]

Denver's Park Hill was a center for segregation in housing as well as in education by the mid-1950s. After the first black family moved into the neighborhood, real estate agents urged white families to sell their homes, lining pockets of speculators. The Urban League initiated its "Project on Changing Neighborhoods" to stem the flight and received assistance from local white ministers. Jews, through the Anti-Defamation League, also joined in the battle. Colorado's state House and Senate wrangled over a fair housing bill and in 1959, the senate passed House Bill 259 with a vote of 24 to 11. At that time, only thirteen states had fair housing statutes, but only Colorado's applied to both public and private housing. A few weeks later, Governor Steve McNichols signed the bill into law.

The law received challenges from the director of the Colorado Anti-Discrimination Commission, from Duke Dunbar, Colorado's attorney general, and from the Colorado Supreme Court. That led organizations such as CORE (Congress of Racial Equality) and other civil rights groups to engage in nonviolent protests. During 1964, female members of CORE did an overnight sit-in outside Governor John Love's office after he refused to strengthen the fair housing law. Yet, Colorado "succeeded in passing the type of anti-discrimination legislation that segregationists in Congress successfully filibustered until passage of the national Civil Rights Act of 1964 and the national Fair Housing Act of 1968."[8]

The passage of the national Fair Housing Act of 1968 did a lot for the country but did not significantly affect Colorado. Colorado's Fair Housing Act, amended and strengthened in 1965, provided more coverage than the national law. The national law did give the state law more publicity, which resulted in more cases brought before the Colorado Civil Rights Commission. In other efforts, the commission adopted a policy "to include discrimination in education and de facto segregation under the Public Accommodations law" and adopted "a policy on the use of tests in employment." Sometimes, psychological and other tests were administered for hiring and promotion, but were not related to job performance.

In higher education, the University of Colorado and the University of Denver ceased asking applicants to state their race and religion. Further, Boulder barbers were pressured to cut the hair of African American students. In 1956, CU's Board of Regents ruled that 1962 would be the date that sororities and fraternities were to end racial discrimination.

The history of African Americans at the University of Colorado has vacillated over time and in some areas, is not quite clear-cut. Although Colorado's constitution of 1876 forbade student classifications based on race and color in public education, de facto segregation existed. The first identifiable African American student attended law school from 1897 to 1899, but there may have been one or more who "passed." An African American male received his bachelor of arts degree in 1914 while the first black woman earned her degree in 1918. By 1939, a total of forty-one degrees had been awarded to thirty-six students over the years. In 1933 and 1935, two African Americans played sports for the university, although they were unofficially barred from football and basketball in the Rocky Mountain Conference. Yet, track coach Frank Potts fielded an integrated team.

Students had to find housing in Boulder's black community and many restaurants in town would not serve them. Because Boulder usually had a summertime influx of tourists from the South, summers saw discrimination become even stricter. Two student organizations that organized early on against racism were the Cosmopolitan Club and the American Student Union, both led by white students at the time. The process would be long and slow, and would take decades, but change was inevitable. In 1976, Rachel Noel would be the first African American on CU's Board of Regents, the same year that CU offered the position of chancellorship to Dr. Mary Francis Berry, making her the first black woman to head a major research university.

The Colorado Civil Rights Commission worked with universities on a number of civil rights issues and helped Colorado State University students resolve complaints, for instance. In the spring of 1969, the commission conducted an ethnic census of all Colorado universities, including both full-time and part-time faculty, plus undergraduate and graduate students in two-year and four-year institutions. The information was used to determine if integration problems existed and their extent, and to see if and how institutions were planning for possible expansion of recruitment and retention efforts.

With all the struggles, successes included the achievements of people such as George L. Brown. He was the third African American to graduate from the University of Colorado Law School, and in 1956, the first African American elected to the state senate. In 1969, Brown became the first executive director of the Metro-Denver Urban Coalition, and in 1973 became Colorado's lieutenant governor. Also in the 1972 election, Penfield Tate was elected mayor of Boulder, and Wellington Webb, future first African American mayor of Denver, was elected a state representative.

A famous graduate student at the University of Colorado was Mildred D. Taylor, author of the novel *Roll of Thunder, Hear My Cry*. While there she helped to create the school's first Black Studies Department, which is still in place under the Center for the Study of Ethnicity and Race in America (CSERA) and which is still involved in issues related to civil rights. Taylor received her master of arts degree in 1969 and worked for two more years on campus before leaving for California.

Wellington Webb ran for state office in 1972 and served as representative from 1973 until 1977. He and Artie Taylor, an African American woman, worked as a team and won seats. He got young people to pass out literature and to knock on doors, also receiving assistance from former mayor of San Francisco, Willie Brown. Webb won with 5,997 votes; his opponents Tom Crowe, an independent, received 801 votes and Emilia Alvarado, the La Raza candidate, garnered 503 votes.

A case that had national repercussions involved petitioner Marlon D. Green, who applied for a pilot position with Continental Airlines, headquartered in Denver. The airline turned down Green's application "because he was a Negro," so he filed suit in 1957. This was in spite of the fact that the Colorado Anti-Discrimination Act of 1957 forbade an employer to discriminate against a qualified person "because of race, creed, color, national origin or ancestry." The commission decided in Green's favor, but the Denver District Court reversed that decision. The commission then appealed to the Supreme Court of Colorado in 1960 and 1962. It took six years for the case to reach the U.S. Supreme Court, where it was argued on March 28, 1963, and decided on April 22, 1963, costing Green his life savings in the process. However, the Supreme Court's ruling awarded Green some justice.

The *Denver Post* obituary for Green reported that there was no written agreement against hiring minorities but that there was a "gentlemen's agreement" in place. Green had attended flight school and had flown for the air force. Nevertheless, the airline argued that whites would not want to fly with a black pilot and further, that a black pilot would not be able to find a hotel room in the South. After winning his case, Green began flying for Continental in 1965 in a career that spanned fourteen years. Green's lawsuit resulted in him receiving the "same salary, seniority, privileges and fringe benefits that he would have been entitled to had he been employed in 1957."[9]

Plaintiffs were not successful in all civil rights litigations regarding racial discrimination in employment, but still, the courts determined if a person's dismissal was based on racial grounds. In 1962, Coors Company hired Booker T. Mays Sr., the first African American to be employed there, but he was terminated in 1969. Mays claimed racial prejudice on the job was the cause of his firing, and he took his case to court. In one example, a supervisor had repeatedly asked Mays if he could "get him a nice colored girl for a date." When Mays reported the behavior, the supervisor denied it, and both men were subjected to a polygraph test to determine which one would be immediately fired for lying. Although the supervisor was the one found to be untruthful, he was not fired as promised. The polygraph debacle was followed by reprimands for minor violations that, according to Mays, amounted to harassment and ultimately his dismissal.

The Colorado Civil Rights Commission found that racism was indeed the cause of Mays's dismissal. Coors appealed the decision to the Jefferson County District Court, which reversed the commission's decision, and then the case went to the Colorado Court of Appeals. After hearing the evidence, the latter ruled that Mays had been treated the same as any other employee.

In a second case involving Coors, the Colorado Court of Appeals heard a 1971 case against the Colorado Civil Rights Commission over the latter's subpoena powers. According to Commissioner Morrison, its investigation revealed that "Coors was not offering equal opportunity to nonwhites, and indeed it was discriminating for reasons of race, creed, color, national origin, or ancestry." The commission issued a subpoena for documents relating to the charges, and Coors refused to comply.

In the ensuing legal activity, the Colorado Court of Appeals ruled that under the 1957 Colorado Anti-Discrimination Act, the commission could investigate discrimination but did not have the power to subpoena witnesses or documents. Further, the commission could "subpoena materials and individuals only in specific cases where discrimination had occurred in fact, not in theory." The complaints had to be in writing and in enough detail to support the charge and the alleged guilty party had to be granted a reasonable amount of time to respond. One interpretation is that the Colorado Civil Rights Commission, in its fervent efforts to eliminate discrimination, overstepped its authority. In any case, Colorado's legal system was fine-tuning various elements related to civil rights litigations.

One interesting case that provides an example of the subterfuge a company utilized to get rid of a person without making it seem racial occurred in the late 1960s. An unnamed airline laid off an unnamed young African American male because of his "natural" hairstyle, one that he wore when he worked for the same airline in another city. Of course, the airline denied it was racially discriminating. The man did seek redress through his union but the union representative was his supervisor, the same person who filed the complaint against the worker, so the union sided with the company following the hearing. The resulting Colorado Civil Rights Commission investigation revealed that the airline used the hair "problem" as an excuse, but the real reason was concern from some that the young man was dating white stewardesses. Further, the hair "problem" was not uniformly applied and was used to force the man to quit. In a conciliation action, the man was rehired, he received his back pay, and he was given the opportunity to take the test for a promotion to senior agent.

Between 1966 and 1969, the commission investigated an increasing number of formal complaints. There were 239 such cases filed in 1965–66, 242 for 1966–67 and 452 in 1967–68. In Denver, two satellite offices opened, and in April 1967, the commission opened a full-time office on the Western Slope in Alamosa. The Pueblo office opened in 1965. To serve the Latino community, another office opened in Greeley, located in Weld County, one of the top-producing agricultural counties in the United States. Part of the impetus for expanding support of civil rights commissions around the country was the issuance of the Kerner Report, which said that the country was moving toward separate and unequal black and white societies.

It might come as a surprise to many that not only were there groups such as the NAACP and the Urban League that were on the forefront of civil rights struggles in Colorado, but also there were groups such as the Black Panther Party (BPP).

Between 1968 and 1971, the BPP played important roles in Denver's struggles, such as criticizing "Denver's police force and elected officials for racist practices." They brought their national ten-point program to Denver and inaugurated a free breakfast program for schoolchildren. Moreover, they "attempted to take control of their community through the local schools, and by recruiting young Black men interested in making a change."[10]

The *Denver Post* archives contain photographs and stories that recorded African American struggles following the signing of the Civil Rights Act of 1964. The following are just a handful of the activities, but they fight the misconception that Denver was "out of the loop" in the struggle for racial equality. Further, they demonstrate that black Coloradans were supporting national civil rights activities.

- March 9, 1965—One hundred people take part in the Boulder Sympathy March to show support for civil rights workers in Alabama. The route began on the University of Colorado campus to downtown Boulder.
- March 9, 1965—Demonstrators hold a five-hour sit-in at Denver's FBI office to demand greater federal protection for civil rights workers in Alabama.
- March 13, 1965—Five thousand people participate in a rally at the state capitol to support civil rights activities in Selma, Alabama.
- June 25, 1968—Protestors file by the Denver Police building to demand that white police officers be replaced with blacks. Further, they offered to assist in the process.
- April 9, 1969—In Fort Collins, Colorado State University's Black Student Alliance led a sit-in inside the administration building to demand the enrollment of more black and Latino students.
- November 2, 1969—Police were called in to break up a disturbance during halftime at the Colorado State University–UTEP football game over the dismissal of fourteen black student athletes at the University of Wyoming.
- September 6, 1971—Lauren Watson, leader of the Denver BPP, plus 150 others, held a memorial rally around the controversial death of Soledad Brother George Jackson at San Quentin Prison.
- February 23, 1972—About thirty students of the Black Student Alliance at the University of Denver burn copies of the student newspaper, which they claim did not adequately report minority affairs on campus.

- January 14, 1975—Black legislators, including state representative and future Denver mayor Wellington Webb and state senator Regis Groff, led a walkout at Governor Dick Lamm's inauguration ceremony, protesting his failure to appoint black applicants to high office.
- August 6, 1975—Black Denver leaders pressured Safeway to keep its store open in the black community and requested that it be maintained in a first-class manner at all times.

From 1975 through today, many black Coloradans believe their community has lost ground in areas of civil and human rights. They point to single-female-headed households, which are sometimes correlated with the incarceration of black males; lack of individual responsibility; the push away from bilingual education; economic policies; resegregation in education, poverty, income, health, and education disparities when compared to whites; the erosion of policies from the 1960s and 1970s that were designed to provide a boost to minorities; and more. In addition, blue-collar jobs have disappeared and college costs have increased.

When Denver's present-day African American mayor, Michael Hancock, views Denver's current situation, he looks to those who were fighting during the civil rights era. Some of them will say that African Americans had it better before that period in some ways. That does not mean they would want to return to those times, but they remembered stronger families and communities. Some would say that "it's those kinds of values of staying together, and working together, and making sure that children are the focal point of the family and that there's a strong family unit around kids is the point these people are trying to make." In the 1950s through the 1970s, education was seen as the answer but today, many see health care, nutritious meals, after-school programs, and support systems outside of school as necessities.

The complex struggle for civil and human rights is an ongoing process for peoples of color. Societies have to obtain those rights and then fight to keep them. In Colorado, blacks and others today owe a lot to those who fought for rights that we all enjoy. However, like Sisyphus of the Greek myth, Coloradans must stay vigilant lest they lose many gains and have to begin all over. Although there have been some dramatic losses in some areas, the "rock" is nowhere near the bottom of the hill. In other areas, that "rock" is still advancing.

In a September 6, 1956, speech to the National Baptist Convention in Denver, Roy Wilkins of the NAACP said the following, which not only enunciated the goals of civil and human rights, but also connected them to overarching religious principles:

The rulers of darkness shall not prevail. Man—all men—of every shade and circumstance everywhere—shall be free in both body and spirit. This is the promise of the great land of America; this is the pattern of God's will.[11]

Notes

1. Summer Burke, "Community Control: Civil Rights Resistance in the Mile High City," *Psi Sigma Siren* 7, no. 1 (January 2012), http://digitalscholarship.unlv.edu/psi_sigma_siren/vol7/iss1/4/.
2. Ibid.
3. Carl Abbott, "Plural Society in Colorado: Ethnic Relations in the Twentieth Century," *Phylon* 39, no. 3 (3rd Quarter, 1978): 251; and Calvin Trillin, "Doing the Right Thing Isn't Always Easy," *New Yorker*, May 31, 1969, 88.
4. Abbott, "Plural Society in Colorado," 252.
5. "Keyes v. School District No. 1," Oyez Project at Illinois Institute of Technology's Chicago-Kent College of Law, November 18, 2014, http://www.oyez.org/cases/1970-1979/1972/1972_71_507/.
6. Calvin Trillin, "Doing the Right Thing Isn't Always Easy," 85–86.
7. James Brooke, "Court Says Denver Can End Forced Busing," *New York Times*, September 17, 1995, www.nytimes.com/1995/09/17/us/court-says-denver-can-end-forced-busing.html.
8. Ibid.
9. Eleanor G. Crow, *A Time for Change and Challenge: Civil Rights in Colorado, 1966–1969*, (Denver: Colorado Civil Rights Commission, 1969), 19–20, https://archive.org/details/ERIC_ED035489.
10. Burke, "Community Control."
11. Davis W. Houck and David E. Dixon, eds., *Rhetoric, Religion, and the Civil Rights Movement* (Waco, Tex.: Baylor University Press, 2006), 202.

Further Reading

Abbott, Carl. "Plural Society in Colorado: Ethnic Relations in the Twentieth Century." *Phylon* 39, no. 3 (3rd Quarter, 1978): 250–60.

Abbott, Carl, Stephen J. Leonard, and Thomas J. Noel. *Colorado: A History of the Centennial State*. 5th ed. Boulder: University of Colorado Press, 2013.

Atchison, Carla Joan. "Nativism in Colorado Politics: The American Protective Association and the Ku Klux Klan." Master's thesis, University of Colorado, 1972.

Athern, Robert G. *The Coloradans*. Albuquerque: University of New Mexico Press, 1976.

Bardwell, George E. *Characteristics of Negro Residences in Park Hill Area of Denver, Colorado, 1966*. Denver: Commission on Community Relations, City and County of Denver, 1966.

Brooke, James. "Court Says Denver Can End Forced Busing." *New York Times*, September 17, 1995. www.nytimes.com/1995/09/17/us/court-says-denver-can-end-forced-busing.html.

Brown-Bailey, Sharon Ruth. "Journey Full Circle: A Historical Analysis of Keyes v. School District No. 1." PhD diss., University of Colorado at Denver, 1998.

Browne, Phiefer L. "Mildred D. Taylor." In *Notable Black American Women*, vol. 2, edited by Jessie Carney Smith, 629–30. Detroit: Gale Research, 1996.

Burke, Summer. "Community Control: Civil Rights Resistance in the Mile High City." *Psi Sigma Siren* 7, no. 1 (January 2012). http://digitalscholarship.unlv.edu/psi_sigma_siren/vol7/iss1/4/.

Calvert, Robert A. "Colorado Anti-Discrimination Commission v. Continental Airlines, 372 U.S. 714 (1963)." In *Encyclopedia of African-American Civil Rights: From Emancipation to the Present*, edited by Charles D. Lowrey and John F. Marszalek, 119–20. Westport, Conn.: Greenwood Press, 1992.

The Colorado Anti-Discrimination Commission et al., Petitioners, v. Continental Air Lines, Inc. Marlon D. Green, Petitioner, v. Continental Air Lines, Inc., 372 U.S. 714 (1963).

Cortese, Charles F. *The Park Hill Experience*. Denver: Colorado Civil Rights Commission, 1947.

Crow, Eleanor G. *A Time for Change and Challenge: Civil Rights in Colorado, 1966–1969*. Denver: Colorado Civil Rights Commission, 1969. https://archive.org/details/ERIC_ED035489.

Culver, Virginia. "Pilot Marlon D. Green Fought Racial Discrimination." *Denver Post*, July 9, 2009. www.denverpost.com/obituaries/ci_12805244/.

Davis, Jack E. "Keyes v. School District No. 1, Denver, Colorado, 413 U.S. 189 (1973)." In *Encyclopedia of African-American Civil Rights: From Emancipation to the Present*, edited by Charles D. Lowrey and John F. Marszalek, 297–98. Westport, Conn.: Greenwood Press, 1992.

Delgado, Richard, and Jean Stefancic. *Home-Grown Racism: Colorado's Historic Embrace, and Denial of Equal Opportunity in Higher Education*. Denver: Latino/a Research Center & Policy Center, University of Colorado at Denver, 1999.

Gray, Juanita R. *Denver Negro Leaders, 1973–1975*. Denver: Juanita R. Gray, 1975.

Hansen, Moya B. "'Try Being a Black Woman!': Jobs in Denver, 1900–1970." In *African American Women Confront the West, 1600–2000*, edited by Quintard Taylor and Shirley Ann Wilson Moore, 207–27. Norman: University of Oklahoma Press, 2003.

Hayes, David M. "The Rocky Road to Racial Integration at the University of Colorado." *Journal of Blacks in Higher Education* 44 (Summer 2004): 96–98.

Leonard, Stephen J. "Black-White Relations in Denver, 1930s–1970s." *Midwest Review* 12 (1990): 56–64.

McBride, Conrad L. "The 1964 Election in Colorado." *Western Political Quarterly* 18, no. 2 (June 1965): 475–80.

Musgrave, Michael David. "Racism in the Weld County Judicial System." BA thesis, University of Northern Colorado, 1975.

Newsum, Dani R. "Cold War Colorado: Civil Rights Liberals and the Movement for Legislative Equality, 1945–1959." MA thesis, University of Colorado, 2012.

Norman, Mary Ann. "Civil Rights in Colorado: An Examination of Five Cases." *Journal of the West* 25 (October 1986): 38–43.

"The Struggle for Racial Equality in Denver, 50 Years after the Civil Rights Act of 1964." *Denver Post*, July 2, 2014. http://blogs.denverpost.com/captured/2014/07/02/civil-rights-denver-50-years-signing-civil-rights-act/7113/.

Taylor, Mary J. "Leadership Responses to Desegregation in the Denver Public Schools, a Historical Study: 1959–1977." PhD diss., University of Denver, 1990.

United States Commission on Civil Rights. Colorado Advisory Committee. *School Desegregation in Colorado Springs, Colorado: A Staff Report of the U.S. Commission on Civil Rights*. Washington, D.C.: U.S. Government Printing Office, 1977.

Watson, Frederick Douglas. "Removing the Barricades from the Northern Schoolhouse Door: School Desegregation in Denver." PhD diss., University of Colorado at Boulder, 1993.

8

Civil Rights in Utah
The Mormon Way
J. Herschel Barnhill

In Utah, the civil rights movement involved three groups—women, African Americans, and American Indians; eventually it also included freedom of religion, as Oklahoma scholar J. Herschel Barnhill reminds us. Two factors were of importance in that state. First, there was the small number of minorities in Utah; in 1960, for example, only 2 percent of the population was black. The second controlling and vital factor was the influence of the Mormon church. Blacks in Utah needed to overcome the antiblack role of the church; as an example, not until 1978 were blacks even eligible to become priests. The author of this article, J. Herschel Barnhill, an Oklahoma resident who earned his PhD at Oklahoma State University, has published other articles about the civil rights revolution, including publications in the *Negro History Bulletin* and the *Red River Valley Historical Review*. He also authored *From Surplus to Substitution: Energy in Texas.*

Each of the states of the West developed its own identity. With respect to civil rights the story unfolded according to the blend of political alignments, economic conditions, and other elements that molded the unique character of each state. Despite that diversity, however, progress toward equality in all states affected the same categories of people—racial and ethnic minorities and women—and came about because of or despite local responses to national currents or policies. Thus, in varying degrees, each state's story dealt with minority movements that resembled

---

"Civil Rights in Utah: The Mormon Way" by J. Herschel Barnhill. Copyright 1986 by Journal of the West, an imprint of ABC-CLIO, LLC. All rights reserved. Reproduced with permission of ABC-CLIO, LLC, Santa Barbara, Calif., and the *Journal of the West.*

the black civil rights movement and the women's liberation struggle. Each of those threads wove its way into what had previously been fabric constructed predominantly by white males. Even the court decisions that enriched the weave came primarily, almost totally, from white male jurists. A final theme common to the saga of civil rights in the West was the preoccupation with economic and political rights to the neglect of another right—freedom of religion.

In Utah, two factors unshared by the other western states produced a civil rights movement that diverged significantly from the pattern. The first factor was the virtual nonexistence of racial or ethnic minorities in the state-precluded development of strong, creative, or individualistic movements working for equality for a group or for an individual. Civil rights cases made their way into the courts with reasonable frequency, but victories came only in consequence of earlier progress elsewhere, as a result of developments in states where minorities had greater strength or in the federal government.

The second factor unique to Utah was the dominant position of the Mormons. The argument about the influence of the Mormon church on the politics of Utah (and, to an extent, the politics of surrounding states) has endured for many years. No final determination could possibly be reached in the limited space of a journal article. Suffice it to say that church members shared a system of values that promoted similarity of response to a given situation. And the consensual reaction appeared often to be the result of bloc voting directed by church leaders more than the result of shared values producing shared views.

Further, since the Mormons expanded well beyond Utah, and because the other states with significant numbers of Mormons sometimes responded to civil rights issues in a fashion strongly resembling that of Mormon Utah, concern existed that there might truly be that monolithic Church of Jesus Christ of Latter-day Saints. The worry, at least superficially, resembled that which arose concerning the influence of the Catholic Church on a Catholic president of the United States. The only conclusion attempted here is that the church long held the power, should it choose to exercise it, to influence its members to pursue actions favorable to church interests. And, sharing the same interests, members had little inclination to resist. Consequently, with but few exceptions, civil rights in Utah developed as the church accommodated or resisted change.

As the predominant power group in Utah, Mormons enjoyed, inevitably, a strong political position both in the state and beyond its borders. Mormon influence had impact in Washington, D.C., as early as the New Deal years. To the 1950s the Mormons had easy access to the presidency: Marriner Eccles worked in the FDR administration and Ezra Taft Benson had the ear of Dwight D. Eisenhower, who regarded Benson's religion as an asset. Also, a general rule seemed to be that all presidential candidates had to make an obligatory visit to the Mormon Tabernacle. And the church had almost as much clout in Idaho and Arizona as it had in its stronghold, the Utah that it dominated. However, despite its strength the church remained quiet unless forced to act, the elders preferring to channel their energies into economic development and missions.[1]

The church did step in to defeat pro–New Deal candidates for the governorship and the senate in 1948 and 1952. And church leaders proved willing to stifle right-wing embarrassments as well. In the 1960s Ezra Taft Benson had become sympathetic with the goals of the John Birch Society, and his son, Reed Benson, served as Utah chairman of the group. Both attacked John Kennedy's New Frontier, causing embarrassment to the church leadership. The Mormons shipped Reed off to Europe and ordered Ezra to be silent. Radical and reactionary Mormons alike suffered the wrath of the church elders, but for the most part the need for intervention was rare. Successful Utah politicians tended to be Mormon and Democratic. Calvin Rampton, governor from 1964 through 1976, and his successor, Scott Matheson, both were probusiness Democrats attractive to Republicans. In keeping with the emphasis on economic growth, moderate elements dominated the Latter-day Saints and the government of Utah.

Political accommodation to promote economic development—that was the Mormon mission in the 1960s and 1970s. The church had concentrated on purifying the state of radicalism and Nathan Eldon Tanner's economic expansionism included acquisition of media in Los Angeles, Kansas City, San Francisco, Chicago, and the District of Columbia. Building from an economic base that produced income estimated at $1 million a day as early as 1962, Tanner invested in traditional enterprises as well as film and computer companies. Supposedly, when conflict developed over church interests, "invariably the church hierarchy would step in, stories would be killed, and programming would be affected" at the church-owned media.[2]

With increased streamlining of economic assets and growth into a worldwide organization, the Mormons also increased their centralized approach to politics. Revived interest in Utah political activity produced the unwritten rule in the legislature that Mormon approval was a necessity for all laws impacting on Mormon interests. Such a rule seemed unnecessary in a legislature whose membership included an estimated 80 percent Mormons. Also, the entire Utah delegation in the federal Congress was Mormon in 1980; naturally the delegation paid attention to the interests of the church. Mormons composed 72 percent of Utah's population in 1980.

By 1960 Utah was 98 percent white. The other 2 percent included 6,961 Indians, 4,371 Japanese, 4,148 blacks (80 percent of them residing in Salt Lake City or Ogden), 629 Chinese, 207 Filipinos, and 483 "other." Even in 1980, after a 37.9 percent explosion in population in only a decade, minorities comprised only approximately 10 percent of Utahans. The largest minority in Utah was Gentiles, non-Mormon whites. And white males, although they might squirm under the rigid moral code that restricted any propensity for vice that they might have, suffered little if any economic or political discrimination. Accordingly, civil rights as a movement had no viable existence in Utah save as an extension of outside forces. The Mormon hierarchy had little need to exert its influence in that arena.[3]

With such a minute minority population, there should have been no need for discrimination in Utah; in fact, the Utah Constitution prohibited segregated schools. The first black pupil in Salt Lake City's high school, however, did not enroll until 1947. And in 1952 Salt Lake City officials refused a black teacher the right to teach in their schools; the teacher had to practice teach at Ogden instead. In 1953 there was only one black graduate student in the state. Blacks were enrolled at all three of the state's universities—Utah, Utah State, and Brigham Young—but even in 1984 only approximately thirty black students attended Brigham Young University. Public pools and clubs were open to minorities by 1953, primarily as a consequence of *Watkins v. Oaklawn Jockey Club* (1950). And organizations such as the Masons and Elks allowed black members. But discrimination persisted in private clubs and organizations, even bowling alleys.[4]

An ancient court case, *De La Ysla v. Public Theatres Corporation* (1933), had affirmed the right of a theater owner to seat customers where he chose; in 1952 blacks in Salt Lake City normally had to sit in the balcony. *Nance v. Mayflower Tavern, Inc.* (1944) affirmed the right of restaurants to refuse service as they chose: only blacks such as Paul Robeson, Adam Clayton Powell, and others of equal prominence, for example, managed to overcome the segregation in accommodations—despite a 1953 Utah law prohibiting such segregation. Even hospitals had restrictions: black patients had either to take private rooms or go elsewhere.[5]

In 1952 there was only one black lawyer and no black doctors in the entire state. And, although the American Federation of Labor and Congress of Industrial Organizations generally eschewed discriminatory practices, a 1947 senate committee in Utah reported that "there is a substantial body of unfair and discriminatory practices in the state's industry." Legislation to outlaw discrimination in employment died in the legislature in 1947, 1949, and 1951. Other discriminatory practices included segregated jails—both city and county—in Salt Lake City; antimiscegenation laws (despite the laws, mixed marriages continued to occur, but their frequency had to be miniscule given the scarcity of minorities within the state); and segregation of blood in Utah's blood banks. There was no discrimination in worship, save of course for the Mormon ban on blacks in the priesthood. And restrictive covenants prevailed.[6]

A 1956 case challenged the restrictive covenants in real-estate agreements that prohibited unauthorized sale to specific ethnic or racial minority group members. In the case of *Gaddis Investment Company et al v. Charles H. Morrison*, Gaddis sued in state court to get his broker's commission. The defendant, Morrison, had listed a property with Gaddis, who found a buyer who paid earnest money. The buyer was black, so Gaddis informed both buyer and seller that the transaction required approval of the Salt Lake City Real Estate Board. The seller responded that he would sell anyway. Thereupon Gaddis returned the earnest money. He then sued for his broker's commission, and a lower court found in his favor. The state supreme court, however, overturned the decision, ruling that the broker had waived his contractual right to a commission. Although an attempt was made to bring Fourteenth Amendment issues before the court, the decision was that racial discrimination was an extraneous matter. By so narrowly defining the case, the court dodged the whole question of restrictive covenants. The practice stood.

In 1961 a state advisory commission reevaluated the status of civil rights in Utah. It reported to the U.S. Civil Rights Commission that conditions were "measurably worse than in previous years."

Discrimination, according to the report, was most likely to occur in lower-class public accommodations; however, discrimination in public accommodations generally continued, as did discriminatory employment practices. Even some labor unions continued to be closed to minorities, and educated blacks continued to leave Utah in search of suitable employment. And attempts to enact civil rights legislation continued to fail in the state legislature. In 1963 three more bills died. In the one bright moment of progress in 1963, the Utah legislature deleted those sections of state law that prohibited marriage between blacks and whites, and between "a Mongolian, member of the Malay race, or a mulatto, quadroon, or octaroon and white person." Even the civil rights revolution that polarized much of the United States during the 1960s failed to stir conservative Utah.[7]

The antiblack rules of the Mormons came under attack from civil rights activists at out-of-state sporting events. Pickets became a common sight at

Brigham Young University out-of-state games, but the church continued to resist the pressure; Brigham Young had, after all, been desegregated for decades, a situation that hardly prevailed at many of the nation's universities, including perhaps some of those that sported pickets. And the Mormon leadership in the 1960s had more pressing concerns, having to deal with the strong conservative wing represented by the Bensons. Once the crisis of the leadership waned, and once the civil rights furor diminished, the Mormons could afford to become more accommodating. The election in 1973 of Spencer Kimball as the new prophet signaled the triumph of the moderates, and in 1978 Kimball had a new revelation, a new definition for the Mormons of racial equality. For the first time in more than a century, as the result of Kimball's revelation, blacks became eligible for the priesthood. With equality in the most important of church offices, blacks could anticipate at least equal treatment in other aspects of life in Mormon Utah.

Another minority whose halting steps toward equality depended on assistance from outside the state, the American Indians of Utah, struggled to little avail to attain their ends. In their case, assistance failed to materialize. Utah's Paiutes and Utes suffered at the hands of the federal government, the state courts, and the Mormon church.

The federal government treated Utah's Indians just as it did those in other states—badly. After World War II the Bureau of Indian Affairs, which under John Collier had attempted to promote autonomy and self-sufficiency on the reservations, came under attack as Communistic and anti-religion, primarily because Collier had deemphasized the influence of missionaries and promoted economic cooperation for his charges. Congress increased pressure for the elimination of the bureau. Further, a commission headed by Herbert Hoover recommended not only the elimination of reservations but also the assimilation of American Indians into mainstream American society. In 1950 Dillon Myer became commissioner of the bureau; his primary goal proved to be the closing down of the reservations. Under Myer, the Bureau of Indian Affairs forced some Indians into urban rehabilitation programs, exerted its influence to eliminate the Indian cooperatives, and sought to convert Indians into farmers. The tribes agreed to relinquish their reservations in return for a money payment and to assimilate themselves into the larger society.

Among the approximately twenty tribes were sophisticated and acculturated groups such as the Menominees of Wisconsin, and fairly backward and extremely poor tribes such as the Southern Paiutes of Utah. The primary reasoning behind Paiute termination was that members of that tribe could not be any worse off under any circumstances than they already were on their reservation. According to Parker Nelson, attorney for the terminated tribes, the difficulty of adjustment to an urban environment caused some Paiutes such distress that they were "actually going out and committing suicide by walking under motor vehicles."[8] Eventually, with the demise of the termination policy, the Paiutes regained control of their land. The theoretically humanitarian gesture of saving the Paiutes from their backwardness lacked sufficient importance to its advocates to survive in the face of opposition.[9]

Another problem facing Utah's Indians was the denial of voting rights. From statehood in 1896 until 1940, Utah law prohibited voting by Indians. In 1940 an opinion by the state attorney general overturned that policy, and Indians voted for the next sixteen years. In 1956 the attorney general issued another opinion, and conditions reverted to their pre-1940 status. According to the opinion, Indians must establish Utah residence just like any other citizen of the United States. That is, they must reside off a military or Indian reservation to establish their eligibility. Further, because no reservation Indian could establish residence without leaving the reservation, there was no obligation on the state to provide voting facilities on that reservation.[10]

Preston Allen, a Ute on the reservation in Duchesne County, sought to vote in the election of 1956. The county clerk, Porter L. Merrell, in accordance with the law as interpreted by the attorney general, denied the request. Allen brought a class action suit against Merrell as both an individual and an agent of the government. Allen initially sought a court order requiring Merrell to provide the ballot. The court refused, however, arguing that "the right to vote, though fundamental to our scheme of government, is not absolute. It derives from the state." And the state had the right to prohibit voting by reservation Indians or any other class of citizen it chose. Allen appealed.

Before the Utah Supreme Court in late 1956, Allen argued that Utah law, in practice, disfranchised only reservation Indians. Accordingly, the law violated the Fourteenth and Fifteenth Amendment guarantees of equal protection of the laws and the right to vote. But the court reaffirmed that the right to vote came not from the federal Constitution but from the state. The "wisdom or desirability" of laws was beyond judicial purview, according to Justice J. Allan Crockett, the highly conservative jurist, who also noted that "it is important that the court proceed with the utmost caution in reviewing legislative acts lest it encroach upon the prerogatives of the legislature."[11] In a supplemental opinion that expressed a logic more suited to the preceding century, an opinion too extreme for the majority of the supreme court, Crockett went on to list additional reasons why the law seemed reasonable. He noted that although Indians had not yet attained equality as citizens, while on the reservation they enjoyed special rights beyond the control of the state: the right to tax, prosecute law violators, pass laws, and so on. Thus they were semisovereign states, a concept discarded by the federal government in the 1870s. Also, because of their unique relationship as wards of the federal government, Indians might be susceptible to federal influence; they were clearly beyond the control of Utah. Crockett's third argument blatantly stated that Indians enjoyed lower taxes and had less interest in politics and government than did average (i.e., white) citizens.[12]

Crockett refused to stop there. According to him it was "common knowledge" that most Utah Indians lived in isolation from one another and from the outside world. Not only did they have a high illiteracy rate, but they also didn't even speak English in their tribal courts and affairs. Furthermore, they did not pay the full costs of government services provided to them. And they just might take over the county government and place an undue burden on the other inhabitants. Thus the law stood as just. According to this jurist, who served for another two decades, the majority of inhabitants of the county should be disfranchised for the good of the Mormon minority. By the time the United States Supreme Court heard the case, the election had passed. Thus, the court ruled the matter moot and remanded it to the Utah Supreme Court and Justice Crockett. There it died.[13]

The third problem confronting Indians in Utah proved to be the Mormon church. Initially Mormon Indian policy strongly resembled that of the United States. Within twenty years of their taking up residence in Deseret, Mormons reduced the Indian population from forty-five thousand to eight hundred. The survivors—Utes, Paiutes, and Shoshones, among others—staggered to the reservation, there to be ignored until the 1940s. During that decade the church developed a new mission to the Lamanites, a humanitarian program for American Indians, which the Mormons called the Indian Placement Service. Under the program, Indian children between the ages of eight and eighteen left their reservation to live with Mormon families during the school year, returning to the reservation for the summer. The humanitarianism of the program might be subject to question; in 1960 Spencer Kimball told a conference of Mormons that the children in the program often were lighter than those who remained on the reservation. Allegedly, some Indians who had converted to Mormonism believed that conversion would whiten them, a belief strongly reminiscent, in its implications that their skin color shamed them, of the pre–civil rights movement attempts of some blacks to lighten themselves or to pass for white. Although the American Indian Movement, social workers, and other concerned parties regarded the Indian Placement Service as tantamount to kidnapping, the Indian Welfare Act of 1978, after lobbying by the Mormon church, exempted the program from its coverage. In contrast to the questionable value of the Indian Placement Service, in 1975 George Patrick Lee, a full-blooded Navajo, became the first Indian member of the First Quorum of Seventy, an oversight group for overseas affairs, which ranked on the third level of the church hierarchy.

The fourth component of Indian misery, the Indian Claims Commission, was the design of Ernest Wilkinson, a Mormon attorney who had worked on two Ute claims cases under a preceding Indian claims law. Congressional enactment was the result of the labors of Pat McCarran of Nevada and Arthur Watkins of Utah. During its thirty-two-year life, the commission ruled on $2 billion worth of claims, awarded roughly $800 million, and rewarded lawyers with fees of $60 million. Among the prominent attorneys who benefited from the commission was Wilkinson, who represented the Ute, Shoshone, Goshiute, Paiute, and others, and who won $50 million for the Utes. But the victory for the Utes had strings: their money went to the United States Treasury, and they received it only as the United States Congress chose to appropriate it for them.

Dissatisfied with the Indian Claims Commission, American Indian groups, including those of Utah, sought court redress on several occasions. The Indians sought to convince the courts that their lawyers had deceived them by representing the claims commission as an agency through which the Indians might reclaim their land. Consistently the courts ruled that the commission had the power, through the claims process, only to determine an equitable means of payment for the land; there was no option that allowed the return of the land. Finally, in 1980, after years of unsuccessful litigation, huge legal fees, and insulting claims commission offers of 1 or 2 percent of current value (offers that logically but not legally would give the Indians the right to return to lands admitted by the commission to be Indian property), the Indians appeared before the United Nations and charged the United States with human rights violations. That action, naturally, accomplished nothing save the release of frustrations accumulated over centuries.

Equally futile was the crusade of Reies Lopez Tijerina's Alianza Federal de Mercedes. That Chicano movement sought between 1963 and 1970 the recognition of the legitimacy of Spanish land grants, a step that would have taken lands from Anglos and granted them to Mexican Americans. Spawned in the turbulence of the civil rights revolution, the Alianza grew quickly, went beyond the law in the manner of the Black Panthers, and faded into a pamphleteering operation within a span of only eight years. As with so much of the civil rights movement, it extended into Utah but had only minimal impact there. After all, Spanish Americans comprised only 60,000 of the 1.46 million citizens of Utah in 1980. They were the .06 in the 1.46 million.[14]

Foreigners fared no better. As of 1970 the state's laws prohibited or restricted the employment of aliens on public works, this even though the Chinese had built the railroad through Utah a century before. Service by foreigners on barber and coal examining boards and employment as certified public accountants, pharmacists, and veterinarians was restricted. Also, Utah statutes prohibited aliens from prospecting on state lands.[15]

Other minorities fell afoul of the definition of morality by the Mormon church. In the late 1970s a church lawyer told officials of the Utah Federation of Labor that the church had defined questions such as right-to-work laws, abortion, and the Equal Rights Amendment as moral issues. Accordingly, debate had become moot on matters of vital concern to much of the nation. On the right-to-work issue the church had sufficient influence even in the 1940s, to guide a successful right-to-work campaign in Utah, Arizona, and Nevada. And in 1965 the Mormon congressmen of Utah received word that they must oppose repeal of the anti-closed-shop component of the Taft-Hartley labor law. One member of the council of twelve reputedly said that loyalty to the church would be determined by the issue. Despite the definition of the issue as a question of fidelity, one congressman, David King of Salt Lake City, voted against the church position; King lost his bid for reelection.[16]

Women's rights also had moral implications in Utah. In 1974 the church stood strong against the Equal Rights Amendment in Virginia, Florida, and Nevada; Utah was a safe state for opponents of the amendment. The amendment failed in each state where the church used its influence. And in the courts of Utah equality for women proved to have a narrow definition. For instance, in the 1973 case of *Kapp v. Salt Lake City*, a woman sued for equal pay for equal work. She won her case before the industrial commission and a district court, but the Utah Supreme Court overturned the decision. The higher court ruled that unquestionably her pay was not equal; nevertheless, even though discrimination was evident, the plaintiff had failed to prove to the court's satisfaction that such discrimination had occurred solely because of her sex. Whereas federal equal pay legislation postulated that inequality of pay was presumed to be due to discrimination, in

Utah the burden rested with the plaintiff to show discrimination. And in the same year the court ruled that sexual differentiation was permissible as long as it served a practical purpose. Although the courts abided by federal guidelines, they continued to do so in as narrow a manner as possible.[17]

Civil rights for blacks, women, and other minorities in Utah came and went at the whim of the church and generally conservative jurists and legislators. Minorities lacked the power to determine their own fates. Although there were occasional challenges through the courts, little of national significance occurred in the story of civil rights development in Utah. One exception sparkled like a diamond in the otherwise murky coal mine of the Beehive State. That exception arose in the area of religious rights.

The issue was polygamy, and on that issue of religious freedom neither the government nor the church had the power to impose restrictions on those who chose to practice their religion in their own way. The Mormon practice of polygamy dated from at least 1843, the year in which Joseph Smith announced his revelation that plural marriage had divine sanction. In 1890, under intense pressure from Congress and the courts, President Wilford Woodruff presented to the church a new revelation, the Woodruff Manifesto, which read in part:

> Inasmuch as laws had been enacted by Congress forbidding plural marriages, which laws have been pronounced constitutional by the court of last resort, I hereby declare my intention to submit to those laws, and to use my influence with the members of the Church over which I preside to have them do likewise.

In 1933, after forty-three years, more than ten church manifestos, and vows by the church to excommunicate and prosecute violators in the courts, polygamy continued; the church issued its final manifesto against the practice. Two years later, in 1935, the Utah legislature enacted legislation making unlawful cohabitation a felony.

The Fundamentalists, those Mormons who denied the legitimacy of the revelation, continued to practice plural marriage. In 1935 the Fundamentalists began publishing *Truth*, a monthly magazine that cited the pioneer Mormon position on polygamy, opposed the official church interpretation, and even accused the church president of practicing polygamy. In 1944 the church succeeded in getting an indictment against *Truth* for obscenity, but in district court the charge was dropped. Other prosecutions during the 1940s tended to rely on the 1935 law, charging various individuals with acts against the public morality. Federal prosecutors in the 1940s relied on the Mann Act of 1910 to charge polygamists with transporting women across state lines for immoral purposes. Such an approach had some success, but polygamy continued in all areas of Mormon settlement, not just in Utah.

Despite a string of successful prosecutions in the 1940s, polygamy failed to die. In 1954 Utah instituted a new approach—enforcement of the so-called "neglected children" statutes. In 1953 Governor J. Howard Pyle of Arizona had called out more than one hundred policemen in an attempt to eradicate a Fundamentalist colony in his state. Accompanied by reporters from radio, television, and the newspapers, the lawmen raided Short Creek, Arizona. Disrupting the residents, who were singing hymns, the police arrested all the adults and made more than 250 children wards of the state. Pyle appeared on radio, saying, "They have arrested almost the entire population of a community dedicated to the production of white slaves." According to Pyle, the state sought custody in order to protect "the innocent chattels of a lawless 'commercial undertaking of wicked design and ruthlessly exercised power.'"[18]

Reaction to the raid was mixed, although generally Arizonans responded negatively. On the other hand, the *Deseret News*, official newspaper of the Mormons, applauded the actions of Pyle and his little band of one hundred. An editorial of July 27, 1953 expressed the hope that the Arizona governor could stamp out polygamy lest it become "a cancer of a sort that is beyond hope of human repair."

In 1954 the case of *State v. Vera Black* began. Black's husband was an Arizona Fundamentalist who had received parole after the Short Creek raid. At the time of the prosecution he was not living with her; therefore she was not engaged in a polygamous marriage. Nevertheless, the state claimed that she was rearing her children in an immoral atmosphere, arguing that the immorality lay in the religion she taught. The state offered to let Black keep her children, requiring simply that she swear to teach those children to follow the marriage and sex laws of the state. Black refused. The state seized the children, and the courts upheld that action.

Children of plural marriages in Utah became in law wards of the state, because, as the court ruled, "There must be no compromise with evil."[19] In response to the decision of the state supreme court, on January 28, 1956 the *Deseret News* applauded. But despite all prosecutions, and despite the guarantee of loss of their children if they were detected, the Fundamentalists continued to practice their religion. They dispersed into less conspicuous areas, abandoning highly visible communities for the anonymity of the cities or congregating in smaller groups, and by the mid-1970s their numbers reached an estimated thirty-five thousand. Plural marriages prospered, even in the cities of the Mormon state.

Despite forty years of persecution, the Fundamentalists retained their religious freedom. In 1970 the *Deseret News* reported that the census bureau had warned its census takers to be alert for possible polygamy among Mormons and Indians. And in 1975 the Salt Lake City *Tribune* reported that "polygamy continues in Utah and surrounding areas. The law says it's illegal and it's banned by the LDS church." But it continued to flourish among the true believers, numbering in the thousands. It continued to grow, and it included the "wealthy and prominent," the "deeply religious," and many who led "well adjusted lives."[20] And in 1983 there appeared at least one indicator that the years of struggle might have a faint hope of culminating in success. In that year a judge in Salt Lake City ordered the federal government to explain in court its reasons for prohibiting polygamy. U.S. district judge A. Sherman Christensen, hearing a case in which a policeman fired for polygamy had challenged the constitutionality of antipolygamy laws, ruled that the government of the United States should be a defendant in the case.[21]

It appeared that Utah might finally break new ground in the civil rights arena. After a dilatory performance in regard to the rights of women, blacks, and other minorities, Utah potentially could be the site of a landmark decision with respect to religious freedom. And ironically the Mormon church, which had fled to Deseret in pursuit of freedom to practice its religion, polygamy and all, without government interference, would take the conservative position.

Notes

1. Peter Wiley and Robert Gottlieb, *Empires in the Sun: The Rise of the New American West* (New York: Putnam, 1982), 156.
2. Ibid., 159. For a discussion of the Mormon media programs, including a listing of LDS-owned radio and television stations, see Leonard J. Arrington and David Bitton, *The Mormon Experience* (New York: Alfred A. Knopf, 1979), 270–71.
3. Dennis L. Wright, "State Legislative Response to the Federal Civil Rights Act: A Proposal," *Utah Law Review* (Winter 1964), 441; *Hammond Almanac, 1983*, 14th ed. (Maplewood, N.J., 1982), 445.
4. Wallace R. Bennett, "The Negro in Utah," *Utah Law Review* 3, no. 3 (Spring 1953), 340–41.
5. Ibid., 342–43; *De La Ysla v. Public Theatres Corp.*, 26 P.2d 818.
6. Bennett, "Negro in Utah," 343–48.
7. Wright, "State Legislative Response," 441–42; *Race Relations Law Reporter* 8 (1963), 253 (hereafter *RRLR*).

8. Wiley and Gottlieb, *Empires in the Sun*, 224–25.
9. Alvin M. Josephy Jr., *The Indian Heritage of America* (New York: Bantam, 1973), 353–54.
10. *Preston Allen for himself & other American Indians similarly situated v. Porter L. Merrell individually & as County Clerk, Duchesne County, Utah*, 305 P.2d 490; John H. Allen, "Denial of Voting Rights to Reservation Indians," *Utah Law Review* 5, no. 2 (Fall 1956), 247; *RRLR* 1, no. 6 (1956), 1067–68.
11. *RRLR* 2, no. 2 (1957), 167; *RRLR* 2, no. 1 (1957).
12. Ibid., 168–69; Ray Allen Billington, *Westward Expansion: A History of the American Frontier*, 4th ed. (New York: Macmillan, 1974), 580.
13. *RRLR* 2, no. 1 (1957), 170; *RRLR* 2, no. 6 (1957), 778; U.S. 932, 77 S. Ct. 809.
14. Matt S. Meier and Feliciano Rivera, *The Chicanos: A History of Mexican Americans* (New York: Hill and Wang, 1972), 270–74; *Hammond Almanac*, 445.
15. "Equal Protection and Supremacy Clause Limitations in State Legislation Restricting Aliens," *Utah Law Review*, no. 1 (1970): 136, 141–42.
16. Wiley and Gottlieb, *Empires in the Sun*, 159, 257–58.
17. Ibid., 161; *Kapp v. Salt Lake City*, 506 P.2d 809, 29 Utah 2d 1970; "Case Notes—Sex Discrimination," *Utah Law Review*, Spring 1974, 162–66. By 1978 even the legitimacy of the antidiscrimination act came under attack, but the court had by then broadened somewhat. The right of the state to involve itself in cases of alleged economic discrimination stood. See *Beehive Medical Electronics v. Industrial Commission*, 583 P.2d 53.
18. Quote in Samuel Woolley Taylor, *Rocky Mountain Empire: The Latter-day Saints Today* (New York: Macmillan, 1978), 101; Jerry R. Andersen, "Polygamy in Utah," *Utah Law Review* 5, no. 3 (Spring 1957), 386–87.
19. Andersen, "Polygamy," 387.
20. Taylor, *Rocky Mountain Empire*, 98, contains both quotes.
21. *Oklahoma City Times*, August 23, 1983.

Further Reading

See selected bibliography, pp. 271–78.

9

Blacks and Whites Together
Interracial Leadership in the Phoenix, Arizona, Civil Rights Movement
Mary S. Melcher

In the desert southwest states of Arizona and New Mexico, a small African American population and competition for recognition with two additional minority groups—American Indians and Mexican Americans—reduced black civil rights abilities. Nevertheless, as will be noted in the following article on the Arizona civil rights movement, African Americans did manage to achieve some successes. Partially this was due to able white and black leaders who worked together, such as Lincoln and Eleanor Ragsdale and white clergymen. They had much to accomplish; blacks in Phoenix existed with abysmal living conditions and segregated theaters, pools, parks, and education. One important early success was the desegregation of the schools in 1953, a year before the U.S. Supreme Court decision in *Brown v. Board of Education*. Mary S. Melcher, PhD, is also the author of *Pregnancy, Motherhood, and Choice in Twentieth Century Arizona*; she worked in public history for most of her career while enjoying the pursuit of multicultural history and the diverse stories of women and men of the Southwest.

Race relations in Phoenix changed dramatically in the 1950s and 1960s. In these years, determined black and white activists worked together in organizations such as the Greater Phoenix Council for Civic Unity, the National Association for the Advancement of Colored People, and the Urban League to break down

---

Originally published in the *Journal of Arizona History* 39, no. 2 (1991), 195–216. Reprinted by permission of the author, Mary S. Melcher, and the Arizona Historical Society.

educational barriers and end social discrimination.[1] Because of the efforts of these educated, middle-class men and women, Arizona schools were desegregated in 1953, one year before the U.S. Supreme Court ruled against public school segregation in *Brown v. Board of Education*. The eyes of the nation turned toward Phoenix and Arizona, where people observed firsthand the effects of desegregation. Today, the veterans of the civil rights movement in Phoenix look back with pride on their accomplishments of the past decades.

Phoenix's founders promoted the city as "a middle class utopia, a demiparadise in the desert." The only southwestern metropolis founded and run exclusively by Anglos, Arizona's capital city was not known for its racial tolerance. Most of its residents (except for American Indians) had come to the sunbelt from other parts of the country, including the East and West Coasts and the Great Lakes. Many with agricultural backgrounds migrated to Phoenix from Oklahoma, Texas, and Arkansas. These newcomers arrived in Arizona with their prejudices intact and tried to recast the Anglo-dominated society of their original homes. The 1920 city directory proudly advertised Phoenix as "a modern town of 40,000 people, and the best kind of people too. A very small percentage of Mexicans, negroes or foreigners."[2]

People of color were excluded from social and economic life in this "demiparadise." Compared to other minorities, African Americans experienced the greatest amount of overt racial discrimination and segregation. Laws limited their employment opportunities, forced them into segregated neighborhoods, denied them access to schools and public accommodations, and restricted their access to medical care.[3]

Educational and social segregation of blacks in Arizona dated back to territorial days. A 1909 law segregated pupils of African descent from Caucasians, except in high schools. Whenever twenty-five or more blacks matriculated to a high school, 15 percent of district residents could call an election to decide whether or not to place black and white students into separate but equal facilities. In fact, facilities were never equal once segregation was decreed.

Blacks experienced discrimination in other ways as well. The 1912 state constitution declared interracial marriages illegal. Reflecting racial bigotry, chapters of the Ku Klux Klan sprang up in Phoenix, Glendale, and Flagstaff in 1916 and 1917. In certain areas of Phoenix, Anglo homeowners banded together and signed restrictive covenants limiting the sale of land to whites only.[4]

Rather than meekly accept discrimination, African Americans found strength in organization. In 1919 black merchants Samuel Bayless and C. Credille formed the Phoenix Advancement League to combat racial injustice. During the Depression, the Colored Businessman's Association aided blacks whom the Community Welfare Council ignored, while the Phoenix Protection League fought employment discrimination. The Phoenix chapter of the Arizona Federation of Colored Women's Clubs also worked to improve conditions for blacks. Likewise, black churches sought to strengthen racial pride and community togetherness. Because as a rule Phoenix banned black organizations from using city auditoriums, the churches served as community halls.[5]

Despite discrimination, a small black middle class emerged during the early twentieth century. Black-owned hotels, grocery stores, restaurants, bars, pool halls, and even a beauty shop provided services to members of the black community. In 1921 Dr. Winston C. Hackett opened the Booker T. Washington Memorial Hospital on Jefferson Street to provide medical care to blacks.[6]

While a few black businesspersons prospered, prior to World War II most blacks (and many Mexican families) lived in poverty in the ghettos of southwest Phoenix. An influx of veterans and migrant cotton pickers after the war exacerbated the already horrible living arrangements. City-county health director Dr. H. L. McMartin decried the dilapidated hovels that served as homes in South Phoenix, along with the open backyard toilets and the crowded wooden shacks that lined the littered streets and dirty alleys. In far too many cases, squatters simply pitched tents and lived without electricity, water, or trash collection.[7]

Blacks who escaped these impoverished conditions still had to contend with segregation in theaters, parks, and swimming pools. At its annual midsummer picnic for children, the *Arizona Republic* diligently separated invitees according to race—blacks, Mexicans, and Anglos. Blacks could neither rent rooms in the city's motels and hotels nor eat in most of its restaurants.

Similar conditions existed in the city's schools. Grade schools were strictly segregated. A "Colored High School" was established in 1914 and renamed George Washington Carver High in 1943. When W. A. Robinson became Carver's principal in 1945, he campaigned aggressively to improve the school. Robinson recruited black teachers with master's degrees from around the country and demanded that district administrators improve facilities at the black high school. Refusing to accept cast-off stock from white schools, he improved the equipment and supplies at Carver and added music and art classes to the curriculum. For the first time, art teacher Eugene Grigsby obtained tools for making pots and jewelry and equipment for developing photographs.[8]

Despite these and other improvements at Carver High School, some Phoenicians still saw educational segregation as a blight on the city. In the late 1940s, white and black activists organized to combat institutionalized racism. Motivated by a deep aversion to segregation, whites strove to understand racial oppression and identify with the blacks who suffered under it. Many of Phoenix's black activists had long personal histories of involvement with the National Association for the Advancement of Colored People (NAACP); several came from middle-class families with a strong heritage of activism. Ted Ragsdale, the uncle of prominent Phoenix black mortician Lincoln Ragsdale, had been lynched because of his work as president of the Oklahoma NAACP. Although meant to inspire fear, the lynching had the opposite effect. As Lincoln Ragsdale explained:

> It didn't put fear. It put aggressiveness in us that we're going to have to work it through the system. You can't work it with a gun because you can't outshoot white folks. There are more white folks than black folks. So you have to work it intellectually, hard work, saving your money. . . . You have to outsmart him.[9]

White men like attorney William Mahoney and physician Fred Holmes could not duplicate the tragic, bitter memories of someone like Ragsdale, yet they were equally determined to challenge segregation in Phoenix. In 1947 Holmes invited Professor Lewis Wirth, a scholar from the University of Chicago, to speak about race relations. About three hundred Phoenicians, blacks and whites, attended the event. After the talk, they organized the Greater Phoenix Council for Civic Unity (GPCCU). In the early years, the group devoted most of its attention to the desegregation of Phoenix public schools. Once they had secured this goal, the GPCCU became an important umbrella organization working for racial justice.[10]

William Mahoney recalled the organization's argument to press for desegregation: "the die is pretty well cast in the South or in an old city like New York or Chicago, but . . . we, here, are present for creation. We're making a society where the die isn't cast. It can be for good or ill." Mahoney and his fellow activists also stressed that "you don't want to educate bigots."[11]

Organizing the GPCCU was not without tension, according to Ruth Finn, a white activist and wife of attorney Herb Finn. Fearful that they would be labeled communists, Fred Holmes proposed that all members sign an oath swearing that they were not "reds." Many of the organizers resented the idea, but went along with it anyway.[12]

Eugene and Thomasena Grigsby were among the blacks who joined the GPCCU. The couple had moved to Phoenix in 1946, when Eugene accepted a teaching position at Carver High School. Through the GPCCU and the Urban League, the Grigsbys met other middle-class blacks, as well as whites, who were interested in changing the racial atmosphere in Phoenix. Segregation-minded Phoenicians saw them as troublemakers as they broke the barriers separating the races in a very segregated city. Attorney Mahoney's activities in organizations such as the GPCCU, the Urban League, and the NAACP probably cost him the business of conservative clients. According to Thomasena Grigsby, Phoenix activists may not have been in the majority, but they had the brainpower. "We were like yeast in bread," she explained. When they came together, things started to happen.[13]

The GPCCU joined with the Arizona Council for Civic Unity, a statewide organization, to press for school desegregation. In their first effort, they spent thousands of dollars to hire California civil rights lawyers Al Wiren and Loren Miller to press their cause. Aware that several desegregation cases were moving toward the U.S. Supreme Court, Wiren and Miller filed suit in federal court to desegregate Arizona schools. U.S. district court judge David Ling dismissed the case, however, instructing the attorneys to exhaust first their remedies in the state courts before appearing in front of the federal bench.[14]

Undaunted, the GPCCU lobbied the legislature and, in 1951, secured a statute giving local school boards the option to desegregate voluntarily. Unfortunately, the law lacked teeth. As independent legal entities, the Phoenix school districts chose not to desegregate. An attempt to achieve desegregation through a ballot initiative failed by a 2–1 margin. Finally, on February 9, 1953, H. B. Daniels, a black attorney, and Herb Finn, a white, argued a case in the Maricopa County Court against high school segregation. The GPCCU having exhausted its legal funds, Daniels paid the five dollar filing fee from his own pocket. In a landmark decision, superior court judge Fred C. Struckmeyer handed down the first legal opinion in the United States declaring school segregation unconstitutional. "A half century of intolerance is enough," Struckmeyer declared.[15] Shortly thereafter, Maricopa County Court judge Charles Bernstein also ruled in Daniels's and Finn's favor, striking down segregation in Arizona grade schools. According to William Mahoney, Arizona became "a footnote in Brown vs. Board of Education," when a clerk from the U.S. Supreme Court requested a copy of Bernstein's opinion in the Phoenix case.[16]

While Mahoney and others were "darn proud" of their victory, some blacks experienced mixed feelings. Teachers at all-black Carver High School had provided excellent educations for black children and enjoyed harmonious relationships with parents. Carver also fielded an excellent football team that compiled a twenty-one-game winning streak between 1951 and 1953. As integration proceeded, coaches in the Phoenix Union High School District recruited Carver's top-rated athletes. Black teachers, meanwhile, were reassigned to other schools in the district. Even parents who rejoiced at desegregation hated to see Carver close its doors.[17]

Although Phoenix set an example for the nation when it integrated its public schools, living conditions for African Americans remained abysmal. Housing and public facilities were still segregated, and job discrimination was rampant. Hoping that Phoenicians would try to improve their image "once the limelight fell on them," civil rights activists turned for help to Thomasena Grigsby. In addition to her work with the GPCCU, the Urban League, and the NAACP, Grigsby also wrote articles for national black newspapers. Approached in 1952 by Lincoln Ragsdale about Phoenix's all-white veterans' cemetery, Grigsby wrote an article for the Chicago *Defender*, a black newspaper. In it, she explained how Ragsdale's mortuary was holding the body of Thomas Reed, a black serviceman killed in Korea whose family wanted him buried with his fellow veterans in Greenwood Cemetery. As Grigsby later explained:

> To talk about that in Phoenix alone wasn't going to do it. The white newspapers weren't concerned about it particularly. The only thing you could do was to get this out of the community. Remember Phoenix has always been a tourist town. People who come to a tourist town want to feel it's peaceful, restful, etc. If they get the idea that this is going on in Phoenix, they might begin to question this [discrimination].

Reed was eventually buried in the previously all-white veterans' cemetery. By publicizing events in Phoenix, Thomasena Grigsby helped break the pattern of segregation.[18]

While Grigsby was employing her journalistic skills to improve racial conditions, Lincoln Ragsdale waged a private battle to live in a white neighborhood. Real estate agents and banks restricted the residential mobility of blacks by refusing to show them houses in white neighborhoods and by denying them loans. Ragsdale bypassed the restrictions by having a white friend purchase a house at 1606 West Thomas Road, far north of the black enclaves in South Phoenix and around Washington and Van Buren Streets in downtown Phoenix. The friend then transferred the title to Ragsdale while the deal was still in escrow. Even so, Ragsdale had bought the house almost sight unseen. The realtors, he explained, "wouldn't let me in."

Although Ragsdale, his wife, Eleanor, and their four children lived in their home on Thomas Road for seventeen years, the neighborhood never accepted them. Vandals spray-painted the word "nigger" on their house, and white playmates mistreated the Ragsdale children. Every new police officer who patrolled the area invariably stopped Ragsdale as he returned late at night. "I looked suspicious," the thriving mortician explained. "And all you have to do to look suspicious is to be driving a Cadillac and be black.... When I'd see him coming with his lights, I'd get my ownership of the car out and show him my driver's license." In the face of injustice, the Ragsdale family kept their house neat and in good repair and "dug in their heels." They realized that their presence in a white neighborhood was a source of pride to many blacks who might lose faith in their own ability to challenge segregation if the Ragsdales moved out.

Lincoln Ragsdale also suffered harassment from the business community, probably because of his outspoken activities as vice president of the local NAACP. The bank repossessed his car after he missed one payment. When he missed a monthly payment on a business loan, the bank threatened to accelerate collection of the $90,000 debt. This would have ruined him in 1964. Fortunately, the bank official with whom Ragsdale was dealing left town, and Ragsdale was able to make two payments through a secretary. His loan remained in force.[19]

Ragsdale and others devoted much of their time to the NAACP. Two branches of the organization had been founded in the Phoenix area during the 1940s—a Maricopa County group headed by H. B. Daniels and a South Phoenix branch under the leadership of Dr. Robert Phillips and his wife, Louise. Their victories, however, were few, and their work mostly consisted of lodging official complaints against discrimination and police brutality.[20] Things changed after the arrival of the Reverend George Brooks in 1953. Young and well-educated, the twenty-seven-year-old clergyman, with the help of Presbyterian elders, organized the Southminster Presbyterian Church in South Phoenix. In 1960 he convinced the two Phoenix-area branches of the NAACP to merge, and within six months Brooks became president of the revitalized Maricopa County NAACP.[21]

As president, Brooks aggressively fought discrimination in employment. At a 1962 U.S. Civil Rights Commission hearing in Phoenix, representatives of the

NAACP and the Urban League decried black unemployment and underemployment in both the private and the public sector. In an effort "to move into every aspect of economic life in this community," Brooks and Ragsdale approached employers and urged them to hire blacks. Brooks recalled their meeting with Valley National Bank president Jim Pattrick:

> Lincoln [Ragsdale] was brash, nasty . . . he would back him up into a corner and I was the good guy. I would pull him out. Then he [Pattrick] would get belligerent again, and Lincoln would back him up again, and I would pull him out . . . that's what you call creative conflict. We didn't know it, but that's what we did.

Regardless, the tactic worked. Pattrick agreed to integrate the Valley National workforce and hired Wilbur Hankins as the bank's first black teller.[22]

Brooks visited other employers, including IBM, Goldwater's, Food City, and Woolworth's. When Woolworth's refused to integrate, black and white clergy and NAACP picketers walked the street in front of the store carrying signs that read: "Stop Discrimination" and "Woolworth's Discriminates Against Black People." According to Brooks, the white ministers, priests, and rabbis were among the NAACP's most reliable supporters; they answered to a higher employer and were available to picket during the day. Eventually, Woolworth's national office ordered its Phoenix store to hire blacks.[23]

Rabbi Albert Plotkin was among the religious leaders who carried a picket sign. As part of the North Phoenix Corporation Ministry, he and other liberal white clergymen made it a point to know black ministers. Many of them joined the NAACP and the Urban League. When George Brooks called on them to picket, they responded with enthusiasm. "He had a rather commanding 'I need you,'" Rabbi Plotkin recalled. "George was the catalyst. He had the personality."[24]

Like other black ministers throughout the country, Brooks was financially independent of the white community. In Phoenix, as elsewhere, the black churches provided financial as well as moral support for the civil rights movement. They also served as meeting places. The Maricopa County NAACP gathered either at the First Institutional Baptist Church or at the Tanner Chapel, both of which were larger than Brooks's own church.[25]

Sometimes, NAACP leaders were able to head off discrimination before it occurred. During the spring of 1962, local rumors reached the Maricopa County chapter that a large company was using the Arizona Welfare Department to hire high school graduates with no previous work experience; the one catch—they had to be white. It appeared that the state employment service was collaborating with private industry to discriminate against blacks. When George Brooks and Herb Eli of the Urban League visited the employment office, they learned that the Motorola Corporation was indeed trying to hire only white workers.[26]

Brooks immediately requested a meeting with Arizona Attorney General Robert Pickrell. "I was *good* that day," Brooks later boasted. "I accused the welfare department and the state employment services of being in collusion with private industry to keep black folks unemployed." When the Phoenix newspapers picked up the story, Motorola quickly integrated its workforce.[27]

In addition to ending employment discrimination, the NAACP also fought to dismantle segregation of public facilities. Barbara Callahan of the Phoenix chapter's Youth Department organized several sit-ins on one summer day in 1960. Energized by events occurring throughout the country, young black Phoenicians sat in at lunch counters downtown. In each instance, they were served. The absence of resistance from white owners and managers suggested to Callahan and Brooks that many Phoenicians were ready to change, and only needed the impetus. Also, blacks were a small minority in Phoenix and, therefore, did not pose a threat to the overwhelming white majority.[28]

Phoenix also mirrored the nation at large in the sense that the NAACP pursued a more confrontational approach than did the Urban League. According to Eugene Grigsby, although the Urban League and the NAACP both worked to halt discrimination, the NAACP was the "pusher, the firebrand." George Brooks agreed, adding that "we were the War Department, and they were the State Department." The NAACP did the "dirty work," and the Urban League cleaned up the mess.[29]

While the Urban League and the NAACP struggled to integrate Phoenix businesses and public facilities, the GPCCU called for a city commission to oversee race relations and stop discrimination. After nearly two years of lobbying, the Phoenix City Council established the Human Relations Commission on July 2, 1963. During its first eight months, the commission investigated numerous complaints from black Phoenicians who had been barred from restaurants, hotels, and places of recreation.

Initially, the commission attempted to persuade businesses to integrate. When it became obvious that persuasion was not working, it recommended passage of an ordinance that would make segregation of public facilities illegal. The city council responded on June 16, 1964, with a Public Accommodations Law. Henceforth, it was unlawful "to discriminate in places of public accommodation against any person because of race, creed, national origin, or ancestry." The Human Relations Commission set up a Public Accommodations Committee to oversee enforcement of the ordinance.[30]

Dr. Martin Luther King's appearances before Phoenix and Tempe audiences in 1964 galvanized activists in the Salt River Valley. Brooks, who had worked with King in Atlanta, invited the civil rights leader to Arizona, and Rabbi Plotkin solicited funds from Jewish businessmen to defray the cost of the visit. In moving speeches on June 3 to 450 Kiwanis members and before a crowd of 3,000 at Goodwin Auditorium on the Arizona State University campus, King called for nonviolent action "to get rid of the last vestiges of segregation." "You may throw us in jail . . . bomb our homes . . . threaten our little children," King resolved, "and—difficult as it is—we will still love you. . . . This is the meaning of nonviolent action."[31]

While King's followers in Phoenix fought segregation, they also worked to improve the cultural life of black youth. As chairman of the Urban League's Education and Youth Committee, Eugene Grigsby organized exhibits and sponsored murals at the juvenile detention home and at public housing projects. The Urban League also held workshops to interest children in art activities and build up a sense of community. Grigsby, former high school principal Morrison Warren, and others stressed the importance of providing role models for black youth. Through education, they helped students understand racism and develop positive self-images.

Grigsby stressed the importance of people learning to live together and to appreciate each other's differences, while accepting their own self-worth. He was appalled by Carver High School students who rejected their African heritage. Some girls in his art class drew self-portraits in which they were blond-haired and blue-eyed. Grigsby remembered, in particular, a girl who wore an ugly blond wig. He was pleasantly surprised one day when she came to school without the wig and wearing her hair in a natural style. "I beamed because she had accepted herself," he explained. "And until one accepts oneself and one's own heritage, then it's difficult for one to accept somebody else and to exchange and share."[32]

A multireligious group hoped to achieve these same goals through Any Town Interfaith Camp. Organizers like Rabbi Plotkin and Nancy Phillips recognized that because of de facto segregation in housing, white children did not meet blacks in their classrooms or neighborhoods. For one week each summer, black, white, and Mexican American boys and girls gathered at the Interfaith Camp to discuss prejudice, race, bigotry, religion, nationality, and family, and to get to know one another. The sessions produced community leaders, including future Arizona House minority leader Art Hamilton.[33]

Phoenix civil rights leaders also fought to preserve for minorities the fundamental right to vote. The task was not an easy one. Activists recall that in the early 1960s some Young Republicans tried to intimidate blacks, Hispanics, and poor people who were waiting in line to cast their ballots. According to Madge Copeland, committeewoman for her predominantly black precinct, Phoenix attorney William Rehnquist mailed letters to voters in her precinct; if they failed to respond, he claimed that they did not live at the addresses where they were registered and tried to have them removed from the voting rolls. Witnesses in South Phoenix reported that Rehnquist asked voters at Reverend Brooks's church, which also served as a polling place, to read from the Constitution. If they were unable to do so, he insisted that they not be allowed to vote. Brooks, who served as election officer, immediately stopped the voting and confronted Rehnquist. "I told him that he was interfering with the people's right of franchise," Brooks stated, "and I was going to call the sheriff and have him arrested." Rehnquist left the polling place.[34]

While some activists fought to ensure democratic voting rights for all, others were concerned by the exclusion of minorities from city government. Prior to the mid-1960s, the Charter Government Committee (CGC) held a tight grip on Phoenix city elections. Formed in 1949 and supported by the likes of newspaper publisher Eugene Pulliam and businessman Barry Goldwater, the CGC rallied Phoenicians behind its slate and selected successful candidates for Phoenix mayor and city council throughout the 1950s. Critics complained that the CGC represented mainly the white middle and upper classes, and indeed nearly all CGC candidates were conservative Republicans who lived in the affluent areas of north Phoenix.[35]

In 1963 some members of the GPCCU formed the so-called Act Committee to challenge the CGC. Functioning independently of the GPCCU, the Act Committee ran a slate of candidates for city council that included Lincoln Ragsdale, Ed Korrick, and Manuel Tena, all of whom were active in civil rights. "We didn't win," Jewish activist Fran Waldman boasted, "but did we shake up city hall! Ed Korrick almost won." The following election year, in 1965, the CGC placed black educator Morrison Warren on its slate, and he won election to the Phoenix city council. Warren was reelected in 1967, and that same year Ed Korrick also gained a council seat, running on former mayor Milton Graham's Citizens' Ticket. Warren lost his bid for a third term in 1969, but two years later

Calvin Goode, another black, was elected to the council as a CGC candidate. The control of Phoenix politics by upper middle-class whites had begun to dissolve.[36]

By the mid-1960s, segregation was illegal in Phoenix. In 1965, the Arizona legislature followed the lead of the U.S. Congress and passed a civil rights act that forbade discrimination in housing, voting, employment, and public accommodations. But outlawing segregation and discrimination did not automatically bring about social and economic integration for blacks. In 1964 the local chapter of the Congress of Racial Equality (CORE) staged a demonstration to protest extreme poverty in South Phoenix. Responding to pressure from CORE and other organizations, then-mayor Graham created Leadership and Education for the Advancement of Phoenix (LEAP), an advisory council that would act as a clearinghouse for federal programs designed to better conditions in the city's poorest neighborhoods.[37]

In 1966 LEAP became a city department administering federal War on Poverty funds. These government-sponsored programs provided new educational and employment opportunities, but many activists continued to express dismay at the incredibly slow economic progress of blacks and Hispanics. Although the federal government had provided $15 million to improve conditions in South Phoenix, little had been accomplished. The majority of the city's blacks and many Hispanics still lived in terrible slums within the 21.2-square-mile target area. Thirty percent of South Phoenix residents subsisted on less than $3,000 a year.[38]

Persistent racial tension in South Phoenix and alleged police harassment erupted into violence on July 26, 1967. Rioters, whom George Brooks described as radical noisemakers (many from CORE), burned down a house belonging to a Mrs. Davis. Brooks played the role of "strong man" in an attempt to calm the situation. "We're not going to do anything foolish in this town," he warned, "and if you do it, you're going to have to come by me."[39]

Brooks debated the issues with the young protestors on a street corner near Osborn Project. Finally, they agreed to meet with Mayor Graham in an effort to obtain more federal monies for fighting poverty and improving education. "We kept moving," Brooks recalled, "but without the kind of volatility we had in other parts of the country." Even so, the riot resulted in over two hundred arrests and the imposition of a curfew. Four days later, Mayor Graham lifted the curfew and began to push for improved training and employment opportunities for minorities.[40]

In Phoenix, as in the nation at large, men generally had exercised leadership in the struggle for equal rights. Unlike in the South, where work in the civil rights movement led many women to reexamine their roles as females, Phoenix women were content to work behind the scenes as volunteers with the GPCCU, the Urban League, and the NAACP. Ruth Finn points out that much of the civil rights activity in Phoenix occurred in the 1950s and 1960s, before many American women challenged traditional assumptions of female roles. Finn and her fellow activist Barbara Callahan speculate that a strong female could have assumed leadership of one of Phoenix's civil rights organizations, but that most women were too busy raising children or saw themselves as helpmates to the men. Phoenix women did not make the connection between racism and sexism as did white women in the national movement.[41]

Nevertheless, several dynamic women played vital roles in the Phoenix civil rights struggle. For years, Fran Waldman singlehandedly organized GPCUU events and won a reputation as "the important woman behind the organization." Barbara Callahan helped young people stage sit-ins during the 1960s, and Madge Copeland labored tirelessly within the Democratic Party to elect blacks to public office. Like their sisters nationally, Phoenix women picketed, lobbied, marched, and shared information. William Mahoney discovered that women were more effective than men in "leaning" on legislators and that they did not hesitate to make their feelings known. They were not worried about offending people in power and operated from deep feelings about the fundamental issue of civil rights. Support from southern white women living in Phoenix assisted the NAACP in its struggle. George Brooks remembers women with long southern drawls discussing the issues at meetings. According to Brooks, they would say "we know what we're talking about. We've been there. We know what they do to black folks in the South." Unfortunately, these courageous women, white and black, have received little public recognition for their work.[42]

By working together, this small band of activists—black and white, male and female—broke down the barriers of racial discrimination and profoundly changed the political and social fabric of Phoenix. At a time when, according to Ruth Finn, "screaming injustices . . . had the moral and legal approval of the courts, the legislature, and the populace," they helped push forward legislation and court decisions that altered the public perception of morality and rendered bigoted behavior unacceptable. Of course, injustices still exist in Phoenix as they do elsewhere. But, Finn observes, "it's a different world" now than it was in 1948.[43]

Today, leaders of the Phoenix civil rights movement recall their efforts with satisfaction and pride. George Brooks believes that his confrontational style alienated many people in the Phoenix power structure. But he has no regrets and is glad that he wasn't a "good boy." Barbara Callahan learned through the movement that people could bring about meaningful change. White activists like Rabbi Plotkin and Nancy Phillips achieved a sense of personal satisfaction through their work with blacks and their successes in swaying public opinion. Councilman Calvin Goode, who as a boy had attended an all-black grade school in Gila Bend, followed the advice he had given to others and became a community leader in Phoenix. Like many of his fellow activists of the 1960s, he looks back on significant accomplishments while pointing to the increasing poverty and joblessness that plague the black community. Even as a wealthy businessman living in Paradise Valley, Lincoln Ragsdale is barred from admission to the local country club. "The snake's head is cut off," he warns, "but his tail is still wiggling." The battle for equality is far from over.[44]

Notes

1. Recent studies emphasize the role of local leadership in the civil rights movement. See, for example, William H. Chafe, *Civilities and Civil Rights: Greensboro, North Carolina and the Black Struggle for Equality* (New York: Oxford University Press, 1980); David R. Colburn, *Racial Change and Community Crisis: St. Augustine, Florida, 1877–1980* (New York: Columbia University Press, 1985); Robert J. Norrell, *Reaping the Whirlwind: The Civil Rights Movement in Tuskegee* (New York: Alfred A. Knopf, 1985).
2. *1920 Phoenix City and Salt River Valley Directory* (Phoenix: Directory Company, 1921), 1.
3. Michael Kotlanger, "Phoenix, Arizona: 1920–1940" (PhD diss., Arizona State University, 1983), 445. Although Mexicans and Mexican Americans also experienced segregation in schools and public accommodations, their status was not mandated by law.
4. Richard Harris, *The First Hundred Years: A History of Arizona Blacks* (Apache Junction: Relmo Publishers, 1983), 7, 47, 52, 59. Roger D. Hardaway, "Unlawful Love: A History of Arizona's Miscegenation Law," *Journal of Arizona History* 27 (Winter 1986), 377–90; Sue Wilson Abbey, "The Ku Klux Klan in Arizona, 1921–1925," *Journal of Arizona History*, 14 (Spring 1973), 10–30.
5. Harris, *First Hundred Years*, 53, 57; Kotlanger, "Phoenix," 458. Occasionally, black organizations were able to rent the Phoenix Union High School auditorium for their events.
6. Kotlanger, "Phoenix," 450; Madge Copeland interview, January 26, 1985. All interviews cited in this article were conducted by the author and are located in the Arizona Historical Foundation, Hayden Library, Arizona State University, Tempe. From 1929 to 1952, Madge Copeland operated the only beauty shop in Phoenix that catered to black women. She was also active in the Democratic Party.
7. Kotlanger, "Phoenix," 459.

8. Calvin Goode interview, January 24, 1990; Sue Perkins interview, February 20, 1986; Copeland interview; George Brooks interview, January 31, 1990; Albert Plotkin interview, January 29, 1990; William Mahoney interview, February 16, 1990; Thomasena Grigsby interview, February 7, 1990; Eugene Grigsby interview, February 12, 1990; Ruth Finn interview, March 30, 1990. Harris, *First Hundred Years*, 65–72; Bradford Luckingham, *Phoenix: The History of a Southwestern Metropolis* (Tucson: University of Arizona Press, 1989), 173.
9. Brooks, Thomasena Grigsby, Eugene Grigsby, Mahoney, Finn, and Plotkin interviews; Lincoln Ragsdale interview, April 8, 1990. Both Mahoney and Finn recalled being asked to leave Phoenix restaurants when they attempted to dine with black friends.
10. Mahoney interview; Fran Waldman interview, July 17, 1990; Greater Phoenix Council for Civic Unity, *To Secure These Rights* (Phoenix: Phoenix Sun, 1961). GPCCU members worked with the National Conference of Christians and Jews, the Urban League, and the NAACP to combat discrimination based upon race and religion.
11. Mahoney interview.
12. Finn interview.
13. Eugene Grigsby, Thomasena Grigsby, and Mahoney interviews.
14. Mahoney and Finn interviews; Joe Stocker, "Remembering a Challenge to Segregation," *Arizona Republic* (Phoenix), December 11, 1988, section C, 2.
15. W. A. Robinson, "The Progress of Integration in the Phoenix Schools," *Journal of Negro Education* 25 (Fall 1956), 371. Frederick C. Struckmeyer, Maricopa County Superior Court Order and Court Opinion No. 72909, February 9, 1953; Elections, Official Canvasses, 1911–1982, Box 1, both in Arizona Department of Library, Archives and Public Records, Phoenix. Mahoney interview. The school desegregation initiative lost by a vote of 104,226 to 57,970. Tucson public schools voluntarily desegregated in 1951.
16. Hayzel Burton Daniels, "A Black Magistrate's Struggles," in *Arizona Memories*, ed. Anne Hodges Morgan and Rennard Strickland, (Tucson: University of Arizona Press, 1984), 337–38; Finn and Mahoney interviews.
17. "Era of Pride and Shame Closed with Carver High," *Arizona Republic*, February 6, 1990, section D, 6; Harris, *First Hundred Years*, 72; Robinson, "Progress of Integration," 373. The Phoenix Union High School District did not appeal Judge Bernstein's ruling. Some blacks later maintained that the district accepted desegregation because Carver High School was too expensive to maintain. Others claimed that PUHSD officials knew that the federal courts would soon outlaw school segregation and therefore decided not to fight Judge Bernstein's ruling. "Citizens' Group Gives Help," *Black Heritage in Arizona* (November 1976), 7.
18. Thomasena Grigsby interview; and her article, "Father Wins Fight to Have Korea Vet Buried in Hometown Cemetery," *Chicago Defender*, January 19, 1952, 1. Grigsby also wrote articles for the Pittsburgh *Courier* and the Norfolk *Journal*, highlighting the activities of exceptional blacks. Claude Barnett of the Associated Negro Press distributed her columns to black newspapers throughout the country.

19. Ragsdale interview. Ragsdale's testimony on housing discrimination in Phoenix appeared in *Hearing Before the United States Commission on Civil Rights, Phoenix, Arizona, February 3, 1962* (Washington, D.C.: Government Printing Office, 1962), 46–49. Housing discrimination is also discussed in GPCCU, *To Secure These Rights*, 9–13.
20. "Black Population Smallest," *Black Heritage in Arizona* (November 1976), 8; Brooks interview.
21. Brooks interview; "NAACP Chapter to Seat Officers," *Arizona Republic*, January 20, 1961.
22. *Hearing Before the U.S. Commission on Civil Rights*, 49–59, 62–63. Brooks and Ragsdale interviews. Ragsdale confirmed that he played the "bad guy" in confrontations with employers.
23. Brooks interview.
24. Plotkin interview. In 1963, George Brooks was elected moderator of the predominantly white Presbytery of Phoenix, which had 15,500 members and fifty-two churches. His position no doubt helped him in the civil rights struggle. See "Negro Moderator for Presbytery," *Arizona Republic*, January 12, 1963.
25. Brooks interview; Aldon Morris, *The Origins of the Civil Rights Movement* (New York: Free Press, 1984).
26. Brooks interview; "Note Sent by Welfare Officer," *Arizona Republic*, April 12, 1962, 11; "Complaint on Hiring Lodged," *Phoenix Gazette*, April 24, 1962, 18.
27. Brooks interview.
28. Barbara Callahan interview, February 24, 1990. Blacks composed 15 percent of the Phoenix population in 1960. See Luckingham, *Phoenix*, 175.
29. Brooks, Callahan, Thomasena Grigsby, and Eugene Grigsby interviews; Robert Weisbrot, *Freedom Bound: A History of America's Civil Rights Movement* (New York: W. W. Norton, 1990), 167.
30. Waldman interview; Human Rights Commission, *First Annual Report . . . 1963–64* (City of Phoenix, 1964), 2–6.
31. "King Calls for Nonviolent Action," *Arizona Republic*, June 4, 1964, section A, 8; Brooks, Plotkin, and Ragsdale interviews; Nancy Phillips interview, March 2, 1990.
32. Grigsby interview.
33. Plotkin and Phillips interviews.
34. Plotkin, Brooks, Goode, Copeland, and Mahoney interviews.
35. Waldman interview; Luckingham, *Phoenix*, 150–53.
36. Waldman interview; "Election Candidate Status, 1963," 9–11, in City of Phoenix File no. 3500, Arizona State Archives, Phoenix. Luckingham, *Phoenix*, 179. Waldman believes that the Act Committee had a direct effect on the CGC's decision to integrate its slate of candidates.
37. *Economic and Cultural Progress of the Negro* (New York: National Urban League, 1965), 133–34; *Arizona Revised Statutes*, vol. 41, sections 1401–42; Luckingham, *Phoenix*, 178; John Crow, *Discrimination, Poverty and the Negro: Arizona in the National Context* (Tucson: University of Arizona Press, 1968), 3; Weisbrot, *Freedom Bound*, 87–92.

38. Luckingham, *Phoenix*, 213–14.
39. Ibid., 214; Brooks interview.
40. Brooks interview; Luckingham, *Phoenix*, 178, 215. Later critics said that much of the money went to fight crime rather than to boost anti-poverty programs.
41. Copeland, Brooks, Plotkin, Goode, Mahoney, and Waldman interviews; Sara Evans, *Personal Politics: The Roots of Women's Liberation in the Civil Rights Movement and the New Left* (New York: Random House, 1980). Paula Giddings, *When and Where I Enter: The Impact of Black Women on Race and Sex in America* (New York: William Morrow, 1984), 261–67, argues that black women were a dynamic force in the black church nationally, where they represented moral and social authority in decision-making. The church played an important role in the civil rights movement, and many black women pressured ministers to open their churches for movement activities.
42. Mahoney and Brooks interviews.
43. Finn interview.
44. Brooks, Callahan, Phillips, Plotkin, Goode, and Ragsdale interviews. William Mahoney believes that his civil rights activities influenced President John F. Kennedy to name him U.S. ambassador to Ghana in 1961.

Further Reading

See selected bibliography, pp. 271–78.

10

The Modern
Civil Rights
Movement
in New Mexico
George M. Cooper

In the following essay, George Cooper notes a situation in New Mexico similar to that in Arizona. African Americans in New Mexico did not always present a united front, they composed a small percentage of the population, and their rights seemed incidental to those of other state minorities. Yet as early as 1947 students at the University of New Mexico successfully boycotted an eatery that refused service to blacks. That led to an Albuquerque public accommodations law and eventually to a statute from the New Mexico legislature. Civil rights activities took place in other cities of the state, such as Carlsbad, Hobbs, Las Cruces, and Santa Fe. George Cooper teaches history at Lone Star College near Houston, Texas. Among his accomplishments, Cooper has served as president of both the East Texas Historical Association and the South Texas Historical Association. His article was previously published in Bruce Glasrud's edited collection, *African American History in New Mexico.*

A discussion of the modern African American civil rights movement often starts with the *Brown v. Board of Education of Topeka* decision handed down by the U.S. Supreme Court in 1954. In many states it is seen as stimulating the drive for equality by the single largest minority in the United States prior to the onset

---

Originally published in *African American History in New Mexico*, edited by Bruce A. Glasrud (Albuquerque: University of New Mexico Press, 2013), 201–12. Reprinted by permission of the University of New Mexico Press and the author.

of the twenty-first century. However, in New Mexico that particular watershed event did not constitute a vital happening for several unique reasons.

Foremost is the fact that at no time during the modern civil rights movement did African Americans in New Mexico ever exceed more than 3 percent of the population of the entire state. African Americans were the third-largest minority in New Mexico in 1950, but they were a distant third, less than 2 percent of the population.[1] With the number of African Americans in New Mexico being so small, their fight for equality and civil rights often included the struggle of the other minorities as well.

Secondly, because of their small numbers and their dispersal throughout the state, African Americans found it difficult to present a unified front significant enough to attract the attention of decision makers in the state. To a large degree, African Americans took few independent actions of their own to alleviate discriminatory practices by the dominant white society. Thirdly, we need to expand our study of the civil rights movement within the restricted area of New Mexico and across the ethnic boundaries of the state, and we must also expand our temporal horizons. The state government of New Mexico long had addressed issues of minority rights; however, in most instances the issue of black rights was incidental to the concerns of other groups. Nonetheless, in some cases the people of New Mexico took corrective action well ahead of the rest of the nation, especially the southern states. The New Mexico state legislature early ratified a fair employment act. In fact, the state passed its fair employment act in 1948, before the U.S. Congress enacted similar legislation. Indeed, the national bill proposing establishment of a permanent Fair Employment Practices Board was sponsored and championed by New Mexico senator Dennis Chavez. In 1951 Carlsbad desegregated its schools to avoid losing accreditation for the entire system, well ahead of cities in neighboring states. Tucumcari integrated its secondary schools at the request of African American parents who didn't want their children to attend out-of-town schools. The state's largest city, Albuquerque, enacted an antidiscrimination ordinance on February 13, 1952.[2] In 1962 the Hobbs City Council appointed a committee comprised of both African Americans and whites to address the issues of racial intolerance in the city. While African Americans played a role statewide, with the exception of the Hobbs committee they were not the only minority involved in the struggle for civil rights in New Mexico.

Toward the end of the 1960s blacks in New Mexico realized some progress in their own civil rights role. Under the leadership of Governor David Cargo in 1969, the state legislature passed and, more significantly, funded civil rights legislation. Cargo also was aggressive in appointing blacks to governmental positions during his administration, naming African Americans to major appointive offices in the state and increasing the number of such appointees to forty-three.[3] There is ample evidence that the state did not ignore the plight of blacks even prior to the Cargo administration, even though few blacks resided in the state to influence policy.

In the introductory chapter to *Minorities and Civil Rights*, Charles Woodhouse argues that African Americans mobilized in the late fifties and sixties not to gain freedom and independence but rather to gain assimilation into the dominant white culture.[4] The lack of assimilation success in most instances was obvious. In New Mexico Hispanics as well as African Americans were excluded by majority choice based on racial differences.[5]

In New Mexico the place of African Americans was further complicated by the fact that they were seen as neither native, conqueror, nor colonist but often as a subservient people brought to the territory by the Spanish and Anglo conquerors. Despite this situation, free blacks were early settlers in the New Mexico territory. Mountain man James Beckwourth married a local and opened a hotel in Santa Fe. Henry Boyer, the father of the founder of Blackdom, was a free teamster with Alexander Doniphan's Missouri Rifles in the Mexican War. Early migrants were in turn followed by the famous Buffalo Soldiers after the Civil War, some of whom chose to remain, but not many.[6] After the turn of the century a larger influx of blacks into New Mexico began when the oil industry developed the southeast quadrant of the state, in what became known as "Little Texas." Even so, the black population of New Mexico was still less than 1 percent of the state's total population in 1940.[7]

Since the precepts of racism appeared to dominate New Mexico society and culture, blacks struggled for equality within the confines of a resistant white society with sometimes hardened attitudes. Few whites accepted that freedom meant more than setting slaves free, that it also meant the necessity for full equality of opportunity for minorities, especially blacks. The combination of racial difference, the lack of visible cultural distinction, and small numbers meant that blacks in New Mexico relied on organizations such as the National Association for the Advancement of Colored People (NAACP) to support and aid them.

Throughout the nation, early leadership in the civil rights movement came from the NAACP. In New Mexico as late as 1950 there was but a single chapter of the NAACP. The only city with a large enough number of blacks to support a chapter was Albuquerque. Leadership of the NAACP tended to come from the black middle class: ministers, lawyers, doctors, barbers, and other professionals. While black professionals made up no smaller a percentage of the whole in Albuquerque than anywhere else, they failed to assume leadership roles or to seek the full benefits of society for their less fortunate brethren according to some critics, such as Black Power sympathizer Roger W. Banks. This shortcoming did not affect the passage of a fair employment practices act by the New Mexico legislature in 1948.

When A. Philip Randolph, head of the Brotherhood of Sleeping Car Porters, and others chastised President Franklin Roosevelt for failure to establish a fair employment practices committee, they threatened a march on Washington. To further accomplish their mission of gaining federal legislation, states with large minority populations organized fair employment board committees, especially in the South and in the industrial North. As support for the legislation grew, other racial and ethnic minorities became active in grassroots support of the legislation. Despite being a state with a large minority population, only one special fair employment practices committee was formed in New Mexico.[8] That a bill passed at all in New Mexico was more a tribute to the bill's sponsor in the U.S. Senate, Dennis Chavez, than it was an upwelling of encouragement in the state for the bill.

Four years later the city of Albuquerque passed an antidiscrimination ordinance after receiving a letter from a California educator who inquired into the discriminatory actions taken by an Albuquerque restaurant owner. The restaurant owner refused service to a dark-skinned student who had entered his establishment to eat while waiting for a train. Claiming that the student was not an African American but rather a medical student from Ceylon, the educator wanted to know if refusal to serve based on racial appearance was a standard practice in Albuquerque and, by implication, in the state of New Mexico. The Albuquerque City Council supposedly sent a letter of apology to the student, prompting R. L. Chambers's acerbic note in the *Crisis* that "there is no record of any Negro being sent an apology for mistreatment in any Albuquerque restaurant or hotel, though the incidents are legion. Apparently, one must be a foreigner to receive hospitality of the city of Albuquerque."[9] A survey conducted on behalf of the city council over the next year and a half found that discrimination against African Americans was widespread in the city, leading to the passage of the ordinance prohibiting racial discrimination in public facilities and businesses in 1952.

Discrimination existed in other aspects of black life in New Mexico, education in particular. Black youths attended segregated schools especially in the area of Little Texas. On the other hand, schools in the northern half of the state, specifically Albuquerque and Santa Fe, were already desegregated by 1952. In Roswell a visiting Santa Fe black high school athlete was refused food service. The student received support from his teammates, both white and Hispanic, who refused to patronize the businesses that had refused service.[10]

Although the schools in the towns of Hobbs and Roswell were segregated in 1952, not all the schools in the Little Texas region were segregated at that time. Three years before *Brown v. Board of Education*, schools in Carlsbad began to integrate, largely due to the cost of maintaining accredited schools for both white and black students. In 1951 the Carlsbad school district received word that the all-black high school in town did not qualify for accreditation. The cost to bring the physical plant up to acceptable levels was $100,000. Unwilling to spend the money but fearing race mixing, the school board considered various ideas, including running two high schools in the same physical plant, one in the morning and one in the evening. Just before the school session ended in the summer of 1951 the superintendent of the Carlsbad School District made an executive decision, integrating both schools into one. Justifying his decision on the basis of cost and bolstering that decision with community input, he announced that the administration had polled the students at Carlsbad High School, the white high school in the district, and found that the students did not oppose desegregation. To prevent problems with the parents, the administration reached out to the ministers in the town and asked them to speak to their congregations on the matter. Few problems resulted once school opened.[11]

That same year Haroldie Kent Spriggs completed eighth grade in Tucumcari and was ready to move on to high school. Although both African Americans and Hispanics lived in a segregated area on the same side of the railroad tracks in Tucumcari, they did not share a segregated school. The Hispanics attended Tucumcari High School with the whites. If black children wanted to attend high school, they were forced to travel out of town, to Clovis, Hobbs, or one of the other towns in Little Texas that had a black population large enough to support a separate school for them. Haroldie's father, not wanting his daughter to attend high school elsewhere, appealed to influential whites who sympathized with him. They convinced the school board to integrate Tucumcari High School, and Haroldie completed her high school education in her hometown.

Although Carlsbad integrated to avoid spending money to bring the African American high school up to code, not all the school boards in Little Texas felt the same, and school districts both addressed the issue and sought to hide it entirely. Hobbs spent $127,000 to build a separate school for black children, ensuring a quality facility, at least temporarily. The schools were also segregated in Las Cruces, the home of New Mexico State University. To avoid facing state regulators, the black high school was not even carried on the records as part of the school system, a problem for graduates who wanted to attend college and had no record of even attending high school, much less graduating. Though the extent of segregated education varied within the state, segregation existed and hindered some African Americans from achieving their goals. On the other hand, desegregation came easier in New Mexico than in many other states, partially due to the small size of the black community.

The small size of the black community unfortunately also hindered African American civil rights achievements. Organizational problems hampered African Americans in New Mexico during the modern civil rights movement, in most cases due to the small number of African Americans in the state. Aside from Albuquerque, few towns in New Mexico had a black population large enough to support even an NAACP chapter. In 1953, chapters existed in Roswell (seventy-one members), Hobbs (seventy-seven members), Clovis (thirty-three members), Carlsbad (sixteen members), and Las Cruces (fifty-six members).[12] There was no chapter in Santa Fe, the state capital. With the exception of Albuquerque, all the chapters were in the southern part of the state and, with the exception of Las Cruces, all in the Little Texas part of southeastern New Mexico. At the time Roswell was the third largest city in the state, but Hobbs was competing to move ahead. Albuquerque and Las Cruces were the seats of the state's two major universities, both of which relied heavily on African Americans in their athletic programs, so one might expect a more urbane, open attitude about race relations in those two towns, yet Las Cruces schools remained segregated until after the *Brown* decision. Roswell and Hobbs had institutions of higher education but inadequate numbers of African American students to permit student organization for expanding black rights.

Though their numbers were small, African American students were a potential organizing force for the civil rights movement, but reports of such efforts were limited. On March 27, 1960, a group of "about 10 young Negroes" entered the McLellan store located in the Bel Aire Shopping Center in Hobbs and sat down at the soda fountain. The group consisted "of both males and females of college age" according to Bud Peters, the manager trainee on duty at the time. When the group was advised that they could not be served at the fountain but could place an order to be taken out, they asked to speak to the manager. Told that the manager was on vacation and that Mr. Peters would have to do, they remained sitting at the counter for ten to fifteen minutes. Peters reported that a couple of white customers left and that two white women got up and stood behind their husbands while the blacks remained at the counter.[13]

The sit-in at Hobbs occurred less than sixty days after the more famous sit-in at Greensboro, North Carolina. The NAACP chapter in Hobbs, just as those throughout the country, was dedicated more to the use of the legal system than to the more confrontational style favored by students who participated in sit-ins. Further, as noted by Richard Stephenson in an article in the *Crisis*, there were no chapters of the Urban League in New Mexico, nor of the Congress of Racial Equality (CORE), both of which were more militant than the NAACP. In fact, none of the major African American civil rights organizations aside from the NAACP had a presence in New Mexico. Yet the sit-in did occur.[14]

It is interesting to note the treatment by the *Hobbs Daily News-Sun* of the sit-in. The story was positioned in the spot reserved for the lead story, the banner headline, and the far right-hand column above the fold. Although the article is quite short, less than six inches of print, the incident is the lead story, but with no byline. Also interesting is the placement of a story immediately adjacent, an Associated Press article, again with no byline, discussing nine weeks of "anti-segregation" demonstrations that generated cross burnings in response by the Ku Klux Klan in Alabama, Georgia, Florida, and South Carolina, "as students in the North and West joined Negroes in their campaign against separate lunch counter facilities."[15] Although the story reveals that charges were brought against some Klansmen, its placement may be more of a warning to the students who participated in the sit-in at Hobbs than a serious attempt at reportage.

The people of Hobbs typified the attitudes of whites in Little Texas. Charles E. Becknell Sr., one of the students in the impromptu Hobbs sit-in, states in his autobiography, *No Challenge—No Change: Growing Up Black in New Mexico*, that in the fifties blacks in New Mexico still had to enter the houses of whites through the back door and were buried in separate cemeteries.[16] Although desegregation was implemented after *Brown v. Board of Education*, schools remained largely segregated at the primary level because blacks and whites lived in separate parts of town. Prior to desegregation, all black students from first through twelfth grade attended the same school. Buildings were primarily old military castoffs, and of course, the books were hand-me-downs from the white schools, well used and frequently abused. At least the teachers were black.

In the week following the Hobbs sit-in, the local president of the NAACP, Leora Willis, appeared before the city council requesting that a city ordinance be created to force integration of eating facilities within the city. The city council refused on the ground that in 1955 the state passed a civil rights law, which could not be superseded by city ordinance. Advising the council that to this point the black youth of the community had been kept under control, Willis urged the council to look at similar ordinances in Albuquerque and Las Cruces. Both of these cities prohibited discrimination in public facilities, imposing a fine of $300 per violation and up to ninety days in jail. A city commissioner's response to the request was, "We will do what we can.... In the meantime, if you people will do everything you can to continue the good relationships, it will help."[17] Obviously, improved race relations were dependent on the black community in Hobbs.

Realizing that school desegregation was merely the first step to full integration in society, the Hobbs City Council took action within three years to more smoothly ease the transition. On December 1, 1962, the council approved the creation of "an interracial committee to seek peaceful solutions to existing problems between Negroes and whites in Hobbs." Speaking for himself, Ralph D. Littleton argued that "the Negro youth of Hobbs . . . has nowhere to go for wholesome recreation or culture."[18] Littleton further complained that police response to fights and other disruptions, which occurred because black youths had no outlet for after-school energy, was frequently slow because police shift changes occurred at the same time schools were being dismissed for the day. Mayor Audrey Kenmitz noted that a city ordinance would have little or no effect because the council would not include an enforcement provision in any ordinance.

Two weeks later the city council created the Hobbs Inter-Racial Council. Mayor Kenmitz immediately appointed three white members and three black members to serve, along with one nonvoting ex-officio member from the city council. Both whites and blacks were represented by clergy: Rev. Jack London of the First Presbyterian Church for whites and Rev. S. V. Brooks of the Church of God in Christ for blacks. Both ministers had roots in Oklahoma, which had its own problems with race. Elementary school teachers were represented on both sides. The final white member was a local pharmacist, also from Oklahoma. Rather than choosing a black professional from the African American community, the mayor selected George Farquhar, a retired building custodian who spent his career at Humble Oil and Refining Company. Farquhar commented,

"I haven't had any experience in this field, but I'm willing to do the best I can to make the council a success."[19] Little mention is made of any work or progress made by the council, but Hobbs integrated with few if any race-related problems.

In the 1960s New Mexico saw a widening civil rights focus. The national turmoil of the period and the success of the African American civil rights movement awoke other minorities to the possibilities of gaining their own rights. In New Mexico the Hispanic population and the American Indian population, always more numerous than African Americans in the state, established their positions and began to assert their numbers. While the American Indian Movement gained headlines with actions in California and the Dakotas, American Indians in New Mexico, notably Paul Bernal of Taos Pueblo, fought for tribal recognition and cultural reclamation. The birth of the Chicano movement in the Southwest, based on the concept of Aztlan centered in New Mexico, Arizona, and the states of northern Mexico, spawned mass action groups throughout the states acquired from Mexico in 1848. New Mexico's Hispanic movement attempted to emulate the success of the black civil rights movement. The difference was that the movement did not look to Mexico for inspiration but returned to its Hispanic roots in New Mexico proper.

The Alianza Federal de Mercedes, or Federal Land Grant Alliance, sought the return of land originally held by descendants of Hispanic settlers in the region. Following U.S. acquisition of the region, some of this land had been granted to non-Hispanic individuals and some was granted communally, becoming federal land. It is the latter that primarily interested the members of the Alianza. At the first annual meeting of the Alianza, on September 1, 1963, the keynote speaker was Dr. Alton Davis, the African American president of the American Emancipation Centennial. He was joined by Mexico's former president Miguel Aleman, expressing Mexico's interest in the success of the Alianza movement.[20]

Although it was highly unusual that the members of the Alianza selected an outsider, much less an African American, as the keynote speaker, the membership had already broken with their tradition of self-reliance and distrust of outsiders by aligning themselves with Reies Lopez Tijerina. Tijerina, an itinerant Protestant, Mexican American preacher from Texas, founded the Alianza por Pueblos Libres (Alliance for Free Communities). Charismatic, enthusiastic, and willing to tolerate violence within the movement, Tijerina was passionate about the goals of the Alianza por Pueblos Libres, and his initial audiences were mesmerized by him. After achieving notoriety in New Mexico, Tijerina wanted to expand his leadership beyond the Alianza por Pueblos Libres, and he became involved with Martin Luther King's Poor People Campaign. Subsequent to King's assassination on April 12, 1967, the leadership of the Southern Christian Leadership Conference (SCLC) decided to move ahead with King's plan for a march on Washington in support of economic opportunity, jobs, and better housing. Tijerina, appointed head of the Hispanic delegation, broke with the SCLC leadership over his desire to include the issue of land grants in the March list of grievances. He also clashed with other equally strong personalities within the Mexican American rights movement, such as Rudolfo "Corky" Gonzales, leader of the Crusade for Justice in Denver, and Jose Angel Gutierrez, founder of La Raza Unida, a political party in Texas. Tijerina's commitment, combined with his tolerance for violence within the movement, eventually led to his arrest, trial, and conviction. His jail term effectively left his movement leaderless. Without his charismatic leadership, the movement subsided and percolated below the surface.[21]

Tijerina saw definite parallels between the struggle of La Causa on a nationwide basis and the African American struggle, but he felt there was a special relationship between New Mexico Hispanos and American Indians. New Mexico American Indians shunned outside assistance and organizations to a greater degree than New Mexican Hispanos. Although desirous of forming some type of an alliance with American Indians, Tijerina was willing to undertake an innovative interracial affiliation with African Americans to gain the property rights he so desperately wanted for the Alianza por Pueblos Libres.[22] Interracial affiliation was considered radical among Hispanos, as was Tijerina's suggestion for linking all claimants into one group, believing in the strength of numbers. The suggestion alienated some of Tijerina's followers, and large numbers of Hispanic New Mexicans rejected the adoption of "Negro tactics." In fact, the U.S. attorney for the Northern District of New Mexico who handled Tijerina's prosecution, Alfonso Sanchez, was himself Hispanic.

Hispanic middle-class attitudes in New Mexico during the 1960s are reflected in a statement that prominent New Mexico Republican Fernando C. de Baca made to a BBC reporter: "The truth is that Hispanics came here as conquerors. African Americans came here as slaves.... Hispanics consider themselves above blacks."[23] Although the statement was made just prior to the 2008 presidential election, C. de Baca explained that he was speaking of his father's generation. His statement reinforces the concept of alienation between the two minorities presented by Thomas Weyr, who explained that blacks and Hispanics distrust each other.[24]

Changes in race relations occurred in New Mexico during the era of the modern civil rights movement, some even before the *Brown* decision. For a number of years Albuquerque had been the only city in the state with a sizable enough black population to support an NAACP chapter, but by the 1950s other cities in the state also had chartered chapters. Although black leaders of the stature of Martin Luther King, or even Reies Tijerina, did not step forward, other blacks did help bring about change, including Charles Becknell Sr. Fewer ministerial leaders seemed to step forward, at least compared to the southern experience. The biggest drawbacks facing black New Mexicans in their efforts to wrest political, civil, and social rights from the white majority were the small size and the scattered nature of the black population of New Mexico. With such a small base from which to work and the lack of a charismatic leader, conditions inhibited the formation of an activist mass movement. Small numbers brought about small gains, particularly in the period from 1955 to 1975. As the third-largest minority in the state, African Americans in New Mexico were almost forced to sit and wait to be included in the efforts made by Hispanics with their own issues and needs.

Notes

1. Campbell Gibson and Kay Jung, "Historical Census Statistics on Population Totals by Race, 1790 to 1990, and by Hispanic Origin, 1970 to 1990, for the United States, Regions, Divisions, and States," table 46, "New Mexico—Race and Hispanic Origin: 1850–1990;" available at http://www.census.gov/content/dam/Census/library/working-papers/2002/demo/POP-twps0056.pdf.
2. R. L. Chambers, "The Negro in New Mexico," *Crisis* 59, no. 3 (March 1952): 149.
3. "Freedom News," *Crisis* 77, no. 4 (April 1970): 165.
4. Charles E. Woodhouse, "Minorities and Politics: An Introduction," in *Minorities and Politics*, ed. Henry J. Tobias and Charles E. Woodhouse (Albuquerque: University of New Mexico Press, 1969), 2.
5. Silvia Pedraza, "Origins and Destinies: Immigration, Race, and Ethnicity in American History," in *Origins and Destinies: Immigration, Race, and Ethnicity in America*, ed. Silvia Pedraza and Ruben G. Rumbaut (Cincinnati: Whitworth, 1996), 16.
6. Bruce A. Glasrud, "New Mexico," in *Encyclopedia of African American History, 1896 to the Present: From the Age of Segregation to the Twenty-First Century*, ed. Paul Finkelman et al. (New York: Oxford University Press, 2009), 3:479.
7. Gibson and Jung, "Historical Census Statistics on Population."
8. Louis Coleridge Kesselman, *The Social Politics of FEPC: A Study in Reform Pressure Movements* (Chapel Hill: University of North Carolina Press, 1948), 50.
9. Chambers, "Negro in New Mexico," 149.

10. Richard Stephenson, "Race in the Cactus State," *Crisis* 61, no. 4 (April 1954): 200–201.
11. Ibid.
12. Ibid.
13. *Hobbs Daily News-Sun*, March 28, 1960, 1.
14. Stephenson, "Race in the Cactus State," 200–201.
15. *Hobbs Daily News-Sun*, March 28, 1960, 1. On black communities in the civil rights movement, see Aldon D. Morris, *The Origins of the Civil Rights Movement: Black Communities Organizing for Change* (New York: Free Press, 1986).
16. Charles E. Becknell Sr., *No Challenge—No Change: Growing Up Black in New Mexico* (Rio Rancho, N.Mex.: Jubilee Publications, 2003), 63–82.
17. *Hobbs Daily News-Sun*, April 5, 1960, 1.
18. Vic Jameson, "Special Committee Appointments for Negroes," *Hobbs Daily News-Sun*, December 4, 1962, 1.
19. Ibid., 5.
20. Frances L. Swadesh, "The Alianza Movement of New Mexico: The Interplay of Social Change and Public Commentary," in *Minorities and Politics*, ed. Henry J. Tobias and Charles E. Woodhouse (Albuquerque: University of New Mexico Press, 1969), 69.
21. Ibid., 69–70.
22. Ibid.
23. Jeff Jones, "GOP Leader Won't Resign," *Albuquerque Journal*, September 24, 2008.
24. Thomas Weyr, *Hispanic U.S.A.: Breaking the Melting Pot* (New York: Harper & Row, 1988), 126.

Further Reading

See selected bibliography, pp. 271–78.

Part IV

The Upper Midwest

The six states in this section make up the eastern edge of the Great Plains. Kansas, Nebraska, South Dakota, and North Dakota stretch north from Oklahoma to the Canadian border. They joined the United States during and after the Civil War. Kansas, after being a battleground over the expansion of slavery in the 1850s, entered the Union as a free state after the Civil War began. Iowa and Minnesota, the easternmost states in this study, entered the Union as free states in the 1850s, while North and South Dakota were settled and entered the Union after the Civil War. The percentage of African Americans declines significantly as you move north from Kansas. During the Civil Rights era, the African American population in Kansas grew steadily from 3.6 percent to 7.6 percent; and in Nebraska from 1.5 percent to 3.1 percent. In Iowa and Minnesota it grew from less than 1 percent to 1.4 percent and 1.2 percent respectively. In the Dakotas, African American population remained less than 1 percent. Despite its relatively small African American population, this region experienced a significant civil rights movement. Kansas, of course, was the site of the lead case in the *Brown v. Board of Education of Topeka* decision; and each of these states had its own distinctive struggle against racial discrimination.

11

Civil Rights in the Dakotas

Betti VanEpps-Taylor

African Americans in North and South Dakota? Well, yes, but not many; more reside in South Dakota than North Dakota. Yet, those black Dakotans endured and worked to create a society that was amenable to their presence as well as one in which they could become contributors and participants. In the following chapter, Betti VanEpps-Taylor provides us with historical background and actions taken by white and black Dakotans to improve relations between the two. Of course, one also must recall that a significant presence exists in the Dakotas by American Indians, principally the Sioux. As in the remainder of the West, organizations acted to help human relations including the NAACP and the South Dakota Advisory Committee on Civil Rights. Progress has been made, but as VanEpps-Taylor notes, in this twenty-first century more changes in race relations remain to be accomplished. VanEpps-Taylor is an independent scholar who teaches at the College of Southern Idaho; her publications include *Forgotten Lives: African Americans in South Dakota* and *Oscar Micheaux: A Biography*.

Few areas of the United States are as unknown to most Americans as the Dakotas. Sparsely populated, with unforgiving wide open spaces, violent winds, and weather extremes, and situated squarely in the middle of the North American continent, they are often thought of as part of the American Outback. Indeed, they were once characterized as part of the so-called Great American Desert. They are lands of endless open prairie, towns and hamlets, farmland, and ranches, and vertically split nearly down the center by the wide, muddy Missouri River. Twelve scattered Indian reservations are home to the remains of the Great Sioux

Nation and assorted smaller tribes. Small towns that once owed their existence to now mostly unused railroad tracks struggle to survive, while luckier ones near the major interstates find ways to thrive as trade centers and oases that relieve the miles of travelers' empty boredom. While some Americans remember with pleasure their visits to the Black Hills and famous Mount Rushmore, they may be uncertain which of the two Dakotas they had visited.

The land that became Dakota Territory in the last days of the Buchanan administration had a long history of settlement: river men, fur traders, wood cutters, hunters, soldiers, fort workers, adventurers—hardy men of all races, including always a smattering of African Americans, successful and otherwise, who came and went, depending on the challenges of the moment. The first territorial officials were appointed in the earliest days of Lincoln's Republican administration. Portions of ceded Indian lands drew an immediate influx of eager Yankee land speculators and land-hungry homesteaders from across the globe. The latter had little idea of the enormous struggle involved in wresting farmland from desolate, unforgiving, mostly treeless prairie country where basic survival was a daily challenge. Backbreaking work combined with language barriers and cultural differences discouraged religious and cross-cultural interactions that might have widened horizons; and safe, conservative values, beliefs, and resistance to change found fertile and lasting ground, generally independent of race or ethnicity.

The early days were characterized by a raucous struggle among early elites who intended that politics and town building would make them rich. Political infighting, long distances between towns, and poor transportation, among other things, led to the eventual conclusion that there should be two separate states, roughly the same size, each allowed to grow up in its own individualistic fashion. At the time, most Dakotans didn't care much; they were too busy trying to survive. It was, however, an era during which national politicians of both parties were deeply interested in creating western states. This combination of local and national interest resulted in the admission of the Dakotas on November 2, 1889, followed in short order by Montana, Washington, Idaho, and Wyoming.

Thus, the two Dakotas grew up together; similar in many basic ways, but with different patterns of settlement. Both states always had transient African American populations whose size varied with economic conditions, seasons, and weather. They also always had small, stable urban African American communities with strong internal leadership, people who thrived as service providers or railroad employees. From the outset, however, in keeping with common unspoken custom, black Dakotans were generally quietly restricted from professions and lifestyles that were seen as "white." Both states also always had a smattering of highly independent African American individuals who chose to settle in widely separated parts of the states, as farmers or ranchers, or as "singletons" who found ways to survive and even thrive in villages and hamlets. In that hard country, individuals have always tended to be accepted by the majority based on whether they "fit in" and brought something of value to the community. Common customs, rather than restrictive laws, set the tone of cross-cultural relationships that included race, religion, and ethnicity, and those customs were respected. People usually knew "where they belonged" and for the most part made it work by staying within the commonly understood boundaries. Still, in a quiet way, patterns and platforms of change were quietly—very quietly—being constructed; changes that would make the new civil rights laws relatively easy to implement when the time came.

The first round of modern federal action with respect to race relations came on July 26, 1948, when President Truman, in Executive Order 9981 effectively desegregated the military. Many ordinary South Dakotans, for example, would remember their direct experiences close at hand with a segregated military when the army created technical training bases at Sioux Falls and Rapid City. Sioux Falls, with its stable black population and strong interracial community leadership, successfully preplanned and effectively managed the peaceful training of more than forty-five thousand trainees in communications, electronics, radio, and other wartime communication skills. These units consisted of segregated black troops, both male and female; and white troops, many with deep roots in the segregated South.

Rapid City, with its long-standing tensions between American Indians who regarded the Black Hills as their homeland and whites who regarded it as their private paradise, was not so fortunate. The air force established a flight training base at the hamlet of Box Elder, just east of the city, and from the outset both black and white troops were stationed there. Planning and preparation to deal with cultural differences had not been particularly effective and there was a long history of "incidents," although the depth of the problem did not become widely public until the early 1960s, long after the military was desegregated.

In the aftermath of World War II, most ordinary Dakotans put aside concerns with racial problems. Thus, in 1954, unless one was among the relatively few people of color living and working in either of the Dakotas, there was little interest in what seemed to be a remote, regional, mostly southern problem. The first comprehensive civil rights legal requirement related to school desegregation.

Brown v. Board of Education was signed on May 17, 1954, but for Dakotans this was a nonissue on its face. Schools had never been segregated, and few, if any towns had more than one high school.

It was only later as the long national struggle for basic human rights and dignity exploded onto the national *televised* evening news, complete with visions of burning buses, fire hoses, blood, and police dogs; when the national conversation turned into a hate-filled, violent, unseemly screaming match; that thoughtful Dakotans began to examine whether this conflagration might have any relevance at all to their towns and neighborhoods.

Even so, the idea that there was a local race problem *with respect to African Americans* was a real stretch for most white Dakotans. But for those who stopped to consider, that was not the case with respect to "Indian Country." North Dakota is home to a group of western Chippewa and the Mandan, Hidatsa, and Assiniboine tribes that Lewis and Clark came to know well; and both states have large populations of Sioux. These indigenous groups are located on four reservations in North Dakota and eight in South Dakota. Relations with American Indians were built on an ambiguous and often bitter history that continues to pervade life in both states. The institutionalized bitterness, anger, and outright bigotry on both sides was widely recognized, but not as a civil rights issue. Rather, incidents when they surfaced tended to assume center stage as long-standing cross-cultural problems. Thus, it was comparatively easy to brush off the idea of race relations problems between Dakota whites and blacks as relatively minor.

And yet over the next two decades, federal civil rights legislation with all its complexities, regulatory changes, and new institutions, descended on the Dakotas, accompanied by a cultural revolution that would call into question many cherished midwestern values. Ten years after *Brown v. Board of Education*, in January 1964 came the Twenty-Fourth Amendment abolishing the poll tax, which was ratified with the last-minute help of South Dakota legislators; followed in July by the sweeping Civil Rights Act of 1964—the one with direct application to critical lifestyle issues like public accommodations, housing, and job access. That one surely would have drawn immediate attention, since it struck directly at the cherished "customs" of behavior that had guided the states from the beginning. A year later Congress passed the Voting Rights Act of 1965.

Previous to these years, the overwhelming majority of white Dakotans had only the most limited exposure to blacks or black culture, and most would have been surprised to know how many African Americans called the Dakotas home. Those who had come to the area and were successful were, for the most part, expert at hiding in plain sight. Except for students in the larger cities where there were small black populations, most young people would have had no exposure whatsoever to African Americans; and television, when available, was still the land of white America, except for the unseemly, disturbing, never-ending newscasts from the civil rights front.

African American populations in both states were indeed small, but many were respected and long established, apparently fitting into their communities in much the same way as people fit into their close-knit Euro-American hamlets, where old languages and customs flourished and were accepted as part of the collective culture. A few widely scattered, longtime successful farmers and ranchers of color also seemed to fit well in their communities. African Americans on the surface seemed to live free and successful lives within the generally understood social customs common to the northern Great Plains.

There were, however, rumblings that suggested all was not well. More than a few white Dakotans were dimly aware of troubling "incidents" when custom clashed with ideas of equality. Custom, for example, allowed restaurants and hotels to discriminate, refusing service to whomever they pleased—which usually meant people of color. In most towns, hotel keepers were notorious for refusing accommodations to respected traveling artists and musicians of color who were frequently billeted in private homes. High school athletic teams learned that in some towns their black teammates would not be permitted in the hotel that welcomed the white players. Many an early stand against discrimination was made out of loyalty to a fellow teammate. African Americans could not even enjoy a haircut in a white-owned barbershop. These and other wearisome public accommodation customs were part of the routine lives of people of color.

Within the educational system, teachers who often considered themselves accepting and liberal, but were poorly informed about black life in general and opportunities for people of color "in the big world" in particular, were notorious for counseling promising students of color away from college and into blue-collar service jobs "to protect them from discrimination."[1]

And the specter of "irregular relationships" between black and white boys and girls across color lines that might have led to intermarriage loomed in the thoughts of concerned parents, black or white. Intermarriage, or miscegenation, had been illegal in North Dakota until 1955, and in South Dakota until 1957—and in their minds, heaven only knew what kind of bad behavior relaxing those cherished boundaries would create. While these incidents were facts of life for people of color, and whites who became aware might have been momentarily offended or sorry but felt helpless, there was little white understanding that these were in fact civil rights issues connected in some way to the rage in the South.

The bottom line was that to live successfully as a person of color in the Dakotas it was necessary to fit in, "know one's place," keep a low profile, and establish reputations for being a member of a law-abiding, contributing community. Local churches and lodges, often based in larger cities or in nearby states with a larger African American population, brought a measure of community and cultural awareness in the midst of a white world.

These were the Dakotas that many experienced well into the 1960s. And these were the Dakotas where frank conversations between African Americans and the white majority were unusual on any level. Some on both sides had been considering the matter, however, and those who were invited to consider issues of race did so under the guidance of clergy and laypeople from mainstream Protestant churches. It was a time of "ecumenism" when those churches were beginning to look for areas of agreement. Social justice, which certainly had its roots in churches of the South, became a topic that could finally come out into the open for frank and honest discussion, at least in the larger cities. Thus, the conversations began—slowly, at first—but then became more open as the civil rights revolution in all its pain and glory began taking over the airways.

In the Dakotas, scholarly studies of the black experience, particularly the recent black experience, are few and far between; and national records, which tend to deal with the nation's larger and more egregious problems, are not terribly helpful to the scholar. There is, however, a good stock of anecdotal lore found in oral histories, disguised in public records, or buried in the memories of those who lived it. These stories allow those with perseverance to tease out the clues and make sense of the quiet groundwork earlier laid by black and white Dakotans with the common sense, goodwill, and foresight to begin building this platform for change. To fully understand, it is useful to look more closely at the demographics common to this sparsely populated part of the world.

Each of the Dakotas has had a constant population of far less than a million, and a historically strong Christian population from heavily Catholic to Protestant, spread across denominational lines. Serious emphasis has historically been placed on post–high school education and there was a large assortment of state universities, state colleges, and private, church-owned colleges and academies. These, particularly the ones owned by mainstream Protestant denominations, would become points of stability as the civil rights revolution brought its changes, especially as they reached out to attract students and staff of color.

Population centers have never been large in terms of the wider world, but Fargo, Bismarck, Grand Forks, and Minot early became the most cosmopolitan of North Dakota cities. Each has a history of small, stable African American populations. Most developed around river transportation and later, the railroads. The populations peaked in the 1920s and waned as the Great Depression and dust bowl drove people to better opportunities elsewhere. The World War II draft, along with war work, also provided impetus for people to relocate; and many chose not to return. Nevertheless, small stable populations found roots and held on.

Yankton, in the southeastern panhandle of South Dakota, was the earliest settlement in Dakota Territory; a jumping-off point for the interior in territorial and homesteading days. It was home to a sizable river transportation and trade center, employers of African Americans. Indeed, the "Yankton Colored Colony" that developed endured well into the twentieth century. Other important towns with black communities included Sioux Falls and Huron. Towns like Mitchell, Pierre, Aberdeen, and Rapid City had smaller populations of the "hiding in plain sight" variety; populations that fluctuated over the years, affected by drought, depression, the availability of jobs, and the general fatigue associated with survival in an unforgiving countryside.

In both states, those who were the first to move to greener pastures were often those with the least to lose and the least opportunity for consistent prosperity on the plains. Inevitably, this was true for black families, especially when nearby cities like Minneapolis–St. Paul, Chicago, Sioux City, Omaha, or even Kansas City offered both opportunity and access to a familiar cultural world.

Currently, few resources document the modern lives of African Americans in the Dakotas, especially North Dakota. In 1994, a group of North Dakota scholars published *African Americans in North Dakota* through the University of Mary Press. This remarkable collection utilized census records, newspaper articles, personal histories, and background documents to track black residents from territory to statehood and after, but ended its research in 1955. In their introduction, the authors state that "a 1980s estimate reported that approximately 300 individuals could possibly be classed as bona fide long term North Dakota residents" while "the 1900 Census found 3,524 black Americans in the state. An analysis of places of residence indicates that most of these individuals were attached in some way to college and Air Force establishments. Perhaps 400 could be considered a permanent type of resident."[2]

These statistics, which also show North Dakota as just 1 percent black in 2007, perhaps explain why North Dakotans did not feel the need for an NAACP chapter until 2009, the one hundredth anniversary of the founding of the National Association for the Advancement of Colored People. Organized in Grand Forks, its stated purpose was to serve all: not only the African American population, but also the 5.4 percent American Indians and the 2 percent Hispanics, together with a growing refugee population from Bhutan, Burundi, Iraq, and other countries. Spearheaded by Grand Forks pastors Rev. Ronald Cooper and Rev. Henry Passmore, both air force veterans who had been stationed in the state and decided to stay, the new organization was designed to be responsive to an increasingly diverse community that could no longer stay on the sidelines as it had during past civil rights struggles.

Official reports from the North Dakota State Advisory Committee of the U.S. Commission on Civil Rights suggest that it may well be past time for the entrance of organizations such as the NAACP. North Dakota has been extremely slow to officially recognize and deal with issues of discrimination and human relations even in the face of documentation. Fact-finding reports assembled in 1996 recap the state's long history of unresponsiveness, lack of funding, inadequate investigation, and lack of judicial enforcement. It did not adopt the Martin Luther King holiday until 1991; and as of this 1996 report, there was no Human Rights Commission to implement any kind of coordinated program in a proactive way. Lack of funds, together with a perceived lack of any existing problem, in spite of evidence to the contrary suggest that there is much work to be done if the state is to effectively manage the myriad of problems the twenty-first century oil boom is already bringing to the western part of the state.

The NAACP has traditionally been a source of public education and mediation among diverse peoples; something at which it has excelled, and something whose time in North Dakota has come, if the state is to make the most of the economic opportunities that are becoming available. Both Grand Forks pastors believe that North Dakota's best days are ahead; a state that will inevitably grow in diversity and is already offering opportunities for people who are seeking "a place where you can excel. There are strong values here, a strong work ethic."[3] In the face of what, on the surface, is a damning report of inaction concerning civil rights violations with respect to gender, race, housing, age, disability, employment, and other problems, an article by Charles Haga suggests what many in the northern Great Plains have known to be true: that civil rights problems in general have not heretofore been pressing issues for the government and the general citizenry of North Dakota.

South Dakota's issues of race relations are slightly different, arguably better documented, and quite advanced compared to what appears to be the North Dakota circumstance. The black population was always larger. Its cultural contacts were relatively broad and included Sioux City, Omaha, and even Kansas City, from which the prominent black newspaper *The Call* reached out to African Americans in the hinterlands. Serious documentation began in 1977 when Sara Bernson, a history major at the University of South Dakota, chose the black experience in South Dakota for her master's thesis. Research and relationships that derived from that project resulted in Bernson partnering with Robert J. Eggers to write *Black People in South Dakota History* in 1977 for the general public. With the help of influential black Yankton businessman and prominent Republican Theodore "Ted" Blakey, it was published in a limited edition by the Yankton Chamber of Commerce. Blakey also made sure that these and stories from his personal collection made it into the *History of Yankton County, South Dakota*, published in 1987.

These foundation studies not only address the lives of African Americans who created the "platform" on which awareness of civil rights would be built, but they also show something of the turmoil that stimulated the understanding that changes were necessary and important. The documents resulted in black history monographs presented at statewide history conferences, and the author's own subsequent research was published by South Dakota History Press in 2008 as *Forgotten Lives: African Americans in South Dakota*. These efforts interested others—writers, lecturers, scholars, and oral historians—in the topic and have ensured that black history remains alive, well, and highly active in South Dakota.

For South Dakota African Americans, civil rights activism had begun early. In 1920 the leadership eyed the horrendous national race riots of the summer of 1919 that sprang up in large postwar northern cities. It was too close for comfort. The result was the organization of an NAACP chapter in Sioux Falls in early 1920, followed immediately by a second chapter in Yankton. A couple of years later the reinvented Ku Klux Klan burst upon the state, sending chills up the spines of those who knew better. Their brief rampage, while posing as a respectable political organization and family-oriented lodge, targeted the area's large Catholic population, immigrants, prostitutes, and ne'er-do-wells rather than African Americans. Nevertheless, black South Dakotans must have breathed a sigh of relief knowing that prudent steps had been taken to protect themselves in case of necessity.

Yankton's black community boasted the first black church in the territory and a small colony of solid citizens, led by the Blakey dynasty. They were a large agricultural family who settled on less desirable Missouri bottomland and turned it into an effective truck gardening empire. Born in the mid-1920s, Theodore "Ted" Blakey became a successful businessman, modeling his cleaning, portering, and pest control business on the success of Maurice Coakley, a successful black businessman in Sioux Falls. As one of the younger members of the Blakey family, he would be well placed to become a significant player in the emerging civil rights revolution.

The Sioux Falls community was always more cosmopolitan and urban. As a prominent political and trade center, it was an attractive location for up-and-coming African Americans. Louise and Harvey Mitchell were one of the earliest and most prominent couples. Arriving in the early twentieth century, they quickly became successful entrepreneurs. They were experts in the barber and beauty field and used it to begin building a bridge between the black and white communities. Harvey Mitchell's downtown barbershop catered to the most prominent white citizens, and Louise Mitchell successfully operated the high-class hair salon located in the prestigious Shriver-Johnson Department Store. This base of operations gave the couple unique access to the white power structure and leadership in the local black community. Together, they founded the California College of Beauty, which trained young people well into the 1950s. Students were black and white, local and from the Deep South, and their training in the science of cosmetology launched a number of successful careers. Graduates would return home and create their own "platforms" of influence.

Louise Mitchell interested herself in many important causes. Realizing that customs would be hard to change, she sought ways to build bridges. To combat the lack of access to lodging for travelers, including prominent entertainers of color as well as those working the harvest circuit, she enlisted the help of the white political structure to create the Booker T. Washington Service Center, which provided both lodging and access to local social services. Through her efforts, Mrs. Mitchell gained Community Chest financial and public support for the new center.

As young men dealing with family disorganization, Maurice Coakley and his brother lived and worked at the center for a time; and the mentorship of the Mitchells helped launch Maurice Coakley into his successful business that in turn, became a model for Ted Blakey. The Booker T. Washington Center remained viable and active through the challenges of World War II and beyond. It became an important launching pad from which various public services, entertainment options, and comfort care were brought to African American servicemen during World War II. It and the other institutions the Mitchells created became focal points for NAACP sponsorship of public education and action on behalf of civil rights changes.

The 1950s and the Cold War brought additional military bases to the Dakotas and strengthened the military role of Ellsworth Air Force Base near Rapid City. But in the early 1960s, the bases created an embarrassing public airing of that beleaguered city's difficult history of race relations. This history even reached a national audience through release of a highly public series of hearings and follow-up reports spearheaded by the newly formed South Dakota Advisory Committee of the United States Commission on Civil Rights. Their report, which is available in the archives of the organization, makes instructive reading about the nature of race relations in the Rapid City area during that period. In 1957, two air force bases were opened in North Dakota. Minot Air Force Base opened as an Air Defense Command and later became a major Strategic Air Command base. Grand Forks Air Force Base was also constructed that year and became a major installation of the Strategic Air Command. Since both bases opened after the military was desegregated, these bases dealt from the outset with a mixed and integrated population. Considering the era in which they were inaugurated, however, it is likely that they experienced similar adjustment problems that may well be documented in further scholarly studies of the state and the era. It is a fact, however, that many veterans of color who served in these military facilities in both states liked the area and returned to settle successfully nearby, bringing to two otherwise homogeneous states a stable population of Dakotans of color.

The mid-1950s and 1960s also brought a new professional class of African Americans. In 1957, Sidney Milburn, a recent honors graduate of the Tuskegee Institute Veterinary School and his wife, a trained teacher, chose the tiny town of Elk Point, South Dakota, located in the state's panhandle, as the place to set up his veterinary practice. Surprised townspeople were at first dubious, and then delighted when the family fit well into the community and enjoyed outstanding professional careers.

Mitchell, South Dakota, is a large town centrally located on the east-west interstate. Its African American population long consisted of the Leonard Williams Sr. family, who had arrived in 1908. Williams had a long career on the railroad, and the couple, respected members of the community, raised a son and daughter in apparent complete acceptance. Leonard Williams Jr. joined the army in World War II, and was recalled after Korea where he served successfully and internationally, retiring as a lieutenant colonel, the first black American to reach that rank in the newly integrated army. Returning to Mitchell in 1968, he turned his attention to public service, serving first as the director of the local YMCA, and then as director of student affairs for the local vocational technical college. In 1986 he entered politics first as councilman, and then as mayor, serving four consecutive eight-year terms and bringing many important changes to the town.

Williams's experience in South Dakota and the military had effectively rendered him color-blind and also an astute observer of twentieth century politics and race relations. In a 1976 interview, he spoke at some length about his home state's subtle, well-meaning, and often mindless racism. He remarked that historical issues of racism were "often addressed in this way: 'You know, I'm not prejudiced, but if I did thus-and-so, why, that would cause me to lose my business and people would say this-and-this-and-this.'" He pointed out that while discrimination might not have been the intent of such remarks, the effect was the same on the lives and attitudes of the areas' small black populations.[4]

Perhaps the most effective black Dakotan in this period was Ted Blakey, whose personal success had freed him to pursue statewide political and social action goals. He had all the right political connections of the self-made man. He began his public career by serving on the school board of the small Grove School, which had provided his elementary education. He helped them establish their Boy Scout troop. He joined the Jaycees, Kiwanis, the SD Civil Defense Organization, Prince Hall Masons, and the Republican Party. In June 1966, he was drafted as president of the South Dakota State Custodians Association and instituted a program that revised and restructured the group into an effective organization. He used that platform to lobby successfully for state legislation to prohibit discrimination in public places. It passed on January 30, 1963.

That year he was further energized by a trip to Washington, D.C., to represent the state at the centennial celebration for the signing of the Emancipation Proclamation. Returning home determined to force change, he took on important local issues of discrimination including a successful challenge that made it illegal for a white-owned barbershop to refuse to cut a black man's hair. Subsequent political contacts in the Greater Kansas City black community led to his appointment as chairman of the state group charged with getting the Twenty-Fourth Amendment to the Constitution ratified. With the help of black leaders Dr. Arnett Matchett, William Mahoney, and his old friend Maurice Coakley, they created a public relations campaign that pressured the state legislature to pass the necessary resolution, which they did on January 23, 1964. South Dakota became the thirty-eighth state to ratify the amendment, which passed just five days later.

Blakey next challenged the new civil rights legislation. With the help of the NAACP, he forced the nationally known Gurney Seed Company to hire his wife, Dorothy, for "clean work" in the offices, thus breaking the hiring practice that relegated people of color: Indians, Hispanics, and African Americans, to "dirty work" in the seed room.

In the meantime, beginning in the mid-1960s, the states' colleges were engaged in active campaigns to attract African American students. This brought a variety of African Americans from all over the country to state and private colleges and universities in both Dakotas. They came—undoubtedly wondering what they had gotten themselves into—and brought with them news from the civil rights battles in the outside world. Black student associations sprang up on surprised white campuses, and some students participated in demonstrations. Many of these students were successful; some stayed to become Dakotans, while others went on to careers elsewhere.

It would be the mid-1970s before real access to the better jobs became widely available to African Americans. For example, in Rapid City in 1975, Ron Randle became the first black public school teacher; in Sioux Falls the city hired its first black firefighter and police officer; and the opening of large national businesses like Citibank, and the establishment of the federal Earth Resources Observation and Science (EROS) Center brought open hiring requirements. Similar circumstances prevailed as well in places in North Dakota.

It is not possible to leave the period under discussion without briefly touching on the way that the civil rights revolution eventually began to impact American Indians who had spawned their own group of activists and militants insistent on change. The violent confrontation between members of the American Indian Movement (AIM) and members of the FBI at Wounded Knee in 1973 grabbed the national spotlight when it resulted in fatalities and trials that focused worldwide attention on the long history of cultural frictions between American Indians and white South Dakotans. Some said that being Indian in South Dakota was like being black in Mississippi. Many white South Dakotans were stung by the criticism; others, who grappled daily with the long heritage of cultural misunderstanding felt polarized and unfairly criticized. Now, these many years later, the issues are not yet resolved, but it is important to note that the civil rights legislation put in place with the assistance of black South Dakotans has helped with constructive transitions and has provided a body of tools that can be implemented to mitigate the old wrongs and reduce the old tensions between American Indians and the white majority.

Social change never comes easy; actions that began in 1948 have taken years to bring change to fruition, and much work remains. However, as the 1980s unfolded and the affirmative action and civil rights precedents began to be formalized, the results of more than two decades of revolution began to create permanent changes in public and private behavior. With behavior changes came gradual changes in private attitudes as well. Today, well into the twenty-first century, North and South Dakota, once bastions of the American "Outback," have assumed new importance as desirable places for people of all races and ethnicities to quietly live the American life.

Notes

1. Betti VanEpps-Taylor, *Forgotten Lives: African Americans in South Dakota* (Pierre: South Dakota State Historical Society Press, 2008), 162–88.
2. Thomas P. Newgard, William C. Sherman, and John Guerrero, eds., *African Americans in North Dakota: Sources and Assessments* (Bismarck, N.Dak.: University of Mary Press, 1994), introduction.
3. Charles Haga, "In NAACP's 100th Year, Grand Forks Charters First North Dakota Chapter," *MinnPost*, June 5, 2009, accessed November 23, 2014, https://www.minnpost.com/politics-policy/2009/06naacps-100th-year-grand-forks-charters-first-north-dakota-chapter.
4. VanEpps-Taylor, *Forgotten Lives*, 199–201.

Further Reading

Bernson, Sara L. "Black History in South Dakota." Master's thesis, University of South Dakota, 1977.

Gatewood, Willard B., Jr. "Katie D. Chapman Reports on 'The Yankton Colored People.'" *South Dakota History* 7 (Winter 1978), 28–35.

Haga, Charles. "In NAACP's 100th Year, Grand Forks Charters First North Dakota Chapter." *MinnPost*. June 5, 2009.

Newgard, Thomas P., William C. Sherman, and John Guerrero, eds. *African Americans in North Dakota: Sources and Assessments*. Bismarck, N.Dak., University of Mary Press, 1994.

Norris, Kathleen. *Dakota: A Spiritual Geography*. New York: Houghton-Mifflin, 1993.

Porter, Kimberly. *North Dakota: 1960 to the Millennium*. Dubuque, Iowa: Kendall Hunt, 2009.

United States Commission on Civil Rights South Dakota Advisory Committee. *Negro Airmen in a Northern Community: Discrimination in Rapid City, South Dakota*. Washington, D.C.: U.S. Government Printing Office, March 1963.

VanEpps-Taylor, Betti. *Forgotten Lives: African Americans in South Dakota*. Pierre: South Dakota State Historical Society Press, 2008.

Wilkins, Robert P., and Wynona Huchette Wilkins. *North Dakota: A Bi-Centennial History*. New York: W. W. Norton, 1977.

12

The Modern Civil Rights Movement in Iowa and Minnesota

Donald H. Strasser and Melodie Andrews

The civil rights revolution emerged in the upper midwestern states of Iowa and Minnesota where a largely apathetic rural white population existed. While white politicians frequently sympathized with the goals of moderate civil rights activists, they were alarmed by the militant stance of groups such as the Black Panthers. The African American communities in these states lived amid de facto segregation, overcrowded and unhealthy residential districts, and low income jobs or unemployment. With the aid of the NAACP, courageous leaders, and the Black Panthers, civil rights activists challenged the racial status quo. Conditions improved, but even today blacks lack the respect and opportunities granted to whites in the Upper Midwest. African Americans in Minnesota are not the only group in need of and seeking equitable rights, so too are American Indians. Donald Strasser and Melodie Andrews are professors emeriti of history at Minnesota State University, Mankato.

On the night of April 27, 1969, as a spring storm raged outside, six members of the Black Panther Party sat in the front room of their headquarters at 1207 11th Street. Surrounded by stacks of Panther literature, their mimeograph machine and typewriter at the ready, they talked late into the evening. Then at 11:47 P.M. their conversation came to an abrupt shattering end as a bomb made of plastic explosives blew out the back of the wooden frame house and created a swath of destruction three blocks wide. Miraculously the front rooms of the headquarters remained standing and the six Panthers escaped injury. Despite the extensive damage, with considerable bravado the Black Panther spokesperson said they would stay at the house and continue their work. "This is war," he declared. "The Vietnamese people do not evacuate because living conditions become miserable and neither shall we."

And where did this act of vigilante violence take place? Did it occur in Chicago or Los Angeles? No, it happened in Des Moines, Iowa. This incident and others like it suggest that a more regionally nuanced understanding of the civil rights movement is required. In matters of racial injustice, the South has always been the central focus of scholarly attention. Only more recently have historians subjected the North to the same hard scrutiny. America's heartland, however, still remains peripheral to the traditional narrative of the civil rights movement. Shining a light on the little-known struggles of black midwesterners for civil rights and equal opportunities makes it abundantly clear that the same racial discrimination that existed in the South and the urban North could also be found in Iowa and Minnesota, and this is why the Black Panther Party established a headquarters in Des Moines. As historian Jason Sokol rightly notes, racial inequality was "a national trait more than a Southern aberration."

In the 1950s, 1960s, and 1970s, black youth in the Midwest saw their futures being denied and started demanding change. In both Iowa and Minnesota, white-dominated state and local governments, fearful of growing black militancy, used repression against radicals like the Black Panthers, but demonstrated increasing willingness to work with black moderates. As a result, blacks in the Midwest achieved some meaningful progress during these pivotal years of the campaign for civil rights.

Iowa's struggle for civil rights, like the national movement in which it took place, was rooted in the past. In the early twentieth century, George H. Woodson, a prominent black Iowa attorney, helped to found the Niagara Movement, the precursor of the National Association for the Advancement of Colored People (NAACP). By the 1950s NAACP chapters in Iowa were fully engaged in legal battles over discrimination there. They were joined by other organizations like the Congress of Racial Equality (CORE) in Davenport and Des Moines, and the Catholic Interracial Council in Davenport and Waterloo. Ad hoc groups also sprang up to deal with local issues of specific concern to the black community. Iowa colleges and churches produced their share of activists as well. As some of these reformers challenged racial injustice at the national level, others worked with white allies to tailor their strategies and tactics to local conditions.

In Iowa, middle-sized cities and small towns, with relatively small black populations, dotted the rural landscape. And even though racial segregation was illegal in the state, it was still practiced in many communities. Local hotels regularly turned away black guests, and many restaurants only served blacks out the back door. Real estate agents would not show homes in white neighborhoods to black clients, and white homeowners refused to sell to blacks. College dormitories excluded black students. "It turns out there was a lot of discrimination in Iowa. A lot of Jim Crow laws in the South were happening here, too," recalled Patti Miller, an Iowa participant in Freedom Summer of 1964 in Mississippi.

As the movement for racial justice unfolded at home, Miller, a music student at Drake University, joined thirty-five other Iowans in traveling to Mississippi in the summer of 1964. The contingent included nineteen students, fourteen teachers, two attorneys, and a Christian layman. Steve Smith, a University of Iowa student, was subsequently arrested for trying to register black voters through the Mississippi Voter project. The Iowa volunteers had been trained in nonviolent tactics and knew they were going into a hostile environment. How hostile became clear on Miller's first day of work in Meridian, Mississippi. That was also the day that authorities found the bodies of three slain civil rights workers. Members of the Ku Klux Klan had murdered them. Miller began her duties in the same office where Andrew Goodman, James Chaney, and Michael Schwerner had worked. She described her first day as "somber."

The center of the civil rights movement in Iowa was Davenport, a medium-sized city on the banks of the Mississippi River. On August 23, 1963, a crowd of two thousand civil rights supporters assembled in Le Claire Park to protest against racial discrimination and to urge the enactment of the Iowa Fair Housing bill. John Howard Griffin, the author of *Black Like Me*, was a featured speaker. Among the complaints raised by protestors was the fact that blacks were denied equal access to Davenport's swimming pool facilities. They were only allowed to use the pool once a week and were required to leave the park early in the evening. While Davenport did not have de jure segregation, it had its share of de facto segregation. For example, Hickey's Cigar Store did not allow blacks to be served at the lunch counter. Davenport blacks also had difficulty in securing decent-paying jobs. The city's blacks were the last hired and the first fired, especially at the factories that had attracted them to Davenport in the first place.

A group of progressive, social justice–minded priests and professors at St. Ambrose College led the movement for change in Davenport. A St. Ambrose student activist, Bill Gluba, later became mayor of the city. In April 1965 Martin Luther King accepted the St. Ambrose *Pacem in Terris* award and called for continued "mass action programs." Rev. Martin Mottet, a young priest at the time, attributed the motivation of the activists to the "Catholic social teaching we were trying to put into practice. It is for the dignity of all people and the unity of the human race."

Unrest and protest occurred in other parts of the state as well. In the summer of 1967 black youths rioted in the northeastern town of Waterloo. Black gangs engaged in a three-hour rampage in the North End, smashing windows, throwing rocks, and looting businesses. The next year young blacks rioted along East Fourth Street following the assassination of Martin Luther King.

The reasons for black unrest in Waterloo were obvious. Over 95 percent of the town's six thousand blacks were confined to housing in East Waterloo, which was sandwiched between a freeway and the Cedar River. Public schools were segregated by neighborhoods and thus by race. Black employment was limited, with 80 percent of blacks working in service jobs or as laborers. The riots prompted white business owners to flee the East Side, further hurting the black economy.

Older blacks in the community, many of whom had migrated to Iowa from Mississippi, were more content with the status quo. Young blacks, with no experience of southern racism, compared their lives to that of the town's whites. One young protester justified the rioting by claiming that picketing and marching had failed to bring about change.

In the aftermath of the rioting, fair housing laws allowed blacks to move to the west side of Waterloo and throughout the metropolitan area. But low-income blacks remained unable to afford the low-cost housing built on the northeast side. And in spite of the laws, blacks continued to be steered to certain areas of town based on race and income.

In 1973 Waterloo adopted a school desegregation plan, which ultimately failed to achieve racial balance. Blacks continued to advocate for more black teachers, more creative teaching methods, and better school facilities. Black high school students complained bitterly over the lack of summer jobs, which were essential if they were to afford to go to college. In the decades that followed, Waterloo blacks continued to experience twice the unemployment rate of whites, and their frustrations mounted.

In Des Moines, Iowa's largest city and the state capital, race relations were even worse. Traditionally blacks and whites lived in two different worlds in that city. Blacks migrated to Des Moines in three waves. During World War I the coal industry imported southern blacks as strikebreakers. The second wave occurred during the economic boom of World War II. By far the largest migration came in the postwar decade of the 1950s. By 1970 the black population was 11,425 out of a total city population of 200,587.

The accumulated grievances of black residents in Des Moines boiled over in the 1960s. Ninety-three percent of the black population was confined to two precincts. Agitation erupted over unequal education, school busing, urban renewal, unemployment, and especially what blacks considered police brutality. Public accommodations such as restaurants, hotels, and movie theaters were segregated. When the black opera singer Marian Anderson visited the city, she was allowed to stay in the Roosevelt Hotel, but she was required to use the freight elevator and not mingle with the white patrons.

Urban renewal projects uprooted black residents and broke up black neighborhoods. The "Model Cities" plan eliminated Center Street, the business and cultural center of the black community in Des Moines. The construction of a new freeway further isolated blacks from the white downtown.

One outraged young activist, Mary Rehm, decided to travel to Los Angeles to seek answers to the racial problems plaguing her community. She was impressed by the Black Panthers she encountered there and intrigued by their programs. Returning to Des Moines she met Charles Knox, a former AmeriCorps VISTA volunteer. Together they established the Black Panther Party of Des Moines. In the tradition of southern black women leaders like Gloria Richardson and Fannie Lou Hamer, Mary Rehm defied the gender barriers to women in the male-dominated world of Black Power politics, and in the process fashioned her own identity and her own liberation.

The rise and fall of the Des Moines Black Panther Party occurred in a relatively short period of time between June 1968 and January 1971. Recruiting from a black population of about twenty thousand, the Des Moines chapter reached a membership of a hundred at its peak. Most of the Panthers were young students or high school graduates, working class, and poor. Some were illiterate and would be taught to read by their Panther comrades. Clive De Patton, one of the leaders, was an exception in being drawn from the black middle class.

Being a member of the Black Panther Party was a way of life: up at 5:00 A.M. to serve in the free breakfast program for poor children, then going to school or to work during the day, and afterward spending the evening reaching out to the black community, selling the Black Panther newspapers, engaging in political discussions, and finally ending the day late at night. In addition to the free breakfast programs usually carried out at local churches, the Panthers sought welfare assistance for poor people, particularly single women with children, and sharply criticized the welfare system for breaking up black families. Charles Knox, the local Black Panther deputy of education, convinced a Catholic church to provide the Panthers with the use of a house in the black community. The house became the Panther headquarters and the scene of endless meetings, political education sessions, and discussions of pressing issues.

Eventually a Black Panther–influenced group, the Black Committee for Student Power, presented a list of demands to the Des Moines municipal school board. The committee insisted on the teaching of black history and the hiring of more black teachers. They also demanded that black students be treated with more respect, that students be more involved in decision-making processes, and that teachers be granted autonomy in regard to the curriculum. Some students went to jail for staging sit-ins, but in time Des Moines teachers successfully formed a union and gained more control over the curriculum. Responding to student demands and his own convictions, Cecil Reed, the only black Republican representative in the Iowa legislature, secured a joint resolution authorizing the teaching of black history in the Iowa public schools.

The midwestern chapters of the Black Panther Party differed from those in Los Angeles and Chicago not only in serving smaller black populations, but also in insisting upon practical solutions over theoretical ones. They were only interested in theories that led to direct action. Also the midwestern chapters were more culturally conservative than those in Los Angeles and Chicago in regard to sexual relations and the use of drugs and alcohol. The midwestern chapters did look to Los Angeles and Chicago for ideas and direction. But following the assassination of Panther leader Fred Hampton in Chicago, the Des Moines chapter cut communications with the Chicago chapter. At issue was the distribution of funds, how to put revolutionary theory into practice, and the Chicago chapter's insensitivity to local concerns. Nationally the Black Panthers were under full-scale government attack, the targets of the FBI's counterintelligence (COINTEL) program designed to infiltrate, discredit, and destroy any organizations the government deemed subversive.

In the spring of 1969 a series of explosions and confrontations rocked Des Moines, and tensions escalated between the Panthers and the police. In early April someone blew up an electrical substation. An interracial recreational center called the "Soul Village" was bombed shortly thereafter. On April 13 the police violently broke up a "Free Breakfast for School Children" rally the Panthers were holding in a local park. Then on the evening of April 27 the house serving as the Black Panther headquarters was blown in half. Because plastic explosives were involved and because the Panthers had received threats from a white paramilitary group calling itself "The Minutemen," the Panthers were certain of the identity of the perpetrators. Police who had been standing in full view of the back of the house claimed they saw nothing suspicious. But as one Panther noted, "Thirty seconds after the explosion, a pig was sitting on the front porch. It usually takes them about an hour to get here." The police immediately accused the Panthers of destroying their own building, and they never conducted a formal investigation into the cause of the blast. They also showed little concern for the damage the explosion caused to more than forty other houses in a three-block radius of the headquarters.

Initially the Panthers wanted to remain in the partially destroyed home as a show of defiance, but they were soon forced to relocate their headquarters. The fortunes of the Panthers now began a downward spiral. The police jailed Mary Rehm and three others for allegedly bombing a police station. They charged another member with the bombing of the Panther headquarters, although there was no evidence of schism within the party or of any personal feuds among members. Defense funds for those charged with crimes drained the meager resources of the chapter. These circumstances, combined with attempted assassinations, police harassment, incarceration, and severed ties with the national party hastened the demise of the Black Panther Party in Des Moines.

The chapter dissolved in the fall of 1970 only to be reborn in January 1971 as the Black Revolutionary Party. This new party supported and exerted influence on a variety of local organizations and constituencies including the local black student union, returning black Vietnam War veterans, Operation Spearhead (a tutorial program), the Free Angela Davis Committee, and the Black Methodists for Church Renewal. Mary Rehm and fellow Panther Joeanna Cheatom continued to help black women to exercise their rights to welfare support. Rehm took the lead in organizing breakfast programs for children and health programs for adults. Throughout the rest of their careers, Rehm and other former Panthers continued their services to the poor. A number of working-class blacks helped by the Panthers went on to become community leaders.

In 1980 Charles Knox and Joeanna Cheatom founded radio station KUBC, which gave the black community of Des Moines a collective voice. Mary Rehm, who adopted the name Sister Hadasha, oversaw the operation as station manager. The radio station kept the community informed about local matters, supplied music and drama, and presented programs on African American history. Because of the political education efforts of the Black Panthers and the presence of a black radio voice, the local police found it more difficult to abuse black suspects without community awareness.

The history of racial oppression in Iowa showed that it would take more than civil rights legislation for blacks to achieve justice and fairness. Looking back in 1991, Representative June Franklin, a black Democrat, credited the Black Panthers with finally forcing the white elite to end housing discrimination in Des Moines. During the brief years of its existence the chapter did manage to bring a measure of empowerment to the black community.

During the 1950s and 1960s, Iowa's neighbor to the north, Minnesota, seemed far removed from the civil rights movement in the South and the racial turmoil on the nation's coasts. The Upper Midwest state embraced the reform spirit of the Populist movement, the Progressive movement, and the Farmer Labor Party. But in reality, Minnesota's political liberalism often obscured from the rest of the nation the state's penchant for anti-Semitism, shameful treatment of American Indians, and racial discrimination against blacks.

The Duluth lynching of three black circus workers in 1920 may have been the most extreme example of racial injustice in Minnesota, but it was far from being the only one. As was the case throughout the North, racial discrimination against blacks was endemic and more de facto than de jure. Racial tensions were high in Duluth long before the lynching because U.S. Steel had brought in southern black field hands to thwart white union strike threats. With the state's relatively small black population concentrated in the Twin Cities and Duluth, outstate white Minnesotans had little direct contact with people of color. As a result, they had few if any opportunities to dispel their beliefs in racial stereotypes. When Mankato State College in south-central Minnesota actively recruited black students in the late 1960s, farmers in Blue Earth County informed the press that, if these blacks were coming to take their land, they would be met with shotguns. Mankato retailers ordered their employees to follow black shoppers around in their stores and watch them closely because they believed blacks were prone to steal.

Minnesota would play its most visible role in the civil rights struggle when the ebullient, loquacious mayor of Minneapolis, Hubert Humphrey, burst onto the national stage at the 1948 Democratic convention. Humphrey challenged his fellow Democrats "to get out of the shadows of states rights and walk forthrightly into the bright sunshine of human rights." He urged the adoption of a civil rights plank for the party platform, which, after a great deal of contention, was finally adopted.

A few years earlier in 1945, Humphrey had won the mayoralty of Minneapolis. Sensitive to the discrimination against Jews and blacks in employment and housing, the reform mayor built a coalition of civic, political, and business leaders to support the successful passage of a fair employment ordinance in 1947. The journalist Carey McWilliams, noting the discrimination against Jewish doctors, professors, and lawyers, had dubbed Minneapolis "the capital of anti-Semitism." The ordinance not only outlawed job discrimination against Jews, blacks, and American Indians, but also created a commission to investigate complaints and propose permanent remedies. Humphrey went on to a distinguished career in the U.S. Senate. He was the floor leader in that body for what became the Civil Rights Act of 1964. The following year he stood next to Johnson as the president signed the Voting Rights Act of 1965 into law.

The one questionable act by Humphrey that tarnished his record on civil rights came when he let his political ambition trump his moral vision at the 1964 Democratic Party convention. As the price exacted by Lyndon Johnson for Humphrey to become his running mate, Humphrey agreed to present a one-sided compromise on the seating of the Mississippi delegation. Two groups had arrived in Atlantic City, a segregated white delegation and a racially integrated one organized by Fannie Lou Hamer's Mississippi Freedom Democratic Party. Humphrey supported the seating of the "lily white" delegates while offering to give the MFDP just two nonvoting observers. The MFDP delegates angrily rejected the proposal, calling it "a sellout." Harold Hughes, the governor of Iowa and head of that state's delegation, invited the MFDP representatives to sit with them, but they decided to leave the convention in protest instead. Although the white delegates were officially seated, they ultimately refused to endorse Johnson and Humphrey. Humphrey's actions contributed to the alienation of frontline civil rights groups such as the Student Nonviolent Coordinating Committee (SNCC) and the MFDP. Johnson and Humphrey went on to a resounding victory in the 1964 presidential election, but black militants began to see Black Power as a more attractive political alternative.

Roy Wilkins of the National Association for the Advancement of Colored People was another Minnesotan who played a leading role in the civil rights movement at the national level. Although born in St. Louis, Wilkins grew up in a low-income, racially integrated neighborhood in St. Paul. It was here that he learned that it was possible "for white people and black people to live next door to one another, to get along—even to love one another." He was nineteen years old when he picked up a Twin Cities newspaper and read about the lynching of three blacks in Duluth. He later recalled that he felt "sick, scared and angry all at the same time" and lost his "innocence on race once and for all" that day.

While earning a degree in sociology at the University of Minnesota, Wilkins worked on the *Minnesota Daily*, and later became the editor of the *St. Paul Appeal*, a black newspaper. Wilkins would go by way of Kansas City, Missouri, to the national scene, where he succeeded W. E. B. Du Bois as editor of the NAACP's *The Crisis*. Then in 1955 he became the NAACP executive secretary and almost immediately arranged for financial credit for civil rights workers in the South. He was a prominent participant in the March on Washington in 1963, the Selma March of 1965, and the March Against Fear in 1966.

Under his leadership the NAACP vigorously supported both the Civil Rights Act and the Voting Rights Act. Samuel Myers, a professor at the Roy Wilkins Center for Human Relations and Social Justice at the Humphrey Institute of Public Affairs of the University of Minnesota, observed that Wilkins's "experience working closely with whites, such as on the editorial board of the *Minnesota Daily*, provided him with a unique set of experiences and insights that perhaps he would not have had if he faced stark segregation in his formative years." Myers labeled Wilkins's biracialism his "Minnesota" approach to civil rights.

Minnesota also contributed volunteers to the dangerous work of black voter registration and political education in the South. Joe Morse, a college student from Winona, Minnesota, traveled to Meridian, Mississippi, in mid-July 1964. He participated in the voter registration project as a Congress of Racial Equality (CORE) member until 1966. Charles Leck, sponsored by the National Council of Churches, spent five weeks as a Freedom Summer volunteer in Canton, Mississippi. This self-described white, middle-class Minnesotan went on to work as a volunteer in a black community on the south side of Minneapolis from 1966 to 1969. The veterans of Freedom Summer returned to their native states not only with tales of courage and sacrifice, but also with some practical applications of their experience. The Jane Addams School for Democracy in St. Paul is a direct descendant of the freedom schools in Mississippi.

Minnesota's struggle for racial equality has always been complicated by the fact that the state is one of the most racially homogeneous in the nation with a long history of white reluctance to face up to the enduring legacy of racism. Germans and Scandinavians founded the state and comprised a majority of the population of Minneapolis in the early twentieth century. When Jews, blacks, and other minorities moved into the city in the 1920s, restrictive covenants established rigid housing segregation. And this was not the only indication of the city's racial bigotry. By 1923 there were ten chapters of the Ku Klux Klan in

Minneapolis alone. Other chapters could be found throughout the state.

On the eve of World War II, 60 percent of blacks in the twin cities of Minneapolis and St. Paul were unemployed, and local industries would not hire them for defense-related work. Urban renewal projects and freeway construction displaced many working-class blacks during the 1950s and 1960s. The largest increase in the black population of Minneapolis occurred between 1960 and 1970, when the civil rights movement was at its peak, but their numbers remained quite small. In 1970, only 34,868 blacks lived in a city with a total population of 434,400, making Minneapolis 93 percent white. In that same year, the black population of Los Angeles numbered 763,000, while 660,428 blacks lived in Detroit. Many rural Minnesota towns had no black residents at all and a few of them had no more than a handful. Worthington, a town of slightly more than 9,000, became the exception in 1964 when Armour and Company transferred two hundred black meatpackers there after it closed plants in Kansas and Texas.

In spite of its small minority population, Minneapolis faced the same racial problems that plagued cities throughout the nation in the 1960s. Job discrimination, urban blight, lack of adequate city services, unresponsive government, inadequate recreational facilities, largely segregated schools, and police harassment and brutality created an atmosphere of unrest in black north Minneapolis. In 1967 an alleged incident of police brutality sent fifty young blacks on a rampage down Plymouth Avenue, breaking windows and setting fires. The next night gunshots prompted 150 rioters on Plymouth Avenue to engage in destruction estimated at $4.2 million. Civil rights leader Harry Davis observed that "the racial anger that bubbled to the surface in places like Los Angeles and Detroit was present in Minneapolis, too." While Martin Luther King reminded Americans "riots are the voices of the unheard."

In 1969 race riots once again erupted in north Minneapolis. One response to the violence was the formation of "Soul Police," a group organized by Harry "Spike" Moss, director of the New Way community center. The "Soul Police" were intended to monitor police activity and protect young blacks from police harassment. The New Way was tuned into the national scene and strongly influenced by SNCC's Black Power stance. Moderate black leaders like Harry Davis criticized the New Way for concentrating on black empowerment and teaching black history. Yet even Davis acknowledged, "It was impossible to be a black man anywhere in America . . . and not be aware of both prevalent racism and a persistent stirring to overcome it." One of the New Way instructors claimed that it was the center that successfully pressured the University of Minnesota to offer courses in black studies.

Hubert Humphrey could not have become a successful reform mayor without the support and advice of important black leaders. For thirty years Nellie Stone Johnson owned and operated Nellie's Alterations in downtown Minneapolis. A local leader of organized labor and a union organizer in the 1930s and 1940s, she became the first black president of Local 665 Hotel and Restaurant Employees Union. She was the first black person elected to citywide office in Minneapolis when she won a seat on the library board in 1945. A lifetime member of the NAACP and also a member of the Urban League, she served as an influential advisor to Humphrey. According to her biographer David Brauer, without Nellie Johnson, Humphrey might not have had the moral conviction and political courage needed to challenge the national Democratic Party on segregation. In 1947, because of her leadership, Minneapolis became the first city in the nation to pass a civil rights ordinance guaranteeing people equal rights in the workplace. She also helped shape Humphrey's famous speech on civil rights at the Democratic National Convention in 1948. As Nellie Johnson later recalled, "There were two basic things that Hubert and I fought for and were hard-nosed about that changed this country: the right of labor to organize and the right of black people to live and not be hung from the hanging tree."

Another important leader of the civil rights movement in Minneapolis was Matthew Little, who came to the city in 1948. One of the first things he observed was that blacks were not allowed to stay in the major hotels. They were also excluded from many jobs. He immediately set to work with the local chapter of the NAACP to bring about change. Speaking later about his long career of civil rights advocacy, he told the *Minneapolis Star Tribune*, "I don't think I'll retire as long as I'm black. And I think I'll be black for the rest of my life."

With Matthew Little's support, Josie Johnson lobbied the Minnesota legislature to pass fair housing laws that banned restrictive covenants and the redlining of mortgage credit, which confined most blacks to one section of north Minneapolis and another in south Minneapolis. Josie Johnson was a committed educator as well as a civil rights activist. In 1963 she led the Minnesota delegation to the March on Washington. As a member of the Urban League and a community organizer, she promoted fair housing and job opportunities for blacks, women, gays, and American Indians. She also became the first black person to sit on the University of Minnesota Board of Regents.

In spite of the concerted efforts of activists like Little and Josie Johnson, blacks made only incremental gains in employment and housing in the 1960s, often on a case-by-case basis. One segregation index gave Minneapolis a 79.3 rating, the same rating it gave to New York City. In 1961 Mayor Arthur Naftalin, the city's first Jewish mayor, sought funds from the city council for job training, welfare assistance, and programs designed to halt police brutality. The resources allocated proved woefully inadequate and Naftalin's initiatives failed, producing even more frustration in the black community.

Another target of civil rights advocates in Minneapolis was public education. After the Supreme Court's historic decisions in 1954 and 1955 banning state-sponsored school segregation, white residents of Minneapolis continued to act as if this was only a problem in the South. But Minnesota's urban school districts often concentrated black, American Indian, and Hispanic students in a small number of schools and then blamed the resulting segregation on naturally occurring residential patterns. "We can't help where people choose to live," was the common response of local school boards. In the 1960s a coalition of groups rejected this argument and began to attack school segregation head on.

The cities with the largest black student populations were Minneapolis, St. Paul, and Duluth. In Minneapolis the racial disparity was most noticeable at the elementary school level. Even though one district's black students comprised only 15 percent of the school-aged population, three of its elementary schools had minority enrollments of over 70 percent. On the other hand, predominantly white elementary schools such as Loring, Wenonah, Audubon, and Lake Harriet had fewer than six black students each, and Pillsbury had none.

In 1962 the local branch of the NAACP, led by Curtis Chivers, engaged in a public relations campaign coordinated with the national organization to expose "Jim Crow schools, northern-style." Chivers joined with James Tillman of the Greater Minneapolis Interfaith Housing Program to draw attention to segregated schools and the solutions necessary to bring about change. Chivers and Tillman were also members of the Minneapolis Human Relations Task Force, which joined the call for an end to school segregation. Additional support was provided by the Urban League and then in the mid-1960s by a biracial group called the Committee for Integrated Education. Finally, in 1967, the Minneapolis Board of Education stepped in and issued clear guidelines regarding racial imbalance. The Minneapolis school system responded with a very limited and half-hearted voluntary busing experiment.

In July 1969, Minnesota Human Rights Commissioner Frank Kent ordered the city of Minneapolis to produce a comprehensive desegregation plan by the end of the year. But as the year 1970 began, the Minneapolis school board had yet to produce a plan, while some board members publicly aligned themselves with an antibusing organization calling itself the Neighborhood School Committee. As the anger of white parents mounted, the police were forced to provide protection for school board members, and especially for Harry Davis, the only black member.

Davis grew up on the north side of Minneapolis in a low-income neighborhood of blacks and Jews. Despite being stricken with polio as a child, Davis became a skilled boxer, a successful businessman, and a civil rights leader. In 1969 he became the first black person elected to the Minneapolis school board. With the backing of the Democratic Farmer Labor Party, he ran for mayor in 1971, losing to the incumbent "law and order" candidate Charles Stenvig. It would be more than twenty years before Sharon Sayles-Belton, a former civil rights volunteer in the South, became the first black mayor of Minneapolis.

The Minneapolis school board did come up with a desegregation plan, but not before a case known as *Booker v. Special School District No. 1* reached the federal courts in 1972. The plaintiff was the fifth-grade granddaughter of Curtis Chivers. In his ruling against the district, the federal judge referred to Bethune Elementary in Minneapolis when he wrote, "It's hard to imagine how a school could be more clearly denominated a 'Black school' unless the words themselves had been chiseled over the door."

The judge announced he would monitor compliance with his ruling and set a goal of no more than 42 percent minority enrollment in any school. Despite his best efforts, however, this goal was never reached. The growth of the metropolitan black population coupled with white flight to the suburbs guaranteed failure. Critics pointed out that success could have been achieved if the suburban districts had been joined with the metropolitan ones, but there was no political will to do that. As a result, Minneapolis joined other northern cities in the resegregation of their schools. And despite a subsequent surge in the black population of Minneapolis to ninety thousand during the 1970s, the Twin Cities remained, as they still do today, the "whitest" large metropolitan area in the United States.

In the prairie states of Iowa and Minnesota blacks experienced the same racial discrimination in employment, housing, education, public accommodations, and treatment by police that blighted the lives of blacks in the South and urban North. The major distinguishing factor in both states was their relatively small black populations, even in their largest cities. In both states small groups of black militants emerged who forced the white-dominated governments to face problems they preferred to ignore. The perceived threats posed by these militants made white state and local officials more amenable to the advice of black moderates. Just as on the national level, government concerns about Black Power led to greater acceptance of the views of Martin Luther King. The ability of moderate black organizations and white religious, civic, and business leaders in Iowa and Minnesota to work together enabled them to achieve some policy and legislative changes that advanced civil rights for blacks and other minorities. But for some midwestern blacks these gains were far more chimerical than real. In 2007 Byron Washington, a longtime activist in Waterloo, told a reporter that for the blacks in his community "in forty years basically nothing's changed. You are talking to a very irate African American man who is tired of his people getting kicked in the ass." The achievements of the civil rights movements in Iowa and Minnesota enlarged the possibilities for change, but the struggle for racial justice and equality remained far from over.

Further Reading

Anderson, Reynaldo. "Practical Internationalists: The Story of the Des Moines, Iowa, Black Panther Party," in *Groundwork: Local Black Freedom Movements in America*, edited by Jeanne Theoharis and Komozi Woodard, 282–99. New York: New York University Press, 2005.

Brauer, David. *Nellie Stone Johnson: The Life of an Activist*. St. Paul, Minn.: Ruminator Books, 2000.

Davis, W. Harry. *Overcoming: The Autobiography of W. Harry Davis*. Afton, Minn.: Afton Historical Society Press, 2002.

Fehn, Bruce, and Robert Jefferson. "North Side Revolutionaries and the Civil Rights Struggle: The African-American Community in Des Moines and the Black Panther Party for Self-Defense, 1948–1970." *Annals of Iowa* 69, no. 1 (Winter 2010), 51–81.

Furst, Randy. "Matthew Little Stood Up For Civil Rights for 60 Years." *Minneapolis Star Tribune*, January 27, 2014.

Kenney, Dave, and Thomas Saylor. *Minnesota in the 1970s*. St. Paul, Minn.: Minnesota Historical Society, 2013.

Nathanson, Iric. "Into the Bright Sunshine—Hubert Humphrey's Civil Rights Agenda." *MinnPost*, May 23, 2011.

Reed, Cecil, with Priscilla Donovan. *The Fly in the Buttermilk: The Story of Cecil Reed*. Iowa City: University of Iowa Press, 1993.

Roberts, Gene. "Many Residents of Waterloo Puzzled." *Nashua Telegraph*, July 26, 1967.

Silag, Bill, Susan Koch-Bridgford, and Hal Chase. *Outside In: African-American History in Iowa, 1838–2000*. Des Moines: State Historical Society of Iowa, 2001.

Wilkins, Roy. *Standing Fast: The Autobiography of Roy Wilkins*. New York: Viking Press, 1982.

13

Challenging the Color Line in Kansas and Nebraska
The Revolution at a Regional Nexus
James N. Leiker

Kansas and Nebraska inhabitants consider themselves westerners, not southerners, and that factor is featured in their mottoes and symbols of "freedom." They, too, have participated in efforts at eliminating racial tensions, often before the remainder of the nation. However, as James Leiker phrased it, "their efforts produced short-term successes but long-term forgettability." On the other hand, protests at the University of Kansas, interracial cooperation at the DePorres Club in Omaha, sit-ins at Wichita, and school integration at Topeka, civil rights activists have made considerable strides in those states. Black Power also played a role in the ensuing struggle. Change was not always easy, however, as racial violence broke out in Omaha and Wichita in the sixties. Leiker is professor of history at Johnson County Community College, and is author of numerous articles as well as *Racial Borders: Black Soldiers along the Rio Grande* and with Ramon Powers, *The Northern Cheyenne Exodus in History and Memory*.

The iconic images are embedded in our collective consciousness: the quiet persistence of students awaiting service at a segregated lunch counter; people hustling to their jobs on foot or in carpools, encouraged by church leaders to boycott public transit; a lawsuit filed by Topeka parents to admit their children to a neighborhood school. Like all conventional narratives, the images have power to illuminate but also distort. The students were not SNCC workers in Greensboro in 1960, but Wichita teenagers in 1958; the community boycott was not that of Montgomery in 1955 but Omaha three years earlier; and the Topeka plaintiffs did not come to court in a car, as they likely did in 1954, but probably in a horse and buggy, the standard conveyance in 1902.

Popular understanding of the civil rights movement seems constrained in time, considered a phenomenon of the 1960s, and geographically, a phenomenon of the South. As activists challenged the color line, scholars' task is to challenge this constraint, starting with a firm grounding in the particulars of place. Unlike their brethren states Texas and Oklahoma, Kansas and Nebraska escape geographers' debates about where the South ends and West begins. There is no overlap here. By virtue of climate and culture, residents claim themselves as distinctly western. But with their largest cities located on the eastern edge of the Great Plains, they also enjoy a proximity to the South—its labor pool, food, music, racial mores—that many other westerners lack. African Americans comparatively had greater personal liberties there; custom rather than law governed discrimination, they could vote, and for the most part, could assemble and form their own organizations. Precisely for these reasons, their efforts produced short-term successes but long-term forgettability. Whites' reactions, resistant and occasionally violent, lacked both the viciousness that confronted the movement elsewhere and the attendant drama that transforms episodes into icons. But their stories hold no less importance and not merely because they preceded better-known protests like Greensboro and Montgomery. Some historians prefer the term "freedom struggle" over "civil rights movement" while others simply prefer "revolution." The latter seems most appropriate when examining community-based activism in Kansas and Nebraska, two states at a nexus of West and South where—to borrow an astronomer's term—a constellation of interests and circumstances aligned to produce fundamental changes. But "revolution," having multiple meanings, can describe something other than change, and as its history reveals, the term is appropriate in that sense as well.

Race relations in Kansas and Nebraska have been framed by residents' regional identity, their need to be different from the South. This is especially evident in Kansans' "Free State" image, which originated during the territorial period when abolitionists fought slavery's westward expansion. Besides rallying the University of Kansas (KU) against its athletic rivals, the (formerly slave-owning) Missourians, and boosting beer sales at the brewery in downtown Lawrence that bears the name, Free State iconography is often touted to establish the state's credentials to racial tolerance. The reality is somewhat different. After ratification of the Fourteenth Amendment in 1867, the legislature approved a bill permitting larger cities to practice school segregation. Twelve years later, a modified bill prohibited segregation in secondary schools and in cities not designated "first-class," defined then as having no less than fifteen thousand people. These measures occurred in the context of nineteenth-century debate as to whether taxpayers owed *anyone* a free education, regardless of race. Reformers gradually won the argument by contending that public schools held the key to assimilating undesirables, and that blacks particularly would progress in separate schools, businesses, even towns away from white people. Thousands of African Americans concurred as the late 1800s saw the establishment of dozens of all-black agricultural settlements like Nicodemus. Most were short-lived but their temporary proliferation suggests that "separate but equal," if implemented on their own terms, offered some blacks reason for optimism.[1]

Some but not all. As the black town experiment ended and parallel communities became the norm, middle-class black elites advocated sharply for the abolishment of separate education. In 1902, the Reynolds family, whose children attended an integrated school just outside Topeka, brought suit when the city's expansion incorporated their district and imposed "first-class" segregation policy. Plaintiffs' chief complaint was not separation but inconvenience, having to send students to a school thirteen blocks away. That case was resolved when the superintendent secured facilities closer to the plaintiffs' home but in subsequent decades, as Topeka grew and continued to absorb outlying areas, other legal challenges would be issued that ultimately pointed forward toward *Brown*. They pointed backward too; in 1879, lawmakers had refused to mandate segregation at the state level but allowed it at local ones, thereby creating a confusing, porous color line that twentieth-century urbanization fractured even further.[2]

Created simultaneously in 1854, Nebraska in some ways has superior claim to the "free state" image. Unlike Kansas, Republican legislators enthusiastically ratified the Fourteenth Amendment on their first full day of statehood, even embedding the words "equality before the law" in their state seal and motto. Like Kansas, middle-class blacks campaigned to end separate education but with more success; after 1867, no school could legally segregate, though many did anyway by custom.[3] Omaha especially illustrates the alignment of industrialization and organized labor that nurtured a "civil rights" mentality. Dwarfing its neighbor Lincoln's population of less than 1,000, Omaha's black numbers more than doubled from 4,426 in 1910 to 10,315 a decade later and grew steadily thereafter. Railroads and meatpacking drew the bulk of these southern migrants to the "Near North Side" where they initially clashed with eastern Europe immigrants.

In 1919, hostility by white veterans, recently returned from overseas battlefields to find the city's packinghouse jobs taken by blacks, led to an outbreak of violence. During that year's "Red Summer," a mob castrated and murdered William Brown, mutilating his body and burning it in a macabre public spectacle.

Brown's death actually proved to be a turning point that mobilized the African American community. An NAACP chapter already had been formed in 1912, and a local branch of UNIA (United Negro Improvement Association) was soon established. Earl and Louise Little, the parents of Malcolm X, reported on the UNIA's activities for local newspapers until they were told to leave town by Klansmen. Other African Americans, seeking bridges to white coworkers, became active in the UMPWA (United Meatpacking Workers of America), imbuing North Omaha with a dual sense of labor consciousness and interracial cooperation that informed their later activism. By the 1930s, redlining and restrictive covenants had confined them to the North Side, just as the Depression increased unemployment and poverty. Despite these setbacks North Omaha entered the civil rights era as a thriving urban community on the edge of the West. As a native later explained, the sense of living in a "ghetto" lay far in the future.[4]

Kansas City developed in similar fashion, recruiting southern manpower to process fattened Great Plains beef. As of 1920, only four companies—Armour, Swift, Wilson, and Cudahy—employed one in eight of Kansas City's black men in the West Bottoms, the world's largest collection of slaughterhouses. That same year, 465 African Americans claimed employment as railroad porters, and another 822 as janitors and domestic servants. While their introduction to industry often came as strikebreakers, blacks' gradual involvement in the CIO (Congress of Industrial Organizations) and the Brotherhood of Sleeping Car Porters drew them closer to whites and rooted them permanently in urban areas. By midcentury, over half of black Kansans lived in only three of the state's 105 counties: Sedgwick (Wichita), Shawnee (Topeka), and Wyandotte (Kansas City). A proliferation of churches, chapters of the NAACP and the biracial Urban League, and a newspaper, *The Call*, all helped to establish civic pride and aid new arrivals.[5]

Kansas City's interwar burst of artistic energy, part of what scholars dub "the Harlem Renaissance," resulted from this transplanting of southern culture into western soil. The precedents of jazz followed migrants from New Orleans's Congo Square and the ragtime of western Missouri, and the art was nurtured in black-owned vaudeville companies like TOBA, the Theater Owners' Booking Association ("Tough on Black Asses," musicians called it). Jazz finally blossomed from the instruments of musicians like Count Basie and Charlie "Bird" Parker, who traveled an entertainment circuit from the famous 18th and Vine district to Omaha's North Side and Lincoln's "Black Heaven" neighborhood. Like music, baseball not only entertained and boosted community spirits but made quiet assaults on the color line. Wichita integrated its team in 1932, and after a decade of barnstorming, the Kansas City Monarchs and their star, Leroy "Satchel" Paige, began playing white southern teams in the late 1930s. Sports journalists commented less on Paige's color than on the rude behavior of players and fans who jeered him. Kansas natives like writer Langston Hughes and artist Aaron Douglass, who studied fine arts at UNL (University of Nebraska–Lincoln), frequently drew on their western experiences for material. Whatever whiffs of universal "New Negro" culture these examples suggest, hometown activists—be they students, clergy, or union organizers—took from them the inspiration to tackle issues of relevance in particular locales.[6]

As in the South, an enlarged military presence eroded the provincialism of western towns that had sustained Jim Crow. Western Nebraska, which knew its share of Klan activity and racial violence, saw constant tension between enjoying the benefits of federal spending and the need to uphold outdated practices. In 1943, when Kearney officials' plan to establish a club for black servicemen ran up against opposition by prohibitionists, the army declared the town's businesses off-limits to all officers and enlisted men, causing Kearneyites to rethink their policy. In Hastings, where one-third of the country's naval ammunition was produced, African Americans constituted almost 20 percent of a civilian labor force 7,500 strong. Still, sailors and civilians complained of discrimination in the town's shops and restaurants and in the depot itself. To improve morale, administrators reassigned an unpopular commanding officer, pressured business owners, and even bused in black women from Omaha to provide dance partners at segregated social events.[7] World War II enhanced the influence of CORE (Congress of Racial Equality), which opened branches in Lawrence, Wichita, Lincoln, and Omaha. CORE's use of direct tactics like "sit-ins," employed with some success by labor during the 1930s, as well as its emphasis on black-white cooperation, characterized the revolution's successful early stage.

In postwar Omaha, the revolution was represented by faces on both sides of the color line, and of the gender line too. They included Rowena Moore, secretary of the local meat cutters' union, who fought for the rights of black women to work in packinghouses; Mildred Brown-Gilbert, publisher of the *Omaha Star*, the city's longest-running black newspaper; and Father John Markoe, a white Jesuit priest at Creighton University who publicly declared his intent "to kick Jim Crow's ass out of Omaha." In 1947, Markoe, Brown-Gilbert, and a half-dozen Creighton students founded the interracial DePorres Club, which operated independently for five years until its affiliation with CORE. Emboldened by growing numbers, DePorres protested discriminatory practices at "whites-only" swimming pools, ice cream and donut shops, and businesses as small as a neighborhood laundromat and as large as the Coca-Cola Bottling Company who refused to hire qualified black applicants. Brown-Gilbert's *Star* published photos and articles to rally the community behind DePorres's Omaha and Council Bluffs Street Railway Company (O&CB) campaign. As of 1947, African Americans were employed in only 96 out of a possible 534 occupations in the city, and activists saw the O&CB boycott as a breakthrough move that would open equal job opportunities. After a two-year struggle, the company relented and hired three black drivers in 1954.[8]

Interracial activism proved less successful in university towns like Lawrence due to students' transitory nature and their perceived outsider status among locals, part of a ubiquitous "town-gown" animosity. Since the 1920s, KU admitted black students but excluded them from dorms, campus organizations, and social activities. When Count Basie performed there in 1939, African Americans had to listen from a crowded, separate room. Humiliations like these inspired a new NAACP branch founded in 1942 by Wesley and Rosa Sims, and a year later an NAACP Youth Council organized by their son Paul. In 1948, when CORE launched a campaign to desegregate the all-white Brick's Cafe, KU football players assaulted the protesters while Lawrence police stood by. Segregation at KU did finally end during the 1950s but the battle to desegregate private businesses in Lawrence proved more difficult. When the Simses challenged licensure of a theater after being evicted for refusing to use the colored section, the city promptly responded by revoking the licensing requirement.[9]

In the state capital, twenty miles from Lawrence, the black community grew bitterly divided over the case that came to define civil rights nationally. Topeka was known as a Jim Crow town; Charles Scott, one of the city's few African American attorneys, recalled that on Kansas Avenue in the mornings all one could see were blacks washing windows. But changes were afoot. The Great Depression and labor shortage of World War II had reduced economic disparities across the color line. If World War I–era urbanization tightened that line by absorbing small towns with no previous tradition of segregation into first-class cities, then post–World War II prosperity destabilized it by drawing men like Oliver Brown—a welder with the Santa Fe Railroad—into good-paying jobs that let them move toward the outer fringes of black neighborhoods, near whites.

Like many black Kansans, Lucinda Todd moved to Topeka from an integrated rural area and was shocked at its racist practices. The case that she and other activists championed had a precedent in *Graham v. Board of Education of Topeka* (1941), which ruled segregation in grades seven and eight to be unconstitutional. Besides integrating junior highs, *Graham* had several repercussions. When the district's integration plan eliminated jobs for six African American teachers, outrage arose in the black community against any further activism. Defying white school officials and even fellow blacks, Todd elicited the help of NAACP director Walter White, who immediately expressed interest in a case aimed at elementary schools. In 1952, NAACP attorneys consolidated the Topeka case with others from South Carolina, Virginia, Delaware, and Washington, D.C., asking the U.S. Supreme Court to remove the "separate but equal" provision of *Plessy v. Ferguson* (1896). After much canvassing, ostracism, harassing phone calls, and even threatening notes, Todd and eleven other families attached their names to *Brown v. Board of Education of Topeka*, named not (as commonly assumed) for alphabetical reasons but for the strategic importance of being represented by a male head of household. Brown's membership in the welders' union, providing him relatively secure employment and thus some protection from economic reprisal, factored in as well.[10]

The furor unleashed by the Warren Court's ruling in May 1954 took many Kansans by surprise. Outside of first-class cities, few whites even knew segregation existed in the state, and booster-minded journalists had carefully avoided reporting on the *Brown* case out of embarrassment. Indeed, NAACP strategists had counted on Kansas's unique history and image to make the point that segregation was a national, not a regional, problem. Ironically, as state attorneys defended segregation's constitutionality in Washington, the Topeka Board of Education in September 1953—eight months before the case's resolution—voted to integrate. This was likely an anticipatory move but as had happened after *Graham*, "integration" in this instance meant black children being taught by white teachers, causing district officials—as predicted—to fire black teachers. Many black Topekans were angry and devastated. One of the plaintiffs in *Brown* later said that the televised images of people suffering in the South, demanding civil rights in the decision's momentous aftermath, filled her with regret and second-guessing about her role in bringing it forward.[11]

More than any city on the plains, Wichita at midcentury became "southernized" in demography and culture. Defense spending during World War II and the Cold War sparked a booming aircraft industry that drew migrants from

Texas and Oklahoma and boosted the population from 160,000 in 1950 to more than a quarter million a decade later. Blacks composed less than 10 percent of that latter total, enjoying few benefits from recent industrialization. De facto segregation prohibited their employment in aircraft manufacturing and, as in Omaha, confined them to the northeast side. One historian calls it a residential ghetto, the walls of which were defended by discriminatory banking and real estate practices. Fresh from recent courtroom successes, the adult chapters of NAACP generally frowned on CORE-style direct action but not so its youth councils. In summer 1958, a dozen teenagers led by twenty-year-old Ronald Walters, president of the Wichita council, launched a sit-in at Dockum's Drug Store, part of the Rexall retail chain. Ron drew support from his mother, Maxine Walters, known for work on behalf of homeless rights, and from local NAACP leader Chester Lewis. In another parallel to Omaha's revolution, a local Catholic church, St. Peter Claver, allowed the protestors use of their basement for meetings to practice civil disobedience. Walters spoke at other churches as well, recruiting volunteers for the campaign that met every Tuesday, Thursday, and Saturday—the nights when Dockum's stayed open late—to integrate the store's lunch counters.

Unlike SNCC's Greensboro sit-ins two years later, the Wichita protest saw no overt violent reaction, although much grumbling by Dockum's white patrons did ensue. When Rexall vice president Walter Heiger announced in August that the company had lost revenue due to the demonstration's bad publicity, he ordered black customers to be served at not only Dockum's but all the chain's stores—a victory beyond what the teenagers had wanted. NAACP-sponsored youths quickly targeted other establishments in Wichita and beyond. In neighboring Winfield in 1959, students at Southwestern College staged a sit-in against barbershops that refused service to a black professor. A year later, the Kansas City youth council used Wichita-like tactics against restaurants there, achieving some success in the form of an antidiscrimination ordinance.[12]

These bursts of grassroots activism, seemingly independent, shared several commonalities that pique the curiosity of historians seeking patterns. By no coincidence did the most significant challenges to the color line emerge in urban parts of Kansas and Nebraska, not simply because that was where most African Americans lived but because the transformation of "cow towns" into "cities" produced fragmented, uneven attempts at separation. Industrialization's economic benefits, for the first time, opened to many blacks the possibility of middle-class status against which the color line stood as an impediment. Families closest to realizing that goal had more to gain by eliminating segregation than those whose chief struggle remained chronic poverty. In at least two cities, Omaha and Topeka, activists "made their bones" in organized labor, learning from unions the advantages of solidarity and direct tactics like strikes and boycotts. Nor should the importance of organized religion be discounted, especially as it pertained to white-black cooperation and mobilizing young people. Men like Creighton's Father Markoe and the many campus ministers who organized busloads of Kansas students from Lawrence, Manhattan, and Wichita in the 1960s to work on southern civil rights campaigns exemplified Reinhold Niebuhr's doctrine of Christian realism—Christianity in action, the same theology that guided King. Finally, since challenging the color line carried risks of retaliation in the workplace—a risk that male breadwinners may have felt more keenly—it is little wonder that women often became the "bridge leaders" who did the unglamorous work of carrying petitions, coordinating between churches, organizing meetings in private homes, and much more. Women like Maxine Walters, Rosa Sims, and Rowena Moore were likely the norms and not the exceptions. In fact, of the thirteen plaintiffs who affixed their names to the *Brown* case, only one, Oliver Brown himself, was male.

Some feminist scholars contend that as civil rights gained the attention of national media it became more "male-centric," with men stepping forward as the face of black equality and women retreating to conventional, supportive roles for the good of the cause. Certainly the revolution in Kansas and Nebraska brought to the spotlight assertive young men whose militancy defined a generation. Chester Lewis of Wichita, one of the few adult chapter presidents who supported direct action, became known as a "young Turk" at NAACP's national level. In 1961, he helped pressure the state legislature to pass the Kansas Act Against Discrimination and create a Kansas Commission on Civil Rights (KCCR) with enforcement power to levy fines or imprisonment. Bruce R. Watkins, a Kansas City mortician, formed Freedom Inc. to mobilize black voters and increase their voice in Missouri politics. No revolutionary cut a more dramatic figure than Omaha's Ernie Chambers. Son of a packinghouse worker and sometime preacher, grandson of Mississippi migrants who arrived on the North Side around World War I, Chambers started in a barbershop—a natural gathering place for political debate. Having established his reputation as a radical activist by 1970, he won election to Nebraska's unicameral legislature as a representative from the North Side, beginning a four-decade political career distinguished for campaigns against the death penalty, promotion of hate crime laws, and divestiture of funds from apartheid South Africa.[13]

Yet by adopting such personalities as symbolic of the revolution, Americans obstructed their own potential to see its eclectic origins clearly. Before the 1960s, the color line was one of many injustices against which reformers struggled. Although the movement's success seemed to peak at mid-decade, it stalled and by the mid-1970s even appeared to be rolling backward. Conservative resistance was part of the problem. While no Southern Manifesto or Bull Connor sprang from their ranks, white Kansans and Nebraskans practiced the more subtle form of discrimination known as white flight, relocating to suburbs and leaving behind urban neighborhoods and schools to deal with ever-shrinking tax bases. In a decision referred to colloquially as "Brown II," the U.S. Supreme Court in 1955 remanded implementation of desegregated schools to the lower courts. Ostensibly an acknowledgement of varying local conditions, the ruling offered a license for delay and evasion. In Topeka, the board of education abolished race as a criterion for school assignment but allowed so many exceptions to the neighborhood boundaries rule that virtually no white parent felt compelled to send their child to classes with blacks. Mary Dudziak has called this a one-way integration approach: "Now that the board was getting out of the business of segregation, it wished to get out of the business of compulsion as well. When it meant controlling the choices that whites might make, compulsion became a dirty word."[14]

Nonetheless, Topeka's integration plan became the model for Kansas school districts. Wichita's reaction to *Brown* basically involved gerrymandering its boundary lines, eventually doubling the size of its district through annexation of rural areas and providing parents more options for schools even if they lived in town. As of 1965, 113 of 130 black teachers in the district taught exclusively at black schools, according to data employed by Chester Lewis to document the glacial speed at which whites apparently intended to integrate. As a Wichita superintendent stated bluntly: "When a school goes beyond thirty percent [black], people [whites] begin to move."[15] Even in Lawrence, the state's most consistently liberal city, conservative resistance ran deep. A group calling itself the Loyal American Whites demanded payment of $500 billion from "the Negro race" for the cost of educating them. The typical Lawrence resident avoided ideas that extreme but, fearful of "artificial forcing" by outsiders and intellectuals, also upheld the primacy of property rights over civil rights. In 1960, protests at "the Plunge," a private swimming pool that excluded blacks, elicited a counterreaction from business owners who claimed the privilege of excluding whomever they wished. New owners skirted the issue when they purchased the facility and vowed to operate it as a private club, exempt from public accommodations laws. Twice during the ensuing decade, voters rejected bond issues to build an integrated municipal pool, leaving Lawrence as one of only three first-class cities in Kansas to lack a public pool for black youths who entertained themselves by gathering on downtown street corners.[16]

To young African Americans like Rick Dowdell, born in 1951 and raised during the heady optimism of the post-*Brown* years, equality was taking its sweet time. A protégé of Wichita activist Leonard Harrison who apparently introduced him to Black Power, Dowdell led a movement at Lawrence High School to add black history and literature courses to the curriculum, even joining other members of the Black Student Union in a walkout. Dowdell also developed a troublesome relationship with local authorities, complaining of police harassment. The turbulence of antiwar protests at KU and the town's proximity to urban Kansas City weighed heavily on law enforcement in the late sixties. After Kansas City police used tear gas to dispel rioters in Swope Park in 1967 and again a year later when six residents were killed and more than five hundred arrested, rumors circulated about black gangs from the metro descending on Lawrence with intent to burn it down. In July 1970, an apparent traffic violation precipitated Rick Dowdell, leading police on a car chase that ended with his death by gunfire. For three nights following, explosions and gunplay interrupted the summer darkness as snipers fired at car windows, white vigilantes patrolled the black neighborhood, and police killed another nineteen-year-old, a white student, who had been standing with a crowd taunting cops at a popular hangout.[17]

Urban violence, to which even college towns like Lawrence were not immune, was not an entirely separate phenomenon from Black Power. But the connection between the two was correlative, not causal. Both emerged from bitter disappointment with interracial activism and the limits of legislation acquired through peaceful protest. At the time of Dowdell's death, thousands of young men just like him were in no mood for continued alliances with whites. Books like Frantz Fanon's *Wretched of the Earth*, which asserted an absolute duality between colonizers and colonized, influenced activists like Stokely Carmichael, who by mid-decade favored the eviction of whites from SNCC and CORE. Despite the nationalists' angry rhetoric ("by any means necessary"), there is no evidence they played a role in organizing the urban protests that swept the country. Black Power's strength counted more in the cultural arena than the political, asserting the importance of racial pride and self-definition. The new militancy became obvious in Omaha fairly early. By 1963, Father Markoe's DePorres Club had been replaced with the Citizens Coordinating Committee for Civil Liberties (4CL), and at Technical High School by BANTU (Black Association for Nationalism through Unity). Not explicitly exclusionary of whites, both rejected traditional approaches in favor of black solidarity. Chambers, an alumnus of Technical High, supported their endeavors, as did Malcolm X, who during a speech in the city of his birth emphasized the international dimensions of the struggle following his trip to Mecca.[18]

Kansas and Nebraska shared the wave of urban unrest through their largest black communities respectively in Wichita and Omaha. In summer 1966, black youths on the latter's North Side clashed with police in separate disturbances for a total of six nights. The confrontations began in grocery store parking lots—the only places teenagers could congregate given the lack of recreational facilities—and erupted into vandalism. During his 1968 presidential campaign, George Wallace spoke at City Auditorium from the same stage that hosted Malcolm X a few years earlier. A melee broke out after Wallace verbally goaded protestors, causing police to use nightsticks and chemical spray to clear the aisles at the Alabama governor's request. During the week of assaults and rioting that followed Wallace's visit, an off-duty cop shot and killed a sixteen-year-old black youth who refused to halt after a possible robbery. Burning and rioting swept the North Side again in 1969 after policemen killed fourteen-year-old Vivian Strong. A year later, Officer Larry Minard was lured to the neighborhood and killed by a booby-trapped suitcase bomb. Two suspects were convicted of first-degree murder and handed life sentences, a case long contested by the NAACP and Amnesty International.[19]

Wichita, and particularly the career of Chester Lewis, offers an even more vivid microcosm of how traditional methods were replaced by black nationalism. As one of the NAACP's "Turks," Lewis continued to employ such methods through the mid-1960s: strikes against discriminatory landlords and legal complaints against companies like Boeing for contract violations. In 1967, black students at East High School and Wichita State University (WSU) protested exclusion from cheerleading squads and other collegiate activities. With tensions high, white and black youths on July 30 clashed in ninety minutes of violence at a parking lot near Sandy's Drive-In, resulting in the stabbing of a TV reporter. Following two days of curfew, a group of black teenagers peacefully entered city hall to complain about police brutality and harassment by whites patrolling their neighborhoods and firing shotguns. Lewis pushed for a citizens' review board over Wichita police and obtained concessions from the Chamber of Commerce for job training and recreational facilities. Most activists of his generation, for whom responses like these were time-tested steps toward progress, shared certain features like steady jobs, service in a desegregated military, or church participation, all of which predisposed them toward a cooperative outlook. Blacks born in the postwar years knew different experiences, faced different problems, and consequently articulated different solutions. When Wichita rioting reoccurred in 1968, the city responded with National Guard troops who marched and drove tanks through the black community. By then, Lewis had had enough. Resigning from the NAACP, he began working with newer organizations pursuing anti-poverty and Black Power movement agendas.[20]

The revolution in Kansas and Nebraska, like the rest of the United States, did not so much end as it lost clear focus. Despite forced proximity on one side of the color line, African Americans had never been monolithic. Even during the movement's heyday, class, religious, and personal differences divided them and prevented unanimity. Hometown activism continued after the 1970s, but through smaller organizations, pursuing fragmented, narrower goals. Jim Crow's well-deserved death certainly opened opportunities for middle-class blacks in white-majority occupations and suburbs. But paradoxically, it hastened socioeconomic decline for those who remained in black-majority communities. Since the massive restructuring of railroads and meatpacking, places like Omaha and Kansas City now have some of the highest poverty and crime rates in the country. One study estimates that Omaha's neighborhoods and schools enjoyed more integration in the late nineteenth century than they do in the twenty-first, partly a consequence of the federal *Milliken v. Bradley* decision (1974), which prohibited lower courts from ordering busing across city-suburb district lines.[21] As the saying goes, "Before the Sixties, the fight was to check into the white hotel. Now, the fight is to have enough money to check into the white hotel." Apparently, the alternative meaning of "revolution" applies as well—the astronomer's definition of revolution as a cycle, a circular movement that returns the traveler to the point of origin, only to begin anew.

However defined, the revolution in Kansas and Nebraska teaches a lesson about regional symbiosis. Here at the eastern edge of the West arrived the South's black workers, processing the beef, loading the boxcars, building the machines—indeed, transforming ranching, transportation, and aircraft construction into iconic symbols of the Central Plains. In turn, the thriving communities sustained by those enterprises provided models for effective challenge to racial discrimination, a testing ground of sorts on relatively safe soil before those same models could be tried on the more hostile terrains of Alabama and Mississippi. Both South and West benefitted from this exchange even if the color line persists—challenged but still intact.

Notes

1. James C. Carper, "The Popular Ideology of Segregated Schooling: Attitudes toward the Education of Blacks in Kansas, 1854–1900," *Kansas History, A Journal of the Central Plains* 1 (Winter 1978): 254–65.
2. Jean Van Delinder, "Early Civil Rights Activism in Topeka, Kansas, Prior to the 1954 *Brown* Case," in *African Americans on the Great Plains: An Anthology*, ed. Bruce A. Glasrud and Charles A. Braithwaite (Lincoln: University of Nebraska Press, 2009), 272–301.
3. James E. Potter, "Equality Before the Law: Thoughts on the Origins of Nebraska's State Motto," *Nebraska History* 91 (2010): 116–21; David J. Peavler Trowbridge, "A Double Mixture: Equality and Economy in the Integration of Nebraska Schools, 1858–1883," *Nebraska History* 91 (2010): 136–51; and Patrick Kennedy, "Nemaha County's African American Community," *Nebraska History* 82 (2001): 11–25.
4. Lawrence H. Larsen and Barbara J. Cottrell, *The Gate City: A History of Omaha* (Lincoln: University of Nebraska Press, 1997, original 1982), 166–74 and 222. The native was future legislator Ernie Chambers.
5. Charles E. Coulter, *"Take Up the Black Man's Burden": Kansas City's African American Communities* (Columbia: University of Missouri Press, 2006), 56–85, 217–28.
6. Brian Carroll, "Praising My People: Newspaper Sports Coverage and the Integration of Baseball in Wichita, Kansas," *Kansas History* 33 (Winter 2010–11): 240–55; Jennifer Hildebrand, "The New Negro Movement in Lincoln, Nebraska," *Nebraska History* 91 (2010): 166–89; Marc Rice, "The Western Black Renaissance in the Kansas City Region," and Richard M. Breaux, "The New Negro Renaissance in Omaha and Lincoln, 1910–1940," in *The Harlem Renaissance in the American West*, ed. Bruce Glasrud and Cary Wintz (New York: Routledge, 2012), 44–57 and 121–39, respectively; Richard M. Breaux, "The New Negro Arts and Letters Movement among Black University Students in the Midwest, 1914–1940," and Audrey Thompson, "Great Plains Pragmatist: Aaron Douglass and the Art of Social Protest," in Glasrud and Braithwaite, *African Americans on the Great Plains*, 205–32 and 233–55, respectively.
7. R. Douglas Hurt, *The Great Plains during World War II* (Lincoln: University of Nebraska Press, 2008), 254–63.
8. Bertha W. Calloway and Alonzo N. Smith, *Visions of Freedom on the Great Plains: An Illustrated History of African Americans in Nebraska* (Virginia Beach, Va.: Donning Company Publishers, 1998), 156; and Amy Helene Forss, "Mildred Brown and the De Porres Club: Collective Activism in Omaha, Nebraska's Near North Side, 1947–1960," *Nebraska History* 91 (2010): 190–205.
9. Kristine M. McCusker, "The Forgotten Years of America's Civil Rights Movement: Wartime Protests at the University of Kansas, 1939–1945," *Kansas History* 17 (Spring

1994): 26–37; and Quintard Taylor, *In Search of the Racial Frontier: African Americans in the American West, 1528–1990* (New York: W. W. Norton, 1998), 283–85.
10. Mark Fiege, *The Republic of Nature: An Environmental History of the United States* (Seattle: University of Washington Press, 2012), 318–57; Paul E. Wilson, *A Time to Lose: Representing Kansas in Brown v. Board of Education* (Lawrence: University Press of Kansas, 1995), 8–26; and Charise Cheney, "Blacks on *Brown*: Intra-Community Debates over School Desegregation in Topeka, Kansas, 1941–1955," *Western Historical Quarterly* 42 (Winter 2011): 481–500.
11. Craig Miner, *Kansas: The History of the Sunflower State, 1854–2000* (Lawrence: University Press of Kansas, 2002), 344–47; Cheryl Brown Henderson, "Lucinda Todd and the Invisible Petitioners of *Brown v. Board of Education of Topeka, Kansas*," in *African American Women Confront the West, 1600–2000*, ed. Quintard Taylor and Shirley Ann Wilson Moore (Norman: University of Oklahoma Press, 2003), 312–27; and Mary L. Dudziak, "The Limits of Good Faith: Desegregation in Topeka, Kansas, 1950–1956," *Law and History Review* 5, no. 2 (Autumn 1987): 351–91.
12. Ronald Walters, "The Great Plains Sit-In Movement, 1958–1960," in Glasrud and Braithwaite, *African Americans on the Great Plains*, 302–19; and Gretchen Cassel Eick, *Dissent in Wichita: The Civil Rights Movement in the Midwest, 1954–1972* (Urbana: University of Illinois Press, 2001), 1–11, 208–28.
13. Eick, *Dissent in Wichita*, 66–82; and Tekla Agbala Ali Johnson, *Free Radical: Ernest Chambers, Black Power, and the Politics of Race* (Lubbock: Texas Tech University Press, 2012).
14. Dudziak, "Limits of Good Faith," 386.
15. Eick, *Dissent in Wichita*, 108–9.
16. Miner, *Kansas*, 344–47; and Brent M. S. Campney, "Hold the Line: The Defense of Jim Crow in Lawrence, Kansas, 1946–1961," *Kansas History* 33 (Spring 2010): 22–41.
17. Rusty L. Monhollon, *"This is America?" The Sixties in Lawrence, Kansas* (New York: Palgrave, 2002), 85–100, 165–86.
18. Johnson, *Free Radical*, 41–65; and William L. Van Deburg, *New Day in Babylon: The Black Power Movement and American Culture, 1965–1975* (Chicago: University of Chicago Press, 1992).
19. Calloway and Smith, *Visions of Freedom*, 124–40; Larsen and Cottrell, *Gate City*, 271–77.
20. Eick, *Dissent in Wichita*, 53–65, 108–23, 129–35, 184–95, 208–28.
21. Larsen and Cottrell, *Gate City*, 308–11; and Trowbridge, "Double Mixture," 151.

Further Reading

See selected bibliography, pp. 271–78.

Part V

The South and the West Collide

Texas and Oklahoma share a racial history that sets them apart from the other western states. Both had a history of slavery that significantly defined the status of their African American population well into the second half of the twentieth century. In this context they share a racial history more in common with the South than the West. Texas also shared with the South the experience of the Civil War, Reconstruction, and the institutionalization of Jim Crow segregation and race-based political disenfranchisement in the late nineteenth and early twentieth century. Oklahoma also practiced segregation during its territorial period, and institutionalized it constitutionally and legislatively when it achieved statehood. Texas also has a significantly higher percentage of African American population than did other western states (ranging from 12 percent to 12.7 percent during the civil rights period). However, this was significantly smaller than the African American population of the other former states of the Confederacy. The percentage of African Americans in Oklahoma's population ranged from 7.2 percent to 6.5 percent larger than any other western state except Kansas. Also, like Texas, Oklahoma achieved initial successes in its civil rights struggle prior to the 1950s. And, like Texas, African Americans were the largest minority population during the civil rights movement.

14

Conceived in Segregation and Dedicated to the Proposition That All Men Were *Not* Created Equal
Oklahoma, the Last Southern State
Paul Finkelman

Geographically, Oklahoma can readily be classified as a western state, with an early economy based on ranching and agriculture. However, white Oklahomans seemed determined to follow a more southern path by excluding blacks in Oklahoma from an equitable existence. Laws and practice created a segregated state, second-class citizenship for blacks, and a wall of separation between white and black. African Americans in Oklahoma challenged white Oklahoma's apartheid, and won a number of U.S. Supreme Court cases between 1915 and 1950. Those victories, however, were followed by grudging noncompliance from whites. Only in 1965 did white Oklahoma politicians relent and begin to enact helpful civil rights legislation. In 2017 author Paul Finkelman, a well-known legal historian, became the President of Gratz College in Pennsylvania. Prior to his recent position, he held the Fulbright Chair in Human Rights and Social Justice at the University of Ottawa and was also the John E. Murray Visiting Professor of Law at the University of Pittsburgh. Among his numerous publications are his recent books *Supreme Injustice: Slavery in the Nation's Highest Court*, produced by Harvard University Press in 2018 and *Slavery and the Founders: Race and Liberty in the Age of Jefferson*, published by Routledge in 2014.

For American historians, the South is easily defined. In the antebellum period the South consisted of the fifteen slave states that existed in 1860. These include the eleven traitorous states that seceded to form the Confederacy and the four slave states that remained loyal to the Union. During the War, Virginia subdivided, with West Virginia entering the Union in 1863. This was the South for the rest of the nineteenth century. Segregated, conservative on most issues, and solidly Democratic at a time when the southern Democratic Party stood for states' rights and segregation. In 1907 Oklahoma became the last southern state to join the Union. Oklahoma is western in some ways, besides its geographical location. The Oklahoma State University football team is, after all, "The Cowboys." Oklahoma City is home to the National Cowboy & Western Heritage Museum, and Tulsa has one of the finest collections of western and American Indian art at the Gilcrease Museum. The state has the fourth-largest number of horses in the nation, at over 326,000, and ranks sixth in the nation for per capita horse ownership, at one for every 10.8 people.[1] But despite these western cultural attributes, Oklahoma came into the Union as a southern state, committed to segregation and the subordination of African Americans. From statehood until the 1970s Oklahoma remained a southern, segregating state with a western twang in its voice.

In 1861 Oklahoma was the "Indian Territory," populated by numerous Indian nations, their slaves, and a few whites. In the 1820s and 1830s the federal government had forced the five "Civilized Tribes" of the Southeast to relocate to Oklahoma. They brought their slaves with them—indeed one of the bizarre aspects of the antebellum period is that many Americans considered these tribes civilized because they participated in the thoroughly uncivilized and barbaric practice of buying and selling other human beings. When the Civil War began, Oklahoma was the only federal territory with a substantial number of slaves. Many Cherokee slave owners fought for white supremacy and human bondage,[2] while others, mostly non–slave owners, aligned with the United States and freedom. To this day there are disputes within the state and within Indian nations over the status of the descendants of the slaves owned by those tribes.

By 1890 the population had changed. There were about 173,000 whites, 22,000 blacks, and about 64,000 Indians. By 1900, on the eve of statehood, there were 670,000 whites, 56,000 blacks, and still about 64,000 Indians. The first census after statehood, in 1910, found just under 1.5 million whites, about 138,000 blacks, and about 75,000 Indians. From the time of statehood until the passage of the 1964 Civil Rights Act the state was always between 87 and 91 percent white. Blacks constituted about 8 percent of the population at statehood, but this percentage dropped steadily, reaching 6.6 percent in 1960. Thus, Oklahoma has always had a smaller percentage of African Americans than any other southern state except West Virginia.

But, despite the relatively small black population, Oklahoma began as a segregated state and maintained segregation until the courts and Congress forced it to integrate. At the state level Oklahoma did not adopt detailed statutes, segregating everything it could as much of the Deep South did. For example, there were no state laws requiring segregating circuses, sports arenas, public parks, theaters, and movie houses.[3] But, the state carefully segregated all forms of education, public and private, all social welfare institutions (such as schools for the deaf, reform schools, hospitals, and industrial schools), the penitentiary, and public transportation on railroads and buses and in stations and waiting rooms. In addition, Oklahoma had its own peculiar segregation laws, such as one preventing blacks and whites from fishing on the same lakes. Other forms of segregation—such as restaurants, hotels, and theaters—were segregated by local ordinances or custom. But where the state did mandate segregation, the legislature and its agencies worked hard to find ways to discriminate against blacks and humiliate them. For example, when federal courts forced the University of Oklahoma to admit blacks to its graduate and professional schools, the university established separate seating in its classrooms and cafeteria, holding on, as long as possible, to some way to assert its relentless hostility to African Americans.

Beyond legislation, Oklahoma had an active Ku Klux Klan in the 1920s. Tulsa, one of the two major cities in the state, was the site of a massive attack on the black community, known as the Tulsa Race Riot of 1921. This was in fact an invasion of the black neighborhood of Tulsa by white vigilantes and the local police force that burned at least twelve square blocks of the city to the ground and led to the deaths of scores or more of African Americans. The state has never offered compensation for the victims of this police-sponsored attack on innocent citizens of the state. Only after the passage of the 1964 Civil Rights Act did Oklahoma begin to dismantle its system of de jure segregation.

Oklahoma publicly endorsed its self-conscious alliance with the South, segregation, and racism in 1949, with the wake of these cases in Oklahoma and elsewhere forcing southern state universities to accept black students in graduate and professional schools. Fearful that this would lead to full integration, fourteen southern states, including Oklahoma, entered into a regional compact for cooperative education. Under this program Meharry Medical School in Tennessee would provide medical, dental, and nursing education for blacks from all the states. Other graduate and professional programs would similarly be developed to avoid integrating flagship campuses across the South. The governor of Oklahoma signed this compact, the state senate and house passed "A JOINT

RESOLUTION giving legislative approval to that certain compact entered into by the State of Oklahoma and other southern states . . . relative to the development and maintenance of regional educational services and schools in the southern states in the professional, technological, scientific, literary and other fields, so as to provide greater educational advantages and facilities for the citizens in the several states who reside in such region."[4] As it had been since statehood, Oklahoma would enter the civil rights revolution of the next decade and a half as a southern state, unalterably committed to segregation and racism. Only after the passage of the 1964 Civil Rights Act did Oklahoma begin to dismantle its system of de jure segregation.

Born with Original Sin: The 1907 Constitution

Oklahoma's first constitution makers wasted little time in staking out their support of segregation. Article I, Section 5 of the constitution affirmed that nothing in the document should "be construed to prevent the establishment and maintenance of separate schools for white and colored children."[5] The state constitution also provided for the continued operation of the "Colored Agricultural and Normal University,"[6] which is today Langston University. A subsequent provision on education mandated, "Separate schools for white and colored children with like accommodation shall be provided by the legislature and impartially maintained."[7] Significantly, the same section defined "colored" as "children of African descent," and defined "white children" to "include all other children."[8] A later provision of the constitution reaffirmed that "the word, or words, 'colored' or 'colored race,' 'negro' or 'negro race,' are used, the same shall be construed to mean or apply to all persons of African descent" while "the term 'white race' shall include all other persons."[9]

This definition made Oklahoma the first state in the nation to formally adopt a "one drop" rule for who was black and who was not. Here the contrast with other states is striking. Three years after Oklahoma became a state, Virginia redefined racial identity, declaring that "any person having one-sixteenth or more of negro blood shall be deemed a colored person."[10] Virginia would not adopt a "one drop" rule for determining race until 1924.[11]

While the state's definition of who was black was more strict than any other southern state, its definition of who was white made Oklahoma unique among the southern states for its inclusiveness. The law said that anyone with *any* black ancestry was "colored," but that "all other persons" in the state were members of the "white race." This meant that Indians and Asians were "white" in Oklahoma.

This was not an oversight. In 1917 the legislature required that death certificates note the "color or race, as white, black, mulatto (or other negro descent), Indian, Chinese, Japanese, or other."[12] Thus, for purposes of statistics and identification Oklahoma recognized the presence in the state of people who were not white, black, or Indian, such as the Chinese and Japanese, but for purposes of segregation in schools or public conveyances, or for marriage, Oklahoma divided its population simply between people of any African ancestry (blacks) and all others, who were legally white. This contrasts with Mississippi, for example, which insisted that children of Chinese ancestry attend schools for blacks, rather than for whites.[13]

Similarly, in 1924 Virginia would redefine race to hold that any person with any nonwhite ancestry was "colored," with the exception that "persons who have one-sixteenth or less of the blood of the American Indian and have no other non-Caucasic blood shall be deemed to be white persons." This is known as the "Pocahontas Rule" because of "the fact that a number of 'white' Virginians had long admitted, even celebrated, their descent from the seventeenth-century union between Pocahontas and John Rolfe. Any otherwise white Virginian, if possessing no more than one-sixteenth Indian ancestry—and no African ancestry—would still qualify as a 'white person.'"[14] Virginia could have such a rule because most whites in the state had no Indian ancestry or had very distant Indian ancestry. But, Oklahoma was created by merging the western part of the state (the Oklahoma Territory) with the Indian Territory. The Indian population was substantial and for more than a half century there had been significant intermarriage between Indians and whites. Indeed, three quarters of the enrolled Cherokee were part white, and a significant number of men of European ancestry were married to women who were Indian, or part Indian.[15] Furthermore, the largest Indian nations—the Five Civilized Tribes—had been slaveholding before the Civil War and many tribal members were as eager as whites to segregate blacks. Thus, Oklahoma developed a simple racial classification. All people were "white" unless they had some (however little) African ancestry and anyone with *any* African ancestry was "colored."

Consistent with the Fifteenth Amendment of the U.S. Constitution, Oklahoma's constitution declared that the state would never enact legislation "restricting or abridging the right of suffrage on account of race, color, or previous condition of servitude."[16] However, three years later the state would amend its constitution in an attempt to disfranchise most blacks in the state, and a few years later the U.S. Supreme Court would strike down this amendment under the Fifteenth Amendment for doing precisely what the state constitution said it would never do.[17] The constitution also banned convict labor,[18] which had been used throughout the Deep South as a way of oppressing blacks.

The 1907 Oklahoma Constitution did not create a full-blown system of segregation, but set the new state on the road to creating a segregated society. At statehood blacks constituted about 8 percent of the state population, and even if they had had equal access to the ballot box (which they did not in fact have) they could not have prevented a state legislature, which was entirely white with one exception,[19] from creating a thoroughly segregated society. And that is exactly what happened.

Creating a Segregated World

Oklahoma became a state on November 16, 1907. The first state legislature met on December 2. Senate Bill No. 1, which was the first law introduced in that body, passed December 18. Its full title indicates what was most important to the people of the new state:

> AN ACT TO PROMOTE THE COMFORT OF PASSENGERS ON RAILROADS, STREET CARS, URBAN, SUBURBAN, INTERURBAN CARS AND AT RAILWAY STATIONS. REQUIRING ALL RAILWAY COMPANIES, STREET CARS, URBAN, SUBURBAN, INTERURBAN CAR COMPANIES, CARRYING PASSENGERS ON THEIR TRAINS OR CARS WITHIN THIS STATE, TO PROVIDE EQUAL BUT SEPARATE COACHES OR COMPARTMENTS, AND SEPARATE WAITING ROOMS AT STATIONS OR DEPOTS, SO AS TO SECURE SEPARATE ACCOMMODATIONS; DEFINING THE DUTIES OF OFFICERS OF SUCH RAILWAY, STREET CAR, URBAN, SUBURBAN, OR INTERURBAN CAR COMPANY; DIRECTING THEM TO ASSIGN PASSENGERS TO COACHES OR COMPARTMENTS SET ASIDE FOR THE USE OF THE RACE TO WHICH SAID PASSENGER BELONGS; AUTHORIZING THEM TO REFUSE TO CARRY ON THEIR TRAINS OR CARS SUCH PASSENGERS AS MAY REFUSE TO OCCUPY THE COACHES OR COMPARTMENTS TO WHICH HE OR SHE IS ASSIGNED, TO EXONERATE SUCH RAILWAY, STREET CAR, URBAN, SUBURBAN OR INTERURBAN CAR COMPANY FROM ANY OF THE BLAME OR DAMAGES THAT MAY PROCEED OR RESULT FROM SUCH REFUSAL; TO PROVIDE PENALTIES FOR THE VIOLATION OF THIS ACT, AND DECLARING AN EMERGENCY.[20]

The law provided for separate water tanks for drinking and separate toilet facilities, in separate waiting rooms. Railroads were required to have separate cars or spaces separated by "a good and substantial wooden partition, with a door therein." Railroads failing to do this faced fines from $100 to $1,000. People violating these rules were subject to fines of $5 to $25. Railroads could run sleeping and dining cars at their discretion, but they had to be "separate." This section of the law did require that railroads had to supply dining or sleeping cars for both races. The railroads were also free to run "special" trains for only one race. Anyone sitting in the racially incorrect section of a train could be fined from $5 to $25, but if the person refused to move when asked by a railroad employee, the person could be found guilty of a misdemeanor and face a fine of $50 to $500. The law asserted that "an emergency exists for the preservation of public safety" and therefore it would take effect in sixty days after its adoption,[21] which was just about enough time for the railroads in the state to implement the law.

The fact that this was the first law introduced in the new state senate suggests the importance that whites placed on racial subordination and segregation. The title of the law, which was "To Promote the Comfort of Passengers on Railroads," illustrates the cynical nature of the state legislature. It is unlikely that any African Americans in the state thought their "comfort" was enhanced in Jim Crow cars. The assertion that "public safety" required segregation on trains similarly underscores the hostility to blacks that was rooted in the new state. Apparently, the thought of sitting next to a black person on a train made whites fear for their personal security.

Preventing interracial marriage was a high priority for this new southern state. The new marriage law went into effect immediately because the statute declared this was "emergency" legislation "for the purpose of the public peace and safety." The law was clear in its goal: "The marriage of any person of African descent, as defined by the Constitution, to any person not of African descent, or the marriage of any person not of African descent to any person of African descent shall be unlawful and is hereby prohibited within this State." Anyone who might marry "in violation" of this law, or any "minister of the gospel, or other person authorized to solemnize the rights of matrimony" who officiated at such a marriage would be charged with a felony, and if convicted be subject to a fine "in any sum not exceeding five hundred dollars, and imprisonment in the penitentiary not less than one nor more than five years."[22]

The state constitution required separate public education for blacks and whites, which the legislature implemented. The new school act was appropriately titled "An Act Providing Separate Schools and School Officers for the White and Colored Races in this State."[23] In a variety of clauses the statute provided fines for educators who taught in integrated schools or students attending integrated schools. The statute also offered a definition of who fit in which racial category: "The term 'colored' as used in the first section shall be construed to mean all persons of African descent, who possesses any quantum of negro blood, and the term 'white' shall include all other persons."[24] Here the legislature reaffirmed that Oklahoma would lead the South in the quest for an implementation of the "one drop" rule.

The education statute applied to private as well as public schools, and provided the highest fines—$100 to $500 per day—for private schools or colleges that allowed integrated education.[25] Certified teachers who taught mixed-race classes could be fined and have their licenses suspended. The law provided for separate school boards for white and black schools, and mandated that "the electors of one race shall not participate in any election pertaining to the schools of the other race."[26] This provision gave some power to black voters, since they would elect their own school boards. The law did not specify whether whites could serve on the school boards for blacks, or vice versa. Most of the law was directed at teachers and school officials, punishing them if they taught in integrated settings. However, the final substantive clause was directed solely at whites, providing special fines if they attended schools with blacks.[27] The goal here was apparently to make clear to white Oklahomans that racial solidarity required that they not breach the high wall of segregation that the legislature was trying to create. The rule would remain on the books until the end of segregation. Subsequent reenactments of this law would also specify fines for blacks attending schools for whites.

The legislature also required that teachers attend summer institutes to upgrade their skills. These institutes were to be segregated, with white teachers being taught by white instructors, while black teachers attended their own institutes with black instructors. However, in a concession to the realities of a rural state with scattered populations, the legislature allowed for integrated institutes where there were fewer than twenty-five teachers in a county. However, even in these circumstances, teachers were free to attend an institute in another county with members of their own race.[28]

The first legislature also passed legislation to fund higher education in the state, including a segregated institution, which has evolved into the modern Langston University.[29] The funding for this school illustrates the immediate cost of segregation. The state issued bonds totaling just under $32,000 for this institution, but issued more than $295,000 in bonds for white higher education.[30] At its first session the legislature divided the revenue it received from the federal land grant college program. The state gave a third of its land grant money to the

University of Oklahoma (which the university shared with a preparatory school), a third was divided among the three normal schools for whites, and Oklahoma A&M University (today Oklahoma State University), received about 30 percent of the revenue. The school for blacks at Langston received just 3.3 percent of the total. At the time blacks made up about 8 percent of the state population. The dollar figures are striking. Oklahoma A&M University received $31,293, the three normal schools each received $11,590, and Langston, which was both an A&M school and a normal school received $3,477.[31] In 1909 the state would distribute surplus funds to the educational institutions. Of the $128,000 available, only $11,000 would go to the Colored Agricultural and Normal University (Langston). The University Prep School associated with the University of Oklahoma received $1,500 *more* than Langston.[32]

Beyond education, the state created some segregated public institutions for blacks, including a "colored orphan home"[33] and the state hospital for the insane, which was to have "an additional building, separate and apart from any other building, for the care of insane persons of the negro race."[34] But the state did not create separate (much less equal) institutions for other social services. Thus, the laws funding the school for the blind and creating the Oklahoma School for the Deaf did not provide for similar institutions for blacks.[35] The law funding the newly created state school of mines did not provide similar funding for a school for blacks.[36] Since the state constitution required separate education for blacks and whites, these institutions would only be available for whites. The legislature made this logic crystal clear when it created the "Oklahoma Industrial Institute and College for Girls," which would provide single-sex education in mathematics, the physical and natural sciences, and economics. The school was open to "all white female citizens of Oklahoma between ages twelve (12) and thirty-five (35)" who could pass examinations in reading, history, arithmetic, and were "known to possess a good, moral character."[37] Young black women would have no opportunity to study these subjects, just as young black men and women could not attend a school for mines or a full university like the one available in Norman. A year later the state would create a combined home for black children who were deaf, blind, or orphans, to "teach and train the unfortunate of the said colored race in the rudiments of English . . . and the practical and primary industries, such as may fit such unfortunates for useful citizenship."[38] The state laws here were not color-blind, and apparently, even blind white Oklahomans needed to be "protected" from being near blacks, even if they could not see them. In 1915 the state would also create a State Training School for Delinquent Negro Boys[39] and five years after World War I ended, the state would finally provide a special cottage at the Tubercular Sanatorium for black veterans.[40] This pattern would continue into the 1960s, as the state built institutions for whites and then later (or never) added them for blacks, and always funded the Jim Crow institutions at a lower rate. Education, health care, and other public services for blacks in Oklahoma were always separate (if they existed at all) and never equal.

The Grandfather Clause

The Oklahoma Constitution of 1907 promised equal access to the ballot, and the legislature did not initially try to interfere with black voting. Indeed, it required blacks to vote for school boards for Jim Crow schools. But the legislature did require that voters indicate their race when registering to vote. Furthermore, voters signing nominating petitions for primary elections had to indicate their race or color.[41] This was a prelude for Oklahoma's audacious attempt to simply disfranchise most black voters. In 1909 one black, Representative A. C. Harmin, was elected to the Oklahoma House of Representatives. When he left the legislature no blacks would again be elected until federally mandated redistricting changed Oklahoma politics in 1964.[42] In 1910, with Harmin in the legislature, Governor N. Haskell called a special session of the legislature to write a constitutional amendment that would disfranchise blacks.[43] The attack on black voting was led by Democrats, and some writers have claimed it was an attempt to disfranchise Republicans, which most blacks were. But, the reality is, the proposed amendment was aimed solely at black voters. The proposal created a literacy test for voting that many whites in the state could not have passed. But, it provided an elaborate escape clause:

> but no person who was, on January 1, 1866, or at any time prior thereto, entitled to vote under any form of government, or who at that time resided in some foreign nation, and no lineal descendant of such person, shall be denied the right to register and vote because of his inability to so read and write sections of such constitution.[44]

Under this provision illiterate whites could vote because their grandfathers (or fathers) could have voted throughout the United States. But a black would not have been exempt from the provision and could only vote if "he be able to read and write any section of the constitution of the State of Oklahoma."[45] This would have been an impossible standard to meet for most people in the state, especially if they were black and being tested by a white election official.

The justice department and the recently formed NAACP challenged this law. The United States was represented by Solicitor General John W. Davis, a great lawyer but also a lifelong opponent of civil rights, whose father, a West Virginia politician, had opposed emancipation. In 1953 he would represent South Carolina in *Brown v. Board of Education*. Joining Davis was Moorfield Storey, the first president of the NAACP and a distinguished Boston lawyer who had been on the staff of Senator Charles Sumner during Reconstruction. But both argued that this provision violated the Fifteenth Amendment to the U.S. Constitution.

Speaking for a unanimous court, Chief Justice Edward White (who had been a Confederate soldier as a young man) noted that the Fifteenth Amendment (ratified in 1870) prohibited any state from denying the vote on the basis of "race, color, or previous condition of servitude." This led to a simple question: "How can there be room for any serious dispute concerning the repugnancy of the standard based upon January 1, 1866 (a date which preceded the adoption of the Fifteenth Amendment)?" There was no answer. Throughout his opinion Chief Justice White argued that the *only* purpose for using 1866 as the cutoff date was to disfranchise blacks and circumvent the Fifteenth Amendment. The court would have none of this nonsense.

This was a huge victory for the young civil rights organization. It was the first civil rights victory in the Supreme Court since the 1880s. It would be a harbinger of a better time for race relations. But it was of little value to blacks in Oklahoma. The case was argued in October 1913, but not finally decided until late June 1915. During this period almost no blacks voted in the state. The legislature immediately passed a new voter registration law, requiring all people in the state to reregister to vote, *unless* they had voted in 1914. But, almost no blacks could vote in 1914. Furthermore the registration period lasted for less than two weeks, from April 30 to May 11, 1916. Not surprisingly, this new law required that voters list their "race" or "color."[46] Almost no blacks were able to register in this period, and so they were then permanently barred from voting in the state. This law effectively disfranchised all black men who had been twenty-one or older in 1916. In the future men (and soon women) turning twenty-one could register, but the process was onerous, and social, economic, and political constraints eviscerated black political participation in the state until the 1940s.

Building a High Wall of Separation

Beginning with the first bill in the state senate—to create separate railroad cars for blacks—Oklahoma pursued and expanded segregation, sometimes with bizarre legislation to segregate, and often with legislation that allowed private and public entities to simply ignore the needs of African Americans. The goals of the legislature were to marginalize and humiliate blacks, to economically cripple them, and to keep them separate from whites.

Illustrative of this was a seemingly innocuous amendment to the railroad segregation law passed in 1911, which allowed the corporation commission "to exempt any station or depot from the requirements of this act ... in any city or town where no negroes reside." At the time there were a number of "sundown towns" in the state (such as Norman, the home of the state university) where blacks were simply not allowed to live. Significantly, the index to the annual statutes listed this change as the "'Jim Crow Law' Amendment."[47] At first glance this might seem like an innocent attempt to relieve railroads of the economic burdens caused by maintaining separate facilities for blacks. After all, why would there need to be separate waiting rooms for blacks in railroad stations located in towns where there were no blacks? But the implications of the law illustrate the aggressive nature of Oklahoma's official racism. Many cities and towns might not have black residents (some were sundown towns), but these same towns might have contained the only railroad station in the area, and rural blacks, living just outside the city limits, would have no place to wait for a train when they came into town to catch one. Nor would black passengers have a place to wait, get a drink of water, or use a toilet, if a train stopped or was delayed in one of these towns. This amendment further decreased the "comfort" of black travelers, even though the separate car law was passed "to promote the comfort" of travelers. The same law also allowed trains to haul "sleeping cars or dining cars ... exclusively for either white or negro passengers separately but not jointly."[48] This meant that whites would have access to such cars and blacks would not.

A mine safety law required that employers provide baths and lockers for miners so they could store their clothing while underground and thoroughly wash when they returned to the surface. But the law required that the "baths and lockers for the negroes shall be separate from the white race."[49] This of course increased the capital costs of operating a mine, and served as an incentive to hire only white miners, so that the company would not have to build duplicate facilities for blacks. The irony of this law is that blacks and whites could work side-by-side underground, travel in the same elevators into the mine, and ride in the same coal cars. But, above ground they were immediately segregated. This language would be repeated in a comprehensive coal mining code passed in 1929.[50]

During the territorial period cities of five thousand or more people were authorized to build public libraries.[51] The law did not segregate these institutions, but it seems likely that they were in fact segregated in practice. In 1911 the legislature confirmed this practice by permitting cities of more than five thousand people, with at least one thousand blacks, to establish a separate reading room or library for blacks, but they were not required to do so. And blacks living in smaller places would have no access to libraries.[52] Here the state did not pretend to offer separate but equal facilities, but rather, separate and unequal or, in most cases, nonexistent facilities.

The huge school law of 1913, which ran nearly one hundred pages, reaffirmed the separate school system in the state, with no major changes.[53] However, buried in this law was provision to annually offer "a farmer's short course . . . embracing practical elementary scientific instruction" relating to agriculture as well as "domestic economy, canning, preserving, and cooking." These were to be given free to "all citizens of the white race over fifteen years of age."[54] Once again, "separate" in Oklahoma meant "nonexistent."

In 1915 the state required that telephone companies "maintain separate booths for white and colored patrons where there is a demand for such separate booths." The state corporation commission was authorized to determine where such booths were needed, based on complaints filed by citizens and public hearings.[55] This law allowed a single individual to force the segregation of telephone booths, and clearly discouraged blacks from using public phones. In addition, it led to the reality that either the corporation commission or the phone company might conclude that there was actually not enough "demand" for phones for blacks, and so all the phone booths, or perhaps all but one in a town, would be available only for whites.

Meanwhile, in 1925 the state authorized the construction of a penitentiary, "provided that such building shall be so constructed as to provide absolute segregation of the white and colored races at all times."[56] This was consistent with all other laws segregating blacks in public institutions.

In 1931 the legislature passed a new common carrier law to provide for segregation on buses, just as it had on trains. The legislature dubbed this the "Motor Vehicle Jim Crow Law." The act required that every bus was to provide "separate compartments [which] shall be equal in all points of comfort and convenience." Bus terminals would have segregated waiting rooms and toilet facilities. Bus companies faced fines of $100 to $500 for failing to comply with this law. The law defined "negro" as "every person of African ancestry." Station managers and bus drivers were expected to enforce this law, and to know, of course, who was white and who was not.[57] With the nation deeply in a depression, which hit Oklahoma particularly hard, the legislature was busy finding new ways to humiliate blacks and to add costs to businesses, such as bus companies, which were struggling in the devastated economy. Perhaps, however, these regulations gave white Oklahomans some comfort, knowing that however bad the Depression was for them, it would now be somewhat worse for their black neighbors.

The Depression and the dust bowl also led to legislation to preserve and develop land and water, and the creation of a Conservation Commission followed.[58] But even in the great outdoors, with the economic crisis raging, the Oklahoma legislature found ways to assert white supremacy and to remind blacks that they were second-class citizens. Thus, the Conservation Commission was authorized "to make segregation of the white and colored races as to the exercise of rights of fishing, boating, and bathing."[59] In 1949 the state required that people designate their race on hunting and fishing licenses. This might have made sense for identification purposes, except that Oklahoma had issued such licenses since statehood. But only in 1949—when blacks were demanding equality and access to the state's law schools and professional schools and less than a month after endorsing the regional compact for segregated graduate education—did the state conclude it needed to find some new way to single out its black citizens.[60] This was one more opportunity for the state to place the stamp of race on an official document.

At this time the legislature also addressed the problem of separate school boards for black and white schools. The decision in *Wilson v. Lane* meant that more and more blacks would be voting. Furthermore, changes in the federal law enforcement might soon lead to more black voters, as the court struck down the white primary and other impediments to black suffrage. This might lead to blacks serving on elected school boards. The legislature solved this problem as part of a full overhaul of the schools in 1949.[61] The comprehensive school law devoted an entire article, covering a number of pages, to "Separate Schools."[62] This new law created unified school districts, which would be authorized to establish a "separate school" within the district. Each school board was allowed to "designate what school or schools in each school district shall be the separate school."[63] Thus, a majority white district would have "separate" schools for blacks living in the district. However, to make sure that there would not be black members of school boards, the legislature further provided that "members of the district school board shall be of the same race as the children who are entitled to attend the school of the district, not the separate school."[64] This law continued to provide fines for teachers providing classes "where members of the white and colored race are received and enrolled." This applied to all schools, including colleges.[65]

End Game

Starting in the 1930s the NAACP, other organizations, and even the federal government began to chip away at segregation.[66] In a number of criminal cases the Supreme Court upheld prosecutions of whites or reversed the convictions of blacks because of racist policies and behaviors that offended the Constitution and were sometimes "shocking and revolting."[67] The court began to intervene in the denial of the right to vote,[68] struck down segregation in some aspects of interstate transportation,[69] upheld state civil rights laws,[70] and refused to allow the enforcement of race-based restrictive covenants in housing.[71] Salary equalization cases had forced school districts in Virginia to pay black teachers at the same rate as whites.[72]

Three cases from Oklahoma were instrumental in the beginning of the end for segregation. In 1939 the U.S. Supreme Court struck down the 1916 voter registration law on the grounds that it was simply a replication of the grandfather clause declared unconstitutional in *Guinn v. United States*. The court noted that "the practical effect of the 1916 legislation was to accord to the members of the negro race who had been discriminated against in the outlawed registration system of 1914, not more than 12 days within which to reassert constitutional rights which this Court found in the Guinn case to have been improperly taken from them."[73] With this decision in place more blacks began to vote, although racial gerrymandering, intimidation, and the general conditions of a thoroughly segregated society prevented any immediate changes in the state's politics.

A decade later there were two important challenges to the denial of graduate and professional education to blacks in the states. In *Sipuel v. Oklahoma State Board of Regents*,[74] a case brought by the NAACP, the Supreme Court ordered Oklahoma to provide Ada Lois Sipuel with a legal education at the University of Oklahoma.[75] Oklahoma had no law school for blacks, and the separate but equal doctrine required that blacks either be given educational opportunity in a segregated school or be allowed to go to the all-white school. The court upheld the concept of "separate but equal," and did not challenge segregation per se. Rather, the court held that since Oklahoma did not have a separate law school for blacks, the only solution was to integrate the state law school at the University of Oklahoma. The court decided *Sipuel* with stunning speed. Four days after oral argument the court issued a short per curiam opinion holding that:

> The petitioner is entitled to secure legal education afforded by a state institution. To this time, it has been denied her although during the same period many white applicants have been afforded legal education by the State. The State must provide it for her in conformity with the equal protection clause of the Fourteenth Amendment and provide it as soon as it does for applicants of any other group.[76]

The state responded with an instantly created law school that Sipuel, who was now married and had become Ada Lois Sipuel Fisher, refused to attend. In *Fisher v. Hurst*[77] the court declined to force the issue on Oklahoma. However, in October 1948 a federal court ordered the University of Oklahoma to admit George McLaurin and five other African Americans to the school's graduate programs. The following June the University of Oklahoma finally admitted Fisher to the law school. She would eventually graduate and become a trustee of the university.

In the wake of Sipuel and McLaurin, Oklahoma stepped away from a full confrontation with the federal government. In June 1949, just before Ada Lois Sipuel Fisher was allowed to enter law school, the state modified its law that prohibited any integrated education. The new law said:

> Provided, that the provisions of this Section shall not apply to programs of instruction leading to a particular degree given at State owned or operated colleges or institutions of higher education of this State established for and/or used by the white race, where such programs of instruction leading to a particular degree are not given at colleges or institutions of higher education of this State established for and/or used by the colored race; provided further, that said programs of instruction leading to a particular degree shall be given at such colleges or institutions of higher education upon a segregated basis. Segregated basis is defined in this Act as classroom instruction given in separate classrooms, or at separate times.[78]

This law allowed the president of the University of Oklahoma to enroll Fisher and McLaurin without fear of adverse legal action. But it also allowed the university to create an elaborate system of internal segregation in an effort to humiliate black students and undermine their chance of academic success. The law reflected Oklahoma's willingness to accept the reality of the federal court decision on integration in graduate and professional education, and at the same time demonstrate the state's hard-core commitment to white supremacy, racism, and segregation.

Once blacks were admitted, however, the university—an institution run by highly educated, sophisticated leaders of the state—simply found new ways to humiliate, intimidate, and harm black students. When McLaurin arrived on campus he "was required to sit apart at a designated desk in an anteroom adjoining the classroom; to sit, at a designated desk on the mezzanine floor of the library, but not to use the desks in the regular reading room; and to sit at a designated table and to eat at a different time from the other students in the school cafeteria." In the face of pending litigation, the university later allowed McLaurin into the classroom, placing him in "the section of the classroom in which appellant sat was surrounded by a rail on which there was a sign stating, 'Reserved For Colored.'" While an appeal to the Supreme Court was pending, the school removed these signs, and in its opinion the court noted that McLaurin "is now assigned to a seat in the classroom in a row specified for colored students; he is assigned to a table in the library on the main floor; and he is permitted to eat at the same time, in the cafeteria as other students, although here again he is assigned to a special table." Even as it modified its overtly crude discrimination, the state insisted on segregation, even in the face of integration. Lois Sipuel Fisher faced similar treatment at the University of Oklahoma Law School. This behavior finally ended with the U.S. Supreme Court's decision in *McLaurin v. Oklahoma State Regents for Higher Education* in 1950 in a short and tart rejection of Oklahoma's petulant behavior.[79]

For the rest of the 1950s Oklahoma continued its systems of segregation in higher education, social institutions, medical facilities, and its separate schools at the elementary and secondary level. But, unlike the Deep South, the state was not willing to confront the federal government with force or violence. Noncompliance or the most grudging compliance was the pattern. Not until the 1960s would the state finally come to terms with integration and jettison its formal opposition to racial equality. Thus the state began to dismantle its segregation laws. In February 1965, in the wake of the 1964 Civil Rights Act, the state repealed laws requiring segregation in public transportation.[80]

Emblematic of this new world was a statute passed in 1965 that did not repeal any existing segregation law, but rather sought to begin to undo the silent, de facto segregation that pervaded the state for six decades. A new education law required that the state board of education "adopt necessary rules and regulations providing coverage of the outstanding events involving and surrounding the history of the Negro race and other minority races and the development of their cultures."[81] Perhaps at this point Oklahoma began to look north and west for traditions and cultural values, even as its residual racism, such as its ban on interracial marriage, remained on the books until the courts finally forced an end to that practice.[82]

Notes

1. The top six states for number of people per horse are Wyoming with 5.1 people per horse, South Dakota with 6.4, Montana with 7.1, Idaho with 8.8, North Dakota with 10.7, and Oklahoma with 10.8. Texas has the most horses, 978,822, but that is only 23 people per horse. These are based on 2005 American Horse Council Foundation numbers and U.S. Census 2004 population data found in Emily R. Kilby, "The Demographics of the U.S. Equine Population," chap. 10 in *The State of the Animals IV: 2007*, ed. Deborah J. Salem and Andrew N. Rowan (Washington, D.C.: Humane Society Press, 2007), 185–86, https://animalstudiesrepository.org/humspre/4/.
2. On the white supremacy and proslavery origins of the Confederacy, see Paul Finkelman, "States' Rights, Southern Hypocrisy, and the Coming of the Civil War," *Akron Law Review* 45 (2012): 449–78.
3. For a discussion of such segregation in the Deep South, see Paul Finkelman, "The Long Road to Dignity: The Wrong of Segregation and What the Civil Rights Act of 1964 Had to Change," *Louisiana Law Review* 74 (2014): 1039–94.
4. *Regional Education Services in Southern States, House Joint Resolution, No. 10*, approved April 26, 1949, *State of Oklahoma: Session Laws of 1949*, 790.
5. Oklahoma Constitution, 1907, art. I, sec. 5. Schools in Oklahoma were already segregated, so this was just a constitutionalization of existing practice.
6. Oklahoma Constitution, 1907, art. XXIV, sec. 19.
7. Ibid., art. XIII, sec. 3.
8. Ibid.
9. Ibid., art. XXIII, sec. 11.
10. *An Act to Amend and Re-enact Section 49 of the Code of Virginia, 1887*, Act of March 17, 1910, *Virginia Session Laws, 1910*, 581. Before this law, people who were less than one-quarter black were considered white. See Peter Wallenstein, "Race, Marriage, and the Law of Freedom: Alabama and Virginia, 1860s–1960s," *Chicago-Kent Law Review* 70 (1994): 371, 407.
11. *An Act to Preserve Racial Integrity*, Act of March 20, 1924, *Virginia Session Laws, 1924*, 534.
12. *An Act in Relation to Vital Statistics*, Act of March 31, 1917, *State of Oklahoma: Session Laws of 1917*, 276, quoted at p. 280.
13. The U.S. Supreme Court upheld Mississippi's student classification law in Gong Lum v. Rice, 275 U.S. 278 (1927).
14. *An Act to Preserve Racial Integrity*, Act of March 20, 1924, *Virginia Session Laws,*

1924, 534–35; Wallenstein, "Race, Marriage, and the Law of Freedom," 409.
15. See Kevin Noble Maillard, "The Pocahontas Exception: The Exemption of American Indian Ancestry from Racial Purity Law," *Michigan Journal of Race and Law* 12 (2007): 351, 363–64.
16. Oklahoma Constitution, 1907, art. I, sec. 6.
17. Guinn v. United States, 238 U.S. 348 (1915).
18. Oklahoma Constitution, 1907, art. XXIII, sec. 2.
19. There were no blacks in the first state legislature. Representative A. C. Harmin served in the second legislative session. George G. Humphreys, *A Century to Remember: A Historical Perspective on the Oklahoma House of Representatives* (Oklahoma City: Oklahoma House of Representatives, 2000), 10, http://www.okhouse.gov/Documents/CenturyToRemember.pdf. After his term, voting restrictions and gerrymandering prevented any blacks from being elected to the state legislature until 1964 when federally mandated redistricting led to the election of Curtis Lawson of Tulsa, John White, and Archibald Hill to the state House and E. Melvin Porter to the state senate. Porter would serve in the state senate for twenty-two years, and for eighteen of them he would be the only black in that body. Robert H. Henry, "Civil Rights Movement," *The Encyclopedia of Oklahoma History and Culture*, Oklahoma Historical Society, http://www.okhistory.org/publications/enc/entry.php?entry=CI010&1=c; and Associated Press, "First African-American State Senator, E. Melvin Porter, Honored on Senate Floor," KGOU, http://kgou.org/post/first-african-american-state-senator-e-melvin-porter-honored-senate-floor.
20. *An Act to Promote the Comfort of Passengers on Railroads*, Act of Dec. 18, 1907, *State of Oklahoma: Session Laws of 1907–1908*, 201. Capitalization in the original.
21. Ibid., sec. 12, p. 204.
22. *An Act Providing for Uniformity of Marriage*, Act of May 22, 1908, *State of Oklahoma: Session Laws of 1907–1908*, 553, 556–57.
23. *An Act Providing Separate Schools and School Officers for the White and Colored Races in this State*, Act of May 5, 1908, *State of Oklahoma: Session Laws of 1907–1908*, 694.
24. Ibid., sec. 2.
25. Ibid., sec. 5.
26. Ibid., sec. 3.
27. Ibid., sec. 7.
28. *An Act Relating to the Holding and Conducting of County Normal Institutes*, sec. 11, Act of May 12, 1908, *State of Oklahoma: Session Laws of 1907–1908*, 675, 678.
29. *An Act Making an Appropriation for the Support and Maintenance of the Colored Agricultural and Normal University at Langston*, Act of June 10, 1908, *State of Oklahoma: Session Laws of 1907–1908*, 118. The legislature also appropriated $50,000 for capital construction on the campus. *An Act Making an Appropriation for the Benefit of the Colored Agricultural and Normal University at Langston*, Act of June 10, 1908, *State of Oklahoma: Session Laws of 1907–1908*, 99.
30. *An Act for Funding the Outstanding Warrants and Other Indebtedness of the State of Oklahoma*, Act of March 6, 1908, *State of Oklahoma: Session Laws of 1907–1908*, 155.

The total budget for the school was $30,600. *An Act Making an Appropriation for the Support and Maintenance of the Colored Agricultural and Normal University at Langston*, Act of June 10, 1908, *State of Oklahoma: Session Laws of 1907–1908*, 118.

31. *An Act for the Division and Distribution of the Income, Interest, and Proceeds from Certain Lands*, Act of May 10, 1908, *State of Oklahoma: Session Laws of 1907–1908*, 395–98; *An Act Making an Appropriation for the Support and Maintenance of the Colored Agricultural and Normal University at Langston*, Act of May 10, 1908, *State of Oklahoma: Session Laws of 1907–1908*, 395–97.

32. *Appropriating Certain Territorial Levies*, Act of March 24, 1909, *State of Oklahoma: Session Laws of 1909*, 84. When the legislature apportioned funds from the sale of public lands, Langston received the income from 100,000 acres of land, while the University Preparatory School received the income from 150,000 acres. Both the University of Oklahoma and A&M University each received the income from 250,000 acres. *Apportionment of "New College Fund,"* Act of March 25, 1909, *State of Oklahoma: Session Laws of 1909*, 461.

33. *An Act Authorizing and Establishing State Orphan Homes*, Act of May 18, 1908, *State of Oklahoma: Session Laws of 1907–1908*, 629.

34. *An Act to Create and Establish an East Oklahoma Hospital for the Insane*, Act of May 6, 1908, *State of Oklahoma: Session Laws of 1907–1908*, 623.

35. *An Act Appropriating Funds for the Maintenance of the School for the Blind*, Act of May 29, 1908, *State of Oklahoma: Session Laws of 1908–1909*, 632–33; *An Act to Create and Establish a School for the Education of the Deaf and Dumb*, Act of May 14, 1908, *State of Oklahoma: Session Laws of 1907–1908*, 617–20.

36. *An Act Creating a State School of Mines*, Act of May 28, 1908, *State of Oklahoma: Session Laws of 1907–1908*, 621–23.

37. *An Act to Establish an Industrial Institution and College for Girls*, Act of May 16, 1908, *State of Oklahoma: Session Laws of 1907–1908*, 614–17.

38. *An Act to Locate and Establish an Institute . . . for the Colored Youth*, Act of March 27, 1909, *State of Oklahoma: Session Laws of 1909*, 546.

39. *An Act Creating a State Training School for Delinquent Negro Boys*, Act of March 30, 1915, *State of Oklahoma: Session Laws of 1915*, 500.

40. *An Act Providing for Additional Ward and Cottage Buildings for White Patients . . . [and] a Separate Ward and Cottage Building for Colored Patient, at the Tubercular Sanatorium for Ex-service Persons*, Act of March 21, 1923, *State of Oklahoma: Session Laws of 1923*, 155. The state by this time also had established a single tuberculosis sanatorium for blacks.

41. *An Act to Provide for the Nomination of Candidates*, Act of May 29, 1908, *State of Oklahoma: Session Laws of 1907–1908*, 358, 364.

42. Humphreys, *A Century to Remember*, 10.

43. For a firsthand discussion of this topic see John Hope Franklin and John Whittington Franklin, eds., *My Life and An Era: The Autobiography of Buck Colbert Franklin* (Baton Rouge: LSU Press, 1997), 145–49.

44. The full amendment is quoted in Guinn v. United States, 238 U.S. 347, at 357.
45. Ibid. Ironically, in 1866 blacks could vote in Massachusetts, New Hampshire, Vermont, Rhode Island, and Maine on the same basis as whites, and could vote in New York if they owned some property. They could also vote in school bond elections in Michigan. Thus, someone might have argued that all blacks in the United States in 1866 would have been "entitled to vote under any form of government"—such as the form of government in Massachusetts. But no one at the time seems to have made this argument.
46. *An Act Relating to Elections, Providing for the Registration of Electors in Every Precinct in the State, Prohibiting Voting without Such Registration*, Act of Feb. 26, 1916, *State of Oklahoma: Session Laws of 1916*, 33, 35, 37, 39.
47. *An Act to Amend Section Seven (7) of Article One (1), Chapter Fifteen (15), Laws of 1907 and 1908*, Act of March 22, 1911, *State of Oklahoma: Session Laws of 1911*, 262, 434.
48. Ibid., 262.
49. *An Act to Promote the Health and Safety of Employees in Coal Mines*, Act of April 1, 1913, *State of Oklahoma: Session Laws of 1913*, 237–38. This language would be repeated in *An Act Relating to and Proving for the Working of Coal Mines*, Act of July 16, 1929, *State of Oklahoma: Session Laws of 1929*, 322, at 341.
50. *An Act Relating to and Providing for the Working of Coal Mines*, Act of July 16, 1929, *State of Oklahoma: Session Laws of 1929*, 322, at 341.
51. *An Act to Provide for . . . Free Public Libraries*, Act of March 8, 1901, *Territory of Oklahoma: Territory Session Laws of 1901*, 146; *An Act to Amend . . . the Laws of 1901 Relating to Free Public Libraries*, Act of March 16, 1903, *Territory of Oklahoma: Territory Session Laws of 1903*, 228.
52. *An Act Amending . . . an Act to Provide for the Establishment and Maintenance of Public Libraries*, Act of March 6, 1911, *State of Oklahoma: Session Laws of 1911*, 200.
53. *An Act Prescribing Laws for the Government of the Common Schools of Oklahoma*, Act of May 22, 1913, *State of Oklahoma: Session Laws of 1913*, 487–584. See 558, 571–78 for specific clauses regulating "separate" schools.
54. Ibid., 552–53. The state had actually passed this provision in 1907 as part of its agricultural law. *An Act to Put into Force Section Seven of Article Thirteen of the Oklahoma Constitution Requiring the Teaching of the Elements of Agriculture*, sec. 16., Act of May 20, 1908, *State of Oklahoma: Session Laws of 1907–1908*, 13, quoted at p. 19.
55. *An Act Providing for Separate Telephone Booths for White and Colored Patrons*, Act of March 30, 1915, *State of Oklahoma: Session Laws of 1915*, 513.
56. *An Act Making Appropriations*, Act of April 10, 1925, *State of Oklahoma: Session Laws of 1925*, 263, quoted at p. 269.
57. *An Act Providing Separate Compartments for the Accommodation of White and Negro Races in Motor Vehicles*, Act of April 20, 1931, *State of Oklahoma: Session Laws of 1931*, 184–86. See chapter 50 and cross-references to highway law for reference to "Motor Vehicle Jim Crow Law," *State of Oklahoma: Session Laws of 1931*, 189.
58. *An Act Conferring Additional Duties and Limitation upon the Conservation Commission*, Act of March 22, 1935, *State of Oklahoma: Session Laws of 1935*, 346.

59. Ibid., 349–50.
60. *An Act Relating to Fishing and Hunting Licenses*, Act of May 20, 1949, *State of Oklahoma: Session Laws of 1949*, 222, 224.
61. *An Act Relating to the Public Schools of Oklahoma*, Act of March 30, 1949, *State of Oklahoma: Session Laws of 1949*, 536–610.
62. *An Act Relating to the Public Schools of Oklahoma*, art. 5, "Separate Schools," Act of March 30, 1949, *State of Oklahoma: Session Laws of 1949*, 536–41.
63. Ibid., 537.
64. Ibid.
65. Ibid.
66. See generally Richard Kluger, *Simple Justice* (New York: Alfred A. Knopf, 1975); Mark V. Tushnet, *The NAACP's Legal Strategy against Segregated Education, 1925–1950* (Chapel Hill: University of North Carolina Press, 1987); and Paul Finkelman, "Civil Rights in Historical Context: In Defense of Brown," *Harvard Law Review* 118 (2005): 973–1027; and Paul Finkelman, "The Radicalism of Brown," *University of Pittsburgh Law Review* 66 (2004): 35–56.
67. Screws v. United States, 325 U.S. 91 (1945). See also Powell v. Alabama, 287 U.S. 45 (1932); Norris v. Alabama, 294 U.S. 587 (1935); Patterson v. Alabama, 294 U.S. 600 (1935); Brown v. Mississippi, 297 U.S. 278 (1936); Smith v. Texas, 311 U.S. 128 (1940).
68. United States. v. Classic, 313 U.S. 299 (1941); Smith v. Allwright, 321 U.S. 649 (1944).
69. Mitchell v. United States, 313 U.S. 80 (1941); Morgan v. Virginia, 328 U.S. 383 (1946). See also Catherine Barnes, *Journey From Jim Crow: The Desegregation of Southern Transit* (New York: Columbia University Press, 1983).
70. Bob-Lo Excursion Co. v. Michigan, 333 U.S. 28 (1948).
71. Hansberry v. Lee, 311 U.S. 32 (1940); Shelley v. Kraemer, 334 U.S. 1 (1948); Hurd v. Hodge, 334 U.S. 24 (1948).
72. Alston et al. v. School Board of City of Norfolk et al., 112 F.2d 992. See also Mark V. Tushnet, *The NAACP's Legal Strategy against Segregated Education, 1925–1950* (Chapel Hill: University of North Carolina Press, 1987), chapters 6 and 7. In addition, see Doxey A. Wilkerson, "The Negro School Movement in Virginia: From 'Equalization' to 'Integration,'" *Journal of Negro Education* 29 (Winter 1960): 17–29.
73. Lane v. Wilson, 307 U.S. 268, 276 (1939).
74. 332 U.S. 631 (1948).
75. See generally, Cheryl Brown Wattley, "Ada Lois Sipuel Fisher: How a 'Skinny Little Girl' Took on the University of Oklahoma and Helped Pave the Road to *Brown v. Board of Education*," *Oklahoma Law Review* 62 (2010): 449.
76. Ibid., 632–33.
77. 333 U.S. 147 (1948).
78. *An Act Relating to the Instruction and Attendance of the Colored Race in Colleges or Institutions of Higher Education of the State Established and/or Used by the White Race*, Act of June 9, 1949, *State of Oklahoma: Session Laws of 1949*, 608.
79. 339 U.S. 637 (1950), quoted at p. 640. The entire report of the case is only five pages long.

80. *An Act Relating to the Transportation of Passengers for Hire*, Act of Feb. 10, 1965, *State of Oklahoma: Session Laws of 1965*, 6. The legislature also repealed its law requiring separate bathing facilities in coal mines. Ibid., 90, and numerous other segregation laws as well.
81. *An Act Relating to Schools*, Act of July 22, 1965, *State of Oklahoma: Session Laws of 1965*, 1076.
82. Loving v. Virginia, 388 U.S. 1 (1967).

Further Reading

See selected bibliography, pp. 271–78.

15

The Civil Rights Movement in Texas
Alwyn Barr

As did white Oklahomans, white Texans too revealed a southern bent when considering its black citizens. But white Texans, of course, had much closer southern ties, as Texas, a slaveholding state, seceded from the Union and joined the Confederacy. Texas's civil rights struggle had a difficult process in front of it; however, as Alwyn Barr illustrates so well, black Texans met the challenge with varied forms of resistance, sometimes via the courts and sometimes with physical resistance. They put pressure on the legislature. Organizations aided black Texans, especially the NAACP. In fact, it was so much a thorn to white Texans, that the state's white attorney general successfully sought the records of the NAACP. Although black Texans today have the right to vote as well as other civil liberties, they still face opposition to their right to vote and especially face antiblack violence in the form of murders and physical beatings. Alwyn Barr, perhaps best known as the dean of historians studying black Texas history, is professor emeritus of history at Texas Tech University. Among his numerous publications are *Black Texans: A History of African Americans in Texas*, and with Robert A. Calvert, *Black Leaders: Texans for Their Times*.

The civil rights movement by African Americans in Texas emerged as a response to the several forms of discrimination developed in the late nineteenth and early twentieth centuries by the state, towns, and various organizations or individuals. Black Texans faced growing segregation or exclusion as well as discrimination in jobs and salaries. Railroads and streetcar companies accepted state laws requiring a combination of segregation and unequal accommodations or exclusion for African

Americans, except in first-class Pullman cars because a separate Pullman car for black passengers would be too expensive for the railroad. African Americans in Texas found their voting rights limited by a state poll tax and the adoption of a white primary by the state Democratic Party that dominated politics at that time. Social separation received further reinforcement by a law making interracial marriage illegal. Few courts called African Americans for jury duty, which led to skewed sentencing practices. As Texas cities grew in the twentieth century, residential segregation increased. Whites controlled most property, while some cities would not grant African Americans building permits in specific neighborhoods. Dallas for a short time created separate districts by law. Fear of violent opposition also limited black efforts to overcome those problems. In Dallas one separate black residential area did include better housing for middle-class families. Some West Texas towns tried to keep African Americans from living there. Black schools in Texas operated with less funds per pupil, fewer days in class, and less pay for teachers than white schools in the state. White assumptions of racial superiority provided support for discrimination and at its extreme, led to a culture of violence aimed at forcing subordination upon African Americans. Texas ranked third among states in the number of lynchings, with estimates ranging from three hundred to five hundred. Ku Klux Klan members in the 1920s attacked and intimidated African Americans as well as other ethnic and religious minorities. White riots against black Texans occurred in some towns. Yet white Texans never achieved complete subordination of African Americans in the state, who in various ways opposed all aspects of discrimination.

Foundations for the mid-twentieth century civil rights movement appeared in the early twentieth century as African Americans organized to express themselves on a variety of issues. Black Republicans retained some role in the state level party. Although the party split at times into white and "black and tan" factions, it did oppose the Ku Klux Klan. African Americans continued to participate in local politics in some towns, seeking improved schools and services. At that level during the 1920s in several larger towns they formed Independent Voters Leagues, with a state organization led by Waco lawyer R. D. Evans and *Houston Informer* editor Clifford Richardson.

To oppose discrimination black Texans in Houston organized the first local affiliate of the National Association for the Advancement of Colored People (NAACP) in 1912 and revived it in 1917. Additional branches numbered thirty in 1919 and counted seven thousand members. State officials sought chapter rolls that could expose people to hostile reactions. That caused some decline of membership in Texas.

African American voting in local primaries led to the creation of white primaries in Waco and Houston. Black challenges led to varied legal results in 1918 and 1921. The Texas legislature in 1923 then adopted a state law requiring white-only primaries that had been developed by the Democratic Party to select candidates for state and national elections in Texas. A state district court rejected a case brought by H. C. Chandler of San Antonio. The NAACP then decided to support a case against the white primary in El Paso, brought by Lawrence A. Nixon, a black doctor who worked to form the local NAACP chapter. The U.S. Supreme Court in 1927 agreed the state of Texas could not require a white primary because the Fourteenth Amendment did not allow a state to withhold "equal protection of the law from any citizen." Then the legislature wrote a new act that allowed political parties to conduct white primaries. Faced with continued rejection at the polls, Nixon challenged the legality of the new law and in 1932 won another Supreme Court decision, which ruled that state action on the issue involved discrimination. Despite success, tension existed between local and national leaders of the NAACP over whether white or black attorneys should present their cases before the courts.

The state Democratic Party, claiming the status of a voluntary organization, then allowed white primaries without any state legislation. In scattered cities—San Antonio, Waco, and Corpus Christi—Democratic leaders allowed some black voters to participate. Democrats in Houston, Dallas, and Fort Worth retained white primaries. Black leaders in Dallas and Houston then organized the Progressive Voters League to support a new legal challenge in 1936 by Richard Grovey, the proprietor of a Houston barbershop and an active member of the Third Ward Civic Club. In that case the U.S. Supreme Court accepted the private association argument and ruled against Grovey.

Thousands of African Americans from Texas responded to the limitations of discrimination in the early twentieth century by migrating to the North, primarily the Midwest, and during the Great Depression of the 1930s to the Pacific Coast states. Others moved from rural areas to growing cities in Texas, however, hoping for better jobs and reduced fears of violence. In those cities middle-class African Americans formed their own chambers of commerce and in 1936 created the Texas Negro Chamber of Commerce led by Antonio Maceo Smith of Dallas. In response to defeat in the Grovey case, NAACP chapters across the state met to organize the Texas State Conference of Branches of the NAACP, electing R. D. Evans as president and Smith as secretary.

African Americans in Texas still faced extensive segregation, as well as the lingering impact of the Great Depression, with 11 percent unemployment in

1940, twice the level for Anglos. Yet within a black population of almost a million the basic foundation for a civil rights movement existed. Over 46 percent of black Texans lived in urban areas where the possibility of cooperation and organization were greater. All the Texas cities and some towns had African American newspapers that informed readers about issues and efforts to overcome discrimination. Although still small, the urban middle class had found leaders willing to challenge discrimination. At the state meeting of the NAACP those leaders developed goals for legal efforts to achieve voting rights, to equalize opportunities in education, and to bring down the barriers of segregation.

In Houston, African Americans sought a court ruling during 1940 that the Democratic Party primary represented the decisive decision in selecting state leaders, because the fall election usually involved limited competition. The plaintiff also argued that county clerks participated in the primary, which conformed to Texas election requirements showing the state played a role in elections. That challenge failed because of an unclear focus, but it led to a call by Maceo Smith for other black groups to aid the efforts of the NAACP. At a conference in Dallas during January 1941 African American leaders agreed to form a Texas Council of Negro Organizations for that purpose.

With that broad support from African Americans in Texas, the Houston and state NAACP leaders arranged for its lawyers, led by W. J. Durham from Sherman, to be joined by attorneys from the national office including Thurgood Marshall. They began a case with Sidney Hasgett as the plaintiff. When the U.S. Supreme Court with new justices changed its view of primary elections, however, the NAACP attorneys decided to present a new case filed in 1942 by black dentist Lonnie Smith of Houston. Two years later the U.S. Supreme Court accepted the argument that the white primary denied black Texans a role in a basic stage of voting for state and national candidates. For African Americans in Texas and across the United States the decision led to celebrations and praise in black newspapers. Thurgood Marshall later declared the Smith case historic because it revived African American voting and began the process of ending racial discrimination. Historian Darlene Clark Hine concluded: "It signaled the beginning of the so-called Second Reconstruction and the modern civil rights movement."

Initially state and local Democratic officials and some newspapers published by Anglos criticized the decision while a few tried to continue black exclusion from primaries. African American participation in Democratic primaries for 1946 reached 75,000, one-third more than that of the general election of 1940. By 1948, the number of African Americans registered to vote rose to 100,000, although they represented less than 20 percent of the adult black population in Texas. Federal judges in the state during the early 1950s ruled against local versions of the white primary that had continued in Fort Bend and Harrison Counties.

The new black voters generally favored candidates, usually Democrats, at the state and national levels, who showed concern for ending other forms of discrimination. Thus African Americans strongly supported Ralph Yarborough in the 1954 Democratic primary against Governor Allan Shivers, who had opposed desegregation. In recognition of the growing black role in politics, the state Democratic Party added W. J. Durham to its executive committee, while the Republicans included black physician L. G. Pinkston on their executive committee.

Despite the lingering impact of the poll tax on working-class voter registration, the number of registered African Americans reached 375,000 in 1964. In the election that fall, black voters in Texas overwhelmingly cast ballots for President Lyndon Johnson and U.S. Senator Ralph Yarborough after they helped pass the Civil Rights Act of 1964. Ratification of the Twenty-Fourth Amendment to the U.S. Constitution in 1964 ended employment of the poll tax in federal elections. Two years later the U.S. Supreme Court declared the poll tax unconstitutional in state elections, thus removing the last legal restraint on African American voting in Texas and some other states. Although the decision came in a nonpresidential election year when voter registration often declined, it worked with the Voting Rights Act of 1965 to stimulate black registration in Texas, which increased to 400,000 in 1966.

Another important U.S. Supreme Court decision required that state legislative districts be reorganized to allow "one man, one vote," and that major cities with large populations should include more than one geographical district. Since residential segregation had concentrated African Americans in most cities, the decision made possible the election of black candidates. Attorney Barbara Jordan joined the Texas senate as its first African American member in over eighty years. A young public relations specialist in Houston, Curtis M. Graves, joined the state House of Representatives. From Dallas came another African American House member, attorney Joseph E. Lockridge. When he died in 1968, a black Methodist pastor with a degree from Southern Methodist University, Zan W. Holmes Jr., filled that position. After congressional redistricting occurred, Jordan ran successfully for a seat in the U.S. House of Representatives where she served as the first black Texan from 1972 to 1978.

African American voter registration continued to grow, reaching 540,000 or 83 percent of eligible black voters, the high point for Texas, in 1968. A clear majority of black voters continued to favor liberal Democrats in the primaries and Democrats over Republicans in state and national elections. In rural areas, however, subtle economic control by whites over jobs and other necessities shaped the decisions of some working-class African Americans. Several towns and cities in the 1960s held at-large elections to avoid the elections of African Americans. At the same time the increase in black voting in some areas led to improved treatment and better services. By the early 1970s some cities in Texas—Houston, Fort Worth, San Antonio, and Austin—included one or more African Americans on their city councils. The number of African Americans serving in elective offices across Texas increased from 29 in 1970 to 158 by 1977 and continued to grow beyond the 1970s.

Key figures in the efforts to overcome discrimination in Texas included some African American women in the urban middle class. First as a volunteer and then as the paid executive secretary of the Houston NAACP branch, Lulu White expanded its membership from 5,679 in 1943 to 12,700 in 1945. A year later she became state director for the Texas State Conference of NAACP Branches. After ten years of recruiting new members for the Dallas branch of the NAACP, Juanita Craft joined White at the higher level as state NAACP organizer. They achieved success by working with ministers in African American churches and leaders of black political, business, and social organizations, as well as labor unions. Conflicts with *Houston Informer* editor Carter Wesley over issues and approaches, as well as health problems, caused White to resign as executive secretary of the Houston branch of the NAACP.

The national NAACP office quickly hired her for its regional staff. Another African American woman, Christia Adair, became executive secretary of the Houston branch. Her more low-key style saw less conflict but also a decline in membership. Yet she continued to work for change in Houston for a decade. She withstood questioning in court for over two weeks by the state attorney general during his attempt to intimidate the NAACP and force it to leave Texas in 1957.

The second major focus of the NAACP in Texas became equality of education. Public schools as well as colleges remained segregated with less funding than their white counterparts. The first step came from a meeting of the Colored Teacher State Association in 1941. It created a Texas Commission on Democracy in Education to challenge all forms of discrimination in that field. *Democracy's Debt of Honor*, published in 1942, set forth its concerns. Prominent African

American and Anglo figures in education soon gathered to form a Commission for the Improvement of Educational Opportunities for Negroes in Texas.

In parallel developments, African American teachers in Dallas during 1941 asked the Dallas school board to eliminate the gap between black and white teachers' pay. Rejection of that request resulted in a court case with Thelma Paige as the plaintiff, aided by the Negro Teachers Alliance of Dallas in 1942, with backing from the Texas Commission on Democracy in Education and the Texas Council of Negro Organizations. By early 1943 the two sides negotiated an agreement for equal salaries, to be instituted by 1946. Across the state several school boards in cities and towns followed that pattern in the next two years. Yet some remained reluctant. Others even fired black teachers who spoke for equalization.

The 1940s also saw the development of concern about the segregated and unequal status of higher education in Texas. There had been two earlier requests by African Americans for admission to the University of Texas. A black student met rejection in 1885, only a few years after creation of the university. George Allen, an employee of a black insurance company, completed registration before being refused admission in 1938. He then pursued his original purpose, with NAACP support, by pressing the state to provide a tuition scholarship so he could attend college in another state. The Texas legislature quickly agreed to that solution, as had other segregated states. Yet other African Americans believed the state should provide equal education in Texas. The Texas Council of Negro Organizations sought more equal opportunities for black college students within the state. The Texas legislature in 1945 changed the name of the only state college for African Americans to Prairie View University, but provided few additional funds to help it expand its offerings.

At that point the NAACP joined the Texas Council of Negro Organizations in support of a legal challenge to the segregated University of Texas. The state NAACP in 1945 began to raise money for a lawsuit while meeting with possible plaintiffs to find one with the necessary qualifications and willingness to face the pressures involved. After several meetings, Lulu White offered the name of Heman M. Sweatt. The next year Sweatt, a post office employee in Houston, sought to enroll in the University of Texas Law School. He and African American leaders met first with university president Theophilus Painter, who then requested a ruling from the state attorney general. Although Sweatt had earned a degree at Wiley College and had served in the military during the Second World War, the university accepted the attorney general's ruling and rejected Sweatt because it was segregated by state law. When Sweatt sued in state court, the judge concluded that Texas should offer an equal education for him since it had no law school for African Americans. The state government then offered Sweatt legal studies with two black attorneys while it established a new university for African Americans in Houston. Soon the state decided to offer Sweatt segregated instruction in a downtown Austin basement with three University of Texas law faculty and use of the university library. At the same time the Texas government acquired Houston College for Negroes, changed the name to Texas State University for Negroes (later Texas Southern University), which would develop law and medical schools. *Houston Informer* editor Charles Wesley viewed those ideas as progress, which led to disagreements with NAACP leaders. The case led to lively debate with white students and the general public divided over the issues of segregation and equality.

Following decisions in state courts against Sweatt, he appealed the case to federal courts in 1948 and ultimately to the U.S. Supreme Court. Those justices in 1950 decided in favor of Sweatt, reasoning that the Houston law school did not match the one at the University of Texas in number of faculty, size of library, funding for students, and several supporting aspects that lent esteem to its graduates. The immediate impact of the Sweatt case remained limited with eighteen African Americans enrolling in University of Texas law, medical, and other graduate programs. Yet the case established an important precedent, not only for desegregation and greater opportunity for black students at the college level, but also for extending desegregation to the public schools.

Desegregation of colleges at the undergraduate level appeared first in areas with limited black population. Del Mar Junior College at Corpus Christi took that step in the early 1950s, as did Amarillo College and Wayland Baptist in West Texas. Breakthroughs at universities began with Southern Methodist University in 1956 followed by the University of Texas. In East Texas white protests slowed change at Texarkana Junior College, but the trend continued. The number of desegregated colleges in Texas rose to thirty-eight in 1958 followed in the 1960s by most others. Integration of faculty, dormitories, student activities, and athletic programs often lagged behind until the mid-1960s.

During 1956 Barbara Smith, an African American student at the University of Texas, earned the role of female lead in the opera *Dido and Aeneas* while two white students would share the male lead. Several white Texans including some legislators expressed strong opposition to what they viewed as approval of interracial personal relations. When the fine arts dean refused to act, the university president, Logan Wilson, ruled Smith could not be in the opera. Many students and some faculty and legislators criticized the decision. In 1981, Smith, singing as Barbara Conrad, joined the Metropolitan Opera. In 1985 the university recognized her as a distinguished alumnus.

Access to restaurants and theaters near college campuses, as well as university dorms, often remained segregated until the early to mid-1960s. The Southwest Conference that included several major universities in Texas did not begin to desegregate its athletic programs until 1965, with some universities moving more slowly in specific sports. Texas Western College at El Paso, a city with a small but active African American population, desegregated more smoothly, including its athletic programs. The basketball team captured national attention in 1966 when its all-black starting players defeated an all-white University of Kentucky team for the NCAA national championship.

After equalization of teachers' pay in the 1940s, several issues remained for African American public schools. About one-third of white schools had been consolidated with more teachers to cover more classes and levels of education. Only one-fifth of black schools had reached that point. Two-thirds of white high schools had attained full state expectations, compared to one-third of African American schools. White schools met twenty-five days longer than black schools. School districts devoted less funds per pupil for African American schools, which shaped the quality of buildings, classroom equipment, libraries, transportation, and athletic facilities. Therefore Texas clearly fit the pattern of segregated and unequal schools that the U.S. Supreme Court found to be illegal by its *Brown* decisions in 1954 and 1955.

Initially most Anglo Texans opposed the decision, which led to temporary rejection, evasion, and limited change in many districts. A few West Texas towns with small numbers of black students desegregated early in the 1950s. Austin, Corpus Christi, El Paso, and San Antonio, as well as sixty-two smaller districts, took limited steps to desegregate in 1955–56. A large group of Anglos opposed to integration at Mansfield kept black students from attending previously white schools in 1956. Texas Rangers sent by Governor Allan Shivers supported the segregationists. President Dwight Eisenhower, running for reelection that year, did not enforce the court order at Mansfield as he did in Little Rock, Arkansas, the following year. The state attorney general, John Ben Sheppard, blocked NAACP efforts by injunction in 1956, seized membership rolls, and tried to force the organization out of Texas. Only after it won in court during 1957 could the NAACP try to rebuild its support, which took two to three years for local branches.

Other forms of opposition to school desegregation in Texas included the organization of White Citizens Councils in East Texas and several laws passed by the state legislature aimed at stopping or limiting progress toward integration. Despite such efforts, the number of school districts that took some action toward desegregation grew to more than 120 in the 1957–58 school year. East Texas districts with larger black student populations, Houston and Dallas among them, continued to resist. To maintain segregation some districts redrew school boundaries, or allowed white students to transfer easily, while others placed black students in separate classrooms or made social events private.

A decade after the *Brown* decision, in 1964, about half of Texas school districts, 373, had integrated. Because those districts generally lay outside East Texas, they included only 5 percent of African American students in the state. That year Congress adopted the Civil Rights Act of 1964, with a provision that federal funds could be withheld from segregated districts. A year later less than 10 percent of Texas school districts still had no plan for integration. By 1966–67 almost half of the black students in Texas experienced some degree of desegregation.

With changes from at-large elections to district elections for the school board in the late 1960s, African Americans won seats on boards in Austin, Beaumont, Dallas, Port Arthur, and a number of other towns. Questions remained, however, about the degree of integration. The Department of Health, Education, and Welfare pressed twenty-six Texas school districts to revise their desegregation plans because two-thirds of black students still attended "racially identifiable schools." In some larger cities the percentage ranged above 80 or even 90 percent. That led NAACP chapters to support challenges of desegregation plans. In response federal judges could pair previously white and black schools, change boundaries between schools, or include busing students to further the desegregation process.

In East Texas the remaining nine African American districts became part of larger districts when a federal judge grouped them with bordering districts during 1970 and 1971. Acceptance of busing by the U.S. Supreme Court in 1971, as one of several means for desegregation, led African American and Hispanic groups to pursue revised school integration plans in several larger cities across the state. White opponents spoke of moving or sending students to private schools, while African Americans expressed concern that their pupils might be the only ones bused. Many white Texans seemed to forget that large numbers of students had ridden buses to school in rural areas. Others did not realize black students in some cases had been walking past white schools to reach more distant black schools during segregation.

Following breakthroughs in voting rights and desegregation of schools and colleges, African Americans in Texas shifted their focus in part to other forms of discrimination. The *Brown* decision also strengthened the black legal opposition to segregation in public places. Such challenges broke down segregation in city and state parks, golf courses, restrooms, and eating facilities in the late 1950s and early 1960s. Most public libraries and hospitals soon opened their doors to African Americans, while public cemeteries also desegregated. Railroad segregation had not been enforced fully in West Texas with its limited black population. As autos took over from passenger trains, segregation became too expensive to maintain. Decisions by the U.S. Supreme Court and the Interstate Commerce Commission officially ended segregation on railroads and buses by the mid-1950s. Separate local waiting rooms in stations held out in some towns until the 1960s.

Students from black and integrated colleges began picketing and conducting sit-ins against continued segregation at theaters and restaurants in the 1960s. One national civil rights leader, James Farmer, came from Marshall, Texas, where his father held a professorship at Wiley College. Farmer became one of the founders of the Congress of Racial Equality in the 1940s. He served the national NAACP as program director in the 1950s, then returned to CORE as its director in the 1960s. In 1969 he received appointment as Assistant Secretary of the Department of Health, Education, and Welfare. Students from Texas Southern University (TSU) began sit-ins at white-owned grocery store and drugstore lunch counters near their university. Members of the NAACP and the Congress of Racial Equality in several Texas cities and towns supported such movements by boycotts of segregated businesses. The Houston Council of Organizations gathered money to pay fines of arrested students. Support came from students of an African American business college and some white students from Rice University. Lunch counters closed at first. A new Progressive Youth Association of students, led by Eldrewey Stearns, a law student at TSU, expanded the efforts to stores such as Woolworth's in the Houston downtown. City hall and some stores desegregated in 1961, although some students faced arrest at other lunch counters. Smaller cities including Austin and San Antonio accepted desegregation in 1960, while sit-ins continued in Dallas. The Civil Rights Act of 1964, backed by President Lyndon Johnson and Senator Ralph Yarborough of Texas, made discrimination by such businesses illegal, although some opposition continued in East Texas into 1965.

Problems of violence and unequal law enforcement lingered in the 1950s. The Ku Klux Klan revived especially in East Texas. In Houston four Anglos whipped Felton Turner and carved KKK on his body in 1960. Police and highway patrolmen claiming self-defense beat or killed apparently unarmed African Americans in Houston, Fort Worth, and East Texas. Those events led black organizations to seek the addition of African Americans to law enforcement at the local and state levels in the 1950s and 1960s. The results varied with forty in Houston, fifteen for Dallas, seven in Fort Worth, and smaller numbers in other communities in 1966. By 1971, black police represented only 2 percent of the Dallas force and 4 percent of the Houston department, compared to African American populations of 20 percent or more in each city. In 1966 the Department of Public Safety including the Texas Rangers continued to be entirely Anglo.

Discrimination also existed in the courts, with a very limited number of black judges. Many prosecuting attorneys sought to excuse African Americans from a jury in any case with a black person on trial. Patterns of sentencing showed that in cases where an African American stood accused of a crime against another African American, conviction led to shorter sentences than for whites. By contrast, black defendants charged with a crime against a white person generally faced longer sentences than whites and almost two-thirds of the executions in Texas.

Participation in various forms of protest could lead to excessive charges that appeared to be a form of intimidation by law enforcement. A Texas Southern University protest leader, Lee Otis Johnson, faced a sentence of thirty years for offering a marijuana cigarette to a disguised policeman. Ernest McMillan and Matthew Johnson led a Student Nonviolent Coordinating Committee boycott of grocers in black Dallas neighborhoods. A judge sentenced them to ten years in prison for $211 in damages at one business. Although that virtually ended SNCC activities in Dallas, Eva McMillan, Ernest's mother, became an advocate of prison reform and an active opponent of the Klan.

Two incidents of violence occurred in Houston. On May 16, 1967, Texas Southern University students gathered on campus to debate how to protest problems of greater punishment for African American students in public schools, unregulated garbage sites in black neighborhoods where one person had drowned, and rumors of a shooting that later proved wrong. Fears of unruly acts brought police to the campus, which led some students to throw rocks and bottles at the officers. When a shot rang out, police thought it came from one of the dorms and fired on those buildings. By one estimate police fired 2,000 times in three hours, while 40 to 60 shots came from the dorms. Police then seized control of the dorms, arrested almost 500 students, and while searching for weapons did considerable damage in the rooms. A ricochet that could have come from either side killed one policeman. A grand jury offered Texas Southern no payment for damages, but charged five students for a riot that led to a death. Without evidence, the indictment was dismissed in 1970.

In following years some Houston police continued to antagonize the black community by shooting African American suspects in the back, beating others, and searching homes without warrants. In 1970 such acts, as well as economic concerns, led to the formation of People's Party II, similar to the Black Panthers in other cities. The members gathered clothes, food, and medicine for the needy, but also created an aggressive image by legally carrying weapons and claiming they would oppose harsh treatment of African Americans by police. Police arrested two of them in an encounter on July 26 while others sought money from passing motorists. Plainclothes officers took a position on top of a building. Claiming they faced gunfire, the police shot five members of the People's Party II, wounding four and killing Carl Hampton, the chairman. Some bystanders thought the police fired first, however, causing one writer to call the shooting an assassination. The white press seldom explained black views of such events, which tended to reinforce negative reactions from a majority of Anglos. Most African Americans saw the event as an extreme version of harassment that existed in other cities. Frustrations led to brief incidents in Midland in 1968 and Lubbock in 1971. Only in the late 1970s and early 1980s did urban police forces hire and promote greater numbers of African Americans.

In another area of concern, African Americans continued to face economic problems, in part because of discrimination. Black farmers declined in number as sharecroppers left to seek jobs in cities during the Depression of the 1930s. Federal assistance to farmers went primarily to white landowners during that period. The revival of industry in World War II attracted even more black workers to urban areas. African Americans in industrial jobs increased to twice the prewar figure, although most held unskilled positions that paid less. Beginning in the 1940s and continuing into the 1950s, the Texas State Conference of NAACP Branches labored with the Texas Negro Chamber of Commerce through the Texas Council of Negro Organizations to have more vocational skills taught in schools. They also worked to attain African American inclusion in defense projects, and to have better employment information available to military veterans. Black chambers of commerce sought cooperation with Anglo chambers to achieve consideration of all individuals seeking work. African American members of unions in major industries pressed for fairer promotion lists. One section in the Civil Rights Act of 1964 made job discrimination illegal. The War on Poverty by the Johnson administration in the 1960s included community action agencies that might offer help finding work and assistance with legal issues, as well as aid with other necessities. Training for greater skills took place at two Job Corps centers in Texas.

African Americans in Houston organized local efforts. Churches, led by Methodist pastor Earl E. Allen, created HOPE Development Inc. to deal with the range of poverty issues. Opportunities Industrialization Centers, a concept initially developed by African American church leaders in Philadelphia, offered skilled job courses to blacks in Dallas, Houston, and Lubbock in the 1960s and 1970s. The Southern Christian Leadership Conference adopted a version of that idea with its Operation Breadbasket efforts in the 1960s. Houston church leaders became involved in 1969 with a boycott of a Burger King in an African American neighborhood after the company rejected an application from black businessmen to operate that franchise. Facing financial losses, Burger King reversed its decision. Similar efforts led by Pluria Marshall and Rev. Bill Lawson produced improved situations for African American employees in several Houston businesses. Yet financial problems of its own brought an end to Operation Breadbasket of Texas in 1978.

Housing discrimination also existed in Texas cities. The seventeen largest in population ranged from 80 to 98 percent segregated in 1960, with twelve at 90 percent or higher levels of segregation. A majority of housing for African Americans remained substandard with no water or street paving, since few contractors showed interest, assuming no market existed for new homes in black neighborhoods. When middle-class African Americans moved into nearby white areas in Houston and Dallas, whites opposed sales and bombs exploded at some black-owned houses. Public housing remained largely segregated. Urban renewal led to improvements in some areas, but brought higher costs that some African Americans could not afford. New freeways disrupted some black areas in Austin and other cities.

The issues related to housing led to new responses. When the city of Dallas decided to enlarge Fair Park, site of the state fair, it seemed ready to pay African Americans far less for their homes in the area than Anglo owners. Albert Lipscomb led the struggle for equitable payments. Similar efforts occurred in other Texas cities.

Because a Mexican American civil rights movement developed during the same decades as the African American movement in Texas and other states, historians have raised questions about the lack of frequent cooperation that included both minorities. They point to the status of Mexican Americans as legally white under state law, different views of immigration, and potential economic competition as possible explanations. Cooperation did occur at times, most often at the local level. For example, African Americans and Mexican Americans in San Antonio voted together in 1948 to place black business owner G. J. Sutton on the board for the city's community colleges. In the state legislature during 1957, Henry Gonzales from San Antonio and Abraham Kazen from Laredo opposed by filibuster five bills supporting segregation. Their efforts defeated three of the bills. At Slaton in West Texas the two minority groups cooperated to make an African American pastor a city commissioner in 1959. They also voted down a proposal for at-large elections. Attorneys for African Americans and Mexican Americans cooperated in court cases to end at-large elections to the legislature in urban areas during the early 1970s. Lawyers from the two groups also consulted at times on similar cases.

The civil rights movement in Texas involved multiple African American organizations—local, state, and national—often working together to bring down the barriers of segregation and discrimination. The movement won two major court decisions, the Lonnie Smith case that ruled the white primary unconstitutional in 1944, and the Heman Sweatt case that began desegregation of higher education in 1950 and paved the way for integration of public schools and other public places. African Americans in Texas continued their efforts through the federal courts, protests, and boycotts during the 1960s and 1970s. They achieved real progress in political participation and representation, in more equitable opportunities in education and economic activities, and in desegregation of public places. After strong early opposition from a majority of white Texans, a slow trend toward the acceptance of change began to appear, more often among a younger generation of Anglos. Despite successes in the years of the civil rights movement, African Americans in Texas still grapple with some racially identifiable schools that have lower performance results. Some working-class neighborhoods still face higher unemployment that may translate into more crime and fewer two-parent families. Those concerns contrast with increased numbers of African American high school and college graduates, businesses, attorneys, physicians, teachers, and others with professional degrees, as well as expanded roles among professional athletes and those in the performing arts.

Further Reading

Barr, Alwyn. *Black Texans: A History of African Americans in Texas, 1528–1995*. 2nd ed. Norman: University of Oklahoma Press, 1996.

Beeth, Howard, and Cary D. Wintz, eds. *Black Dixie: Afro-Texan History and Culture in Houston*. College Station: Texas A&M University Press, 1992.

Behnken, Brian D. *Fighting Their Own Battles: Mexican Americans, African Americans, and the Struggle for Civil Rights in Texas*. Chapel Hill: University of North Carolina Press, 2011.

Cole, Thomas R. *No Color Is My Kind: The Life of Eldrewey Stearns and the Integration of Houston*. Austin: University of Texas Press, 1997.

Glasrud, Bruce A., and Merline Pitre, eds. *Black Women in Texas History*. College Station: Texas A&M University Press, 2008.

Goldstone, Dwonna. *Integrating the 40 Acres: The Fifty-Year Struggle for Racial Equality at the University of Texas*. Athens: University of Georgia Press, 2006.

Hine, Darlene Clark. *Black Victory: The Rise and Fall of the White Primary in Texas*. 2nd ed. Columbia: University of Missouri Press, 2003.

Kellar, William Henry. *Make Haste Slowly: Moderates, Conservatives, and School Desegregation in Houston*. College Station: Texas A&M University Press, 1999.

Ladino, Robyn Duff. *Desegregating Texas Schools: Eisenhower, Shivers, and the Crisis at Mansfield High*. Austin: University of Texas Press, 1996.

Lavergne, Gary M. *Before Brown: Heman Marion Sweatt, Thurgood Marshall, and the Long Road to Justice*. Austin: University of Texas Press, 2010.

Martin, Charles H. *Benching Jim Crow: The Rise and Fall of the Color Line in Southern College Sports, 1890–1980*. Urbana: University of Illinois Press, 2010.

Osborn, William S. "Curtains for Jim Crow: Law, Race, and the Texas Railroads." *Southwestern Historical Quarterly* 105 (January 2002): 393–427.

Pitre, Merline. *In Struggle Against Jim Crow: Lulu White and the NAACP, 1900–1957*. College Station: Texas A&M University Press, 1999.

Shabazz, Amilcar. *Advancing Democracy: African Americans and the Struggle for Access and Equity in Higher Education in Texas*. Chapel Hill: University of North Carolina Press, 2004.

Zelden, Charles L. *The Battle for the Black Ballot: Smith v. Allwright and the Defeat of the Texas All-White Primary*. Lawrence: University Press of Kansas, 2004.

Part VI
Epilogue

16

Western Civil Rights since 1970

Albert S. Broussard

In this chapter, which serves also as our epilogue, Texas A&M University historian and scholar Albert S. Broussard argues persuasively that the civil rights revolution during the 1960s continued to demand equality, yet the results were mixed. During the 1970s and beyond, continued actions on the part of African Americans in the West also resulted in mixed receptions. As Broussard points out, even the election of a black president did not alleviate the secondary status of black citizens in the West. Overall gains were made that particularly benefitted the middle classes; however, those accomplishments did "little to close the inequality gap between blacks and whites." Among Broussard's first-rate publications is his study of the black West, *Expectations of Equality: A History of Black Westerners*.

The 1960s had been a transformative decade for many black western communities, as well as the entire nation. Although African Americans had staged sporadic protests in numerous western cities during the World War II era and beyond, and in many respects predated the southern civil rights movement, these acts of civil disobedience had not sparked a mass movement until the 1960s. During the 1960s, virtually every major western city in the nation, including far-flung urban centers in Alaska and Hawaii such as Anchorage, Fairbanks, and Honolulu, staged protests and demonstrations to demand racial equality. Like their counterparts in the northern states and the South, western leaders achieved uneven success in their quest to achieve full equality or to eradicate every remaining vestige of white racial privilege. Yet significant gains were made in politics, in access to housing in both the central cities and suburbs, and in the growth of the black middle and professional classes. Moreover, African Americans gained access to colleges and professional schools, both public and private, at an increasingly impressive rate after the 1970s. Despite these gains, however, black westerners continued to lag behind their white counterparts in almost every area. Moreover, increasing competition with Latinos and Asians for jobs, housing, and public space made even holding on to prior gains difficult in some western cities.

Black westerners faced an increasingly resistant white population during the 1970s and beyond. White backlash had reared its head in every region of the nation, as the white middle class grew weary of black demands for racial justice and economic gains. The fractious race riots of the 1960s, as well as the rise of Black Power and militant black rhetoric, also alienated many white westerners, and even former allies such as white liberals and Jews criticized the movement toward affirmative action because it smacked of quotas in their view. In light of this atmosphere, African Americans appealed to the courts and federal agencies like the Equal Employment Opportunity Commission (EEOC), an outgrowth of the 1964 Civil Rights Act. The EEOC, which Congress included as title seven of the historic Civil Rights Act of 1964, possessed the statutory power to not merely investigate complaints of racial discrimination and sexism, but also to compel organizations to cease and desist such practices. Additionally, the EEOC had the authority to take an organization or company to court and seek monetary damages in behalf of the aggrieved party. Not only did African Americans benefit from this law, but white females, Latinos, Asians, and American Indians also made important inroads in breaking down discriminatory employment barriers and creating a more welcoming workplace.

The role of federal organizations such as the EEOC proved particularly important for black westerners because of a systemic pattern of racism in many public and private companies throughout the western states and territories. Although western black workers had made important inroads into many skilled and white collar jobs, as well as gained access to heretofore white unions such as the building trades and maritime unions, numerous public sector jobs were slow to integrate. Indeed, some western cities were under federal court order to hire additional black policemen and firefighters as late as the early 1970s, a policy that their unions fought, despite a persistent and long-standing practice of discrimination. The city of Austin, Texas, was in the process of approving an agreement with the Department of Justice in 2014 to hire more black firemen, evidence that discriminatory hiring practices persisted into the twenty-first century. Western cities also failed to keep pace with their northern counterparts in hiring and promoting black educators. A smattering of black teachers began to teach in the large urban centers of western cities in the wake of the massive in-migration of southern black migrants during the World War II years. These teachers were generally assigned to teach in predominantly minority school districts and few had the opportunity to earn promotions to counselors, principals, or other administrative positions within their school district.

A similar pattern persisted at western colleges, universities, and professional schools throughout the 1960s and 1970s. True, law schools and professional schools had come a long way since 1950 when the U.S. Supreme Court ordered the University of Texas Law School to admit Heman Sweatt, an African American student, and to cease its brutal discrimination of George McLaurin at the University of Oklahoma. Every college and university in the West, including those in Alaska and Hawaii, had opened their doors to black students by 1970, albeit in modest numbers. Many of these public colleges, such as the University of Washington at Seattle, the University of California at Berkeley, the University of San Francisco, and San Francisco State University, established specific programs to enroll a limited number of black students and to assist in their transition to the collegiate experience. Other schools simply opened their doors to black students who qualified for regular admission without fanfare. Thus by the early 1970s, western colleges enrolled a small cohort or a critical mass of black students for the first time from a breadth of social and economic classes, and in virtually every instance students formed organizations such as black student unions to create a sense of community (or unity) among African Americans.

Black westerners made perhaps their most impressive gains in the political arena. Buttressed by an expanding black western population in the postwar era and continued migration of African Americans to western cities during the 1950s and 1960s, black political candidates made their first serious bids for elective office. Although the largest number of black officeholders resided in the southern states in the wake of the 1965 Voting Rights Act, the gains in western states with considerably smaller numbers of black residents was nevertheless impressive. By 1990, a staggering eight thousand black elected officials were recorded throughout the nation, 60 percent of whom resided in the South, where African Americans comprised a sizable voting bloc. Because the number of African Americans was never as sizable in the West, black politicians depended on white, Latino, and Asian voters to support their candidacy. And in a surprising number of cases, this is precisely what happened. In 1973, Tom Bradley, a native of Calvert, Texas, and a former Los Angeles police officer, defeated incumbent Los Angeles mayor Sam Yorty in a closely contested election. Bradley's victory marked the first time a person of African descent had served as mayor of Los Angeles since Francisco Reyes, a mulatto from central Mexico, served as the alcalde of the pueblo of Los Angeles in the 1780s. Bradley served five terms as mayor—twenty years—in the largest city in the West and the second-largest city in the nation, which was no small accomplishment. In 1986, Bradley lost a close election to George Deukmejian in his bid to become California's first African American governor.

Conservative southwestern cities such as Dallas and Houston also changed politically, as African Americans voted in much larger numbers following the passage of the Voting Rights Act in 1965. In Texas, for example, the number of African Americans who were registered to vote in 1976 stood at 65 percent. It had stood at 35 percent in 1960. By 1977, largely on the strength of the black vote, 158 African Americans held office in Texas cities. Barbara Jordan serves as a case in point, as well as an example of a black woman who succeeded to elected office. Jordan, a product of Houston's Fifth Ward, was a fiery orator who possessed a keen intellect and a powerful will to succeed. She attended Boston University Law School, after which she returned to Houston and entered statewide politics. In 1967, Jordan won a seat in the Texas state senate, the first African American of any gender to do so since 1883. Breaking both racial and gender barriers, Jordan was elected to the U.S. House of Representatives from the Eighteenth District. In doing so, Jordan became the first woman of any race from a southern state to serve in Congress. Highly respected among her congressional peers, Jordan led a distinguished career in that body, and was selected to present the keynote address at the 1976 Democratic National Convention. Jordan is best known, however, for her role—or service—as a member of the House Judiciary Committee during the 1974 Watergate hearings. Jordan presented a brilliant speech in defense of the Constitution and her faith in and commitment to the rule of law, neither of which were practiced during the Nixon administration.

Many other western cities elected African American mayors after 1970, including San Francisco (Willie Brown), Seattle (Norman Rice), Denver (Wellington Webb), Oakland (Lionel Wilson), Dallas (Ron Kirk), and Houston (Lee P. Brown). That the majority of these political leaders were elected from states in the far west or in the mountain states with the exception of Texas, speaks to the significance of the black voting bloc in those states as well as the successful coalitions that African Americans established with moderate white voters. This was particularly true in the far west, where the black population remained a relatively small percentage of the region's total population. In the case of one western city, San Francisco, the African American population declined sharply after 1970, dropping faster than any large city in the nation between 1970 and 2005. Still, San Francisco's voters elected Willie L. Brown Jr., a popular and flamboyant state legislator who had served as chairman of the state's powerful House Ways and Means Committee, as mayor for two terms. Progressive white voters proved crucial to Brown's election, as they did for Tom Bradley in Los Angeles, Norman Rice in Seattle, and Wellington Webb in Denver. Indeed, the support of white liberals, labor, Hispanics, and moderate white Democrats proved crucial in electing black public officials in the majority of western cities during the post–World War II era.

One important constituent that is often overlooked when assessing the rise of either progressive white or black politicians in the West is the LGBT community. By the early 1970s, the gay community recognized the importance of political power in their quest to achieve respect and to change a series of archaic laws and public attitudes about homosexuality. Modeling their activities after the civil rights campaigns of the 1960s, political organizing first bore fruit on the East Coast, but western cities were not far behind. By 1971, gay rights organizations supported the candidacies of Dianne Feinstein for the San Francisco Board of Supervisors; Willie Brown for the California State Assembly; George Moscone for city supervisor, state senator, and later mayor of San Francisco; and Phillip Burton for congressman. Los Angeles followed the lead of San Francisco and Northern California. Working through the liberal wing of the Democratic party, the Stonewall Democratic Club emerged as one of the most significant and powerful organizations in Los Angeles County. These political endorsements were especially important for black westerners, argues historian Robert Self, as "both San Francisco and Los Angeles gay politics featured alliances with African Americans that became a hallmark of liberal urban political coalitions in the late 1970s and throughout the 1980s." Regrettably, for many politicians, black or white, an open alliance with gay and lesbian organizations was anathema in the early 1970s, so black politicians rarely touted these relationships. Only the Black Panther Party, based in Oakland, California, openly supported the rights of gays and lesbians in their quest for equality under the law. Indeed, African American churches were openly hostile to gays, claiming that the Bible did not condone their sexual practices and that homosexuality was unnatural. Cecil Williams's Glide Memorial Church in San Francisco proved one of the rare exceptions in the early 1970s.

Black elected officials in the West, however, were as powerless as their counterparts in other major cities such as Chicago (Harold Washington), Cleveland

(Carl Stokes), Detroit (Coleman Young), or New York (David Dinkins), to improve the lives of their African American constituents, to stop police brutality and racial profiling, to provide affordable housing, or to close the income gap between black and white workers. Nor could black politicians, despite their broad mandate from the voters, stem the steady tide of white middle-class flight from the central cities in the West to the suburbs, or reverse the racial composition of western schools, which had increasingly become dominated by black, brown, and Asian students after 1970. Despite their best intentions, these men and women did not have the means to deliver.

Although the majority of black westerners resided in the inner cities, many remained trapped due to marginal jobs, lack of transportation, or inadequate incomes to move to better neighborhoods. Yet many black westerners moved to suburban communities between 1970 and 2000. By 1990, more than half of all Americans resided in suburbs, continuing a pattern that had begun following World War II when inexpensive housing became available to many middle-class Americans. The majority of black westerners, however, were virtually shut out of these housing developments either by stealth or racially restrictive deeds. This was true even of black veterans, who had far greater difficulty securing low-interest loans from the Veterans Administration's Servicemen's Readjustment Act (GI Bill) than white veterans. Nevertheless, and despite numerous obstacles in their path, by 1970 approximately 250,000 blacks a year moved to the suburbs, a dramatic increase in the space of a decade. Black westerners moved to suburban communities for essentially the same reasons as middle-class whites, Asians, and Latinos. Suburbs offered more spacious housing, higher quality schools, access to shopping malls and industrial parks, and a much safer environment in which to raise families. The most important reason was the relocation of jobs to suburbs, which attracted people of all races and ethnicities. The majority of the nation's retail and manufacturing jobs were based in the suburbs after 1970, and many high-tech companies were based in the San Francisco Bay Area suburbs known as Silicon Valley. The growth of the tech industry in particular fueled the growth of the U.S. economy by the 1990s and 2000s, as companies such as Yahoo, Google, Samsung, Apple, and Facebook dotted the western landscape, employed thousands of people at high wages, and contributed to the expansion of suburban growth. As historian Herbert G. Ruffin has shown, however, African Americans did not benefit to the same degree as other groups in securing high-tech jobs due in part to a historic and persistent pattern of racism in the Silicon Valley region.

The changing legal landscape nationally also contributed to the rapid growth of African American suburbanites in the West and throughout the nation after 1970. The Fair Housing Act passed in 1968 prohibited discrimination in the sale, lease, or rental of housing based on race. Similarly, reversing a long-standing policy, the Federal Housing Administration (FHA) no longer refused to guarantee mortgages when African Americans and other "undesirable" minority groups moved into white neighborhoods. Earlier, California had led the way, when in 1966 the California Supreme Court overturned Proposition 14, a popular referendum that had prohibited the state from denying any property owner the right to sell, rent, or lease their property to anyone at their discretion. Prior to its passage, property owners could, at their whim, deny housing to ethnic and racial minorities. Such was the case when a white property owner refused to sell his home in South San Francisco to an Asian American in the early 1950s. To be sure, these laws did not eradicate housing discrimination completely, but they opened the door more widely to African Americans and others who wished to escape the central cities and move to more desirable housing. Changing public attitudes also contributed to the lessening of racism in housing after 1970. Nowhere in the West did whites riot or mobilize large and hostile white neighborhood organizations to keep blacks out of white neighborhoods and public housing as they did repeatedly in northern and midwestern cities in the early twentieth century. Blacks and Latinos may well have been viewed as unwelcome guests, but their presence did not spark either mob violence or wholesale white flight.

Black western suburbanites fared considerably better economically than their counterparts in the inner city. California, the largest western state, serves as a case in point. By 1990, nearly two-thirds (61 percent) of California's black labor force held white-collar jobs, and many of these African American workers lived in suburbs. The California suburb of Inglewood had reputably the highest income of any predominantly black city in the nation. Bucking the trend of many black majority cities, Inglewood also had one of the lowest rates of poverty. In addition to steady employment, black suburbanites sent their children to higher performing schools with other middle-class children, increasing the likelihood that they would attend college and professional schools. Suburbs also had a much stronger tax base than inner cities, so municipal services such as sanitation and road maintenance were performed on a regular basis. The low crime rates in suburbs compared to those in the inner city also meant that black children, as well as their parents, would less likely be victims of crime. These advantages, which were considerable, also meant that a growing class and spatial divide would emerge between African Americans who were trapped in the inner cities and those who resided in suburbs, a process that sociologist William Julius Wilson described poignantly in his book *The Truly Disadvantaged*. Many of these individuals, the products of single-parent families, multigenerational poverty, poorly performing schools and indifferent teachers, crime, and high unemployment, felt trapped and hopeless.

These frustrations occasionally boiled over into urban unrest, such as the 1965 Watts Riot or the 1992 uprising in Los Angeles that claimed more than sixty lives and the destruction of several billion dollars in property. Each incident involved a perceived miscarriage of justice, police brutality in the case of the Watts Riot, and an unjust jury verdict in the acquittal of the police officers accused of excessive force in the arrest of Rodney King, an African American who had been stopped for speeding and resisting arrest. But Los Angeles proved the exception in the West, for no other western community exploded in a similar fashion. This held true despite a growing gang problem, the infusion of drugs such as crack cocaine, methamphetamine, and heroin in both the inner cities and suburbs, and the spatial separation between the black middle class and African Americans in the inner city. Violence, however, did not abate. Rather, African Americans were far more likely to turn their violence toward each other.

Much of the violence in inner-city black western communities was related directly or indirectly to illegal drugs. To think that drugs had not been present and readily available in western cities would be naive. However, an epidemic of heroin, crack cocaine, and other illegal drugs flooded into predominantly low-income communities after 1970, causing a myriad of problems. By the 1990s, the jails and prisons throughout the West as well as the nation overflowed with black and brown faces, particularly young black men in the prime of life. By 1996, the nation's state and prison population reached 1.2 million. By the year 2000, it exceeded 2 million, giving the United States the distinction of having the largest prison population in the world. African Americans composed half of all prisoners in the United States in 1998, even though they composed about 13 percent of the nation's population. Every western state after 1970 swelled its prison rolls with African Americans, and California, the most populous state in the nation, once again led the way. In the Golden State, four times as many blacks served time in prison as were enrolled in the state's colleges and universities. Texas was not far behind: African Americans, who represented only 12 percent of the Lone Star State's population, made up 39 percent of all inmates on death row in 1998. Critics of the nation's drug policies would be incorrect to blame conservatives for these disparities in sentencing, as the war on drugs launched by Presidents George H. W. Bush and Bill Clinton cut across party lines. Yet, the disparities in the penalties and sentencing for drug use did smack of racial profiling. Individuals, for example, who used or sold crack cocaine, the drug most closely associated with African American inner-city communities, received much harsher sentencing than those caught using or selling powder cocaine, a drug used predominantly by whites. Not surprisingly, more than 80 percent of the people serving time in U.S. prisons for distributing or possessing crack cocaine in 2009 were African American. Congressional lawmakers finally recognized the injustice, and voted in 2010 to reduce the disparity in sentencing between crack and powder cocaine.

Black westerners also struggled to provide adequate health care to themselves and their families in light of their low wages, lack of access to medical facilities and primary health care doctors, and the preponderance of single-parent, low-income families in black neighborhoods. Poverty instead of race remained, perhaps, the single greatest barrier to adequate health care, although access to health care remained a major barrier to African Americans and other people of color in the West due to cutbacks in popular social programs. Not surprisingly, black western families registered the highest poverty rate in the region. Roughly seven in ten black families nationally were headed by single parents by 2000, and these individuals were typically poor, uneducated, and marginally employed, and they occupied some of the worst housing in the inner cities. These neighborhoods were magnets for the drug trade, gangs, and prostitution, all of which contributed to high crime rates.

Black westerners had the shortest life span of any racial or ethnic group in the West. Black males, according to the Centers for Disease Control, had the shortest life span of any group in 2007 at 70 years, compared to 76 years for white males and 80.8 years for white females. Black females averaged 76.8 years, only four years behind white females. Black children also lagged behind white children in almost every indicator of sound health. They suffered from more childhood diseases than white children, and were more likely to suffer from asthma, obesity, poor nutrition, and learning disabilities. The lack of prenatal care also contributed to these health problems, as well as environmental factors such as living in more polluted areas where smog, industrial waste, or toxins were evident. Poverty and an inadequate education also made it more difficult for many of these parents to provide proper food and nutrition to themselves and their children, exacerbating their conditions.

Black westerners have also been affected by the HIV-AIDS epidemic in greater numbers than other groups in the West. Slow to grasp the severity of this disease and critical of homosexual practices in general, black leaders initially discounted its impact on black western communities. The conflicting responses to the HIV-AIDS crisis also reveal that African Americans were as divided as most Americans about how to cope with this disease, who was largely responsible, and whether the victims deserved the compassion of black leaders and the general public. Black southern leaders, such as Baptist ministers and black evangelicals, for example, were more critical of homosexuality in general, as civil rights leader Bayard Rustin learned in the early 1960s when Dr. Martin Luther King Jr. distanced himself from Rustin on the advice of J. Edgar Hoover, director of the FBI. But the criticism of homosexuality was not limited to southern black preachers. Western writers such as Eldridge Cleaver and Ishmael Reed criticized homosexuality as unmanly during a time in the black freedom struggle when African American men were often portrayed as hypermasculine—clearly a stereotype, but an image that Hollywood embraced and showcased in dozens of black exploitation movies during the 1970s and 1980s. Curiously, this stereotype was one of the few that many African American men embraced as a sign of "manhood," for it emphasized excessive bravado, exaggerated sexual prowess, and toughness. This view, however, was challenged by western black filmmakers such as Marlon Riggs, whose controversial film *Tongues Untied*, presented a far different image of some black males. Similarly, the "coming out" of high-profile black athletes as gays and lesbians such as Jason Collins in the National Basketball Association, Sheryl Swoopes and Brittney Griner in the Women's Basketball Association, and Michael Sam at the University of Missouri spark a lively discussion as well as a reexamination of sexual orientation and sexual identity and its meaning in the African American community.

The HIV-AIDS epidemic continued to wreak havoc on African American western communities in the twenty-first century, even during a time when the rate was falling in other regions. For example, even as the number of people globally who died from AIDS was declining by 2009, the number of AIDS deaths in the black population continued to rise. The Black AIDS Institute, an independent advocacy group, reported that nearly 600,000 African Americans lived with HIV by the turn of the twenty-first century, and that nearly 30,000 African Americans become infected each year. In 2004, AIDS was the leading cause of death for black women between the ages of 24 and 35, and black females were 13 times more likely to die of the disease than white females. The severity of the disease in the black community serves as still another indicator of the racial-economic inequality among African Americans in the West and in the nation.

African American westerners pressed for civil rights on college campuses more boldly after 1970 than ever before. Emboldened in part by an increase in the number of black students enrolled in public and private colleges, the successes of the civil rights movement nationally, the Vietnam War protests, and new forms of organizing, African American students demanded a greater voice in a variety of campus affairs after 1970. Wherever black students matriculated in the West between 1970 and 1980, some forms of protest were bound to follow. At San Francisco State College, black students had formed a broad coalition with other ethnic minorities and progressive whites in 1969 to form the Third World Liberation Front, and pressed for the creation of a Black Studies program. After waging a five-month strike, a program was established. Similar, though milder forms of civil disobedience were waged at other western colleges including Stanford, the University of California at Berkeley, and the University of Kansas. In virtually every instance of black student unrest, students demanded an increase in the number of black students, the hiring of black faculty and administrators, and the inclusion of African American and ethnic studies courses in the college's curriculum. Students also challenged college administrators to improve the racial climate on their campuses to make the college experience more welcoming to African Americans and students of color. Western colleges and universities such as the University of Washington at Seattle (1969), the University of Utah (1968), the University of Kansas (1970), and Stanford University (1969), among others, each responded by establishing African American Studies programs. Other schools, however, resorted to short-gap measures designed to pacify student and community protestors, and never devoted the resources to make these programs academically viable and sustainable. Few colleges or universities followed the lead of Stanford University, which hired the eminent black sociologist St. Clair Drake to lead its nascent African American Studies program in 1969.

Although African Americans made important inroads in gaining admission to many western colleges, universities, and professional schools during the 1970s, progress slowed considerably in many states following the 1978 Supreme Court case *Bakke v. Regents of the University of California*. Even though a divided court ruled in Allan Bakke's favor, it also upheld the legality of affirmative action programs as one of many factors that college admissions officials could consider in weighing an applicant's qualifications. In 2003, the U.S. Supreme Court upheld a similar ruling in *Grutter v. Bollinger*, when a white applicant argued that she had been discriminated against on the basis of race in her application to attend the University of Michigan Law School. Once again, the court ruled that affirmative action was legal, provided that it was only one of many factors that colleges considered in the admissions process. Justice Sandra Day O'Connor, speaking for the court's majority, affirmed the importance of diversity in training leaders of every race and ethnicity. On the same day, the court ruled an affirmative action program at the University of Michigan unconstitutional because it gave too much attention to race for admission to its undergraduate college.

Western admissions officers were hard-pressed to increase the number of underrepresented racial and ethnic minorities such as African Americans, Latinos, and American Indians at their colleges given these restrictive barriers and, predictably, college admission remained relatively flat for these groups in most western states. But opponents of affirmative action went even further, placing ballot initiatives before their voters to eliminate race completely from the college admissions process. Funded by a conservative coalition that opposed affirmative action, California voters approved Proposition 209, a statewide initiative passed in 1996, which outlawed the use of affirmative action. Michigan voters passed a similar initiative in 2006 that was upheld by the U.S. Supreme Court in 2014. Proposition 209, probably a sign of what African Americans and Latinos can expect to see in other western states, hurt, but it did not cripple African American college enrollment in California, the nation's most populous state. But these legal barriers, as well as the rising cost of college admissions, made it more difficult to diversify college campuses. Janet Napolitano, president of the University of California system, stated that "across the university, the percentage of African Americans and American Indians enrolled in 2012 remained lower than the corresponding percentages in 1995." Napolitano lamented that in some years the entering classes of the University of California law school and business school did not have a single black student, "despite considerable outreach efforts." The UC system could report that Latino students, the state's largest ethnic minority group, had made gains, but still lagged considerably behind their explosive growth in the nation's population. This trend did not bode well for African American students throughout the West and the nation who saw higher education as an avenue to obtain a steady job or as a means of upward mobility. It also meant that the competition for college and professional school admission would become even more competitive in the future.

Black westerners also struggled to obtain affordable health care, a problem made all the more acute by high rates of obesity, smoking, hypertension,

HIV-AIDS, and poverty. President Barack Obama, whom black westerners supported overwhelmingly in 2008 and 2012, offered Americans a ray of hope when he signed the Affordable Care Act in March 2010, the nation's first system of comprehensive health care. Obamacare, as it is popularly known, required every American to purchase health care or pay a fine. The controversial law also encouraged states to expand their Medicaid programs to embrace more low-income Americans, and many states complied readily. Others, like Texas, despite possessing the highest rate of uninsured people in the nation, refused to expand its Medicaid program. The far western and mountain west states in general were quicker to adopt Medicaid expansion, but many western states rejected the concept even though the federal government agreed to fund the states' expansion and additional coverage in full for a period of three years. Thus the states of Texas, Alaska, Idaho, Kansas, Montana, Nebraska, Oklahoma, and Wyoming all rejected federal dollars, even though their taxpayers would have borne no additional costs. Although it is too early to predict what impact the Affordable Care Act will have on black westerners, they are certain to benefit from the expansion of Medicaid because they have higher rates of poverty than whites in most western states. Additionally, the broad spectrum of health problems that have plagued black communities for decades and have resulted in a lower life expectancy for African Americans than whites, as well as higher rates of infant mortality, suggest that black westerners and low-income westerners would benefit enormously from Medicaid expansion in their states.

Despite the 2008 election of Barack Obama, the nation's first African American president, significant disparities remained between black westerners and other ethnic and racial groups. Median household income nationally as late as 2006 was $32,132 for blacks compared to $50,673 for whites, a sign that blacks had lost—not gained—ground. Fewer blacks also owned their own homes (48 percent) than whites (75 percent), reflecting the enormous disparities in assets between the two groups. Since the majority of whites had their wealth tied up in their homes, African Americans were at a decided disadvantage. Even more disturbing, 24 percent of African Americans lived below the poverty rate, twice the national average (12.3 percent) and three times the poverty rate of whites (8 percent). Clearly, the plethora of Great Society programs to reduce poverty had not made a long-term impact on African Americans.

Nor had the election of dozens of black mayors, state representatives, congressmen, local officials, or even an African American president closed the economic gap between blacks and whites. Similarly, the plethora of African Americans and Latinos elected to local school boards did little to stem the tide of white flight from the central cities or close the achievement gap between black, brown, and white children in western schools. Indeed, civil rights, perhaps with the exception of the reauthorization of the Voting Rights Act in 2006, had faded from the national scene, and neither political party regarded it as a major campaign issue. In fact, no president beyond the 1980s, including George H. W. Bush, Bill Clinton, George W. Bush, or Barack Obama pushed any *new* civil rights initiatives. And although President Barack Obama campaigned on the theme of "hope and change," this campaign slogan and political rhetoric apparently did not include race or civil rights when he won office. To the contrary, President Obama affirmed repeatedly to the press that he did not wish to be regarded as the "black president," and he seldom spoke out on racial issues during his first term (2008–12). Thus President Obama's election in 2008 and his reelection in 2012 illuminated a stark reality: electoral politics, even the election of an African American president, served as a poor vehicle to affect the type of wholesale societal and economic change that would be necessary to significantly improve the condition of many African Americans. Unless progressive black and white politicians allied to push through legislation that significantly improved issues such as education, health care, housing, and employment, little changed in the day-to-day lives of many black westerners and other people of color.

Passing progressive legislation alone, however, will do little to close the inequality gap between blacks and whites. Such legislation largely benefits the middle class of all races, at the exclusion of those who are impoverished, poorly educated, or lack the will and guidance to navigate successfully in an information-age society. As black westerners and other people of color navigate their way through the twenty-first century, they will require policies or assistance aimed and targeted specifically at their disparities such as quality education, job training, better parenting skills, child care, transportation, housing, health care, and a reduction of crime in their communities, including drug trafficking, if they ever hope to bridge the gap between the haves and the have nots. These challenges appear formidable on their face, but black westerners faced equally difficult challenges throughout the twentieth century in their ceaseless quest for equality and dignity.

Further Reading

Behnken, Brian D. *Fighting Their Own Battles: Mexican Americans, African Americans, and the Struggle for Civil Rights in Texas*. Chapel Hill: University of North Carolina Press, 2014.

Broussard, Albert S. *Expectations of Equality: A History of Black Westerners*. Wheeling, Ill.: Harlan Davidson, 2012.

Eick, Gretchen Cassel. *Dissent in Wichita: The Civil Rights Movement in the Midwest, 1954–72*. Urbana: University of Illinois Press, 2001.

Flamming, Douglas. *African Americans in the West*. Santa Barbara, Calif.: ABC-CLIO, 2009.

Glasrud, Bruce, ed. *African American History in New Mexico: Portraits from Five Hundred Years*. Albuquerque: University of New Mexico Press, 2013.

Kurashige, Scott. *The Shifting Grounds of Race: Black and Japanese Americans in the Making of Multiethnic Los Angeles*. Princeton, N.J.: Princeton University Press, 2008.

Miller, Paul T. *The Postwar Struggle for Civil Rights: African Americans in San Francisco, 1945–1975*. New York: Routledge, 2010.

Ruffin, Herbert G., II. *Uninvited Neighbors: African Americans in Silicon Valley, 1769–1990*. Norman: University of Oklahoma Press, 2014.

Self, Robert. *American Babylon: Race and the Struggle for Postwar Oakland*. Princeton, N.J.: Princeton University Press, 2003.

Sides, Josh. *L. A. City Limits: African American Los Angeles from the Great Depression to the Present*. Berkeley: University of California Press, 2003.

Sonenshein, Raphael J. *Politics in Black and White: Race and Power in Los Angeles*. Princeton, N.J.: Princeton University Press, 1993.

Stevenson, Brenda. *The Contested Murder of Latasha Harlins: Justice, Gender, and the Origins of the LA Riots*. New York: Oxford University Press, 2013.

Sugrue, Thomas J. *Sweet Land of Liberty: The Forgotten Struggle for Civil Rights in the North*. New York: Random House, 2008.

Taylor, Quintard. *In Search of the Racial Frontier: African Americans in the American West*. New York: W. W. Norton, 1998.

Taylor, Quintard, Lawrence B. De Graaf, and Kevin Mulroy, eds. *Seeking El Dorado: African Americans in California, 1769–1997*. Seattle: University of Washington Press, 2001.

Taylor, Quintard, and Shirley Ann Wilson Moore. *African American Women Confront the West, 1600–2000*. Norman: University of Oklahoma Press, 2003.

Whitaker, Matthew C. *Race Work: The Civil Rights Movement in the Urban West*. Lincoln: University of Nebraska Press, 2007.

Selected Bibliography

Each chapter contains its own list of citations or short bibliography for the area it represents. The following selected bibliography is the volume editors' list of suggested further reading that transcends regional boundaries or is especially significant. This is not a compilation of the sources cited in previous chapters.

Alexander, Thomas G. "The Civil Rights Movement in Utah." In *Utah: The Right Place*, 388–91. Rev. ed. Salt Lake City: Gibbs Smith, 2007.
Allen, Robert L. *The Port Chicago Mutiny*. New York: Amistad Press, 1993.
Anderson, Frederick E. *The Development of Leadership and Organization Building in the Black Community of Los Angeles from 1900 through World War II*. Saratoga: Century Twenty One Publishing, 1980.
Anderson, Reynaldo. "Practical Internationalists: The Story of the Des Moines, Iowa, Black Panther Party." In *Groundwork: Local Black Freedom Movements in America*, edited by Jeanne Theoharis and Komozi Woodard, 282–99. New York: New York University Press, 2005.
Asante, Molefi Kete. *Maulana Karenga: An Intellectual Portrait*. Malden, Mass.: Polity Press, 2009.
Barnhill, J. Herschel. "Civil Rights in Utah: The Mormon Way." *Journal of the West* 25, no. 4 (1986): 21–27.
Barr, Alwyn. *Black Texans: A History of African Americans in Texas, 1528–1995*. 2nd ed. Norman: University of Oklahoma Press, 1996.
Bauman, Robert. *Race and the War on Poverty: From Watts to East L.A.* Norman: University of Oklahoma Press, 2008.
Beeth, Howard, and Cary D. Wintz, eds. *Black Dixie: Afro-Texan History and Culture in Houston*. College Station: Texas A&M University Press, 1992.
Behnken, Brian D. *Fighting Their Own Battles: Mexican Americans, African Americans, and the Struggle for Civil Rights in Texas*. Chapel Hill: University of North Carolina Press, 2011.
———, ed. *The Struggle in Black and Brown: African American and Mexican American Relations during the Civil Rights Era*. Lincoln: University of Nebraska Press, 2011.
Bernson, Sara L. "Black History in South Dakota." Master's thesis, University of South Dakota, 1977.

Bernstein, Shana. *Bridges of Reform: Interracial Civil Rights Activism in Twentieth Century Los Angeles*. New York: Oxford University Press, 2011.
Bloom, Joshua, and Waldo E. Martin Jr. *Black against Empire: The History and Politics of the Black Panther Party*. Berkeley: University of California Press, 2013.
Bracey, Earnest N. *The Moulin Rouge and Black Rights in Las Vegas: A History of the First Racially Integrated Hotel-Casino*. Jefferson, N.C.: McFarland, 2009.
———. "The African Americans." In *The Peoples of Las Vegas*, edited by Terry L. Simich and Thomas C. Wright, 78–97. Reno: University of Nevada Press, 2005.
Brauer, David. *Nellie Stone Johnson: The Life of an Activist*. St. Paul, Minn.: Ruminator Books, 2001.
Bringhurst, Newell G. "Eldridge Cleaver's Passage through Mormonism." *Journal of Mormon History* 28 (Spring 2002): 80–110.
Broussard, Albert S. "The Honolulu NAACP and Race Relations in Hawaii." *Hawaiian Journal of History* 39 (2005): 115–33.
———. *Black San Francisco: The Struggle for Racial Equality in the West, 1900–1954*. Lawrence: University of Kansas Press, 1993.
———. *Expectations of Equality: A History of Black Westerners*. Wheeling, Ill.: Harlan Davidson, 2012.
Brown, Elaine. *A Taste of Power: A Black Woman's Story*. New York: Anchor Books, 1993.
Brown, Scot. *Fighting for US: Maulana Karenga, The US Organization, and Black Cultural Nationalism*. New York: New York University Press, 2003.
Bunch, Lonnie G., III. *Black Los Angelenos: The Afro-American in Los Angeles, 1850–1950*. Los Angeles: California Afro-American Museum, 1988.
Burke, Lucas N. N., and Judson L. Jeffries. *The Portland Black Panthers: Empowering Albina and Remaking a City*. Seattle: University of Washington Press, 2016.
Campbell, Cloves C., with Yuvonne C. Brooks. *I Refused to Leave the 'Hood*. Phoenix: Cloves C. Campbell Sr., 2002.
Campney, Brent M. S. "Hold the Line: The Defense of Jim Crow in Lawrence, Kansas, 1946–1961." *Kansas History* 33 (Spring 2010): 22–41.
Carper, James C. "The Popular Ideology of Segregated Schooling: Attitudes toward the Education of Blacks in Kansas, 1854–1900." *Kansas History, A Journal of the Central Plains* 1 (Winter 1978): 254–65.
Carroll, Brian. "Praising My People: Newspaper Sports Coverage and the Integration of Baseball in Wichita, Kansas." *Kansas History* 33 (Winter 2010–11): 240–55.
Cheney, Charise. "Blacks on *Brown*: Intra-Community Debates over School Desegregation in Topeka, Kansas, 1941–1955." *Western Historical Quarterly* 42 (Winter 2011): 481–500.
Cleaver, Kathleen, ed. *Liberation, Imagination, and the Black Panther Party*. New York: Routledge, 2001.
Cole, Thomas R. *No Color Is My Kind: The Life of Eldrewey Stearns and the Integration of Houston*. Austin: University of Texas Press, 1997.
Coleman, Ronald G. "Blacks in Utah History: An Unknown Legacy." In *The Peoples of Utah*, edited by Helen Z. Papanikolas, 115–40. Salt Lake City: Utah State Historical Society, 1976.

Coughtry, Jamie. *Lubertha Johnson: Civil Rights Efforts in Las Vegas, 1940–1960s.* Las Vegas: University of Nevada Oral History, 1988.

Coughtry, Jamie, and R. T. King. *Woodrow Wilson: Race, Community and Politics in Las Vegas, 1940s–1980s.* Reno: University of Nevada Oral History Program, 1990.

Coulter, Charles E. *"Take Up the Black Man's Burden": Kansas City's African American Communities, 56–85, 217–28.* Columbia: University of Missouri Press, 2006.

Crouchett, Lawrence P. *William Byron Rumford, the Life and Public Services of a California Legislator: A Biography.* El Cerrito, Calif.: Downey Place Publishing House, 1990.

Crowley, Joseph N. "Race and Residence." In *Sagebrush and Neon*, edited by Eleanore Bushnell, 55–73. Reno: University of Nevada Press, 1973.

Decker, Stefanie. "African American Women in the Civil Rights Era, 1954–1974." In *Black Women in Texas History*, edited by Bruce A. Glasrud and Merline Pitre, 159–176. College Station: Texas A&M University Press, 2008.

De Graaf, Lawrence B., Kevin Mulroy, and Quintard Taylor. *Seeking El Dorado: African Americans in California.* Seattle: University of Washington Press, 2001.

Delton, Jennifer A. *Making Minnesota Liberal: Civil Rights and the Transformation of the Democratic Party.* Minneapolis: University of Minnesota Press, 2002.

Derrick, W. Edwin, and J. Herschel Barnhill. "With 'All Deliberate Speed': Desegregation of the Public Schools in Oklahoma City and Tulsa, 1954–1972." *Red River Valley Historical Review* 6, no. 2 (1981): 78–90.

Dixon, Aaron. *My People are Rising: Memoir of a Black Panther Party Captain.* Chicago: Haymarket Books, 2012.

Dudziak, Mary L. "The Limits of Good Faith: Desegregation in Topeka, Kansas, 1950–1956," *Law and History Review* 5, no. 2 (Autumn 1987): 351–91.

Dulaney, W. Marvin. "The Rise, Fall, and Rebirth of the NAACP in Dallas." In *Lone Star Legacy: African American History in Texas*, edited by Delicia Daniels, 35–43. Houston: Aquarius Press, 2011.

———. "Whatever Happened to the Civil Rights Movement in Dallas, Texas?" In *Essays on the American Civil Rights Movement*, edited by W. Marvin Dulaney and Kathleen Underwood, 66–95. College Station: Texas A&M University Press, 1993.

Eick, Gretchen Cassel. *Dissent in Wichita: The Civil Rights Movement in the Midwest, 1954–1972.* Urbana: University of Illinois Press, 2001.

Flamming, Douglas. *African Americans in the West.* Santa Barbara, Calif.: ABC-CLIO, 2009.

———. *Bound for Freedom: Black Los Angeles in Jim Crow America.* Berkeley: University of California Press, 2005.

Geran, Trish. *Beyond the Glimmering Lights: The Pride and Perseverance of African Americans in Las Vegas.* Las Vegas: Stephens Press, 2006.

Glasrud, Bruce A. "Civil Rights Revolution." In *African Americans in the West: A Bibliography of Secondary Sources*, 54–56. Alpine, Tex.: Center for Big Bend Studies, 1998.

Glasrud, Bruce A., and Laurie Champion, eds. *The African American West: A Century of Short Stories.* Boulder: University Press of Colorado, 2000.

Glasrud, Bruce A., and Merline Pitre, eds. *Black Women in Texas History.* College Station: Texas A&M University Press, 2008.

Glasrud, Bruce A., and Cary D. Wintz, eds. *The Harlem Renaissance in the American West*. New York: Routledge 2012.

Goldberg, Robert A. "Racial Change on the Southern Periphery: The Case of San Antonio, Texas, 1960–1965." *Journal of Southern History* 49, no. 3 (1983): 349–74.

Goldstone, Dwonna. *Integrating the 40 Acres: The Fifty-Year Struggle for Racial Equality at the University of Texas*. Athens: University of Georgia Press, 2006.

Graves, Carl R. "The Right to Be Served: Oklahoma City's Lunch Counter Sit-Ins, 1958–1964." *Chronicles of Oklahoma* 59, no. 2 (1981): 152–55.

Green, William D. *Degrees of Freedom: The Origins of Civil Rights in Minnesota, 1865–1912*. Minneapolis: University of Minnesota Press, 2016.

Henderson, Cheryl Brown. "Lucinda Todd and the Invisible Petitioners of *Brown v. Board of Education of Topeka, Kansas*." In *African American Women Confront the West, 1600–2000*, edited by Quintard Taylor and Shirley Ann Wilson Moore, 312–27. Norman: University of Oklahoma Press, 2003.

Henderson, Joyce. *C. L. Dellums: International President of the Brotherhood of the Sleeping Car Porters and Civil Rights Leader*. Berkeley: The Regents of the University of California, 1973.

Hildebrand, Jennifer. "The New Negro Movement in Lincoln, Nebraska." *Nebraska History* 91 (2010): 166–89.

Hine, Darlene Clark. *Black Victory: The Rise and Fall of the White Primary in Texas*. 2nd ed. Columbia: University of Missouri Press, 2003.

Holland, Matt. *Ahead of Their Time: The Story of the Omaha DePorres Club*. Charleston, S.C.: CreateSpace Independent Publishing Platform, 2014.

Horne, Gerald. *Fire This Time: The Watts Uprising And The 1960s*. Cambridge, Mass.: Da Capo Press, 1997.

Jeffries, Hasan Kwame. "Searching for a New Freedom." In *A Companion to African American History*, edited by Alton Hornsby Jr., 499–511. Malden, Mass.: Blackwell Publishing, 2005.

Jeffries, Judson. *Huey P. Newton: The Radical Theorist*. Jackson: University Press of Mississippi, 2002.

———, ed. *Comrades: A Local History of the Black Panther Party*. Bloomington: Indiana University Press, 2007.

———, ed. *On the Ground: The Black Panther Party in Communities across America*. Jackson: University Press of Mississippi, 2010.

Jensen, F. Kenneth. "The Houston Sit-In Movement of 1960–1961." In Howard Beeth and Cary D. Wintz, eds., *Black Dixie: Afro-Texas History and Culture in Houston*, 211–22. College Station: Texas A&M University Press, 1992.

Johnson, Tekla Agbala Ali. *Free Radical: Ernest Chambers, Black Power, and the Politics of Race*. Lubbock: Texas Tech University Press, 2012.

Jones, Charles, ed. *The Black Panther Party (Reconsidered)*. Baltimore, Md.: Black Classic Press, 1998.

Joseph, Peniel, ed. *The Black Power Movement: Rethinking the Civil Rights–Black Power Era*. New York: Routledge, 2006.

———. *Waiting 'Til the Midnight Hour: A Narrative History of Black Power in America*. New York: Henry Holt, 2006.
Karenga, Maulana. *Kawaida and Questions of Life and Struggle*. Los Angeles: University of Sankore Press, 2008.
Kellar, William Henry. *Make Haste Slowly: Moderates, Conservatives, and School Desegregation in Houston*. College Station: Texas A&M University Press, 1999.
Kluger, Richard. *Simple Justice: The History of Brown v. Board of Education and Black America's Struggle for Equality*. New York: Vintage Books, 1977.
Kun, Josh, and Laura Pilido, eds. *Black and Brown in Los Angeles: Beyond Conflict and Coalition*. Berkeley: University of California Press, 2014.
Kurashige, Scott. *The Shifting Grounds of Race: Black and Japanese Americans in the Making of Multiethnic Los Angeles*. Princeton, N.J.: Princeton University Press, 2010.
Ladino, Robyn Duff. *Desegregating Texas Schools: Eisenhower, Shivers, and the Crisis at Mansfield High*. Austin: University of Texas Press, 1996.
Lang, William L. "The Nearly Forgotten Blacks on Last Chance Gulch, 1900–1912." *Pacific Northwest Quarterly* 70 (April 1979): 50–57.
Lavergne, Gary M. *Before Brown: Heman Marion Sweatt, Thurgood Marshall, and the Long Road to Justice*. Austin: University of Texas Press, 2010.
Lemke-Santangelo, Gretchen. *Abiding Courage: African American Migrant Women and the East Bay Community*. Chapel Hill: University of North Carolina Press, 1996.
Leonard, Kevin Allen. *The Battle for Los Angeles: Racial Ideology and World War II*. Albuquerque, N.Mex.: University of New Mexico Press, 2006.
Luper, Clara. *Behold the Walls*. Oklahoma City: Jim Wire, 1979.
Martin, Charles H. *Benching Jim Crow: The Rise and Fall of the Color Line in Southern College Sports, 1890–1980*. Urbana: University of Illinois Press, 2010.
———. "Oklahoma's Scottsboro Case: The Jess Hollins Rape Case, 1931–1936." *South Atlantic Quarterly* (Spring 1980): 174–88.
Mayes, Keith A. *Kwanzaa: Black Power and The Making of the African-American Holiday Tradition*. New York: Routledge, 2009.
McBroome, Delores Nason. *Parallel Communities: African Americans in California's East Bay 1850–1963*. New York: Garland Publishing, 1993.
McCusker, Kristine M. "The Forgotten Years of America's Civil Rights Movement: Wartime Protests at the University of Kansas, 1939–1945." *Kansas History* 17 (Spring 1994): 26–37.
McMillan, James B. *Fighting Back: A Life in the Struggle for Civil Rights*. Reno: University of Nevada Press, 1997.
Melcher, Mary S. "Blacks and Whites Together: Interracial Leadership in the Phoenix Civil Rights Movement." *Journal of Arizona History* 39, no. 2 (1991): 195–216.
———. *Pregnancy, Motherhood, and Choice in Twentieth Century Arizona*. Tucson: University of Arizona Press, 2012.
Melendez, A. Gabriel, M. Jane Young, Patricia Moore, and Patrick Pynes, eds. *The Multicultural Southwest: A Reader*. Tucson: University of Arizona Press, 2001.
Miller, Paul T. *The Postwar Struggle for Civil Rights: African Americans in San Francisco, 1945–1975*. New York: Routledge, 2010.

Moore, Shirley Ann Wilson. *To Place Our Deeds: The African American Community in Richmond, California, 1910–1963*. Berkeley: University of California Press, 2000.

Murch, Donna Jean. *Living for the City: Migration, Education, and the Rise of the Black Panther Party in Oakland, California*. Chapel Hill: University of North Carolina Press, 2010.

Newton, Huey P. *War Against the Panthers: A Study of Repression in America*. New York: Harlem River Press, 1996.

Orleck, Annelise. *Storming Caesars Palace: How Black Mothers Fought Their Own War on Poverty*. Boston: Beacon Press, 2005.

Osborn, William S. "Curtains for Jim Crow: Law, Race, and the Texas Railroads." *Southwestern Historical Quarterly* 105 (January 2002): 393–427.

Overstreet, Everett Louis. *Black on a Background of White: A Chronicle of Afro-American Involvement in America's Last Frontier, Alaska*. Anchorage: Alaska Black Caucus, 1994.

———. *Black Steps in the Desert Sands: A Chronicle of African-American Involvement In the Growth of Las Vegas, Nevada*. Las Vegas: Native Son Bookstore, 1999.

Pearson, Hugh. *The Shadow of the Panther: Huey Newton and the Price of Black Power in America*. Reading, Mass.: Addison-Wesley, 1994.

Pieroth, Doris. "With All Deliberate Caution: School Integration in Seattle, 1954–1968." *Pacific Northwest Quarterly* 73, no. 2 (1982): 50–61.

Pitre, Merline. *In Struggle Against Jim Crow: Lulu White and the NAACP, 1900–1957*. College Station: Texas A&M University Press, 1999.

Potter, James E. "Equality Before the Law: Thoughts on the Origins of Nebraska's State Motto." *Nebraska History* 91 (2010): 116–21.

Pulido, Laura. *Black, Brown, Yellow, and Left: Radical Activism in Los Angeles*. Berkeley: University of California, 2006.

Raymond, Emile. *Stars for Freedom: Hollywood, Black Celebrities and the Civil Rights Movement*. Seattle: University of Washington Press, 2015.

Richardson, Larry S. "Civil Rights in Seattle: A Rhetorical Analysis of a Social Movement." PhD diss., Washington State University, 1975.

Robison, Kenneth G. "Breaking Racial Barriers: 'Everyone's Welcome' at the Ozark Club, Great Falls, Montana's African American Nightclub." *Montana the Magazine of Western History*, 62, no. 2 (Summer 2012): 44–58.

Ruffin, Herbert G. *Uninvited Neighbors: African Americans in Silicon Valley, 1769–1990*. Norman: University of Oklahoma Press, 2014.

Rusco, Elmer R. "The Civil Rights Movement in Nevada." *Nevada Public Affairs Review* 2 (1987): 75–81.

Sartain, Lee. "Student Activism, the NAACP, and the Albuquerque City Anti-Discrimination Ordinance, 1947–1952." *New Mexico Historical Review* 93 (2018): 127–47.

Saxe, Allan. "Protest and Reform: The Desegregation of Oklahoma City." PhD diss., University of Oklahoma, 1969.

Seale, Bobby. *Seize the Time: The Story of the Black Panther Party and Huey P. Newton*. New York: Random House, 1970.

Self, Robert O. *American Babylon: Race and the Struggle for Postwar Oakland*. Princeton, N.J.: Princeton University Press, 2003.

Shabazz, Amilcar. *Advancing Democracy: African Americans and the Struggle for Access and Equity in Higher Education in Texas*. Chapel Hill: University of North Carolina Press, 2004.
Sides, Josh. L.A. *City Limits: African American Los Angeles from the Great Depression to the Present*. Berkeley: University of California Press, 2003.
Singler, Joan, Jean Durning, Bettylou Valentine, and Maid Adams. *Seattle in Black and White: The Congress of Racial Equality and the Fight for Equal Opportunity*. Seattle: University of Washington Press, 2011.
Smith, Jeffrey Harrison. "The Omaha De Porres Club." Master's thesis, Creighton University, 1967.
Smurr, J. W. "Jim Crow Out West." In *Historical Essays on Montana and The Northwest*, edited by J. W. Smurr and K. Ross Toole, 149–203. Helena, Mont.: Western Press, 1957.
Stephens, Ronald J. "The Influence of Marcus Mosiah and Amy Jacques Garvey: On the Rise of Garveyism in Colorado." In *Enduring Legacies: Ethnic Histories and Cultures of Colorado*, edited by Arturo Aldama, with Elisa Facio, Daryl Maeda, and Reiland Rabaka, 139–58. Boulder: University Press of Colorado, 2011.
Sugrue, Thomas J. *Sweet Land of Liberty: The Forgotten Struggle for Civil Rights in the North*. New York: Random House, 2009.
Taylor, Quintard. "The Civil Rights Movement in the Urban West: Black Protest in Seattle, 1960–1970." *Journal of Negro History* 80, no. 1 (1995): 1–14.
———. *In Search of the Racial Frontier: African Americans in the American West 1528–1990*. New York: W. W. Norton, 1998.
Taylor, Quintard, and Shirley Ann Wilson Moore, eds. *African American Women Confront the West: 1600–2000*. Norman: University of Oklahoma Press, 2003.
Theoharis, Jeanne, and Komozi Woodard, eds. *Freedom North: Black Freedom Struggles Outside the South, 1940–1980*. New York: Palgrave Macmillan, 2003.
———. *Groundwork: Local Black Freedom Movements in America*. New York: New York University Press, 2005.
Tolbert, Emory J. *The UNIA and Black Los Angeles: Ideology and Community in the American Garvey Movement*. Los Angeles: Center for Afro-American Studies, UCLA, 1980.
Trowbridge, David J. Peavler. "A Double Mixture: Equality and Economy in the Integration of Nebraska Schools, 1858–1883." *Nebraska History* 91 (2010): 136–51.
Van Delinder, Jean. "Early Civil Rights Activism in Topeka, Kansas, Prior to the 1954 *Brown* Case," in *African Americans on the Great Plains: An Anthology*, edited by Bruce A. Glasrud and Charles A. Braithwaite, 272–301. Lincoln: University of Nebraska Press, 2009.
———. *Struggles Before Brown: Early Civil Rights Protests and their Significance Today*. Boulder: Paradigm, 2008.
Vincent, Theodore G. *Black Power and the Garvey Movement*. San Francisco: Ramparts Press, 1971.
Walters, Ronald. "The Great Plains Sit-In Movement, 1958–1960," in *African Americans on the Great Plains: An Anthology*, edited by Bruce A. Glasrud and Charles A. Braithwaite, 302–19. Lincoln: University of Nebraska Press, 2009.

---. "Standing Up in America's Heartland: Sitting-in Before Greensboro." *American Visions* 8, no. 1 (1993): 20–23.

Watson, Jonathan. "The NAACP in California, 1914–1950." In *Long Is the Way and Hard: One Hundred Years of the NAACP*, edited by Kevern Verney and Lee Sartain, 185–99. Fayetteville: University of Arkansas Press, 2009.

Whitaker, Matthew C. "'Creative Conflict': Lincoln and Eleanor Ragsdale, Collaboration, and Community Activism in Phoenix, 1953–1965." *Western Historical Quarterly* 34, no. 2 (2003): 165–90.

---. *Race Work: The Rise of Civil Rights in the Urban West*. Lincoln: University of Nebraska Press, 2005.

Wilson, Paul E. *A Time to Lose: Representing Kansas in Brown v. Board of Education*, 8–26. Lawrence: University Press of Kansas, 1995.

Wintz, Cary D. *African American Political Thought: 1890–1930*. New York: M. E. Sharp, 1996.

Zelden, Charles L. *The Battle for the Black Ballot: Smith v. Allwright and the Defeat of the Texas All-White Primary*. Lawrence: University Press of Kansas, 2004.

---. "'In No Event Shall a Negro Be Eligible': The NAACP Takes on the Texas All-White Primary, 1923–1944." In *Long Is the Way and Hard: One Hundred Years of the NAACP*, edited by Kevern Verney and Lee Sartain, 135–53. Fayetteville: University of Arkansas Press, 2009.

Index

Abarr, John, 104
Aberdeen, S.Dak., 173
Adair, Christia, 241
Adams, John, 35
Advisory Committee to the Civil Rights Commission: in Montana, 90, 97; in Nevada, 72, 74, 76–78; in North Dakota, 174; in South Dakota, 167, 177
affirmative action, 58, 62, 180, 256, 265–66
Afro-American Association, 59–60
Afro-American Studies Center, 62
air force, 91–97, 102, 169, 177
airlines, discrimination in, 114–16
Alabama State College, 58
Alamogordo, N.Mex., 17
Alamosa, Colo., 116
Albina district (Portland), 28–29, 33
Albrier, Frances, 44
Albuquerque, N.Mex., 16–17, 153–63
Albuquerque Civil Rights Ordinance (1952), 16
Aleman, Miguel, 161
Alianza Federal de Mercedes (Federal Land Grant Alliance), 130–31, 161
Alianza por Pueblos Libres (Alliance for Free Communities), 161–62
Allen, Cassius, 13

Allen, Earl E., 249
Allen, George, 242
Allen, Preston, 128
Alston v. School Board of City of Norfolk (1940), 14
Alvarado, Emilia, 114
American Civil Liberties Union, 55, 73
American Federation of Labor (AFL), 45–46, 49–50, 52
American Federation of Labor–Congress of Industrial Organizations (AFL-CIO), 76, 125
American Indian Movement (AIM), 130, 161, 179
American Indians: and American Indian Movement, 59, 130, 161–62, 179; and definitions of race, 12, 216–17; and discrimination, 11–12, 72, 90, 127–30, 167–70, 179; and education, 266; population of, 91, 102, 104, 125, 174, 214; relocation of, 214; and voting rights, 128–29
American Student Union, 113
Amnesty International, 207
Anaheim, Calif., 53, 56
Anderson, James, 82
Anderson, Marian, 185

Anti-Defamation League, 76, 112
Arizona Council for Civic Unity, 140
Arizona Federation of Colored Women's Clubs, 138
Arizona State University, 145
Armour and Company, 191, 199
Associated Negro Press, 150
Atlantic City, N.J., 189
Austin, Tex., 241, 243–46, 256

Bailey, Robert, 76, 78, 80–81
Bakersfield, Calif., 53
Bakke, Allan, 265
Bakke v. Regents of the University of California, 265
banks, discrimination in, 142–43
Banks, Roger W., 156
BANTU (Black Association for Nationalism through Unity), 207
Baptist Ministers Alliance, 30
barbershops, 33, 93, 113, 171, 176, 178, 203–4
Barlow, Norman, 102–4
Barnett, Claude, 150n18
Barrett, Francis (Jr.), 102
Barrett, Frank A. (Sr.), 102
Bass, Charlotta Spears, 43
Bayless, Samuel, 137
Beasley, Delilah, 43–44
Beaumont, Tex., 245
Becknell, Charles E., Sr., 159, 163
Beckwourth, James, 155
Bennett, Marion, 78
Benson, Ezra Taft, 124
Benson, Reed, 124
Berkeley, Calif., 53
Bernal, Paul, 161
Bernson, Sara, 175
Bernstein, Charles, 140, 150n17
Berry, Mary Francis, 113
Bethune, Mary McLeod, 49
Big Strike of 1934, 49–51
Billings, Mont., 91

Birth of a Nation, The (1915), 26, 41–44
Bismarck, N.Dak., 173
Black, Vera, 133
Black, Willie, 103
Black AIDS Institute, 264
Black Committee for Student Power, 186
Black Panther Party (BPP): in California, 5, 18, 35, 60–62, 185, 259; in Chicago, 186; in Colorado, 116–17; in Des Moines, Iowa, 181–82, 185–88; in Seattle, 18, 35–36, 61, 116
Black Power movement, 5, 18–19, 189, 195–96, 206, 256; in California, 54, 59–60; in Kansas, 206, 208; in Minneapolis, 191; in Montana, 96; in the Pacific Northwest, 25, 34–36
Black Revolutionary Party, 187
Black Student Alliance, 103, 117
black student organizations. *See* student organizations
Black Student Union, 35–36, 206
black studies programs, 36, 59, 61, 100, 114, 186, 191, 206, 265
Blair, Omar D., 111–12
Blakey, Theodore "Ted," 175–79
Boeing, 26, 207
bombings, 110, 181, 186–87, 207, 249
Booker T. Washington Community Center, 27, 47
Booker T. Washington Memorial Hospital, 138
Booker T. Washington Service Center, 176
Booker v. Special School District No. 1, 194
Boston University, 258
Boulder, Colo., 113–14
Boulder Sympathy March, 117
Box Elder, S.Dak., 169
Boyer, Henry, 155
Bradley, Tom, 55, 257–59
Brauer, David, 192
breakfast programs, 36, 60, 117, 185–87
Breckenridge, Eugene H., 27

Bridges, Harry, 49–51
Brigham Young University, 103, 125, 127
Brisker, E. J., 35
Brooks, George, 142–48, 151n24
Brooks, S. V., 160
Brotherhood of Sleeping Car Porters (BSCP), 27, 43, 45–46, 49, 51, 156, 199
Broussard, Albert S., 4
Brown, Edmund G. "Pat," 57
Brown, Elaine, 62
Brown, George L., 114
Brown, H. Rap, 35
Brown, Lee P., 258
Brown, Oliver, 201–2, 204
Brown, William (Omaha), 199
Brown, Willie L., Jr. (San Francisco), 55, 114, 258–59
Brown-Gilbert, Mildred, 200–201
Brown v. Board of Education of Topeka (1954), 3, 7, 54, 103, 153, 170, 202–5, 223, 245–46
Bryant, Clora, 40
Buffalo Soldiers, 155
Bunch, Lonnie G., 39
Bureau of Indian Affairs, 127
Burton, Phillip, 259
buses: and school integration, 33–34, 108–12, 193–94, 208, 215, 245; segregation on, 225–26
Bush, George H. W., 263, 268
Bush, George W., 268
Butte, Mont., 91

Caldwell, Philip, 96
California Alien Land Law of 1913, 41
California College of Beauty, 176
California Colored Convention, 40–41
California Committee for Fair Employment Practices (CCFEP), 57
California Constitution, 59
California Fair Housing Act (a.k.a. Rumford Act), 57

California Federation of Colored Women's Clubs, 49
California Highway Patrol, 60
California Master Plan, 57
California Relief Administration, 47
Callahan, Barbara, 144, 148–49
Call, The, newspaper (Kansas City), 175, 199
Campbell, John A., 101
Cannady, Beatrice Morrow, 26
Cannady, Edward, 26
Cargo, David, 154–55
Carlsbad, N.Mex., 154, 157–58
Carmichael, Stokely, 18, 35, 206
Carter, Alprentice "Bunchy," 54, 62
Carver High School, Phoenix, Ariz., 138–41, 145, 150n17
casinos, discrimination in, 72, 75–80
Casper, Wyo., 102, 104
Cassey, Peter Williams, 40
Catholic Interracial Council, 182
Cayton, Horace, 26
C. de Baca, Fernando, 162
Center for the Study of Ethnicity and Race in America (CSERA), 114
Central Area Civil Rights Committee (CACRC), 31, 34
Central District (Seattle), 30–35
Chambers, Ernie, 204, 207
Chambers, R. L., 156
Chandler, H. C., 238
Chaney, James, 183
Charter Government Committee (CGC), 146–47, 151n36
Chase, James, 37
Chavez, Dennis, 154, 156
Cheatom, Joeanna, 187
Cheyenne, Wyo., 102
Chicago, Ill., 186, 259
Chicano movement, 107–8, 130–31, 161
Chisholm, Shirley, 97
Chivers, Curtis, 193–94

282 INDEX

Christensen, A. Sherman, 134
churches: African American, 47, 93–94, 101, 138, 143, 160, 176, 259; in civil rights movement, 32, 143, 152, 172, 185, 204, 249; integrated, 95, 97, 126–27
Church of Jesus Christ of Latter-day Saints (LDS). *See* Mormon church
Citizens Committee for Fair Employment, 27
Citizens Coordinating Committee for Civil Liberties (4CL), 207
City Club of Portland, 35
Civic Unity Committee, 26
Civil Rights Act of 1964, 59, 73, 80, 91–92, 103, 170, 189–90, 214–16, 229, 240, 245–49, 256
Civil Rights Acts of 1875, 9
Civil Rights Cases of 1883, 9
Civil Rights Commission, 126, 142
Civil Rights Congress (CRC) (1946–52), 55
civil rights movement, definition of, 4
Civil War, 90, 93, 165, 214, 217
Civil Works Administration (CWA), 13
Cleaver, Eldridge, 264
Cleveland, Ohio, 259
Clinton, Bill, 263, 268
Clovis, N.Mex., 157–58
Coakley, Maurice, 176, 178
COINTEL program, 62, 186
colleges: discrimination in, 100, 113–14, 125, 183, 201, 207, 215, 228–29, 243, 257, 265–66; segregation in, 14, 215, 220–21, 227–29, 241–43, 256
Collier, John, 127
Collins, Jason, 264
Colorado Anti-Discrimination Act (1957), 114–15
Colorado Anti-Discrimination Commission, 112
Colorado Civil Rights Commission, 113, 115–16
Colorado Constitution (1876), 113

Colorado Springs, Colo., 108
Colorado State University, 113, 117
Colored Businessman's Association, 138
Colored Teacher State Association, 241
Colored Women's Clubs, 101
Commission for the Improvement of Educational Opportunities for Negroes in Texas, 242
Committee for Integrated Education, 193
Communist Party USA, 55
Community Welfare Council, 138
Compton, Calif., 54
Concerned Black Citizens (CBC), 36
Congress for Equality (CORE), 18
Congress of Industrial Organizations (CIO), 50, 199
Congress of Racial Equality (CORE), 9, 206, 246; in Arizona, 147; in California, 58; in Colorado, 112; in Iowa, 182; in Kansas, 200–201; in Minnesota, 190; in Nebraska, 200; in Nevada, 73; in New Mexico, 159; in Washington, 25, 29–31, 33–34
Conrad, Barbara, 244
Continental Airlines, 114–15
Coolidge, Calvin, 46
Cooper, Ronald, 174
Coors Company, 115
Copeland, Madge, 146, 148
Corpus Christi, Tex., 238, 243–44
Cosmopolitan Club, 113
Cotton, Anthony J., 97
Council of Churches, 76, 78, 190
Count Basie, 199, 201
court decisions: and affirmative action, 62, 265–66; and American Indians, 128–29; and colleges, 14, 227–29, 243–44, 257; and criminal cases, 227; and employment, 52, 114–15; and Equal Rights Commission, 79–80; and housing, 31, 46, 82, 112, 126, 261; and pay, 14, 131, 227; and public accommodations, 40, 54, 80,

125, 202; and school integration, 3, 7, 40, 109–11, 140, 194, 202, 205, 208, 245; and transportation, 9, 246; and voting, 14, 16, 83, 128–29, 217–18, 223, 226–27, 238–40
Craft, Juanita, 241
Credille, C., 137
Creighton University, 16, 200–201, 204
Crockett, J. Allan, 128–29
Crouchett, Lawrence P., 39
Crowe, Tom, 114
Crowley, Joseph, 82
Crusade for Justice, 162

Dallas, Tex., 237–42, 245–49, 258
Daniels, H. B., 140, 142
Davenport, Iowa, 182–83
Davis, Alton, 161
Davis, Harry, 191, 194
Davis, John W., 223
Davis, Sammy, Jr., 72
De Graaf, Lawrence, 39, 57
De La Ysla v. Public Theatres Corporation (1933), 125
Dellums, C. L., 45, 48, 50, 57, 62
Dellums, Ron, 55, 62
Democratic National Convention, 97, 188–89, 192, 258
Democratic Party: and allegiances, 48, 84, 124, 148, 240–41, 259; and civil rights platform, 188–89, 192; and legislation, 57, 78, 84, 101; and malapportionment, 84; in nineteenth century, 93, 214, 237; and voting rights, 9, 14, 16, 222, 238–40
Denman, Kenny, 35
Denver, Colo., 108–18, 162, 258–59
Denver Public Schools, 109–11
Department of Health, Education, and Welfare, 245–46
Department of Housing and Urban Development (HUD), 35
De Patton, Clive, 185

DePorres Club, 16, 201, 206
desegregation. *See* school integration
Des Moines, Iowa, 182–87
Detroit, Mich., 191, 260
Deukmejian, George, 258
Devin, William F., 26
Dial, William, 78
Dickerson, Harvey, 79
Dining Car Cooks and Waiters Union, 50
Dinkins, David, 260
Division of Negro Affairs, California, 49
Dixon, Aaron, 35–36
Dixon, St. John, 58
Dockum Rexall Drug Store, 17, 203
Doniphan, Alexander, 155
Dorsey, James W., 99
Doss, Ulysses S., 100–101
Double-Victory movement (1941–45), 51
Douglass, Aaron, 200
Dowdell, Rick, 206
Doyle, William, 109
Drake, St. Clair, 265
Drake University, 183
Drive for Equal Employment in Downtown Seattle (DEEDS), 31
Du Bois, W. E. B., 8, 41, 48, 190
Dudziak, Mary, 205
Duluth, Minn., 12–13, 188–193
Dunbar, Duke, 112
Dunbar Art and Study Club, 94
Dungan, Flora, 77
Durham, W. J., 239–40
Durning, Jean, 30
Dwyer, Robert J., 76
Dyer Anti-Lynching Bill, 43

East St. Louis race riot (1917), 43
East Texas, 243–47
Eaton, Lloyd, 103–4
Eccles, Marriner, 123
Edmonds, Jefferson L., 46
Eggers, Robert J., 175

Eisenhower, Dwight D., 3, 124, 244
El Capitan Casino, 72, 79
Eli, Herb, 144
Elko, Nev., 84
Elk Point, S.Dak., 177
El Movimiento, 19
El Paso, Tex., 238, 244
employment discrimination. *See* job discrimination
employment training. *See* job training
Equal Employment Opportunity Commission (EEOC), 256
Equal Rights Amendment, 131
Equal Rights Commission (ERC), 75–81
Equal Rights League, 42
Evans, R. D., 237–38
Executive Order 8802, 15, 51

fair employment legislation, 15, 24, 27, 57–58, 154, 156, 189. *See also* job discrimination
Fair Employment Practices Commission (FEPC), 15, 51–52
Fair Housing Act (1968), 62, 82, 112–13, 261
Fair Housing Act (California), 39, 59
Fair Housing Act (Colorado), 113
fair housing legislation, 29–32, 39, 46, 57, 59, 82–83, 112–13, 183, 192, 261. *See also* housing, integrated; housing segregation, discrimination, and restrictive covenants
Fair Housing Listing Service (FHLS), 31
Fanon, Frantz, 60, 206
Fargo, N.Dak., 173
Farmer, James, 54, 246
Farmer Labor Party, 188, 194
Farquhar, George, 160
Federal Bureau of Investigation (FBI), 62, 117, 179, 186, 264
Federal Housing Administration (FHA), 57, 261
Feinstein, Dianne, 259

Fellowship of Reconciliation (FOR), 9
Fifteenth Amendment, 9, 14, 25, 128, 217–18, 223
Fike, Edward, 82
Finn, Herb, 139–40
Finn, Ruth, 139, 148
First AME Church (African Methodist Episcopal), 32, 35
First Great Migration (African American, 1915–40), 15, 40–41
Fisher v. Hurst, 228
Flamming, Douglas, 48
Flory, Ishmael, 50
Foley, Roger, 75
Fong, Bew Hong (Bill), 72
Fort Collins, Colo., 117
Fort Worth, Tex., 238, 241, 247
Fourteenth Amendment, 14, 25, 42, 126, 128, 197–98, 228, 238
Franklin, June, 188
Freedom Inc., 204
Freedom Rides, 9, 25, 29, 58
Freedom Schools, 34
Freedom Summer of 1964, 183, 190
freeway construction, 185, 191, 249
Fresno, Calif., 53
Frey, William, 62
Frye, Marquette, 60
Frye, Rena, 60

Gaddis Investment Company et al v. Charles H. Morrison, 126
Gaines, Lloyd, 14
Gandhi, Mohandas, 54
Garrott, Homer L., 46
Garvey, Marcus, 43–45
General Federation of Women's Clubs, 101
gerrymandering, racial, 56, 110, 205, 227, 231n19, 245
Ghee, Frank, 96
Ghee, Mary, 96
GI Bill (Veterans Administration's

Servicemen's Readjustment Act), 260
Gillette, Wyo., 104
Glendale, Ariz., 137
Gluba, Bill, 183
Goldwater, Barry, 146
Gonzales, Henry, 250
Gonzales, Rudolfo "Corky," 108, 162
Goode, Calvin, 147, 149
Goodman, Andrew, 183
Gossett, Larry, 35
Graham, Milton, 146–47
Graham v. Board of Education of Topeka (1941), 202
Grand Forks, N.Dak., 173–74
Graves, Curtis M., 240
Great Depression, 13, 45–49, 138, 173, 199, 201, 226, 238, 248
Greater Minneapolis Interfaith Housing Program, 193
Greater Phoenix Council for Civic Unity (GPCCU), 139–41, 144, 146, 148, 150n10; Act Committee of, 146, 151n36
Great Falls Interracial Council, 95
Great Falls Public Library, 89, 94, 97
Great Falls, Mont., 89–97, 104
Greeley, Colo., 116
Green, Marlon D., 114–15
Green, William, 46
Greensboro, N.C., 58, 197, 203
Greenspun, Hank, 75
Griffin, John Howard, 183
Griffith, D. W., 26
Grigsby, Eugene, 138, 140, 144–45
Grigsby, Thomasena, 140–41, 150n18
Griner, Brittney, 264
Groff, Regis, 118
Gross, Benjamin Franklin "Ben," 55–56
Grovey, Richard, 238
Grovey v. Townsend, 14
Grutter v. Bollinger, 265
Guinn v. United States, 227
Gutierrez, Jose Angel, 162

Hackett, Winston C., 138
Haga, Charles, 174
hairstyles, 116, 145
Hamer, Fannie Lou, 185, 189
Hamilton, Art, 146
Hampton, Carl, 248
Hampton, Fred, 186
Hancock, Michael, 118
Hankins, Wilbur, 143
Hardeman, Maurice, 55–56, 58
Hardin, William Jefferson, 101
Harlem Renaissance, 19, 199
Harmin, A. C., 222, 231n19
Harris, Robert, 96
Harrison, Leonard, 206
Hasgett, Sidney, 239
Haskell, N., 222
Hastings, Neb., 200
Hawkins, Augustus F. "Gus," 48, 55, 57
Hawkins Act, 57
Hawthorne, Nev., 72, 79
Hayden, Carl, 91
health care, 36, 263–64, 266–67
Heiger, Walter, 203
Helena, Mont., 90–91, 97–99
Hernandez-Ramos, Flo, 108
Hill, Archibald, 231n19
Hill, E. Shelton "Shelly," 27
Hine, Darlene Clark, 239
HIV-AIDS epidemic, 264–65
Hobbs, N.Mex., 154, 157–61
Hobbs Inter-Racial Council, 160–61
Hoggard, J. David, 78
Holmes, Fred, 139
Holmes, Zan W., Jr., 240
Hoover, Herbert, 127
Hoover, J. Edgar, 264
HOPE Development Inc., 249
Horgan, William, 72, 74, 76
Horne, Gerald, 39
Hotel and Restaurant Employees Union, 192

hotels, discrimination in: in Arizona, 138; in Colorado, 115; in the Dakotas, 171; in Iowa, 183; in Minnesota, 192; in Montana, 98, 100; in Nevada, 72, 76, 79; in Wyoming, 102
housing, integrated, 56, 109, 189. *See also* fair housing legislation
housing segregation, discrimination, and restrictive covenants, 11–12, 260–61; in Arizona, 137–38, 141–42; in California, 41, 44, 46, 52, 55–56; in Colorado, 112; in Iowa, 183–84; in Kansas, 205; in Minnesota, 190, 192–93; in Montana, 93, 97, 101; in Nebraska, 199; in Nevada, 82; in New Mexico, 157, 159; in Oklahoma, 227; in Oregon, 28–29; in Texas, 237, 240, 249; in Utah, 126; in Washington, 30–31. *See also* fair housing legislation
Houston, Charles Hamilton, 13
Houston, Tex., 16, 237–49, 258
Houston College for Negroes, 243
Houston Council of Organizations, 246
Howard, Norman C., 97–98
Howard, Raymond C., 98–100
Huggins, John, 62
Hughes, Harold, 189
Hughes, Langston, 200
Hulse, James, 78
Human Relations Commission, 144–45
Human Rights Commission, 32, 174
Humphrey, Hubert, 188–89, 192
Huron, S.Dak., 173

Independent Voters Leagues, 237
Indian Claims Commission, 130
Indian Placement Service, 129–30
Indian Welfare Act of 1978, 130
Inglewood, Calif., 261
International Brotherhood of Boilermakers, 52
International Longshoreman Association (ILA), 49–50

International Longshoremen's and Warehousemen's Union (ILWU), 49–50
interracial marriage laws. *See* miscegenation laws
Interstate Commerce Commission, 246
Iowa Fair Housing bill, 183

Jackson, George, 117
Jackson, Phyllis, 62
Jackson, Mance, 30, 32
Jacobs, Alma Smith, 89–95
James, Joseph, 52
James Crow, 39, 41, 43–44, 51
Jeffries, Hasan Kwame, 4
Jet Magazine, 96
Jim Crow, definition of, 39
Job Corps, 249
job discrimination, 12–13, 52, 58, 93, 224, 256; and firing, 23–24, 115–16; and hiring, 16, 25–31, 100–102, 114–16, 125–26, 143–44, 179, 191, 201, 248–49; and housing segregation, 44–45; and legislation, 15, 75, 80–81; and pay, 16, 26, 242. *See also* fair employment legislation
job training, 30, 49, 169, 176, 248–49
Johnson, Bertha, 78
Johnson, Jangaba Augustine, 33
Johnson, Josie, 192
Johnson, Lee Otis, 247
Johnson, Lyndon B., 92, 189, 240, 246, 249
Johnson, Matthew, 247
Johnson, Nellie Stone, 13, 192
Jordan, Barbara, 240, 258

Kaiser Aluminum Company, 23–24
Kansas Act Against Discrimination, 204
Kansas City, Mo./Kans., 175, 178, 190, 199, 203–4, 206, 208
Kansas City Monarchs, 200

Kansas Commission on Civil Rights
   (KCCR), 204
Kapp v. Salt Lake City, 131
Karenga, Maulana, 60–61
Kazen, Abraham, 250
Kearney, Neb., 200
Kellar, Charles, 76
Kelley, Robin D. G., 5
Kenmitz, Audrey, 160
Kent, Frank, 193
Kerner Report, 116
Keyes, Wilfred, 109–10
Keyes v. School District No. 1, Denver, Colorado, 109–11
Kimball, Spencer, 127, 129
King, David, 131
King, Martin Luther, Jr., 54, 59, 110, 112, 145, 162, 183–84, 191, 195, 264; holiday of, 174
King, Rodney, 262
Kirk, Ron, 258
Knight Fundamental Academy, 111
Knox, Charles, 185–87
Korrick, Ed, 146
Ku Klux Klan, 104–5, 137, 159, 175, 183, 190–91, 199–200, 215, 237, 246–47

LaMar, Leo, 94
Lamm, Dick, 118
Langston University, 216, 220–21, 232n32
Laramie, Wyo., 103
La Raza de Colorado: El Movimiento, 108
La Raza Unida, 162
Laredo, Tex., 250
Las Cruces, N.Mex., 158, 160
Las Vegas, Nev., 71–84
Latinos, 19, 54–56; in the Dakotas, 174; and housing, 41, 138, 147; in New Mexico, 161–62; and schools, 108–9, 157, 245, 266; and voting rights, 250
Lawrence, Kans., 197, 200–201, 205–6
law schools, 14, 99, 113, 226–29, 242–43, 257, 266

Lawson, Bill, 249
Lawson, Curtis, 231n19
Laxalt, Paul, 81–83
Leadership and Education for the Advancement of Phoenix (LEAP), 147
League of Women Voters, 76
Leck, Charles, 190
Lee, George Patrick, 130
Legal Defense and Education Fund (LDF), 13–14
Lemke-Santangelo, Gretchen, 47
Lewis, Chester, 203–5, 207–8
LGBT community, 259, 264
life span, 263
Lincoln, Neb., 198, 200
Ling, David, 140
Lipscomb, Albert, 249
Lipsitz, George, 40
Liston, Sonny, 79
Little, Earl, 199
Little, Louise, 199
Little, Matthew, 192
Little Rock, Ark., 244
Little Texas (N.Mex.), 155, 157–59
Littleton, Ralph D., 160
Lockridge, Joseph E., 240
London, Jack, 160
Long, George, 16
Long Beach, Calif., 53
Los Angeles, Calif., 5, 15, 38–62
Love, John, 112
Lubbock, Tex., 248–49
Luper, Clara, 17
lynching, 12–13, 26, 139, 188–90, 237

Mahoney, William, 139–41, 148, 152n44, 178
malapportionment, 83–85
Malcolm X, 35, 61, 199, 207
Malmstrom Air Force Base, 91, 94–97, 104
Mankato State College, 188

Mansfield, Glen, 24, 27
Mansfield, Mike, 91–92
Mansfield, Tex., 244
March on Washington, 9, 32, 51, 190, 192
Marcus, David, 55
Markoe, John, 200–201, 204, 206
Marsh, Terry B., 96
Marsh, Vivian Osborne, 49
Marshall, Pluria, 249
Marshall, Tex., 246
Marshall, Thurgood, 13–14, 16, 46, 55, 239
Marshfield, Ore., 26
Matchett, Arnett, 178
Matheson, Scott, 124
Mathews, H. Clyde, Jr., 76, 78, 81–82, 84
Matsch, Richard, 112
Maxey, Carl, 33, 36
Mays, Booker T., Sr., 115
McCarran, Pat, 130
McKinney, Samuel, 32
McLaurin, George, 14, 228–29, 257
McLaurin v. Oklahoma State Regents (1950), 14, 229
McMartin, H. L., 138
McMillan, Ernest, 247
McMillan, Eva, 247
McMillan, James B., 76
McNichols, Steve, 112
McWilliams, Carey, 189
Mead, Washington, 23
Mendez, Sylvia, 55
Mendez v. Westminster, 54–55
Meridian, Miss., 183, 190
Merrell, Porter L., 128
Merritt College (Oakland), 61
Metcalf, Lee, 91–92
Metro-Denver Urban Coalition, 114
Mexican American civil rights movement, 19
Meyer, Estelle Reel, 101
Midland, Tex., 248
migration of African Americans, 9, 11, 15, 25–26, 108, 184–85, 238, 257. *See also* First Great Migration; Second Great Migration
Milburn, Sidney, 177
Miller, E. R. "Boots," 73
Miller, Loren, 46, 55, 140
Miller, Patti, 183
Milliken v. Bradley, 208
Milpitas, Calif., 56
Minard, Larry, 207
Mine, Mill, and Smelter Workers Union, 93
mining, segregation in, 224, 235n80
Minneapolis, Minn., 12–13, 191–94
Minot, N.Dak., 173
miscegenation laws, 11–12, 74–75, 90, 102–3, 126, 137, 171, 219, 237
Mississippi Freedom Democratic Party, 189
Mississippi Voter project, 183
Missoula, Mont., 91, 99–100
Missouri ex rel. Gaines v. Canada (1938), 14
Mitchell, Harvey, 176
Mitchell, Louise, 176
Mitchell, S.Dak., 173, 177–78
Model Cities program, 35, 185
Model Schools Program (MSP), 34
Montana Club, 98–99
Montana Constitution (1972), 92, 101
Montana Federation of Colored Women's Clubs (NFCWC), 94
Montana State Prison, 91
Montana State University, 90
Montana Women's Political Caucus, 97
Montgomery, Ala., 197
Moore, Rowena, 200, 204
Mormon church, 103–4, 122–134
Morse, Joe, 190
Moscone, George, 259
Mosk, Stanley, 75
Moss, Harry "Spike," 191
Mottet, Martin, 183
Moulin Rouge, 72

Murray, Donald, 14
Murray, George, 35
Myer, Dillon, 127
Myers, Samuel, 190
Myrdal, Gunnar, 15

NAACP Youth Council, 17, 201
Naftalin, Arthur, 193
Nance v. Mayflower Tavern, Inc. (1944), 125
Napolitano, Janet, 266
National Association for the Advancement of Colored People (NAACP), 18–19, 223, 227; in Arizona, 136, 139–44, 148, 150n10; in California, 40–46, 52–58; in Colorado, 116, 118; in the Dakotas, 173–79; in Iowa, 182; in Kansas, 17, 199, 201–4, 207–8; in Minnesota, 189–93; in Montana, 94–97; in Nebraska, 199, 207; in Nevada, 72–79; in New Mexico, 16–17, 155–60, 163; in Oklahoma, 17, 227; in the Pacific Northwest, 25–36; in Texas, 14, 16, 236–48; in Wyoming, 104–5
National Basketball Association, 264
National Conference of Christians and Jews, 73, 150n10
National Council of Negro Women (NCNW), 47, 97
National Housing Act (1949), 57
National Industrial Recovery Act of 1933, 49
National Negro Labor Council, 27
National Urban League, 3, 25–33, 47, 58, 112, 144–45, 193
National Youth Administration, 48–49
Negro Consolidated Realty Board of Los Angeles, 59
Negro Equity League, 42
Negro History Week, 56
Negro League baseball, 95
Negro Teachers Alliance of Dallas, 242

Negro Welfare League, 42
Neighborhood School Committee, 194
Nelson, Bruce, 49
Nelson, Parker, 128
New China Club, 72, 76
New Deal, 13, 19, 48–49
New Mexico State University, 158
New Orleans, La., 15, 199
newspapers, African American, 26, 141, 150n18, 175, 190, 199–201, 239
Newton, Huey P., 54, 60–62
New York, N.Y., 260
Niagara Movement, 182
Nicodemus, Kans., 198
Niebuhr, Reinhold, 204
Nixon, Lawrence A., 238
Noel, Rachel B., 111, 113
Norman, Okla., 221, 224
North Las Vegas, Nev., 83–84
North Richmond, Calif., 52
North Side (Omaha), 198–200, 204, 207

Oakland, Calif., 5, 18, 43–47, 53, 60, 62, 258–59
Obama, Barack, 267–68
O'Callaghan, Donal "Mike," 83
O'Connor, Sandra Day, 266
Odegaard, Charles, 36
Ogden, Utah, 125
Oklahoma City, Okla., 17, 214
Oklahoma Constitution (1907), 218, 222
Oklahoma Industrial Institute and College for Girls, 221
Oklahoma School for the Deaf, 221
Oklahoma State University, 214, 221, 232n32
Omaha, Neb., 16, 175, 197–208
Omaha and Council Bluffs Street Railway Company (O&CB), 201
Omaha Star newspaper, 200–201
one drop rule, 216–17, 220
Ontario, Calif., 53
Operation Breadbasket, 249

Operation Windowshop, 32
Opportunities Industrialization Centers, 249
Oregon Bureau of Labor, 28
Organization of African American Unity, 61
Ozark Club, 93–94

Paige, Leroy "Satchel," 200
Paige, Thelma, 242
Painter, Theophilus, 242
Palo Alto, Calif., 56
Park Hill (Denver), 109–12
Parker, Charlie "Bird," 199
Passmore, Henry, 174
Patterson, Floyd, 79
Pattrick, Jim, 143
Pearson v. Murray (1935), 14
People's Party II, 248
Peters, Bud, 159
Pettis, Timothy, 26
Phillips, Louise, 142
Phillips, Nancy, 145, 149
Phillips, Robert, 142
Phoenix, Ariz., 55, 136–52
Phoenix Advancement League, 138
Phoenix Protection League, 138
Phoenix Union High School District, 141, 150n17
Pickrell, Robert, 144
Picture Floor Plans Inc., 33–34
Pierre, S.Dak., 173
Pinedale, Wyo., 102
Pinkston, L. G., 240
Pittman, Tarea (Ty) Hall, 43
Plessy v. Ferguson (1896), 9, 40, 202
Plotkin, Albert, 143, 145, 149
police: and African American officers, 46, 117, 247, 256; and police brutality, 16, 61, 191, 193, 206–7, 215, 247–48, 262; and police harassment, 117, 142, 147, 186–88, 191, 194, 201, 206; and schools, 160; in Utah, 133–34

poll taxes, 9, 170, 237, 240
Pomona, Calif., 53
population, 87, 165; in Arizona, 137; in California, 38, 41–42, 47, 53, 258–59; in Colorado, 109; in the Dakotas, 172–74; in Iowa, 185; in Kansas, 203; in Minnesota, 191, 194; in Montana, 91, 95; in Nebraska, 198; in Nevada, 73, 83–84; in New Mexico, 154–55; in Oklahoma, 214, 218; in the Pacific Northwest, 25–26, 37; in Texas, 239; in Utah, 125, 131, 134; in Wyoming, 104
Port Arthur, Tex., 245
Porter, E. Melvin, 231n19
Portland, Ore., 16, 24–29, 33–36
Portland Commission on Inter-Group Relations, 28
Portland Development Commission, 35
Portland Fire Department, 27
Portland Public Schools, 33
Potts, Frank, 113
poverty, 138, 147, 208, 249, 263, 267
Powell, Adam Clayton, 125
Prairie View University, 242
President's Committee on Fair Employment Practice, 27
Pride, Charlie, 95
prisons and jails, 126, 218, 225, 247, 262–63
Progressive Voters League, 238
Progressive Youth Association, 246
Proposition 14 (California, 1964), 59, 261
Proposition 209 (California, 1996), 266
protests, 5–9, 58–59, 112, 206, 247; for athletics, 103–4; of businesses, 30–31, 201–5; of discrimination in Iowa, 183–84; for housing, 27, 32–33; of job discrimination, 117–18; of Las Vegas businesses, 74–76, 79; of mistreatment, 26, 206; of movies, 26, 41–43; of poverty, 147; of schools, 35–36, 207, 265
public accommodations: discrimination in, 33, 72–80, 93–94, 98, 101–3, 125,

143–45, 183, 201, 203; segregation in, 138, 215, 221–22, 225–26, 232n40, 246
Public Accommodations Law, 144–45
Pueblo, Colo., 116
Pulido, Laura, 40
Pulliam, Eugene, 146
Pyle, J. Howard, 133

race, definitions of, 216–17, 220, 226, 230n10
radio stations, African American, 187–88
Ragsdale, Eleanor, 142
Ragsdale, Lincoln, 139, 141–43, 146, 149, 151n19, 151n22
Ragsdale, Ted, 139
railroads, segregation in, 218–19, 223–24, 236–37, 246
Rampton, Calvin, 124
Randle, Ron, 179
Randolph, A. Philip, 45, 48, 156
Rapid City, S.Dak., 169, 173, 177, 179
Reconstruction, 9–11
redevelopment, 28, 29, 185, 191, 249
Reed, Cecil, 186
Reed, Eddie, 95
Reed, Ishmael, 264
Reed, Thomas, 141
Reed College, 28
Regents of the University of California v. Bakke (1978), 62
Rehm, Mary, 185, 187
Rehnquist, William, 146
Reichert, Arlyne, 89, 92
Reno, Nev., 71–78
Republican Party: and allegiances, 48, 84, 124, 237, 240–41; and legislation, 79, 82–84, 178, 186, 198, 222; and malapportionment, 84; in nineteenth century, 9, 93; and voting rights, 146, 222
restaurants, discrimination in: in Arizona, 150n9; in Colorado, 113; in Iowa, 183; in Montana, 89–90, 98,
100; in Nevada, 72; in New Mexico, 156, 158–59; in Texas, 246; in Utah, 125
Reyes, Francisco, 258
Reynolds, Phil, 28
Reynolds v. Sims (1964), 83
Rhinehart, Naseby "Doc," 99–100
Rhodes, Rudolph "Zip," 99–100
Rice, Norman, 258–59
Rice University, 246
Richardson, Clifford, 237
Richardson, Gloria, 185
Richmond, Calif., 53
Riggs, Marlon, 264
riots, 175, 191, 256, 261; in California, 5, 262; in East St. Louis, 43; in Iowa, 184; in Kansas, 201, 207–8; in Kansas City, 206; in Minneapolis, 191; in Omaha, 207; in Phoenix, 147; in Portland, 35; in Texas, 237, 247–48; in Tulsa, 215; in Wichita, 207–8
Riverside, Calif., 53
Roberts, Frederick M., 48, 55
Robeson, Paul, 125
Robinson, W. A., 138
Roncalio, Teno, 102, 104
Roosevelt, Franklin Delano, 48, 51, 156
Roseboro, John, 95
Ross, Nellie Tayloe, 101
Roswell, N.Mex., 157, 158
Roybal, Edward, 56
Rumford, William Byron, 43, 55, 57
Rumford Act, 39
Russell, Charles, 74
Russell, Richard B., 91
Rustin, Bayard, 264

Sacramento, Calif., 53, 61
Safeway, 27, 30, 58, 118
Salt Lake City, Utah, 125–26, 131, 134
Sam, Michael, 264
San Antonio, Tex., 238, 241, 244, 246, 250
San Bernardino, Calif., 53
Sanchez, Alfonso, 162

San Diego, Calif., 53, 58
Sandoval, David, 108
San Francisco, Calif., 42, 50, 52, 53–54, 258–60
San Francisco State University, 35, 59, 61, 257, 265
San Jose, Calif., 46, 53, 56–57, 59
San Jose State College, 58–59
San Quentin Prison, 117
Santa Ana, Calif., 46, 53
Santa Fe, N.Mex., 157–58
Sawyer, Grant, 74–75, 77, 79–81
Sayles-Belton, Sharon, 194
school integration: in Arizona, 141; in Colorado, 108–12; in Iowa, 184; in Kansas, 198, 202; in Minnesota, 194; in Montana, 98; in Nebraska, 208; in New Mexico, 154, 157–60; in the Pacific Northwest, 34–35; in Texas, 244–45, 250. *See also under* colleges
school segregation: in Arizona, 137–40, 150n15, 150n17; in California, 40, 55; in Colorado, 109–11; in the Dakotas, 170; in Kansas, 198, 202, 205; in Minnesota, 193–94; in Montana, 90, 98; in Nebraska, 208; in New Mexico, 157–60; in Oklahoma, 215–16, 219–21, 225–27, 230n5; in the Pacific Northwest, 29, 33; in Texas, 237, 241, 244, 245; in Utah, 125; in Wyoming, 102–3. *See also under* colleges
Schrunk, Terry, 28
Schuyler, George S., 97
Schwerner, Michael, 183
Scott, Charles, 201
Scott, Eddie B., 76, 78, 82
Seale, Bobby, 35, 60–61
Sears, 27–28
Seattle, Wash., 25–33, 36, 258–59
Second Great Migration (African American, 1940–1970), 15, 51, 55, 59
Self, Robert, 259

Selma, Ala., 117, 190
Shelley v. Kraemer, 46
Sheppard, John Ben, 244
Shivers, Allan, 240, 244
Short Creek, Ariz., 133
Simmons, Jimmy, 104
Simmons, Juanita, 102
Simpson, Milward, 103–4
Sims, Paul, 201
Sims, Rosa, 201, 204
Sims, Tracy, 58
Sims, Wesley, 201
Sioux City, Iowa, 175
Sioux Falls, S.Dak., 169, 173, 175–76, 179
Sipuel, Ada Lois (Fisher), 14, 227–28
Sipuel v. Oklahoma State Board of Regents (1948), 14, 227–28
sit-ins, 9, 117, 148, 200; and education, 186; and housing, 32–33, 112; and public accommodations, 16–17, 75–76, 144, 159, 203, 246
Skorpen, Erling, 78
Slate (student organization at UC Berkeley), 58
Slaton, Tex., 250
Slattery, James, 78, 82, 84–85
slavery, 9, 11, 25, 213–14
Smick, A. H., 33
Smith, Alice, 72
Smith, Antonio Maceo, 238
Smith, Barbara, 243–44
Smith, Emma Riley, 94–95
Smith, Joseph, 132
Smith, Lindsay, 79–80
Smith, Lonnie, 16, 239, 250
Smith, Maceo, 239
Smith, Mary Anne, 56
Smith, Steve, 183
Smith v. Allwright (1944), 14, 16
Social Welfare Committee, 73, 78
Society to Underwrite Racial Equality (SURE), 73

Sokol, Jason, 182
Sonenshein, Raphael, 39
Soul Police, 191
South Central Los Angeles, 48, 52
Southern Christian Leadership Conference (SCLC), 18, 162, 249
Southern Methodist University, 240, 243
South Phoenix, 138, 142, 146–47
Southwestern College, 203
Sparks, Nev., 74
Spokane, Wash., 23, 26–27, 33, 36–37
Spokane Committee on Race Relations (SCRR), 26
sports: and African American players, 95, 113, 117, 141, 200, 244, 264; and discrimination of African Americans on traveling teams, 99–100, 103–4, 157, 171
Spriggs, Haroldie Kent, 157
Springer, Charles, 78
Squaw Valley, Calif., 75
St. Ambrose College, 183
Stanford University, 58, 265
State v. Vera Black, 133
Stearns, Eldrewey, 246
Steele, Percy, 58
Stenvig, Charles, 194
Stephenson, Richard, 159
Stokes, Carl, 260
Storey, Moorfield, 223
St. Paul, Minn., 189, 191, 193
Strong, Vivian, 207
Struckmeyer, Fred C., 140
Student Nonviolent Coordinating Committee (SNCC), 18, 58, 189, 191, 206, 247
student organizations, 35, 59, 61, 113, 179, 187, 257
suburbs, 17, 57, 110, 194, 205, 260–62
Sullivan, Robert E., 90
Sumner, Charles, 223
sundown towns, 224

Sunnyhills Cooperative, 56
Sutton, G. J., 250
Sweatt, Heman Marion, 14, 242–43, 250, 257
Sweatt v. Painter (1950), 14
swimming pools, discrimination at, 111, 138, 183, 201, 205–6
Swobe, Coe, 82
Swoopes, Sheryl, 264

Taft-Hartley Act (1947), 56, 131
Tanner, Nathan Eldon, 124
Tate, Penfield, 114
Taylor, Artie, 114
Taylor, Mildred D., 114
Taylor, Quintard, 32, 49
teachers, African American: and black history, 186; and desegregation, 17, 141; and job discrimination, 102, 125, 202; lack of, 179, 184, 256–57; and pay, 14, 16, 237, 242, 244; and segregation, 138, 159–60, 205, 219–20, 227; and women, 109
Tempe, Ariz., 145
Tena, Manuel, 146
ten-point platform (Black Panther Party), 60–61, 117
Texarkana Junior College, 243
Texas Commission on Democracy in Education, 241–42
Texas Council of Negro Organizations, 239, 242, 248
Texas Negro Chamber of Commerce, 238, 248
Texas Southern University, 243, 246–48
Texas State Conference of NAACP Branches, 238, 241, 248
Texas State University for Negroes, 243
Texas Western College, 244
Theater Owners' Booking Association, 199
theaters, discrimination in, 93, 125, 201

Third World Liberation Front, 265
Thirteenth Amendment, 25
Thurman, Howard, 54
Tijerina, Reies Lopez, 130, 161–62
Tillman, James, 193
Todd, Lucinda, 202
Topeka, Kans., 196–97, 199, 201–5
Topeka Board of Education, 202
transportation, segregation in, 9, 218–19, 223–26, 229, 236–37, 246
Travis, Geraldine W., 97
Trillin, Calvin, 110
Trotter, Joe William, 39
Truman, Harry S, 94, 169
Tucumcari, N.Mex., 154, 157
Tulsa, Okla., 215
Turner, Felton, 247
Turner, Frederick Jackson, 11
Twenty-Fourth Amendment, 170, 178, 240

UAW Local 560, 56
unemployment, 44–45, 143–44, 184, 191, 199, 238–39, 250
Union Bethel African Methodist Episcopal (AME) Church, 93, 96
unions, 13, 15–16, 49–52, 56, 58, 93, 98–99, 126, 204, 256
United Meatpacking Workers of America (UMPWA), 199
United Negro Improvement Association (UNIA), 43–45, 199
United Service Organization (USO), 94
University of California, Berkeley, 58, 61, 257, 265–66
University of California, Los Angeles, 58, 62
University of Chicago, 139
University of Colorado, 111, 113–14, 117
University of Denver, 113, 117
University of Iowa, 183
University of Kansas, 197, 201, 206, 265
University of Kentucky, 244

University of Maryland, 14
University of Michigan, 266
University of Minnesota, 190–92
University of Missouri, 264
University of Montana, 99–100
University of Nebraska, 200
University of Nevada, 74
University of Nevada, Reno, 78
University of New Mexico, 16–17, 153
University of Oklahoma, 14, 215, 221, 227–29, 232n32, 257
University of San Francisco, 257
University of South Dakota, 175
University of Texas, 14, 242–43, 257
University of Utah, 125, 265
University of Washington, 35–36, 257, 265
University of Wyoming, 103, 117
Unruh Act, 57
Urban League. *See* National Urban League
urban renewal. *See* redevelopment
US Organization, 5, 60
U.S. Steel, 12, 188
Utah Constitution, 125
Utah Federation of Labor, 131
Utah State University, 125

Van Delinder, Jean, 7
Vanport, Ore., 28
Vaughns, John L., 23–24
Vietnam War, 59, 96
Voluntary Racial Transfer (VRT), 34
voter registration, 58, 183, 190, 223, 227, 240–41, 258
voting rights, 9, 233n45; in Arizona, 146; in California, 47–48, 55–56; in Nevada, 83; in Oklahoma, 217–18, 222–23, 226–27, 231n19; in Texas, 237–41; in Utah, 128–29; in Wyoming, 101
Voting Rights Act, 5, 170, 189–90, 240, 257–58, 268

Waco, Tex., 238
Waldman, Fran, 146, 148, 151n36
Walla Walla, Wash., 26
Wallace, George, 207
Walters, Maxine, 203–4
Walters, Ronald, 17, 203
War Manpower Commission, 51
War on Poverty, 60, 147, 249
Warren, Earl, 3
Warren, Morrison, 145–46
Washington, Byron, 195
Washington, D.C., 178
Washington, Harold, 259
Washington State Board Against Discrimination in Employment (WSBADE), 24, 27, 33
Waterloo, Iowa, 182, 184, 195
Waters, Maxine, 55
Watkins, Arthur, 130
Watkins, Bruce R., 204
Watkins v. Oaklawn Jockey Club (1950), 125
Watson, Lauren, 117
Watts (Los Angeles), 41, 46, 60
Watts Riot, 5, 60, 262
Webb, Mayfield, 29
Webb, Wellington, 114, 118, 258–59
welfare assistance, 185–87, 193
Wesley, Carter, 241
Wesley, Charles, 243
West Coast Regional Welfare Conference, 74
Western Addition (San Francisco), 41, 52
West Oakland, 41, 52
Westside (Las Vegas), 72, 83
West Texas, 237, 243–44, 246, 250
Weyr, Thomas, 162
Wheeler, John M., 33
White, Edward, 223
White, John, 231n19
White, Lulu, 241–42
White, Walter, 202
White Citizens Councils, 245

white-only primaries, 14, 16, 238–40, 250
Wichita, Kans., 17, 196, 199–200, 202–5, 207–8
Wichita State University, 207
Wiley College, 242, 246
Wilkins, Roy, 118, 189–90
Wilkinson, Ernest, 130
Williams, Cecil, 259
Williams, Leonard, Jr., 177
Williams, Leonard, Sr., 177
Williams, Mrs. Willie, 33
Willis, Leora, 160
Wilson, Lionel, 258
Wilson, Logan, 244
Wilson, William Julius, 262
Wilson, Woodrow, 83
Wilson v. Lane, 226
Winfield, Kans., 203
Winnacker, Martha Kendall, 39
Wiren, Al, 140
Wirth, Lewis, 139
women: as activists, 5, 30, 36, 47, 62, 97, 112, 148, 152n41, 185, 204, 241; in the church, 93–94, 152n41; and job discrimination, 109, 200; and life expectancy, 263–64; in politics, 97, 111, 113, 258; and women's clubs, 47, 49, 94, 101, 138; and women's rights, 123, 131
Women's Basketball Association, 264
Woodhouse, Charles, 155
Woodruff, Wilford, 132
Woods, Clyde, 40
Woodson, George H., 182
Woolworth's, 58, 143, 246
Works Progress Administration and Work Projects Administration, 48
World War I, 184, 201
World War II, 15, 17–18, 20; and employment, 94, 108–9, 201–3, 248; and migration, 184, 257, 260; and military, 89, 95, 101

Worthington, Minn., 191
Wounded Knee, S.Dak., 179
Wretched of the Earth, The, 60, 206
Wright, Herbert, 16
Wyoming Civil Rights Act (1957), 103–4
Wysinger v. Crookshank (1890), 40

Yankton, S.Dak., 173, 175–76
Yarborough, Ralph, 240, 246
Yorty, Sam, 257
Young, Coleman, 260
Young Women's Christian Association (YWCA), 47, 74, 76